The International Politics of the Asia-Pacific, 1945–1995

The two major conflicts of the Cold War era were fought in Korea and Vietnam, pointing to the economic and political importance of the Asia-Pacific to the competing superpowers. In recent years, the area has emerged as a force in international politics in its own right and has acquired a new self-confidence that has found expression in astonishing economic achievement.

Michael Yahuda analyses the complex development of international politics in the region from 1945 to 1995, focusing on the influences that have shaped its political geography. Examining the conflicts in Korea and Vietnam against the backdrop of the Cold War, this study highlights how superpower relations were reflected in local struggles for independence and shows the interplay between international, regional and local politics, charting the changing alignments of the major powers and the local political consequences. The policies of the four major powers are considered separately. The book concludes with an assessment of the post Cold War uncertainties that have eroded Asia-Pacific self-confidence, such as the possible threat from China and doubts about the United States' desire to continue its stabilizing role in an area in which it has proved difficult to establish a basis for regional order.

Michael Yahuda is Reader in International Relations at the London School of Economics and Political Science, University of London.

The International Politics of the Asia-Pacific, 1945–1995

Michael Yahuda

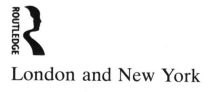

London and New York

First published 1996
by Routledge
11 New Fetter Lane, London EC4P 4EE

Simultaneously published in the USA and Canada
by Routledge
29 West 35th Street, New York, NY 10001

Reprinted 1997, 1998

Phototypeset in Times by Intype London Ltd
Printed and bound in Great Britain by
T.J. International Ltd, Padstow, Cornwall

British Library Cataloguing in Publication Data
A catalogue record for this book is available from the British Library

Library of Congress Cataloguing in Publication Data
A catalogue record for this book is available from the Library of Congress

ISBN 0–415–05756–6 (hbk)
ISBN 0–415–05757–4 (pbk)

For Ellen

Contents

Preface

This historically-based analysis by Michael Yahuda of the changing condition of international politics in a diverse Asia-Pacific is both timely and comprehensive. It is timely because the recent end of the Cold War has had the effect of transforming a strategic environment which has long been distinguished by a close and turbulent junction of regional and global tensions. That longstanding junction has given way to a new and uncertain balance or distribution of power concurrent with a regional registration of self-confidence based on economic achievement but without its translation into a coherent regional consciousness. In order to address the changing and challenging circumstances of post Cold War Asia-Pacific, resident states have established unprecedented multilateral institutions for interrelated economic and security dialogue and this study provides a sound scholarly perspective from which to assess their respective roles and aptitudes for managing regional order.

That scholarly perspective is based on the comprehensive way in which this study traces the international political experience of the Asia-Pacific since the end of the Pacific War and the onset of decolonization. To that end, Michael Yahuda concentrates attention on the interactions between three factors which have shaped political and security developments. He examines in turn the impact regionally of the dynamics of the former central strategic balance, the conflicts and accommodations involving the regional major powers and then the problems of identity and national security of the new or newly-established states. This masterly encapsulation brings the reader back to the point of entry of the volume at which the new-found significance of the Asia-Pacific with its economic dynamism and embryonic multilateral institutions is discussed. A prominent feature of the analysis is the place of China in a region where Russia is a minor force, where Japan is loath to assume a conventional security role and where the USA is seen to lack a former resoluteness. Michael Yahuda concludes this work of vast scope and intellectual depth by posing the intriguing question of whether or not China in its resurgent mode may well provide a new basis for reviving the erstwhile and troublesome junction between regional and global politics.

Michael Leifer

Acknowledgements

I should like to express my gratitude to the members of the seminar on the international politics of the Asia-Pacific that has been held at the London School of Economics for more years than I care to remember. In particular I am grateful to the many distinguished scholars and practitioners who presented papers. The writing of this book has benefited enormously from the thorough discussions of those seminar meetings.

A special debt of gratitude is owed to my colleague and editor Professor Michael Leifer. He commented carefully on each chapter and then critically appraised the book as a whole. It would otherwise have been much the poorer. Of course I alone am responsible for such shortcomings as may remain.

Introduction

The Atlantic Era is now at the height of its development and
must soon exhaust the resources at its command. The Pacific Era,
destined to be the greatest of all, is just at its dawn.

(Theodore Roosevelt, 1903)[1]

It still remains to be seen whether the 'Pacific Era' has at last begun
to unfold one hundred years after President Roosevelt proclaimed
its dawn. But one important difference between his time and the
eve of the twenty-first century is that the Asian countries have long
since ceased to be pawns of the major external powers and have
increasingly become masters of their own destinies. Accordingly, it
is more appropriate to describe the region as the Asia-Pacific.

The emergence of the Asia-Pacific as a region in international
politics is a modern phenomenon. Indeed it might best be conceived
as a region that is still in the process of evolution and whose identity
has yet to be clearly defined. It is a product of several developments
associated with the modernization and globalization of economic,
political and social life that has involved the spread of what might
be called industrialism and statehood throughout the world. Derived
from Europe and still bearing the marks of their origin, these great
forces have shaped and continue to shape what we understand to
be the contemporary Asia-Pacific. At the same time their implan-
tation in this part of the world has involved accommodation and
adaptation to prior non-European traditions and institutions. Thus
although the states of the Asia-Pacific may be defined in common
legal terms (involving concepts of sovereignty, territoriality and
citizenship) that would be recognizable to Europeans of the nineteenth century, the governance of the states of, say, contemporary
China, Japan or indeed Indonesia cannot be fully understood without reference to their respective different historical antecedents.

The regional identity of the Asia-Pacific may be said to derive from geopolitical and geoeconomic considerations rather than from any indigenous sense of homogeneity or commonality of purpose. Unlike Europe the Asia-Pacific cannot call upon shared cultural origins or proclaim attachment to common political values as a basis for regional identity. But the Asia-Pacific can claim to have been located at an important geographical junction of post Second World War politics where the competing Cold War interests of the two superpowers intersected with each other, with those of the two major regional powers and with those of the smaller resident states. The way in which these different sets of competing and cooperative interests have interacted has given this region its distinctive if evolving identity, which has acquired recent significance through geoeconomic factors. The development of what the World Bank has called 'the East Asian Economic Miracle' has transformed East Asia from a region of poverty and insurgency into one of the most important centres of the international economy. The pattern of consistent high rates of economic growth and an increasing share of the world's GNP and trade that began with Japan, and became true of the four little dragons (South Korea, Taiwan, Hong Kong and Singapore), has become true of southern China and most of the countries of the Association of Southeast Asian Nations (ASEAN – Brunei, Indonesia, Malaysia, Philippines, Singapore and Thailand). Vietnam too is on the threshold of participating in the miracle.[2] The continuing economic dynamism of the region and the confidence that resident governments have drawn from their economic achievements has enhanced a new sense of national pride and assertiveness that is in the process of acquiring regional expression.

It was only once the great powers began to treat the diverse countries of the area as a distinct arena of international politics and economics that it became possible to identify the area with some sense of coherence. It was first treated as a separate geographical region at the Washington Conference of 1921–22 when the great powers of the day formally agreed to fix the ratio of the warships they would deploy in the Pacific. That was designed to limit the geographical and military scope of the challenge of Japan – the first state in the Asia-Pacific to adapt to the modernizing imperatives. By the 1930s the Japanese not only repudiated the agreement that had restricted their naval deployments, but they sought to exclude the Western powers altogether from the region as proposed in the scheme formally declared in 1938 as the East Asia Co-Prosperity Sphere. It had appeared in different guises earlier in the decade as in the concept of a 'New Order in East Asia'.[3] Japan's initial victories over the Western powers and its attempts to encourage anti-Western sentiments around the slogan 'Asia for Asians' stimulated local nationalism.[4] However, the brutality and domineering behaviour of the Japanese conquerors undermined their image as liberators and engendered fears and animosities among local peoples that have yet to be expiated more than fifty years later. However, the Japanese sphere of military operations also defined the sphere of the allied response in the Pacific War. The several agreements among the war time allies, beginning in 1941, followed by the Quebec Conference of 1943 which set up the South East Asian Command, continued with the 1943 Cairo Declaration and culminated in the Yalta and Potsdam agreements of 1945, helped to give parts of the region greater geo-political coherence. But they also marked the last time in which the region would be defined by the great powers in accordance with their interests without even informing the local states let alone consulting them.

It was not until after the Pacific War (fought in part to deny Japan an exclusive sphere) when the local countries of the region acquired independence and began (or in some cases resumed) to assert their own identities and to develop patterns of conflict and cooperation among themselves, that the region began to be shaped by its variety of indigenous forces. But the region was still largely defined in terms of the international struggle for the balance of power with the Soviet Union and communist China replacing Japan as the object of Western (primarily American) containment.

The evolution of the region therefore may be seen as beginning with great power arrangements to accommodate the distribution of power within the Asia-Pacific to the global balance of power. Or put another way, it began with the recognition by the Western powers of the rise of Japan as a major power within a geographically circumscribed part of the world. Following the defeat of Japan a new balance of power emerged as, under the impact of the Cold War, the United States sought to contain the challenge of the two major communist powers. That was seen to be linked to the struggles for independence from colonial rule and the subsequent attempts to consolidate independence and build new nations. In some states communist forces led the nationalist challenge and in others they constituted a threat, sometimes by armed insurgencies, to incumbent governments. Local élites tended to seek external support and patronage. Thus linkages were formed between external balance of power considerations and regional and local conflicts that were defined primarily in terms of the Cold War.

The next major stage in the development of the region was its transformation from being only an object of geopolitical interest to the great powers, to one in which its constituent members as independent states sought to articulate an independent approach to international politics in the guise of what later was called nonalignment. The first notable expression of this was the Asian–African conference in Bandung, Indonesia, in 1955. Although this helped to identify what was later called the Third World as a new dimension in international politics and indeed contributed to developing the agenda that emphasized anti-colonialism and the need for economic development, it was unable to overcome the differences of interests and competing security concerns of the resident Asian states. Indeed the enormous diversities of the region have militated against the development of the kind of integrative regionalism associated with Western Europe since the end of the Second World War. Interestingly, the one relatively successful regional organization, the Association of Southeast Asian Nations (ASEAN), formed in 1967, is, as its name implies, restricted to Southeast Asia and was designed in practice to enhance the effective independence of its members. Far from seeking to integrate the region by merging sovereignty and unifying the operations of their economies, the national leaders sought to strengthen their hard won and vulnerable separate systems of government. They sought to reduce the challenges to their domestic rule by containing intra-regional disputes through the recognition of the junction between the stability of the region and that of the domestic order of member states.[5]

The Asia-Pacific became a region of global significance as it counts among its resident members both the global powers, the United States and the Soviet Union (although the latter's successor state, Russia, is less than global in its scope) and the major regional powers of international significance, China and Japan. The two major wars of the Cold War were fought in the region and developments within the region have contributed to changing global alignments of great import. Thus the transformation of China from an ally of the Soviet Union to a position of revolutionary isolationism and then to alignment with the United States helped to undermine the congruence between ideological and strategic affinities that typified the early stages of the Cold War. The Chinese 'defection' from the alliance with the Soviet Union introduced a third factor into the global strategic equation which was increasingly regarded as tripolar. But the main ramifications of this change were felt within the region where the Soviet–American axis of conflict was joined by a parallel Soviet–Chinese one whose outcome was a Sino–American alignment and the end of the Vietnam War (or Second Indo-China War) and then the outbreak of the Cambodian War (or Third Indo-China War). Similarly, developments within the region played a part in the ending of the Cold War for the world as a whole, but its impact upon the communist regimes in Asia has been altogether different from that of their European former counterparts.

The end of the Cold War and the disintegration of the Soviet Union was not accompanied by the collapse of the key communist regimes in the Asia-Pacific, in China, Vietnam and North Korea. As a result, an element of the Cold War has survived in the region as they fear the political agenda of the United States, the sole surviving superpower. The end of bipolarity has brought to an end the central strategic balance that had hitherto dominated international politics and as a result it has detached regional and sub-regional conflicts from the larger global axis of conflict to which they had previously been joined. The ending of the international and then the regional dimensions of the Cambodian conflict facilitated a settlement brokered by the United Nations and has reduced the ensuing domestic struggles within the country to primarily local significance. The Korean conflict has also been transformed, but its resolution is more complex as it involves two separate states in an area of geopolitical significance to four of the world's greatest powers. In so far as it involves a global dimension it centres on the possible acquisition by the North of nuclear weapons and the challenge to the Nuclear Non-Proliferation Treaty regime.

The new strategic situation in the region is regarded as uncertain since it is suspected that the United States government may not have sufficient domestic support in the long term to sustain the level of forces deployed in the West Pacific necessary to serve the objective of upholding stability. Immediate concerns about the management of the rising power of China prompted the establishment in 1993 of the ASEAN Regional Forum (ARF) as an embryonic regional security organization. It may be seen as paralleling the Asia Pacific Economic Cooperation forum (APEC) that was established in 1989 and which, although also essentially consultative in character, has been boosted by American led attempts since 1993 to enlarge its scope to promote an Asian–Pacific community dedicated to free trade. The global economic significance of the region has already been noted, but the political and strategic significance of the region's economic dynamism should also be appreciated. Although less immediately visible, these economic changes are beginning to challenge the character and the distribution of global power. They have already transformed thinking about the character of security and political stability of so-called third world states.

Accordingly, this book is concerned with the inter-play between the interests of the great, the regional and local powers in this part of the world. These may conveniently be depicted as operating simultaneously at three levels – the global, the regional and the local. During the period of the Cold War the first may be said to have involved the dynamics of the central balance between the United States and the Soviet Union, the manner in which that impacted upon the other two levels and the way in which these also fed back into the first. The second involved the conflicts and accommodations affecting the major regional powers in their relations with the other two levels. The third involved the problems of identity and security as played out by the élites of the new or newly established states.

At the local level security tended to be defined especially in the first two or three decades after the Second World War less in terms of conventional military threats than in terms of the survival of the ruling élites and the socio-economic systems that sustained them. In the period immediately after that war the states of contemporary East and Southeast Asia either re-established themselves anew after civil war and alien military occupation or they acquired independence from colonial rule. The experience contributed to shaping their territorial bounds (and territorial claims) as well as the character of their social and economic development. Their domestic political cultures and their views of the outside world were also shaped by historical experiences that in most cases long predated the advent of the Europeans and the modern era. Nevertheless the majority of what might be called these new states were not secure initially in their social and political orders – and indeed some are still insecure or have acquired new sources of instability.

These domestic insecurities have had regional and international dimensions, first, because competing élites have sought support from beyond their own states and external powers have in turn competed for regional influence by supporting them; and second, because the outcomes were sometimes perceived as potentially significant for the management of the central or global balance of power by the two superpowers, the United States and the Soviet Union.

Therefore, this book will examine the interactions between three factors which have shaped the evolution of the political and security developments in the region since 1945. These may be characterized as first, the impact of the dynamics of the central balance; second, the conflicts and accommodations involving the regional great powers; and third, the problems of identity and national security of the new or newly established states. The junctions and disjunctions of security and political interests between these three levels may be seen as having occasioned such patterns of order or disorder as have emerged from time to time within the region. The book will conclude with an assessment of the impact of the end of the Cold War upon the region and of the new significance of the region in international politics.

THE REGION: AN OVERVIEW

The region may be defined in a broad fashion so as to include the littoral states of the Pacific of North, Central and South America, the island states of the South Pacific, Australasia, Northeast, Southeast and South Asia. A more common definition includes the states of North America, Australasia, Northeast and Southeast Asia. But in order to keep this study manageable, the Asia-Pacific has been defined somewhat narrowly to include the two superpowers, the United States and the Soviet Union (and its more circumscribed successor, Russia); the two regional great powers, China and Japan; and the local countries of Northeast and Southeast Asia. Other parts of what may legitimately be regarded as the Asia-Pacific namely, South Asia, Australasia, the South Pacific, Canada and parts of Latin America will be included only in so far as is necessary to explain the international politics of the others.

Even as defined in this relatively restricted way the scope of the region is immense and hugely diverse. That in itself is detrimental to the emergence of an indigenous sense of a common regional identity. Leaving aside the United States and the former Soviet Union, who have claims to being Asian–Pacific countries in their own right, the region embraces eighteen countries and territories that vary from China at one extreme with a territory of more than 9,561,000 sq. kms and a population in 1995 of 1,200 million people to Singapore at the other with a territory of only 625 sq. kms and a population of 2.7 million people. The two countries also serve to point up further disparities as the per capita GNP in Singapore in 1993 was US$14,210 compared to US$370 in China (although it should be noted that in terms of purchasing power parity the

Chinese figure was US $1,680. That was still only 7.6 per cent of that of America as compared to 71.2 per cent for Singapore).[6] As can be seen from these figures, China still essentially belongs to the Third World whereas Singapore is classified as a Newly Industrialized Country or Economy (i.e. NIC or NIE). The economic disparities of the region would loom even larger if Japan were to be compared with Vietnam or Burma.

In addition to these geographical and economic factors attention is usually drawn to the wide divergences in religion, culture, historical associations, social traditions, language, ethnicity and political systems that further divide the region. Many of these divisions cut across state borders and not only make for tensions between regional states, but also exacerbate the problems of nation building and consolidating state power from within. This is particularly true of the states of Southeast Asia where the colonial experience promoted links with the metropolitan power. Thus the Indo-Chinese states were tied to France; Burma, through India, was oriented to Britain, as were Malaya and Singapore. Indonesia, however, was attached to Holland (with the island of Borneo divided between the Dutch and the British). The Philippines was under Spanish rule until 1898 when it was taken over by the United States and was remade in its image. Indeed some of the states were actually the creations of the colonial powers. Indonesia and Malaysia, for example, in their present forms do not have precise historical antecedents although their nationalistic élites draw on pre-colonial traditions. At the same time the borders which all the Southeast Asian states inherited from the colonial period have left them with territorial disputes with neighbours and the colonial legacy has also left them with highly complex domestic communal problems highlighted, for example, by the ethnic Chinese.

The region is also marked by considerable diversity in its security arrangements. The situation in the Asia-Pacific for most of this period and certainly for the duration of the Cold War was more fluid than in Europe where two tightly coordinated military alliance systems confronted each other across clearly defined lines in seemingly implacable hostility. And although it was in the Asia-Pacific that the two major wars of the Cold War were fought, in Korea and in Vietnam, the fact that they were 'limited' and that they did not become general wars is indicative of the greater flexibility that applied in the region. It was possible to insulate conflicts and prevent them from engulfing the region as a whole. The different countries of the region did not on the whole join multiple or regional alliance systems. The alliance systems that have predominated in the region have tended to be of the bilateral kind – typically between a super-power and a regional partner. Such arrangements allowed for significant variation within the region as to how the links or junctions between the global, regional and local levels could apply at any given time. China's evolution from a close ally of the Soviet Union in the 1950s to being aligned with the United States in the 1970s perhaps illustrates the point most clearly.

The diversity within the region and the fluidity of the security arrangements are indicative of the absence of what might be called a regional order. There is as yet no basis for the establishment of a regional order if by that what is meant is the existence of stable relationships based on accepted rules of conduct between states, of shared views about the legitimacy of government within states and of common assumptions about the inter-relationships among regional and external states.[7]

Until the establishment of ARF in 1993 there were no intra-regional political institutions that linked together the various parts of the region and even ARF is best considered as an embryonic rather than a fully fledged security organization. Unlike the situation in Europe, there are no effective institutional arrangements that would facilitate collective consideration by the states of the Asia-Pacific of the security problems of, say, Northeast Asia such as the disputed territories between Japan and Russia or the division of Korea. Similarly, the complexities involving the questions of Taiwan and Hong Kong are left to the parties directly involved. Even the one inter-state organization in the region that is usually regarded as a successful example of a regional organization among Third World countries, ASEAN, has studiously refrained from attempting to become a conventional security organization. Its members may have agreed on certain principles of state conduct, such as the unacceptability of military intervention by a regional state to change the government of a neighbour, which formed the basis for their diplomatic campaign against Vietnam's actions in Cambodia. But the governments do not necessarily feel confident about the long term durability of their respective political systems, nor do they share a common view about the principal security threats to the region, and nor do they agree about the roles that external powers should play in Southeast Asia.

Not surprisingly, these divergencies have combined to militate against the development of a regional consciousness comparable to that of the more homogeneous Europeans. Such regional consciousness that has emerged is of relatively recent origin and has been confined largely to the economic sphere and then only in part. It has been articulated by élites within the worlds of business, academe and government. It has taken the form of a variety of trans-Pacific non-governmental or semi-governmental organizations that so far have been largely consultative in purpose. But especially since the end of the Cold War influential voices within the region have called for the upgrading of regional institutions so that they should be both more comprehensive in membership and better able to address formally matters of security as well as of economics. These may be regarded as an open acknowledgement of the absence of such a facility so far.

Nevertheless, in surveying the evolution of the region into the world's most dynamic centre of economic growth and technological change it is clear in retrospect how important the role of the United States has been in providing the security structure and economic environment that has made this possible. In the absence of a multi-lateral security treaty organization along the lines of NATO, the United States put in place in the 1950s a series of bilateral security treaties or their equivalents of sufficiently broad geographical scope as to provide for a series of military bases and facilities that made a Pacific Rim strategy militarily viable. The United States established treaties that have endured with Japan and South Korea in Northeast Asia, with the Philippines and Thailand (the Manila Pact) in Southeast Asia and a treaty with Australia and New Zealand (the effective membership of the latter has been in abeyance since 1985). This Pacific perimeter defence structure was further buttressed by the American bases in Guam and Hawaii and the Philippines until 1992 and by its special arrangements with island groups in the Central and Southern Pacific (notably the Marshall Islands). These separate arrangements were overseen administratively by the Commander-in-Chief for the Pacific of the US Navy.

The result has been that while the United States perceived its strategic role in the Asia-Pacific area as part of a larger strategic rationale that was both global and regional in scope, its series of bilateral partners have tended to perceive their part in narrower parochial or self interested terms. The latter have tended to judge the value of their strategic association with the United States mainly in terms of particular national interests or even in terms of those of the local holders of political power. Hence the frustration the United States experienced in the 1980s and early 1990s in re-nego-tiating its bases treaty with the Philippines or in finding a mutually acceptable arrangement with New Zealand over the question of disclosure of whether visiting American ships carry nuclear weapons. Since the end of the Cold War there has been widespread support within the region for the continued deployment of American forces in the West Pacific as essential for stability in the region. Even China has refrained from calling for an American withdrawal – at least in the short term. But at the same time there has been apprehension within the region that American domestic opinion may not support the deployment in the long term. Continuing trade disputes and criticism within the region of America as part of the resistance to the perceived attempt to export American political values have added new complexities to the strategic relationship.

From the perspective of international politics it is striking that the main convenient dividing point in the history of the region during the Cold War period should also be the main turning point in American policy towards the region. The transformation of the pattern of global alignments and role of China in 1969–71 which changed the balance of power within the region was interconnected with profound changes in American strategic policies as marked by the Nixon Doctrine of 1969 that forswore further commitment of American ground forces to major combat on the Asian mainland and by the Sino–American alignment of 1971–72. These developments reflected both the escalation of China's disputes with its giant communist neighbour to the level of armed conflict and the ending of the military phase of America's policy of containment in Asia. This found institutional expression in abolishing the military structure of the Southeast Asian Treaty Organization (SEATO) in February 1974 and then the organization itself in June 1977. During the 1970s in the Asia-Pacific, the congruence between ideological and strategic affinities was erased. Yet the American system of bilateral alliances survived the change, especially that with Japan. Even though the alliance with Taiwan had to be formally abrogated in 1979, a way was found through the domestic legislative mechanism of the Taiwan Relations Act to preserve much of the substance of the former treaty. Containment was still practised, but more indirectly through diplomacy and assisting third parties to resist the territorial expansion of Soviet power, either through its proxy Vietnam in Indo-China, or directly, as in Afghanistan.

In addition to providing a militarily secure international environment for its allies and associates in the region through the exercise of hegemonic power the United States also provided an international economic environment that has facilitated the remarkable growth of the economies of most of these friends. By opening its domestic markets and by applying liberal economic principles without demanding reciprocity (at least not until recent times) the United States has made it possible for first Japan and then the East Asian NIEs to follow policies of rapid economic growth that combined various mixes of export orientation and import substitution. To be sure the United States has benefited from Asian–Pacific economic dynamism, but its benefits have become disproportionate to the costs. According to *IMF Direction of Trade Statistics*, in 1985 the United States accounted for nearly 40 per cent of the value of the total trade of the East Asian countries as compared to 15 per cent that was counted as trade among themselves. But even excluding America's trade with Japan its total trade with Asia was valued at $158.8 billion and that involved a trade deficit of $43.9 billion which was not far behind the trade deficit with Japan of $52.5 billion. In 1980, however, according to the same IMF source, the United States had a trade deficit with Japan of $12.2 billion and a trade *surplus* of $1.5 billion with the other East Asian countries. Thus in the 1980s the American trade deficit with the East Asian countries as a whole leapt from just over $10 billion to nearly $100 billion. By 1993 the overall American deficit with Asia and Japan had grown to $121.2 billion. Japan by contrast enjoyed a surplus with Asia and America combined of $104–115 billion.[8]

Although the seeds for the economic transformation of the region were sown earlier, it was not until the 1970s (in the case of Japan) and the 1980s (for the East Asian NIEs) that the region began to be recognized as a centre of economic growth and technological development of global significance. Unlike the security issues where the United States is still unquestionably the dominant (if not unchallenged) military power, American economic leadership in the region has long been contested by Japan. As early as 1965 a leading Japanese scholar depicted graphically Japan's envisioned role as the leader of a 'flying-geese formation' to characterize the future economic development of East and Southeast Asia. With Japan in the lead economic dynamism would be diffused first to the NIEs who in turn would be followed by some of the ASEAN countries and possibly China, Vietnam, North Korea, Burma and even the Soviet Union.[9] Yet even as Japan's trade with Asia has leaped in total value from $7.9 billion in 1970 to $49.5 billion in 1980 and to $147.6 billion in 1989, it has always enjoyed a surplus. The trade surplus in 1989 came to $17.6 billion and in 1993 to $50.1 billion.[10] It is clear that although American trade may have declined as a proportion of overall Asian trade, access to its domestic markets on a non-reciprocal basis was still of great significance to the economic dynamism of the region in the 1990s.

Thus in terms of the region as a whole it is the United States that has provided the general security and other 'public goods'[11] as its friends and allies have benefited while pursuing their more parochial concerns. For some time, Americans have been debating whether their country has been declining as a hegemonic power. But since the ending of the Cold War, governments, business élites and academics in East Asia have begun to question whether the United States will continue to provide the secure strategic and economic environments that have proved to be so advantageous to the countries in the region. Within the United States there is uncertainty about the character of the emerging post Cold War period and the role that the United States should play now that it is effectively the only superpower left. There is also uncertainty whether the United States will continue to provide the economic 'public goods' in the Asia-Pacific as it has done so far.

The economic success of the western oriented countries in the region since the 1970s has doubtless contributed to stabilizing their political systems and to encouraging the development of more democratic forms of political representation. Yet in most instances the consolidation of statehood is too recent and the sources of conflict both within and between the states of the region too apparent for any complacency to emerge in this respect. Indeed these uncertainties contribute to the difficulties in developing regional security institutions.

This is true even in Southeast Asia where the Association of Southeast Asian Nations (ASEAN) in 1992 marked its 25th anniversary as a generally acknowledged successful regional organization especially in the Third World. Yet its members do not share a common strategic outlook. They differ in their assessments of the sources of threats to regional security and on the extent to which they should seek to exclude the external great powers. Moreover even after three or four decades of independence the member states still find that communal problems, challenges from fundamental Islam, intra-mural disputes about borders and territory have been contained rather than solved.

Relations within the region are also complicated by historical legacies from different eras. The legacy of the colonial period still endures in many respects in Southeast Asia long after the European powers were compelled to retreat from Asia. For example, at certain levels communications and social/educational ties with the former metropolitan powers are easier and more visible than those with neighbouring countries. The legacies of historical relations of even earlier eras continue to complicate more contemporary arrangements. This is most evident in the case of China which is central to the concerns of the region as a whole. Its sheer size and the memory of China's traditional assertion of superiority and its former claims to bestow legitimacy on local rulers sustain unease among its neighbours in the region. That memory also contributed to giving a keen edge to the response within the region to the sponsorship by China's communist rulers of revolutionary insurgencies that challenged social order and the local regimes for nearly forty years after the end of the Pacific War. Not surprisingly, unease remains about the character of China's appeal to the ethnic Chinese residents in the region who exercise an economic influence disproportionate to their relatively small numbers and who have become major investors in China. These concerns are exacerbated by China's territorial claims especially in the South China Sea where as recently as 1995 naval forces were deployed to advance them.

The ways in which traditional and contemporary sources of conflict can combine to accentuate problems may be seen from a brief consideration of the recent history of Indo-China which has been the most persistent focus of major power conflict in the region. Long standing enmities between some of the local and regional forces were interrupted by the French colonial intervention in the nineteenth century. The series of wars that followed the Pacific War saw these ancient enmities become enmeshed with the external involvement of the two superpowers. At the risk of oversimplifying, it can be argued that the settlement of the Cambodian conflict as an international problem in the early 1990s only became possible once the more distant great powers disengaged, leaving the historically engaged neighbouring countries to accept a settlement based on the current distribution of power between them. Above all, once the Soviet Union was no longer able or willing to support Vietnam, the Vietnamese found that they could no longer sustain their position in Cambodia. Vietnam, which in 1986 had shifted its main priority to domestic economic reform and development, then sought to mend relations with China. These developments de-linked the Cambodian conflict from the global and regional rivalries that had hitherto blocked all attempts at a settlement. With the conflict localized, it became possible for the United Nations to tender its services in an attempt to reconcile the differences between the warring factions. Meanwhile there can be little doubt about the enhanced position of the regional 'victors' China and, up to a point, Thailand.

In Northeast Asia too the legacies of the conflicts of previous centuries as well as of the Pacific War and the Cold War continue to shape the international relations of the region. Meanwhile, here, too, the resolution of long term conflicts has in some, but not all, respects eased with the ending of the superpower confrontation. The disengagement of the major external sources of conflict has not of itself solved the conflicts of Korea, nor the territorial dispute between Russia and Japan, or still less the China–Taiwan problem, but by being disentangled from the wider global conflict of the Cold War it has become possible to reduce the stakes of the conflicts and to introduce greater flexibility into their management.

The ending of the Cold War provides a convenient point to look back at the previous forty-five years to identify the underlying themes that have shaped the agenda of international politics in the Asia-Pacific region and to establish the points of junction and disjunction between the global, regional and local levels of politics noted earlier. But the ending of the Cold War has also ushered in a new era characterized less by a tangible sense of new order than by one of transition and uncertainty.

The ending of the bipolar divide between the United States and the former Soviet Union has broken the basis of the linkage that used to enmesh some regional questions with global issues. Indeed the character of what is of global concern has changed. For example, the potential conflict between the two Koreas has ceased to be regarded as a possible trigger that could ignite a third world war; rather it is now seen as being of local or, at most, of regional significance. But the possible acquisition of nuclear weapons by the North is perceived with alarm as an issue of global importance.

The world has become more complex and its lines of conflict more disparate. In retrospect the Cold War era provided the United States government with an organizing framework that bound together questions of global strategy with those of ideology, politics, and even economics. Now that that framework has gone it is proving to be much more difficult for Washington to develop a coherent strategy to address the new situation. It can no longer override domestic concerns and special interests by invoking the strategic imperatives of foreign policy. In fact, now that the global agenda has changed, it is the domestic arena that is claiming attention in the United States. These developments have raised new concerns within the Asia-Pacific as to whether the American public and Washington will have the political will to maintain current force levels in the region and to fulfil the commitments of the United States. As a result there is unease within the region that a new distribution of power may be in the process of emerging that may prove disruptive to the relative stability of the last decade.

The impact in the Asia-Pacific of the ending of the Cold War has been altogether different from that in Europe. The Asian communist regimes (with the exception of Mongolia – which in any case had many of the characteristics of an Eastern European satellite of the Soviet Union) have not collapsed. The East Asian economic miracle continues to unfold as it has spread to the ASEAN countries and most spectacularly to China itself. But as China stands on the threshold of developing the economic weight to match its leaders' great power aspirations, new questions have arisen, or perhaps old questions have emerged afresh, about its capacity to survive as a unitary state. Meanwhile its weaker neighbours seek to draw China into closer engagement with the region, particularly through participation in the new regional organizations ARF and APEC.

This book will first provide an historical overview of the region as a whole as it has evolved since 1945. It will be subdivided chronologically so as to facilitate discussion of the possible links between local developments and changes in the balance of power at both regional and global levels. Subsequent chapters will analyse separately the interests and policies of the two global powers, the United States and the Soviet Union/Russia, as these have taken shape within the region. That will be followed by chapters on China and Japan, respectively, as the two major regional powers of global significance. The final chapter will examine the implications for the region of the ending of the Cold War and consider the prospects for the immediate future.

NOTES AND REFERENCES

1 Cited by Bernard K. Gordon, 'Pacific Futures for the USA.' in Lau Teik Soon and Leo Suryadinata (eds) *Moving into the Pacific Century: The Changing Regional Order* (Oxford: Heinemann, 1988) p. 3.

2 The World Bank, *The East Asian Miracle: Economic Growth and Public Policy* (Oxford: Oxford University Press, 1993).

3 F. C. Jones, *Japan's New Order in East Asia: its rise and fall 1937–45* (London: Oxford University Press, 1954); and Robert J. C. Butow, *Tojo and the Coming of War* (Princeton: Princeton University Press, 1961).

4 Interestingly, the Japanese government decreed immediately after the attack on Pearl Harbor in December 1941 that the term, 'the Far East'

(*kyokuto*), an 'obnoxious' reflection of the notion that 'England was the centre of the world', was no longer to be used, and that henceforth the war was to be known as that of 'Great East Asia' (*Daitoa*). See Christopher Thorne, *The Far Eastern War: States and Societies 1941–45* (London: Counterpoint, Unwin Paperbacks, 1986).

5 Michael Leifer, *Asean and the Security of South-East Asia* (London: Routledge, 1989) Chapter 2, 'The Evolution of ASEAN: Faltering Steps in Regional Reconciliation' pp. 17–51.

6 All figures are drawn from the *Far Eastern Economic Review Asia 1994 Yearbook*.

7 This account of regional order is derived from accounts in Hedley Bull, *The Anarchical Society* (London: Macmillan, 1977) Chapter 3; Stanley Hoffman, *Primacy or World Order* (New York: McGraw Hill Book Co., 1978) Chapters 3 and 4; and Michael Leifer (ed.) 'The Balance of Power and Regional Order' in Leifer (ed.) *The Balance of Power in East Asia* (London: Macmillan, 1986). The question of order should be distinguished from that of regime, to which it is closely related, as the latter is usually related to principles and procedures as these apply to a particular issue area.

8 The range of the Japanese surplus arises from discrepancies in the IMF statistics between those listed for the US and those for Japan, see *IMF Direction of Trade Statistics Yearbook 1994*.

9 Kaname Akamatsu, cited by Takashi Inoguchi, 'Shaping and Sharing Pacific Dynamism' in Peter A. Gourevitch (ed.) *The Pacific Region: Challenges to Policy and Theory* (The Annals of the American Academy of Political Science, September 1989) p. 48.

10 As before, these figures are drawn from the *IMF Direction of Trade Statistics Yearbooks*.

11 See Robert Gilpin, *The Political Economy of International Relations* (Princeton: Princeton University Press, 1987) for a discussion of this and theory of 'hegemonic stability', pp. 74, 86–87.

Part I

The significance of the Cold War

1 The impact of the Cold War and the struggles for independence, 1945–54

It was the advent of the Cold War in the late 1940s and early 1950s that brought about a junction in the Asia-Pacific between the international, regional and local dimensions of politics and military strategy. More precisely, it was the Korean War, begun in June 1950, that effectively integrated the Asia-Pacific into the Cold War system that had first emerged in Europe. But unlike the situation in Europe where the Cold War divided the protagonists into two clearly defined camps of opposing ideological, economic and political systems separated by an 'iron curtain', the divisions in Asia were less clear cut and were still being contested long after they had been settled in Europe. Moreover, in Asia there also emerged a non-aligned dimension registered at the Asian–African Conference held in Bandung in 1955 . The difference between Asia and Europe was also apparent from the way the Second World War was conducted in the two theatres and from the different consequences of that war in each sector. The European war had been fought over established states between vast land armies which ended in a division of Europe between the Soviet and Western victorious armies. The war in the Asia-Pacific was won essentially through American naval and air power culminating in the dropping of the two atomic bombs. This left a scramble for power in many parts of Asia involving both civil wars and struggles for independence against the returning colonial powers.

Although the Pacific War had provided a strategic rationale for treating the region as a whole, the Western allies came to treat Northeast and Southeast Asia separately. As the United States concentrated its forces on the assault on Japan itself, Britain was in effect entrusted with winning the war in Southeast Asia with initial responsibility for Burma, Thailand and Malaya, including Singapore and Sumatra. In July 1945, the rest of the Dutch East Indies, excluding the island of Timor, as well as Indo-China south of the 16th parallel of latitude was transferred to the Southeast Asia Command under Admiral Mountbatten. Indo-China, north of the 16th parallel, was allocated to the China command of Chiang Kai-shek and the rest was designated as the South-West Pacific Command.[1] This division of labour was to accentuate the differences between the two sub-regions of Northeastern and Southeastern Asia in the early years after the war since the immediate agenda for the north centred on relations between the United States and the Soviet Union and the domestic evolutions of China and Japan, whereas that of the south turned on the struggles for independence with the returned colonial powers. As became evident from the American involvement in the struggles in Indo-China from the late 1940s, it was the advent of the Cold War that began to link the two sub-regions together from both global and local perspectives. It was only then that the results of local struggles for power or independence were regarded as having implications for the global distribution of power and influence. That provided a basis, on the one hand, for competing local élites to seek and to obtain external patronage and, on the other hand, for the external powers to extend such support for their own competitive advantages.

NORTHEAST ASIA

The immediate aftermath of the Pacific War was shaped by the understandings reached at the Yalta Conference which in turn reflected the realities of American maritime hegemony in the Pacific and Soviet dominance of the landmass of Northeast Asia.[2] The result was a division into spheres of interest. The United States exercised predominance in the Pacific Ocean, including the Philippines, Okinawa and Japan. The Soviet Union regained Sakhalin and the Kuriles as well as obtaining rights in Manchurian railways and ports and gaining Chinese recognition of the independence of its protégé, the former Outer Mongolia. Headed by the British, the colonial rulers sought to restore their positions in Southeast Asia. China had been expected to emerge as a sovereign power and to join the other three great powers in establishing a trusteeship over Korea.[3] In the event a trusteeship did not emerge in Korea. Instead a hasty agreement about the division of responsibility for accepting the Japanese surrender was concocted between the Americans and the Soviets which to the agreeable surprise of the former was observed unilaterally by the Soviet forces who stopped at the 38th Parallel even though American forces had yet to arrive.[4]

The American view of international order was not confined to balance of power considerations, it also put a premium upon domestic stability in the form of democratic institutions within states.[5] The linchpin of Roosevelt's original post war strategy in the Asia-Pacific was that a 'united and democratic China' would emerge, capable of exercising decisive influence as one of the great powers in the kind of post war order envisaged in his 'Four Freedoms' speech of January 1941 and in the Atlantic Charter which he announced with Churchill in August that year. The Charter asserted such principles as denial of territorial aggrandizement, guarantee of the right of self determination for all nations, creation of an open liberal economic system and international cooperation to preserve peace and security. Although these principles were incorporated with Soviet agreement in the United Nations Charter at the San Francisco meeting in 1945, and despite Soviet attendance at the Bretton Woods meetings that agreed the framework for a world economy based on free trade, it became clear that the Soviet Union had no intention of following them in terms as understood in the West. By 1946 the American disillusionment with Soviet behaviour in Poland was affecting American attitudes in the East.[6]

Nevertheless, the American disappointment with China's failure to live up to their wartime expectations, coupled with the failure of the 1945–46 Marshall mission to avert a civil war did not lead the American administration to cast the rivalry between the nationalists and communists within the framework of the Cold War at that point.[7] The origins of the Cold War were in Europe and that was the main focus of the attentions of both the Soviet Union and the United States. The Truman Doctrine of March 1947 which elevated the specific obligations being undertaken in Greece and Turkey to a universal commitment to 'support free peoples who are resisting attempted subjugation by armed minorities or outside pressures', was in fact made some time after the Americans had already begun to assist those two countries. As many have argued, the high moral tone and the universal character of the Doctrine was directed as much at mobilizing the American public back home as it was aimed abroad. By this stage a good part of American problems stemmed from the absence of means to carry out the growing international commitments the US was undertaking. Immediately the war had ended the US began a rapid and extensive de-mobilization of its armed forces. These had stood at 12 million at the end of the war with Germany, and had come down to 3 million by July 1946 and to 1.6 million a year later. Defence spending followed a similar trajectory. In 1945, the last year of war, it had reached $81.6 billion; in fiscal 1946 it came down to $44.7 billion and in fiscal 1947 it dropped to $13.1 billion.[8]

Just as the hoped for cooperation with the Soviet Union was being replaced by confrontation, the American capacity to meet even the needs of Western Europe had diminished. The Truman Doctrine was designed at least in part to galvanize the American public. It was a factor in building support for the Marshall Plan for Europe and in providing further aid for Chiang Kai-shek. But the disappointment with China had already led to a reconsideration of the American interest in retaining forces in Korea south of the 38th parallel. Indeed by 1947–48 it had been decided to withdraw them. Meanwhile the United States had begun to regard Japan not only as a country that had to be encouraged to develop along liberal lines, but also as one that had to undergo reconstruction as a potential ally and as a source of stability in Northeast Asia.[9]

Despite Soviet apprehensions, the United States government had no intention of intervening in the Chinese civil war. As the communist victory loomed the US government took the view that deep indigenous forces were at work and that the costs of intervention were unacceptably high and had little chance of success. Although there is evidence to show that Mao Zedong and Zhou Enlai on their side had hoped to cultivate relations with the United States, perhaps for economic reasons and to avoid becoming exclusively dependent upon the Soviet Union, nothing came of their private overtures. Leading US administration figures also hoped to wean the Chinese communists from Moscow along the path pioneered by Tito.[10] Whether or not such developments amounted to a 'lost chance', Sino–American relations diverged more and more markedly in the course of the nine months from the establishment of the PRC (People's Republic of China) in October 1949 until the outbreak of the Korean War in June 1950. At home anti-communist hysteria, sparked in part by the administration's own Cold War rhetoric and fanned by Senator McCarthy's campaign against so-called domestic traitors, including those in the State Department who were alleged to have contributed to the 'loss' of China, contributed to the difficulties in deciding upon foreign policy by rational calculations of measured interests. Meanwhile, Mao publicly encouraged hostility towards the United States, proclaimed his adherence to the Soviet Union in July when Liu Shaoqi was secretly sent to Moscow, and in December 1949 went himself to Moscow to negotiate an alliance that was eventually signed in February 1950.

Nevertheless the Truman Administration had decided early in 1950 that US interests in Taiwan were not important enough to prevent its conquest by the Chinese communists. Even the Joint Chiefs of Staff, who recognized the damage that it would cause to American strategic interests, were unwilling to recommend military intervention because the limited American forces available might be needed for higher priority use elsewhere.[11] With the Yalta system having broken down in the Asia-Pacific because of the communist victory in China, US policy became less than consistent and coherent. Its policy of limited assistance to the Kuo Min Tang (KMT or Nationalist) Government 'pleased no one and gained nothing'.[12] In January 1950 as Mao was still embroiled with difficult negotiations with Stalin, first Truman made it clear on 5 January that the US would not defend Taiwan and then on 12 January Acheson stated at the National Press Club that the American defence perimeter in Asia ran from the Aleutians through Japan and Okinawa to the Philippines. Korea was not included among those listed as being of vital strategic importance to the US; instead it was said to be under UN protection.

The perimeter defence concept would have been badly flawed if indeed the PRC had taken over Taiwan. But had the US sought to defend Taiwan it would have undoubtedly ensured the enmity of the PRC by undermining its national aims of unifying China, thereby driving it still further towards the Soviet Union. The trouble was that the policies designed to serve the US Administration's long term policy goal of weaning China away from its Soviet ally were not in accord with its own short term strategic interests. Being still disillusioned with the KMT but bound by a Republican Congress to extend aid to Chiang Kai-shek, the administration still clung on to the hope that a separate Taiwan might emerge under different auspices.

Thus on the eve of the Korean War the US perimeter defence strategy involved a strong commitment to the defence of Japan and to upholding the liberal domestic system that was evolving there under the American aegis, and it also included Okinawa and further south, the Philippines. But despite American aid to the Chiang Kai-shek regime in Taiwan and to the Syngman Rhee regime in South Korea, commitment to them was more qualified. Although there was some support for these regimes among Republicans in Washington, there was no fundamental disagreement among the leaders of the Truman Administration that even though it was in American interests to uphold them the means to do so had been stretched very thin. The main American priority was Europe and care had to be taken to avoid being over-committed elsewhere.

On the communist side there was continued distrust between China and the Soviet Union despite the alliance between them. Nevertheless both Mao and Stalin had given Kim Il-Sung the go-ahead to seek to reunify Korea by force. Yet it is still not clear how each had calculated the security interests involved. Clearly they had reason to believe that the Americans would not intervene, but they did not appear to have contingency plans ready in case they did.[13] Moscow was absent from the Security Council at the crucial time in June 1950, ostensibly in protest at the exclusion of the PRC from the UN. Western analysts have found no evidence to suggest that the Chinese were involved in the preparations for the war or that they intended to become involved in it.[14] The Soviet Union had played the major part in establishing and arming the Kim regime right up to late Spring 1950, and it is possible that Stalin may have approved Kim's war plans with a view to increasing the Soviet influence over China. Although Kim had been effectively put in place by the Soviet forces in 1945 the character of his relations with Stalin remain unclear. How much of a free hand did he have? Was there any idea of tying in Kim's plans with Mao's plans to attack Taiwan? Despite the increased availability of archival material many questions remain. But there can be little doubt that both sides regarded the existence of a friendly regime (which at that time could only have meant a communist one) on their Korean borders as vital to their respective securities. In that sense Korea was more important to the Soviet than to the American side.

Although the Cold War had already begun to influence the international politics of the Asia-Pacific as was demonstrated by the US despatch of aid to Indo-China in May 1950, the Korean War had the effect of drawing a sharp demarcation line in Northeast Asia between the communist countries on one side, and the so-called 'free world' on the other, that was to last for the next twenty years. The North Korean attack on the South across the 38th parallel on 25 June 1950 may have been regarded by Kim Il-Sung as a national civil war to unite his artificially divided country, but in the international climate of the time it was bound to have been seen as more than that. In Washington it was immediately regarded as a new instance of communist aggression and a test of Western resolve, especially after the success in countering the Soviet blockade of

West Berlin a year earlier. The impact in Europe of the possible successful communist use of force in Asia was very great and the North Korean's sudden attack was an important element in the decision to establish a unified NATO command. The consequence in Asia was President Truman's immediate announcement that an economic embargo would be imposed on China and that the US Seventh Fleet would be interposed in the Taiwan Straits, thus preventing a pending Chinese communist attack upon the island. Truman's intention was to deny Taiwan as a potential base to the Soviet Union in the western Pacific.[15] The effect of the decision on Mao was to confirm his view that the Americans supported Chiang Kai-shek in the hope of invading the Chinese mainland to reverse the result of the Chinese civil war.[16] In retrospect the Chinese were to argue that this was the decisive turning point in their relations with the Americans.

However, it was the crossing of the 38th parallel by the American dominated UN forces in October 1950 (after their defeat of the forces of the North) and their approach to the Chinese border in total disregard of Chinese warnings to desist, that led to military intervention by the Chinese. What was seen by the UN as a move towards uniting Korea was perceived by Mao as a threat to China's security and the survival of his newly established revolutionary regime. Local, regional and international political and security issues became enmeshed in an apparently seamless web.

Instead of seeking to distinguish between primary and secondary strategic interests, the outbreak of the Korean War caused the Truman Administration to define its interests in absolutist terms and to try to apply the strategic doctrine of containment in Northeast Asia as laid out in NSC 68 of 1949 – the first comprehensive attempt to extend Cold War strategic thinking to Asia. Following the European pattern a sharp geographic line was drawn on the map between two opposed systems whose security was ultimately guaranteed by each of the superpowers. The line ran between Japan and the USSR in the Sea of Japan and along the armistice line (roughly the 38th parallel) between North and South Korea and through the Taiwan Straits between Taiwan (the Republic of China – ROC) and the Chinese mainland (the People's Republic of China – PRC). The disposition of some of the off-shore islands in the Straits was to become the ostensible cause of two major crises in the Cold War era. At the same time it is important to recognize that the strategic divide that was underlined by a political and ideological bifurcation between the US and the USSR as global powers was mirrored not only by a regional divide, as described above, but by local ones in which both Korea and China were split into two separate states claiming exclusive jurisdiction of the whole country. The sharpness and immobility of the line drawn between 'East' and 'West' was paralleled by a stalemate in the civil war between the divided states. The competitive junction between the two global powers and their local allies had become very close indeed.

The Korean War itself may be regarded as essentially a domestic or civil war that had unanticipated international consequences.[17] Despite the release of new source materials in the last few years, the motives and the calculations of the different communist leaders are still unclear. Both Kim Il-Sung of North Korea and Ho Chi Minh of Vietnam visited Moscow during the course of Mao's negotiations with Stalin. Kim obtained Stalin's approval to go to war and apparently that of Mao too, whose advice to Kim to pursue a more guerilla based strategy was ignored.[18] The veil of secrecy on Mao's relations with Stalin has been lifted to reveal extraordinary degrees of distrust. As Mao put it a dozen years later:

> After the victory of the revolution [Stalin] . . . suspected China of being a Yugoslavia, and that I would be another Tito. . . . When did Stalin begin to have confidence in us? It was at the time of the [Korean] War from the winter of 1950. He then came to believe that we were not Tito, not Yugoslavia.[19]

Whether by accident or by design the Korean War was beneficial to Moscow in that it put to an end for a long time the possibilities of an accommodation between Beijing and Washington.[20]

Despite the enormous destruction unleashed upon Korea and its people and the high rate of casualties of the opposing armies,[21] the Korean War is credited as the first limited war of the Cold War era in which the US and the USSR exercised calculated restraint so as to avoid its widening. Both sides, for example, connived in effect to suppress news of extensive clashes between the Soviet and American air forces.[22] It should be noted, however, that at the end the Eisenhower Administration threatened to use nuclear weapons so as to bring to an end the armistice negotiations that had been dragging on for two years.

The Korean War also prompted the US to seek to include Japan in attempts to strengthen the 'free world' in the region. This involved preparing for the conclusion of a peace treaty and for tying Japan into some kind of regional alliance. The administration's special envoy, John Foster Dulles, who visited Japan in early 1951 was unable to persuade the Japanese to rearm and settled instead for a policy of economic cooperation by which Japanese productive capacity would be used in support of the war effort. American ideas of establishing a regional Pacific Pact also foundered on allied residual distrust of Japan and on differences between them. In the build up to the Peace Treaty itself the US signed a Mutual Defense Treaty with the Philippines in August 1951 and one month later a similar treaty with Australia and New Zealand. The Japanese Peace Treaty was also signed in September in San Francisco. Japan and the US signed a Mutual Defense Treaty and the following year the American occupation came to an end as Japan resumed full sovereignty.

Despite American efforts the end result was a Cold War alignment in Northeast Asia very different from the one that emerged in Europe. Although the first hot war of the era had been fought in this part of the world, regional ties were relatively weak on both sides of the divide. On the Soviet side its dominance over Eastern Europe was not matched in Northeast Asia. It exercised influence but not control over North Korea and the PRC was too big, independent and proud to be dominated in that way especially as it proved itself to be a major power on the battlefields of Korea where for the first time in modern history Chinese forces had fought a modern Western army to a standstill. On the American side too there was no Asian Pacific equivalent to the Marshall Plan let alone NATO. Instead there were a series of primarily bilateral treaties across the Pacific.

SOUTHEAST ASIA

The end of the Pacific War saw the return of the colonial powers to a very changed world. The legacy of the Japanese had been, first, to have shattered the myths of colonial white superiority and, second, to have accelerated the nationalist drive for independence. Three levels of foreign relations may be identified in the early evolution of the foreign relations of the states of Southeast Asia. The process of acquiring independence and the character of the post colonial settlement involved relations with former rulers. In some cases these endured in relative harmony well beyond the transfer of sovereignty. The second level involved local reactions to great power involvement in the region. The third involved intra-regional relations among the resident states.[23] More broadly their different roads to independence became embroiled in the wider struggles of international politics that centred on Cold War issues and they greatly influenced the subsequent alignments and international roles of the new states.

The international aspects of the end of the Pacific War also contributed to shaping the subsequent development of independence in the resident states. The SEAC under British leadership lacked the resources to cope with the sudden and unexpected surrender of the Japanese forces in Southeast Asia. This led to delays in establishing a significant SEAC presence in the Dutch East Indies and French Indo-China in particular. Nationalist groups filled the vacuum which led to armed confrontations as the Dutch and the French later returned in force. Indeed armed struggle that inevitably acquired external dimensions became a feature of the acquisition of independence in both territories. The impact of the communist victory in the Chinese civil war in the late 1940s was also widely felt in the region as an inspiration and source of support for insurgents and as a challenge to incumbent élites.

The Philippines became independent as a close associate of the United States and it was not until the US abandoned its bases there at the end of the Cold War that the Philippines began to move away from the highly ambivalent position that sought to balance its professed Asian identity with its dependence on America. This pattern was evident from the acquisition of independence. The US had promised independence even before the war and it moved towards it speedily once it had ended. The Philippine Republic was inaugurated on 4 July 1946, but from the outset the Filipino élite accepted a dependency on the United States to which it was indebted for its continued dominance of the country. The American Supreme Commander General Douglas MacArthur chose to overlook the collaborationist record of much of this élite as the principal resistance movement to the Japanese was the communist led Hukbalahap (People's Anti-Japanese Army). The United States contributed to the economic rehabilitation of the Philippines, but at the same time it insisted upon a Trade Act that benefited American agrarian and manufacturing interests. In March 1947 it was agreed to perpetuate the huge American bases on Filipino territory. By 1949 the communist led Huks turned to armed struggle against the corrupt ruling élite. This led to greater American military aid and to relative success in containing the insurgency. In January 1950 the American Secretary of State, Dean Acheson, declared the Philippines to be part of America's strategic defence perimeter in the Pacific.

The Filipino élite has been called bi-national on account of the attachment to the US.[24] By virtue of geography and history the Philippines has been set somewhat apart from the other Southeast Asian countries. Compared to them the historical influences of Indian and Chinese cultures have been relatively small. There was no national centre or state before the Spanish conquest in the sixteenth century. Islam had spread from Borneo and from what is now Indonesia to the island of Luzon, but it was driven back south by the vigorous extension of Catholicism by the missionaries who accompanied the *conquistadors*. Having in effect created the Philippines as a state, the Spaniards also left their mark on the social structure, leaving behind a wealthy *mestizo* élite based on large rural estates who have come to dominate politics, as well as a legacy of extensive rural poverty. Not surprisingly, the Philippines has often been depicted as a piece of Latin America located off-shore of East Asia. The newly independent country 'acquired a reputation [in Asia] for being a spokesman for American interests'.[25] Indeed right until the closure of the American bases at the end of the Cold War, the Filipinos' sense of identification with Asia continued to be ambivalent. Notwithstanding shared linguistic and ethnic origins with their near neighbours, Indonesia and Malaysia, the Philippines remained somewhat aloof from their regional concerns. In 1963 it formed the Association of Southeast Asia (ASA) with Malaya and Thailand – the other two pro Western states of the region – which soon foundered because of the Filipino claim to Sabah. The Philippines became involved in the Vietnam War under the influence of the United States. Its membership of the Association of Southeast Asian Nations (ASEAN) did not make a substantive difference initially, but over time the intra-regional dimension carried increasing weight in Filipino foreign policy. However, the Philippines remained the Asian state with the closest ties to the United States.[26]

Indonesia by contrast professed great attachment to what became known as non-alignment. This may be traced to the impact of the complex struggle for independence when the great powers were found wanting and to the Indonesian sense of an entitlement to exercise the leading position in Southeast Asia. Interestingly, despite the anti-communist outlook of the Indonesian army there was a tendency among its senior officers to feel that they had much in common with their Vietnamese equivalents because their respective struggles for independence involved anti-colonial armed struggle. In fact the Indonesian road to independence involved both armed struggle and diplomacy.

Indonesian independence was first declared on 17 August 1945, two days after the surrender of the Japanese. The latter had left behind a trained Indonesian military force and an active youth movement. The British arrived in September to be followed by the Dutch a month later to confront a mass movement. The Dutch established influence over the outer islands and attempted to crush the independence movement by two 'police actions'. By the time of the second in December 1948 the international political environment had changed to the advantage of the Indonesians. In the first two or three years after the Second World War the American sentiment in favour of national independence as against old world colonialism was tempered by the need to shore-up the weakened West European countries and their fragile democracies against the perceived communist and Soviet threat. But by late 1948 a new dimension had entered the equation as the impact of the Cold War began to be felt in Southeast Asia too. The Americans now began to fear that the appeal of communism to the peoples of Asia would grow if the nationalists were to be continually frustrated in their rightful quest for independence. Moreover the Americans took note of the crushing of the communist uprising in Mediun by the Indonesian Republican forces earlier in September 1948. The Dutch then came under increasing American pressure to concede. Paradoxically, it was the success of the second 'police action' in December that hastened their end. Amid a context in which the Indonesian army had begun a guerilla campaign a negotiated settlement was eventually reached and the Republic of the United States of Indonesia was formed, initially under UN auspices, in December 1949. These events reaffirmed the Indonesian attachment to independence, as in a bipolar world the Soviet Union had proved to be untrustworthy because of Mediun and the United States unreliable because of inconsistency.

This left two sets of tensions that were to dominate Indonesian politics and foreign relations for a long time thereafter. First, a tension developed between the army and the politicians, and second, a tension emerged between the efficacy of struggle and diplomacy in the conduct of foreign affairs. The army came to see itself as even more than the ultimate protector of the Indonesian state and under President Sukarno's Guided Democracy, the army became part of the uneasy triumvirate in charge of the ship of state. In the end, after the failed 1965 coup, it eventually took over supreme power in 1966 under the leadership of General Suharto. Until his fall Sukarno combined elements both of struggle and diplomacy in his assertive foreign policy. This was most evident in his successful campaign to annex West Irian (the former West New Guinea) in 1963, where he played off the United States and the Soviet Union, and in the unsuccessful attempt to undermine the newly formed Malaysia in his campaign of *Konfrontasi* of 1963–66. Notwithstanding the diplomatic support of the United States in the struggle for independence, and even on the West Irian question, Indonesia became firmly wedded to the non-aligned position of Asian nationalists and indeed became a leading exponent of it.[27]

In contrast to the Dutch in Indonesia and the French in Indo-China, the British sought to encourage Malaya on the road to independence and indeed there was a Malay élite that was close to Britain and espoused democratic values. But the British task was complicated by the consequences of having encouraged the settlement of migrant labour from China, in particular in the nineteenth and early twentieth centuries. By the outbreak of the Pacific War the Chinese and also Indian immigrants had come to account for nearly half the population. During the occupation the Japanese cultivated the resentful Malays at the expense of the Chinese who had been greatly influenced by stories of the resistance of their kith and kin and fellow nationals to Japanese aggression in China itself. During the war the British supported the communist-led and Chinese dominated resistance against the Japanese. Their support was in many ways similar to that of the Americans for the communist-led Vietnamese resistance to Japan at the same time.

After the war the British were unable to persuade the ethnic Malays of the virtues of a projected Malayan Union with equal citizenship for Chinese and Indians, despite excluding the Chinese dominated city of Singapore. It was rejected by the newly formed United Malays National Organization (UMNO) which dominated the alternative Federation of Malaya established in 1948. The Malayan Communist Party (MCP) with its constituencies among the Chinese communities found that its political effectiveness within the trade unions was being curtailed and it turned to armed struggle in June 1948. That insurrection also reflected the changing international circumstances associated with the beginnings of the Cold War and the inspiration of the pending victory of the communists in the civil war in China and of the armed struggle begun by the communist-led Vietminh against the French.

The British declared a state of emergency in June 1948. The Emergency lasted officially until 1960; a rump insurgency force continued to operate in the jungles of the Thai–Malay borders until the late 1980s. But the back of the insurgency was broken in the early

1950s after the resettlement of some half a million (Chinese) squatters on whose support the insurgents depended. The costs to the victorious side were nevertheless enormous. Against guerillas whom at no stage numbered more than 8,000 men, were deployed 40,000 regular British and Commonwealth troops, 70,000 Malay police and some 200,000 home guards. But the Emergency itself led to the establishment of the Malayan Chinese Association (MCA) in February 1949, made up of anti-communist Chinese Chamber of Commerce members and educated professionals. A pact between the two communal organizations UMNO and MCA at municipal elections in 1952 at the expense of a multiracial rival eventually paved the way to independence in 1957.[28]

The only country in Southeast Asia that did not experience colonialism, Thailand, nevertheless had to make difficult adjustments in order to adapt to the post war conditions. It chose a path of adhering closely to the United States, primarily because it was the dominant power and also because Thailand's regional interests coincided with the Cold War objectives of the United States in the area.

The military government that came to power following a coup in 1932 which overthrew the absolute monarchy, accommodated to the power of Japan and allowed its armies transit to British held Burma and Malaya. Immediately after the Japanese surrender a new Thai government headed by a civilian member of the 1932 coup group who had led a war time resistance to Japan nullified the arrangements made with Japan and promised to return with compensation the territories the Japanese had granted the Thais from Burma and Malaya. The United States helped the Thai government, which was now headed by its former minister to Washington, to resist pressure for further concessions from Britain. At the end of complex diplomacy Thailand also gave up territories in Laos and Cambodia and was admitted to the United Nations at the end of 1946. Thailand has enjoyed a continuity of diplomatic style that goes back a long time in history.

> Though it is often wrongly construed as one of neutrality, in fact it has always been a diplomacy which has been 'hard' towards small neighbours and 'soft' towards the dominant regional power: China before the Opium Wars, then Britain, then Japan, and, particularly evident ever since 1954, the United States.[29]

Interestingly, even earlier Thailand had sent a contingent to participate in the Korean War which contributed to securing benefaction from the United States. Thailand became a party to the 1954 Manila Pact with the US that secured a formal American commitment to come to the defence of the country and Bangkok became the headquarters of the South East Asia Treaty Organization (SEATO).

Burma, one of the historic political centres in Southeast Asia, became a province of British India in the nineteenth century, which led to an inflow of immigrants from India. Burmese nationalism before the Pacific War had a distinctive anti-Indian flavour. In 1937 Burma was separated from India and given considerable control over domestic affairs. During the Japanese occupation it was granted nominal independence in 1943, but this proved to be illusory and although the British return was welcomed in 1945 there was now impatience for independence. The leader of the nationalist movement, Aung San, was a former student leader who had been commander of the Japanese sponsored Burmese National Army. The British offered independence within dominion status that in the end was rejected. Aung San along with six of his colleagues in the Cabinet were assassinated in July 1947 before the formal transfer of power had been completed. Association with the Commonwealth had already been rejected and the Republic of the Union of Burma became formally independent in January 1948. But faced with ethnic rebellions, opposition from China's communist leaders combined with a lack of interest in its security by Britain and the United States, the new Burmese government opted for a policy of what Michael Leifer has called 'non-offence' especially towards its giant neighbour to the north.[30] By the early 1950s it became active in voicing the concerns of Asian neutralism (in the Cold War) and it was one of the key Asian powers that met in Colombo to help convene the first Asian–African summit conference in Bandung in 1955.[31]

Vietnam was the most important country in Indo-China and its history after 1945 was dominated by the armed struggle for independence from France led by the communist-directed Vietminh, that began in 1946 and culminated in the Geneva Agreements on Indo-China of July 1954. This resulted in the recognition of the independence of Laos and Cambodia and of a communist North Vietnam and a non-communist South. These eight years of armed struggle, later known as the first Indo-China war, brought together the three main dimensions of conflict: the global, the regional and the local. It also began a process of international and regional conflict that was not to be concluded before the end of the Cold War itself. At this stage the conflict initially involved the intensely nationalistic and fervently communistic Vietminh against the returning French forces who had desperately and largely unavailingly sought to recruit a credible Vietnamese nationalistic alternative to the Vietminh. The two warring parties were soon to be backed by the victorious Chinese communists on the one side and by the Americans on the other. American support became possible only after the Elysée Agreements of March 1949 which gave the Indo-Chinese states nominal independence.

Once the Vietminh in the North had secured access to Chinese communist support after the latter's domestic victory in 1949, the terms of the war turned remorselessly against the French. Up to that point the French forces were in possession of most of the cities and towns in Vietnam, but had difficulty in controlling the rural areas. Thereafter the Vietminh were able to escalate their fighting capabilities from guerilla to positional warfare. The French finally conceded that they should withdraw after their defeat at Dien Bien Phu in May 1954.[32] That surrender has been called 'the worst defeat any Western colonial power ever suffered on the battlefield at the hands of an Asian people'.[33] The war, which drew in the external powers, became the primary agency that led to what has been called the internationalization of the problems of Southeast Asia. Within the context of the Cold War it highlighted an American concern with the domestic conditions of the state of the area. It provided a framework for placing the domestic developments and the contending élites of the countries of the region within a Cold War syndrome that at its height joined them with the axis of international as well as regional conflict.

THE GENEVA CONFERENCE

The Geneva Conference of 1954 which convened to address the Korean and Indo-Chinese issues may be seen as the bench-mark that signalled the completion of the integration of East Asia into the Cold War system. It also confirmed China's great power status (even though John Foster Dulles is reputed at one point to have refused to shake the hand of Zhou Enlai). It affirmed the stalemate of the Korean armistice and helped to end what turned out to be the first Indo-China war.

The Geneva Agreements of July 1954 effectively ended the French presence in Indo-China. They arranged a partition of Vietnam that, although provisional in principle, resulted in practice in a victorious communist regime in the North beyond the 17th parallel and an

insecure anti-communist regime in the South. The two were supposedly to be united through elections to be held two years hence.
The Geneva settlement also called for an independent but neutral
Cambodia and Laos. The Geneva Agreements satisfied the Chinese
government by preventing an immediate American military intervention – which was one of the routes that Mao feared the Americans might follow in order to attack China itself.[34] Moreover,
following the Korean War the Chinese adopted a new diplomatic
stance that favoured peaceful co-existence so as to be better able
to concentrate on economic development at home and cultivate
newly established Asian governments. The post Stalin Soviet leaders
also sought to reduce tensions with the Americans. That is why
the two communist giants had combined to put pressure on the
Vietnamese communists to give up ground they controlled below
the 17th parallel. Twenty-five years later, after the 1979 Chinese
attack on Vietnam, the Vietnamese leaders publicly revealed their
anger at what they regarded as the Chinese betrayal at Geneva.[35]

The Americans too were displeased with the Agreements and,
together with the government of South Vietnam they refused to
accept the Final Declaration. The United States, however, did not
block the Geneva settlement because of the position of its European
allies, notably the British and the French, but neither did it wish to
condone formally the communist victory. The American representative confined himself to declaring that his government would regard
any attempt to upset the terms of the settlement by force as a threat
to peace. Dulles himself regarded Geneva as confirming that 'the
tide is running against us in the channel of [his] tough policy. If we
are to continue to pursue it we shall lose many of our allies . . .'[36]

By the middle of 1954 the Cold War had left its mark on Southeast
as well as on Northeast Asia. The Philippines and increasingly Thailand were closely tied to the United States. North Vietnam, as a
communist state, belonged to the socialist camp and South Vietnam
sought to consolidate its precarious statehood under American protection. The fragile states of Laos and Cambodia were nominally
neutral by an agreement of the regional and external powers. Burma
had perforce to choose inoffensive neutrality. Indonesia was increasingly identifying its independent course in what came to be called
non-alignment. Malaya, which was still subject to the Emergency
had yet to be granted independence as its colonial ruler gradually
asserted mastery of the one Cold War insurgency still active in the
region. But it was clear that in the aftermath of independence, which

would not long be delayed, the Malay élite would lean to the British side.

More generally, the very different paths by which the countries of Southeast Asia acquired independent statehood were to have marked effects upon their subsequent political developments and upon their foreign relations. Some, especially Thailand and divided Vietnam, could draw on traditions of national identity and statehood that long antedated the colonial era, and others such as the Philippines, Malaysia and Indonesia were new successor states to the previous colonial order. Although these too could draw on pre-colonial antecedents this was true of only parts of the new states such as the old trading principalities in parts of what is now Indonesia. Nation building for the very new states encompassed a wider task than the enormous problems of seeking to establish good governance. The conduct of foreign affairs became an essential part of the new nation building as it provided potent new symbols for evoking national unity.

Yet in many respects some of the profound challenges that confronted the older and the newly established states in the aftermath of independence were similar. In varying degrees, with the exception of the Indo-Chinese states, they were led by westernized élites with limited experience in government who had to deal with wide disparities in cultural and political traditions and with deep divisions between town and country. Their inadequate infant administrations had to tackle the still destructive remains of the war and to develop their national economies, quite often against the legacies of one sided economic development of the colonial period. The attempts by their leaders to strengthen national consciousness frequently met with only limited success when faced with ethnic, religious and local particularisms. Moreover none of the new states was free of border or territorial disputes. The rhetoric of Asian solidarity often failed to take into account the realities of differences within and between states, the limited capacities of governments and the paucity of the opportunities to cooperate to solve common problems. Moreover none could really escape the patterns of alignments set by the Cold War.

NOTES AND REFERENCES

1 Evelyn Colbert, *Southeast Asia in International Politics 1941–1956* (Ithaca: Cornell University Press, 1977) p. 53.
2 For accounts of the Yalta Conference see, Diane Shaver Clemens, *Yalta*

(New York: 1970); and Russell D. Buhite, *Decisions at Yalta: An Appraisal of Summit Diplomacy* (Wilmington, Delaware: 1986). For a considered judgement see John Lewis Gaddis, *Russia, the Soviet Union and the United States* (New York: McGraw-Hill, 1990) pp. 165–67 and, for a perspective by a Beijing based political scientist, see Wang Jisi, 'An Appraisal of U.S. Policy toward China, 1945–55, and Its Aftermath' in Harry Harding and Yuan Ming (eds) *Sino–American Relations, 1945–1955* (Wilmington: Scholarly Resources, 1989) p. 290.

3 See the discussion by Akira Iriye, 'Security and Stability in Northeast Asia: A Historical Overview' in Martin E. Weinstein (ed.) *Northeast Asian Security after Vietnam* (Urbana: University of Illinois Press, 1982) p. 9.

4 See the account by Bruce Cummings, *The Origins of the Korean War*, 2 vols (Princeton: Princeton University Press, 1981 and 1990); and by Max Hastings, *The Korean War* (London: Michael Joseph, 1987).

5 See the parallel discussions in Iriye, 'A Historical Overview' *op. cit.* pp. 3–5, 10–15. See also John Lewis Gaddis, 'Korea in American Politics, Strategy, and Diplomacy, 1945–50' in Yonosuke Nagai and Akira Iriye (eds) *The Origins of the Cold War in Asia* (University of Tokyo Press, 1977) pp. 277–80.

6 Gaddis, 'Korea in American Politics . . .' (*op. cit.*) p. 278.

7 See the argument and citations by Aruga Tadashi, 'The United States and the Cold War' in Nagai and Iriye (eds) (*op. cit.*) p. 78.

8 John Lewis Gaddis, *Strategies of Containment* (Oxford: Oxford University Press, 1982) p. 23.

9 See the point made by the US Joint Strategic Survey Committee in April 1947 noted in Akira Iriye, 'Continuities in US–Japanese Relations, 1941–49' in Nagai and Iriye (eds) *The Origins of the Cold War in Asia* (*op. cit.*) p. 403. It should be recognized, however, that the entire thrust of Iriye's argument is to show that until 1949 US policy in Asia operated within the pre-Cold War 'Yalta system'.

10 For discussion of these issues see Dorothy Berg and Waldo Heinrichs, *Uncertain Years: Chinese American Relations 1947–1950* (New York: Columbia University Press, 1980); Nancy Bernkopf Tucker, *Patterns in the Dust: Chinese–American Relations and the Recognition Controversy, 1949–1950* (New York: Columbia University Press, 1983); and Steven M. Goldstein, 'Sino–American Relations, 1948–1950: Lost Chance or No Chance?' in Harry Harding and Yuan Ming (eds) *Sino–American Relations, 1945–1955* (*op. cit.*) pp. 119–42. For an analysis based on recently available Chinese sources see Chen Jian, *China's Road to the Korean War: The Making of the Sino–American Confrontation* (New York: Columbia University Press, 1994) Part Two. For a considered analysis of the position of the Truman Administration see John Lewis Gaddis, *The Long Peace: Inquiries into the History of the Cold War* (Oxford: Oxford University Press, 1987) Chapter 6.

11 Ralph N. Clough, *Island China* (Cambridge, Mass: Harvard University Press, 1978).

12 Suzanne Pepper, 'The KMT–CCP conflict 1945–1949' in John K. Fairbank and Albert Feuerwerker (eds) *The Cambridge History of China,*

Vol. 13, Republican China 1912–1949, Part 2 (Cambridge: Cambridge University Press, 1986) p. 786.

13 For an account of the Chinese side see Chen Jian, *China's Road...* (*op. cit.*) and for an account of the Soviet side see Kathryn Weathersby, *Soviet Aims in Korea and the Origins of the Korean War, 1945–1950: New Evidence from Russian Archives* (Washington, DC, Woodrow Wilson Center: Cold War International History Project, Working Paper No. 8, November 1993). See also her *New Findings on the Korean War*, Cold War International History Project Bulletin No. 3 (Washington, DC, Woodrow Wilson Center: Fall 1993). All these are based on archival sources that became available only recently. It should be noted that the findings must be treated with caution as access to the Russian archives is incomplete and Chinese documentation is still only available second-hand through the writings of Chinese official scholars who have had access to the archives.

14 For more detailed discussion of the Soviet and Chinese positions see Chapters 6 and 7. For an account of the prevailing Western view of the Chinese role at the time see Mineo Nakajima, 'Foreign Relations: from the Korean War to the Bandung Line' in Roderick MacFarquhar and John K. Fairbank (eds) *The Cambridge History of China, Vol. 14, The People's Republic, Part 1: The Emergence of Revolutionary China 1949–1965* (Cambridge: Cambridge University Press, 1987) pp. 271–72. For the best account of Sino–Soviet relations at this time that is based on new archival materials and on the accounts of participants, see Sergei N. Goncharov, John W. Lewis, and Xue Litai, *Uncertain Partners: Stalin, Mao, and the Korean War* (Stanford: Stanford University Press, 1993). See also the previous note.

15 Gaddis, 'Korea in American Politics . . .' (*op. cit.*) p. 289.

16 Hao Yufan and Zhai Zhihai, 'China's Decision to Enter the Korean War: History Revisited', *The China Quarterly*, No. 121, March 1990, pp. 94–115.

17 For accounts of the background to the Korean War in addition to those cited in note 13, see Bruce Cummings, *The Origins of the Korean War*, 2 vols. (*op. cit.*); Max Hastings, *The Korean War* (*op. cit.*); Rosemary Foot, *The Wrong War* (Ithaca: Cornell University Press, 1985); Allen S. Whiting, *China Crosses the Yalu: The Decision to Enter the Korean War* (Stanford: Stanford University Press, 1960).

18 See Hao and Zhai, footnote 15. But Goncharov, Lewis and Xue show that Mao could hardly have objected to Kim's proposed war because of fear of American intervention when he himself had secured a promise of Soviet support for his proposed invasion of Taiwan. He could hardly have expressed fears about American intervention in Korea without tacitly admitting to Stalin the likelihood of similar involvement in Taiwan, thereby jeopardizing his support. *Uncertain Partners* (*op. cit.*) p. 146.

19 Mao's speech of 24 September 1962 in Stuart Schram (ed.) *Mao Tse-tung Unrehearsed* (Harmondsworth: Penguin, 1974) p. 191.

20 O. B. Borisov and B. T. Koloskov, *Sino–Soviet Relations 1945–1973: A Brief History* (Moscow: Mysl Publishers, third supplemental edition, 1980) p. 117.

21 According to Jon Halliday and Bruce Cummings, 2 million North Korean civilians and 500,000 soldiers, and at least 1 million Chinese soldiers died on the communist side. They estimate that 1 million South Korean civilians died. See Halliday and Cummings, *Korea: The Unknown War* (London: Viking, 1988), p. 200. Max Hastings gives the following figures for the UN side: '1,319,000 Americans served in the Korean theatre, and 33,629 did not return. A further 105,785 were wounded.... The South Korean army lost 415,000 killed and 429,000 wounded.' The figures for the remaining thirteen states that sent combat forces were 3,063 killed and 11,817 wounded. See Hastings, *The Korean War* (London: Pan Books, 1988) p. 407.

22 Jon Halliday, 'A Secret War' in *Far Eastern Economic Review* 22 April 1993, pp. 32–36.

23 Michael Leifer, *The Foreign Relations of New States* (Melbourne: Longman Australia, 1974) p. 2. Much of the subsequent discussion of Southeast Asia in this chapter draws on Chapters 1 and 2 of this book.

24 See the general argument of Alfred W. McCoy, 'The Philippines: Independence without Decolonisation' in Robin Jeffrey (ed.) *Asia – The Winning of Independence* (London: Macmillan Press, 1981), in particular pp. 50–53.

25 Leifer, *Foreign Relations . . . (op. cit.)* p. 11.

26 Evelyn Colbert, *Southeast Asia in International Politics (op. cit.)* pp. 90 ff. See also D. G. E. Hall, *A History of South-East Asia* (London: Macmillan, Fourth Edition, 1981) pp. 899–905; Milton Osborne, *Southeast Asia, An Introductory History* (Sydney: George Allen & Unwin, 1979) pp. 44–46; and Peter Lyon, *War and Peace in South-East Asia* (Oxford: Oxford University Press, 1969) pp. 39–46.

27 The above account relied on Lyon, *War and Peace . . . (op. cit.)* pp. 55–67; Anthony Reid, 'Indonesia: Revolution without Socialism' in Robin Jeffrey, *Asia, The Winning of Independence (op. cit.)* especially pp. 140–55; Osborne, *Southeast Asia (op. cit.)* pp. 139–46; John R. W. Smail, 'Indonesia' in Mark Borthwick, *Pacific Century, The Emergence of Modern Pacific Asia* (Boulder: Westview Press, 1992) pp. 230–33; and Michael Leifer, *Indonesia's Foreign Policy* (London: George Allen & Unwin, 1983).

28 The above account has drawn mainly on Lee Kam Hing, 'Malaya: New States and Old Elites', in Jeffrey (ed.) *Asia, The Winning of Independence (op. cit.)* pp. 213–57; and Milton Osborne, *Region of Revolt* (Australia: Pergamon Press, 1970) pp. 71–82.

29 Peter Lyon, *War and Peace . . . (op. cit.)* p. 34. This account has also drawn on Evelyn Colbert, *Southeast Asia in International Politics (op. cit.)* p. 90 ff.; and D. G. E. Hall, *A History . . . (op. cit.)* pp. 896–98.

30 Leifer, *Foreign Relations . . . (op. cit.)* p. 14.

31 This account has relied mainly upon Peter Lyon, *War and Peace . . . (op. cit)* pp. 46–55; and Hall, *A History . . . (op. cit.)* pp. 770–88, 878–85.

32 For an excellent account of the French experience see Bernard B. Fall, *Street Without Joy: Indochina at War, 1946–54* (Harrisburg: Stackpole, 1961).

33 Martin Borthwick, *Pacific Century* (Boulder: Westview Press, 1992) p. 237.

34 Hao and Zhai, 'China's Decision . . .' (*op. cit.*) p. 106.
35 *Chinese Aggression Against Vietnam* (Hanoi: Foreign Languages Publishing House, 1979).
36 For a full account of the Geneva Conference see Robert F. Randle, *Geneva 1954: the Settlement of the Indo-Chinese War* (Princeton: Princeton University Press, 1969). For the quote by Dulles see Gaddis, *The United States and the End of the Cold War* (*op. cit.*) p. 69.

2 The application of bipolarity, 1954–70

This was the period when international politics in the Asia-Pacific, as elsewhere in the world, were greatly shaped by the attempts of the United States and the Soviet Union to consolidate their respective sides of the Cold War as part of the management of central balance of power between them. Although the alliance patterns in the Asia-Pacific were bilateral and much more volatile than in Europe – as attested by the collapse of the Sino–Soviet alliance into acrimony and bitter rivalry – they nevertheless reflected the essential bipolar character of international politics of the period. Most of the countries in the region were linked to one or other of the two superpowers and the changing character of Soviet–American relations had a discernible impact upon the points of conflict and cooperation in the region.

Perhaps one of the most important ways in which the operation of bipolarity was distinctive in the Asia-Pacific during this period centred on the role of China. As a relatively independent strategic actor that had proved its entitlement to great power status in the Korean War, China moved from being a close ally of the Soviet Union in the early 1950s to become its most implacable adversary by the end of the 1960s. Indeed for much of the 1960s it challenged both the superpowers simultaneously. Moreover, within the Asia-Pacific region itself China exercised considerable weight independently of all other powers. However, it was not until relations were opened with Washington at the beginning of the 1970s that the main features of a broader strategic triangle involving Beijing as well as Moscow and Washington became evident. Nevertheless, as we now know, the Eisenhower Administration sought to drive a wedge between China and its Soviet ally by a policy of calculated toughness towards the former so as to increase pressure upon the alliance beyond breaking point.[1] The irony is that when that point was reached during the Kennedy and Johnson Administrations the United States became too focused on Vietnam to exploit it. Hence tripolarity did not fully emerge until 1971–72 when Chairman Mao and President Nixon recognized their common interest in managing an augmented Soviet threat.

If the unity of the communist side of the bipolar divide in the Asia-Pacific was threatened by the nationalist sentiments of independent governments (and that included North Vietnam and to a degree North Korea as well as China)[2] the pro-Western side was also characterized by greater diversity than obtained in Europe. The Cold War rhetoric that characterized the application of the containment policy of the bipolar period was even less appropriate here than in Europe. Thus India – the world's largest democracy – enjoyed closer relations with the Soviet Union than with the United States. The Indian attachment to non-alignment stopped it from joining the Western alliance systems in the early years especially as Pakistan became allied to the United States. Once the conflict with China deepened as a result of the border skirmish of 1959 and open warfare in 1962, India's links with the Soviet Union were correspondingly consolidated. The notion that the Cold War consisted of a conflict between the 'free world' and that of communist dictatorships did not accord with the situation elsewhere in Asia. Although the economies of the pro-Western states in East Asia were oriented towards the market, the majority were not ruled by 'free' democratic governments. Additionally, with the possible exception of Japan, most governments especially in Southeast Asia were fragile in their exercise of power and fearful of a variety of challenges to their survival. These came not only from communist insurgencies that exploited rural discontent, but also from ethnic unrest, disorders based on religious forces, and from separatist elements – all of which could be aided and abetted from the outside, and not necessarily by communist forces alone.[3]

Unlike the European theatre, the threat to the pro-Western side beyond Taiwan, Korea and to a degree Vietnam, was not on the whole one of conventional military assault. If the two superpowers tended to approach these regional and local preoccupations from the global perspectives of bipolarity, local élites and governments sought external support and even patronage with their own more parochial security interests in mind. The conjunction between the two worked best in the cases of Korea and Taiwan where the divisions of the Cold War and the respective civil wars coincided. But as we shall see, even there the correspondence was less than complete. In Southeast Asia the conjunctions were on the whole less clear cut. Even in the case of Vietnam, where after 1954 the United States may be said to have had a global strategic interest in assisting the regime in the South to survive the threat from the North, it did not follow, as the prominent 'realists' Hans Morganthau and George Kennan pointed out at an early stage, that the American interest was so vital that the fall of the South would undermine its standing in the central balance with the Soviet Union. Moreover they also argued that American power could not substitute for effective government backed by popular support.[4]

The nationalist sentiments of the majority of the countries of the Asia-Pacific did not coincide with the Cold War cleavage. Many of the states had newly emerged from colonial or semi-colonial rule and were economically less well developed. Their leaders claimed to have much in common that transcended the East–West divide. Led by the five powers which met in Colombo in April 1954 many sought to establish a separate and distinctive international identity that was epitomized by the Asian–African Conference that met in Bandung in April 1955. Leaders of communist and anti-communist governments rubbed shoulders together in the name of Asian–African unity as they sought to register their own separate international agendas. Although conflicts of interests soon shattered the rhetoric of the solidarity of the Bandung spirit, the conference paved the way for the development of the Non-Aligned Movement and other Third World-ist institutions. Yet, whatever their public protestations, governments faced by domestic or external challenges to their survival and to the national security of their states often turned for support to precisely the same external great power they were otherwise denouncing – usually the United States.

The actual balance of power between the Soviet Union and the United States was more uneven in the Asia-Pacific than in Europe. Despite its credentials as a Pacific power the Soviet Union was much more of a European power. Its political, historic and cultural heartland was in Europe. The Soviet Far East was more of an outpost of empire. It was strategically important, but it was little populated and it was of minor economic significance. Consequently, the Soviet economic impact on the region was restricted to its communist allies, possibly India and to a point Indonesia and Afghanistan.[5] As for the bulk of the Asia-Pacific the significance of the Soviet Union was limited to strategic considerations. The United States, by contrast, bestrode the Pacific like a colossus. Until brought low by the war in Vietnam during the late 1960s the United States exercised its hegemonic economic power with great self-confidence. It sponsored and oversaw the re-emergence of Japan and provided the favourable 'public goods' that facilitated the astonishing economic dynamism of the Pacific Rim. The means available to the United States to influence if not actually control international developments in the region far exceeded those available to the Soviet Union.

Accordingly, this chapter will first consider the application of the American strategy of containment before proceeding to discuss the attempt to establish Asian and African solidarity and the two off-shore island crises in the Taiwan Straits that shaped the conduct of Sino–American relations. It will then turn to the communist side of the Cold War divide by examining the collapse of the Sino–Soviet Alliance before evaluating the significance of the second Indo-China war. It will conclude with an assessment of the impact of the development of bipolarity on the other points of conflict in the region.

THE AMERICAN STRATEGY OF CONTAINMENT IN THE ASIA-PACIFIC

Containment became more than a strategy designed to limit the possible expansion of Soviet power – as was originally envisaged by George Kennan who had first coined the term.[6] It became inflated with the aim of stopping the expansion of communism wherever it seemed likely to spread. In much of the rhetoric of the American government communism was seen as both monolithic and international with its centre in Moscow. Arguably, in Europe this was very much one and the same, where the confrontation with Soviet power was more than a matter of balance of power, as it constituted a clash between two incompatible systems. The military divide was bolstered by a clash of ideologies, by fundamental differences in running the economies and by radically different political systems. The dividing line between the two was soon tightly demarcated by heavily militarized borders. In Asia, however, the division was less clear cut and there was not the same correspondence between the spread of communism and the expansion of Soviet or Chinese power. Containment, as applied by the United States government, was not a doctrine that allowed for the greater subtlety and discrimination that Asian conditions required. Moreover, unlike the West European countries, few of the Asian states allied or associated with the United States could be described as democratic. Consequently, there was the danger that the United States anti-communist crusade in the name of the free world could backfire if it were perceived to be carried out to support an unpopular dictatorial regime.

There was an economic corollary to the strategy which involved the United States in extending massive economic assistance in order to rehabilitate the economies of the 'free world' so as to strengthen the resilience of their societies against the appeals of communism. The Marshall Plan that was extended to facilitate the economic recovery of Western Europe had originally been offered to Europe as a whole, including the East, and it only became a keystone of containment after its rejection by Moscow in late 1947 and the communist coup in Czechoslovakia early in 1948. Although no such grand scheme was applied to Asia, the United States extended economic aid both in the form of investment and technical assistance and in the form of favourable trade policies. Japan was the main focus of attention. In the event it became the principal economic beneficiary of the Korean War as the provision of supplies to the Western war effort helped to re-establish Japanese industry. In general terms these policies played an important part in helping the reconstruction of South Korea and Taiwan which contributed to ensuring the survival of the respective regimes. In Southeast Asia the situation was complicated by the political problems attendant upon nation-building in newly independent states in the aftermath of colonial rule. The conditions of most of the states seemed so fragile that in the 1950s and 1960s, beginning with Eisenhower, successive American presidents persuaded themselves that were South Vietnam to 'fall' to communism a domino effect would be created in which the rest of the states in Southeast Asia would also fall.[7]

The evolution of the American strategy of containment was of major significance in shaping the development of the Asia-Pacific as a whole. The doctrine of containment actually followed by the Truman Administration owed more to the formulation of a document drawn under the leadership of Kennan's successor, Paul H. Nitze, than it did to the original view as articulated by the former. The Nitze version known by its bureaucratic code name, NSC-68, 'derived its view of American interests primarily from its perception of the Soviet threat' which had the effect of denying the utility of distinguishing between those American interests that were peripheral and those that were vital. It went on to argue that American interests depended on the perception of power as well as the reality of power itself. In other words the balance of power depended as much upon appearances as upon rational calculation of strategic significance and advantage. If America 'even appeared to be losing ground to its adversaries, the effects could be much the same as if that loss had actually occurred'. The document also called in effect for America to ensure that it always negotiated with the Soviet Union from a position of strength. The purpose of policy in Asia was to deny any further advances to communism in any form. Although the significance of nationalism even for communists was appreciated, it was nevertheless held that countries that came under communist sway necessarily followed a path of hostility towards the United States.[8] The application of the NSC-68 version of containment was prompted by the Korean War. That war was also significant as it occasioned massive rearmament by the United States which led to the 'militarization of containment' that was to have profound consequences especially in East Asia.[9]

The Eisenhower Administration sought to improve upon the earlier containment policy which it criticized for surrendering the initiative by being essentially a strategy of response. Its 'New Look' strategy was designed to seize the initiative and reduce costs by reacting to the adversary's 'challenges in ways that were calculated to apply to one's strengths against the other side's weaknesses, even if this meant shifting the nature and location of the confrontation'. Nuclear weapons were a key element in that strategy, but the strategy also involved building alliances, conducting psychological warfare, carrying out covert actions and, when appropriate, holding negotiations. The two concepts most readily associated with Secretary of State John Foster Dulles were nuclear 'brinkmanship' and 'massive retaliation'. Resort to them was threatened in the 1954 and 1958 crises over the off-shore islands of Quemoy and Matsu precisely because they could not be defended by conventional means. But had nuclear weapons been used it would have been difficult to argue that the interests at stake really justified the resulting devastation or the risks of possible retaliation. Typically, Dulles argued that the issue at stake was Taiwanese morale. If Taiwan were lost the security of the entire Western Pacific would be damaged and Southeast Asia would come under communist influence.

John Lewis Gaddis, the principal historian of containment, has faulted the Eisenhower Administration particularly for lacking confidence in its own supposed reliance upon the independence and nationalism of Third World countries especially. Accusing the administration of 'hyperactivity' he argued that the attempts to tie Third World governments in alliances coupled with unilateral security

guarantees were overbearing and in reality unenforceable. Moreover, accusations about the 'immorality' of Third World 'neutralism'
only made matters worse. Although the administration hoped to
split China from the Soviet Union, no strategy had been devised
for exploiting the consequences. As early as 1954, General Ridgway,
who had succeeded MacArthur in Korea, had pointed out that that
would require bringing 'Red China to a realization that its long
range benefits derive from friendliness with America'. That was
ruled out by Eisenhower himself on the grounds that the requisite
diplomatic contacts were unacceptable as they would pose problems
with allies, destroy Chiang Kai-shek and be resisted by an American
people still 'emotional' about China.[10]

The Kennedy Administration, followed by that of Johnson,
favoured a symmetrical rather than the asymmetrical response
espoused by the previous administration. The earlier emphasis upon
nuclear brinkmanship that entailed either inaction or a response
that was wholly disproportionate to the original provocation was
sharply criticized for lacking credibility. The new strategy of 'flexible
response' called for an appropriate and careful response to any act
of aggression be it a limited or general war, conventional or nuclear,
large or small. Top priority went to decreasing reliance upon
nuclear weapons and to developing mobile forces capable of fighting
and assisting allies in fighting different types of war. Accordingly, a
much enhanced counter-insurgency capability was developed replete
with so-called 'special forces' so as to be able to counter wars of
national liberation. At the same time the Kennedy Administration
continued with the programme of acquiring a greater variety of
nuclear weapons. Alongside the strategy of 'flexible response' came
that of graduated response through carefully controlled escalation
and crisis management. Ironically, given the outcome in Vietnam,
the Kennedy Administration also saw itself as favouring the forces
for change and the new emergent classes in Third World countries.

Gaddis argued that the fundamental reason the Kennedy and
Johnson Administrations regarded the 'loss' of such a small and distant country as South Vietnam in such catastrophic terms was
because of their undifferentiated view of American security
interests: 'They tended to view the American stake there as determined exclusively by threats and obligations. The security of the
United States, indeed of the entire non-communist world, was
thought to be imperiled wherever communist challenges came up
against American guarantees.' There was an element of self fulfilment in this since the more the policies towards Vietnam were

upheld as necessary to safeguard credibility the more American credibility required those policies to be successful.

Furthermore the employment of a supposedly calibrated ladder of escalating responses to persuade the other side to desist or to compromise could work only if there were a clear adversary who accepted that the other side was willing and able to escalate to a point that would be destructive of its key values. Since the escalatory responses in Vietnam were aimed at several targets (Hanoi and the Vietcong directly, Moscow and Beijing indirectly), and since the United States had long indicated that there were limits beyond which it would not go in the war lest it bring in Chinese and Soviet forces, the strategy became ensnared in finding what Gaddis calls disparagingly, 'some middle ground between the insanity of nuclear war and the humiliation of appeasement'. The very disproportionate character of the American commitment brought about its own undoing. Despite the huge American military presence the communists carried out uprisings in the main cities of South Vietnam in early 1968. Although the communist Tet Offensive was eventually defeated it became a political success as President Johnson threw in his hand by refusing to escalate further and by refusing to run for re-election. It fell to the new President Nixon to change the direction of American international politics that brought means and ends into closer alignment and that opened the way to cooperation with China and to détente with the Soviet Union.

In terms of actual policy, the Eisenhower Administration attempted to consolidate its containment strategy in East Asia by concluding a series of treaties that aimed ultimately at establishing a multilateral arrangement that would bring together the various parties in a collective defence pact against communist expansion. The preambles of the American security treaties with the Philippines and ANZUS of 1951 and that with South Korea of 1953 all referred to the development of 'a more comprehensive system of regional security in the Pacific area'. In the spring of 1954 (i.e. coincidental with the Geneva Conference) and into the summer the United States was active in promoting a multilateral security pact for Southeast Asia that bore fruit of a kind in September in the signing of the Collective Defense Treaty for Southeast Asia – the Manila Pact. Formally speaking, the Southeast Asia Treaty Organization (SEATO) was established the following year in Bangkok. The United States, Britain, Australia, New Zealand, France, Thailand, Pakistan and the Philippines agreed to act together 'in accordance with [their] constitutional practices' to counter an 'armed attack' if they could unanimously agree on its designation and they further agreed to consult if any signatory felt threatened. South Vietnam, Cambodia and Laos were not signatories, but the provisions of the treaty were extended to them gratuitously by a protocol attached to the treaty. The highly qualified security commitments of the Manila Pact and SEATO in particular compared unfavourably with the more explicit ones of NATO and of the bilateral pacts the United States had signed in the region.

In the event SEATO did not provide a basis for the collective defence of South Vietnam. Moreover it was noticeable that even in its attenuated form the Manila Pact did not attract other Asian members such as Indonesia, Burma, Ceylon (as it then was) or India. Asian non-alignment was already beginning to become a factor in international politics. Meanwhile Cambodia, in 1955, rejected the gratuitous protection on offer as being inconsistent with its neutrality and Laos was eventually excluded from it by the outcome of the Geneva Conference of 1962. Thus the underlying rationale of the Manila Pact had already been removed before it could be invoked in 1964. The Americans were left to intervene unilaterally.

The first Taiwan off-shore island crisis, 1954–55

The People's Republic of China (PRC) nevertheless felt that in 1954 it had cause for alarm especially as it became clear that a mutual defence treaty was in prospect between Washington and Taipei. That provided the occasion for the first off-shore island crisis of 1954–55. It can be seen as an example of how local, national, regional and international issues were enmeshed. From Beijing's perspective the Taiwan question not only involved the question of China's national security, but it also constituted the tail end of the uncompleted civil war and, above all, it was a question of sovereignty and territorial integrity. Taiwan was the last remaining province beyond Beijing's control and there was fear that a treaty with the Americans that was linked to the other American allies would put Taiwan, with international endorsement, permanently beyond the reach of the PRC short of a world war.

By shelling the islands close to the Chinese shore Beijing was first declaring its determination to lay claim to Taiwan as well; second, it was implicitly warning off America's allies from the putative alliance; third, it was complicating the American position by compelling it to include the protection of those islands in its treaty commitment so as to make it more difficult to establish Taiwan as a separate entity; and finally, it was hoping to begin a dialogue with the United States so as to break out of the economic embargo and isolation imposed upon it by the United States. Taipei sought an American commitment that would both ensure it relative equality with America's other Asian allies and that would uphold its occupation of the off-shore islands in the hope of an eventual return to the mainland to overthrow the communist regime. Constituting the Republic of China the Chiang Kai-shek government saw itself as the legitimate representative of the whole of China and, as Chinese patriots, its leaders were unwilling to contemplate a separate Taiwan. Indeed one of the American concerns was that a collapse of morale on the island might cause the regime to make its own deal with Beijing. The American interest was to link Taiwan in the emerging security system of the Asia-Pacific and so complete the cordon of containment. To this end it did not wish its security commitments to be subject to military conflicts over islands where the PRC enjoyed overwhelming geographical advantage. Still less did it wish the crisis to lead to splits with allies.[11]

In the event none of the other American security agreements in the region mentioned Taiwan and the United States and the Republic of China (Taiwan) signed a Mutual Defense Treaty on 2 December 1954, but it was carefully limited to the defence of Taiwan and the Pescadores (Penghu) islands. On 29 January President Eisenhower signed the Formosa Resolution, passed by Congress, giving him the discretion to defend the off-shore islands should he judge that necessary for the security of Taiwan itself. Meanwhile Eisenhower gave separate assurances to Chiang Kai-shek about the off-shore islands of Quemoy and Matsu, but not about the more northerly Dazhen (Tachen) islands which were evacuated and then promptly taken over by the PRC. That reassured Beijing, as it confirmed the statements emanating from Washington that President Eisenhower opposed any plans for invading the mainland. If the US were unwilling to support Taipei in holding on to outposts such as the Dachens it was unlikely to lend support to a beachhead on the mainland. At the same time and against its better judgement, the United States had in effect been manoeuvred into supporting Taipei's occupation of Quemoy and Matsu on the grounds that their loss would undermine the morale on Taiwan. But in truth that suited both Beijing and Taipei at the time as it precluded the formal separation of Taiwan from the mainland. The outcome in the end was mixed for all sides. The United States was able to include

Taiwan within its Western Pacific security perimeter, but it had to give up on its hope of a collective defence system amid uncertainties about the character of its commitment to Quemoy and Matsu. In the process of reaching that point Washington had threatened the possible use of nuclear weapons and had given a practical demonstration of how points of no geopolitical significance to the United States could influence its main interests. If the readiness 'to go to the brink' over such an issue was designed to assure allies in principle of American resolve, in practice it frightened them off lest they be dragged into conflicts in which the general interest was not apparent.

The Bandung Conference, April 1955

In contrast to the group of countries that were to set up SEATO, Ceylon had earlier taken the initiative to bring together in Colombo the prime ministers of Burma, India, Indonesia, itself and Pakistan. Other than Pakistan they held that military pacts increased insecurity and they favoured Nehru's policy of 'neutralism'. This was defined in terms of the 'five principles of peaceful co-existence' agreed to by India and China in April 1954.[12] That agreement of the two great Asian powers was reached at a time when there was a prospect of an imminent American military intervention in Vietnam. A year later some thirty countries held the first ever Conference of Asian and African nations in Bandung, Indonesia. They demonstrated their desire to be heard on matters of international affairs especially on issues of peace and cooperation. The delegates talked loudly about affairs for which they had no responsibility and in subdued tones about those such as Korea, Vietnam or Kashmir, for which they did. They were divided about cooperation with the West and the communist countries. No bloc or permanent organization emerged from the meeting. It solved none of the questions on which the participants had conflicts of interest and it made little difference to the distribution of power. But it was of great symbolic significance as for the first time it articulated a Third World voice that was to become a growing feature in international politics thereafter. It provided an opportunity for leaders to meet who would otherwise have found it difficult to do so.

It also provided the occasion for China to establish what would now be called its Third World credentials.[13] In the not inconsiderable person of Zhou Enlai, Chinese diplomacy presented a more reasoned face to several leaders of anti-communist governments. He helped to convert Prince Sihanouk of Cambodia to accept the desirability of the neutral status of his country. The Conference also provided the occasion for the signing of a nationality treaty with Indonesia. Reversing the old Republican or KMT position on the dual nationality status of overseas Chinese that had been the cause of constant friction with Southeast Asian governments, the new treaty in effect enjoined the Chinese residents to choose either Indonesian or Chinese nationality. The new approach was designed to mollify governments in the region more generally who had professed concern about the potential 'fifth column' aspects of their resident Chinese. In the event the agreement was not ratified until 1960 and it meant that those traders who retained Chinese nationality became subject to laws that prohibited aliens from trading in rural areas. The PRC duly protested at these harsh laws, but in the interests of placating Indonesia, with whom the Chinese sought to be on good terms, the PRC undertook to repatriate those Chinese who wished to return to China. Some of the tens of thousands who were repatriated were descendants of migrants who had left China several generations before.[14] The episode demonstrated some of the difficulties of the Chinese position in seeking simultaneously to cultivate friendly relations with Southeast Asian governments and to protect the interests of resident Chinese nationals to whom in any case the PRC was not well placed to offer practical assistance. Moreover, in practice neither the PRC nor the governments and peoples of Southeast Asia punctiliously observed the distinctions between the different nationality credentials of the Chinese resident in the area.

To return to the Bandung Conference, Zhou used the setting as a platform on which to demonstrate his government's 'reasonableness' especially in contrast to the position of the United States. He skilfully used the occasion to appeal for a dialogue with the United States that in effect brought the first Taiwan off-shore crisis to an end. This led to an agreement to hold Sino–American talks at ambassadorial level in Geneva.

The 'Bandung spirit' soon evaporated. Local disputes between member states proved to be no easier to resolve. Thailand and the Philippines, whose leaders had apparently been impressed by Zhou Enlai's performance, still refused to recognize the PRC. Although the PRC had abandoned its earlier revolutionary approach in favour of a more conventional diplomacy, especially towards its Asian neighbours, profound problems remained. Although relations had improved with India as indicated by their agreement of April 1954 by which India recognized Chinese sovereignty over Tibet (thereby giving up its residual interest in the region as the successor to the British Raj) there were still outstanding boundary questions and a more intangible sense of rivalry between the two major Asian powers with the different political visions embodied in their respective political systems. Indeed, remaining boundary and territorial questions were problems that affected China's relations with all its neighbours. It became evident that these could raise serious problems when the negotiations with a compliant Burma took four or five years before eventually an agreement was reached, even though there was manifest goodwill on both sides. China's neighbours suspected that a newly reunified China would be influenced by the legacy of the more distant past when imperial China exercised a kind of superior overlordship over the other Asian rulers. The communist issue deepened the distrust: Beijing was seen as a supporter of local communist parties dedicated to the overthrow of the newly established and fragile regimes by subversion and by rural insurgencies. It was feared that China would seek to exploit domestic weakness and intra-regional disputes. Moreover the PRC's new approach towards the nationality of the millions of ethnic Chinese resident in Southeast Asia, welcome as it was, did not dispel the distrust about their potential as a fifth column; still less could it address the many communal problems they faced; and China's residual patrimonial attitudes suggested a responsibility that, in reality, it lacked the capacity to discharge. These misgivings about China intensified in 1958 when Chinese foreign policy shifted away from the moderation of Bandung towards a more militant revolutionary line, that was in part caused by the failure to improve relations with the United States.[15]

If some of the earlier hopes that a sense of Asian solidarity would promote a wider sense of community failed to materialize, the Bandung Conference was not without a lasting impact. It placed the Third World and its concerns firmly on the international agenda. It contributed to de-legitimizing colonialism and to widening the demands for independence. In foreign policy terms it was the precursor of the Non-Alignment Movement. Although the separate visions and interests of the independent states and their leaders before too long undermined the 'spirit of Bandung' the conference marked the emergence of the Third World as a factor in international politics.

The second off-shore island crisis, 1958

As in the previous crisis, the issue combined elements of local and international questions. In fact the second crisis may be said to have followed from the failure to solve the deeper problems inherent in the first. The price that the United States and China each demanded of the other for improving relations was concessions regarding Taiwan that neither was in a position to make. The Sino–American Geneva talks had begun in August 1955 in a favourable international atmosphere. The treaty ending the military occupation and division of Austria had been signed in May and the four powers, the US, the USSR, Britain and France, had just concluded their summit meeting. But the Sino–American talks soon foundered on their irreconcilable positions. The Americans wanted Beijing to agree to renounce the use of force in the Taiwan area and the PRC wanted the Americans to agree to withdraw from the area. The only agreement they were able to reach was on the subject of citizens of each country held or detained by the other.

Over the next two years the Americans sought to consolidate the status quo and establish a *fait accompli* that would give Beijing no alternative but to accept international opinion that the situation was similar to Germany, Korea, Vietnam and even Ireland. By 1958, having failed to obtain a renunciation of force by Beijing vis-à-vis Taiwan and having succeeded in maintaining Taiwan's participation in numerous international fora, the United States suspended the talks. Angered by the breakdown of the link with the US that had been forged with such difficulty and having found that its policy of peaceful co-existence with Washington and Taipei had not turned out well, Beijing chose to take the initiative once again by generating a crisis on the off-shore islands.

In the summer of 1958 Beijing began an orchestrated campaign over the Taiwan question that culminated in carefully considered bombardments of Quemoy in which days of intensive shelling would be followed by lighter shelling. The US Navy escorted Taipei supply ships to within three miles of the island. Having decided that the loss of Quemoy could lead to the loss of Taiwan, amid talk of the use of nuclear weapons Eisenhower and Dulles issued a public warning to Beijing on 4 September. The following day Beijing stopped the shelling and on 6 September Zhou announced that the PRC would accept an American offer to resume talks. On 7 September the Soviet leader Khrushchev felt safe to warn Eisenhower that an attack on the PRC would be considered as an attack on the

Soviet Union. From 8 September until 6 October Beijing resumed intensive shelling and then announced a cease-fire. On 25 October Beijing announced that it would resume shelling but only on odd days – a state of affairs that was to continue for the following twenty years.[16]

For Mao and Zhou Enlai the Taiwan problem had two aspects, an international one involving the United States, and a domestic one involving the KMT. Their consistent aim was to negotiate the removal of the former before proceeding to settle the latter. The off-shore islands were never considered as a separate issue, rather they were thought of as a way of bringing pressure to bear on Washington over its Taiwan commitment as a whole. The fact that the exercise was never repeated suggests that Mao and his colleagues recognized that to do so could be counter productive: Washington might be pressed to respond to international sentiment and to growing voices at home that the off-shore islands were not worth the high stakes invested in them. In other words the danger from Beijing's perspective was that rather than being a peg to which the United States was tied in a noose (as Mao had once put it), the islands might be discarded and thus pave the way for a more formal separation of Taiwan from the mainland. From the perspective of Washington the successful management of the crisis proved something of a pyrrhic victory – at least for the strategy of nuclear brinkmanship that underlay it. The disproportionate response paved the way for the development of the new strategy of flexible response. But it left Taiwan firmly embedded within the American scheme of containment. It was not until that issue had been addressed between Beijing and Washington in 1971 that their bilateral dispute over Taiwan could be reconsidered in 1972.

THE COLLAPSE OF THE SINO–SOVIET ALLIANCE

The breakdown of the alliance was a complex and protracted affair that took about ten years to unravel from its beginnings in 1956. The Sino–Soviet alliance, which seemingly had been cemented by the Korean War, began to unfold as differences of interest began to emerge. Many factors played their part, given the participants' previous history, the vast differences of culture between them and the disparities in their socio-economic conditions. But as these had been obtained when the alliance was first established the most significant factors that occasioned the collapse of the alliance were those of international politics and strategy. As the senior ally, the Soviet

Union could not allow China to place its global strategic interests in jeopardy. For its part, an independent China could not be expected to subordinate itself to the degree of compliance demanded by its Soviet ally. As the major communist powers the character of their relations affected the character of the relations between the Soviet Union and the other communist states, as well as the character of the international communist movement as a whole. All these relations were expressed in ideological terms and, since ideology was at the heart of the legitimacy of Communist Party rule in both the Soviet Union and China, the legitimacy of the regimes in Moscow and Beijing was necessarily affected by their disagreement. That may explain why by the early 1960s both sets of leaders were condemning the other as traitors to the communist cause. Ultimately for Marxist–Leninists there could only be one correct view and no true comrade would persist in publicly putting forward a contrary view.[17]

At the heart of the dispute were their respective relationships with the United States. After establishing his authority as successor to Stalin, Khrushchev sought to diffuse some of the tension with the United States partly in order to carry out reforms at home, but primarily because of the unacceptable risks associated with nuclear weapons and the high costs of maintaining a military confrontation with the United States and its allies. To this end he sought to reach various understandings with the United States and declared an interest in preventing local wars and wars of national liberation from escalating into conflicts between East and West. Ironically, in the mid-1950s the Chinese leaders had also sought to diffuse tensions with the Americans because they wanted to concentrate upon economic development at home. But unlike their Soviet colleagues, Mao Zedong and Zhou Enlai found an obdurate Eisenhower Administration that refused to respond in kind. As was noted earlier, Dulles took the view that the way to drive a wedge between the two communist giants was to keep up the pressure on China. Not only were the Chinese denied the diplomatic openings that became available to their Soviet colleagues, but they also found no evidence, as far as they were concerned, of the United States having developed more moderate or reasonable approaches as claimed by Khrushchev. Consequently the Chinese leaders found that the Soviet leaders tried to prevent them from standing up for what they regarded as their sovereign and irredentist rights and from supporting wars for national liberation in the Third World. For example, in 1959 Khrushchev publicly charged the Chinese leaders in Beijing with seeking 'to test the international stability by force'. For their part, the Soviet leaders were unwilling to allow the Chinese to determine the nature of Soviet dealings with America.

A major turning point was the refusal of the Soviet Union in 1959 to supply China with a sample atomic bomb. The logic of the situation in fact was for the United States and the Soviet Union to combine together to restrain China from developing its own nuclear weapons. Indeed that was one of the factors that led to the signing of the Test Ban Treaty in 1963. Undaunted however the Chinese tested their first device the following year.[18] Meanwhile the Soviet Union declared itself neutral in the border conflict that had reared up suddenly in 1959 between China and India. In 1960 it withdrew all its several thousands of experts from China. Taking their blueprints with them, they dealt the Chinese economy a severe blow at a time of low ebb as the country faced famine and economic downturn after the disastrous Great Leap Forward. By 1962 the Soviet Union was to be found alongside Britain and the United States in support of India after its humiliating defeat by China in their border war. Thereafter the Chinese and Soviet leaders took opposite positions on all the key international issues. In 1963 and 1964 the Chinese deepened the inter-state conflict when they publicly raised the issue of the 'unequal treaties' imposed by Tsarist Russia on the weak Qing Dynasty, and other border disputes, which they argued had yet to be settled.

By this stage they had each condemned the other as betrayers of communism and of the interests of their own people. Not even the removal of Khrushchev in 1964 (which coincided to the day with the testing of China's first nuclear device) changed the situation. Meanwhile Mao, having condemned the Soviet leaders as revisionists who had used state power to bring about a counter-revolution by peaceful means, began to identify similar alleged revisionists alongside him in China. This was to culminate in the Cultural Revolution. Clearly foreign and domestic policies had become closely inter-connected.

The impact of the collapse of the Sino–Soviet alliance on the rest of the international politics of the Asia-Pacific was not immediately obvious. As observed earlier, the United States, which had played a role in fomenting it, seemed to have no plans to exploit it. The Kennedy and Johnson Administrations took the view that difficult though it was, they could do business with a post revolutionary Soviet leadership, but not with the revolutionary Chinese whose aggressiveness had to be stopped. It was only with the advent of

Nixon and Kissinger that the Americans took positive steps to take advantage of the conflict between the two communist giants. Nevertheless the impact of the communist schism was real enough. It divided the communist world on national lines thus weakening the general appeal of communism and its effectiveness as a force for change. The conflict also provided greater opportunities for independent manoeuvre to the smaller communist powers, which in the Asia-Pacific meant primarily North Korea and North Vietnam. Although the Soviet Union in 1963 withdrew its assistance from Vietnam this was resumed after Khrushchev's ouster. Curiously the United States chose to start bombing North Vietnam in 1965 just as the Soviet premier was visiting Hanoi to determine the character of Soviet aid. The Soviet Union not only became the main supplier of advanced weaponry to the North during the war with the United States, but it also began to reduce Chinese influence in Vietnam. However, for reasons of geography and ethnicity the communist parties of Southeast Asia (with the exception of the Philippines until 1969) continued to accept Chinese patronage.

The most immediate impact of the Sino–Soviet dispute was felt in the Third World where the two competed for power and influence among the newly independent countries and for the allegiance of the various liberation movements. The dispute complicated the attempt to reconvene the Bandung Conference in Algeria in 1965. China's greater militancy and its opposition to India may have won it adherents among the more radical governments and movements, but that served to alienate others, especially in Southeast Asia. The experience of Indonesia is instructive in this regard.

The rise of President Sukarno from the mid-1950s and the progressive weakening of parliamentary government was accompanied by a more assertive foreign policy that focused on the acquisition of West Irian (or Dutch New Guinea) from the Netherlands which had refused to include it in the transfer of sovereignty in 1949. The failure to elicit full support from the still American dominated General Assembly of the United Nations resulted in expropriation of Dutch economic interests in Indonesia in late 1957. This tended to consolidate the interests of Java and the central government against the outer islands. This was further confirmed by the government's declaration of an archipelagic principle on 13 December. That challenged American claims to rights of passage through the high sea. Accordingly, covert American aid was offered to a rebellion that broke out in early 1958, centred in Sulawesi and Sumatra. Britain, Taiwan and the Philippines were also seen as active in the rebel cause. The failure of the rebellion by the summer helped to bring about an uneasy coalition between President Sukarno as the country's leader, the Army as the defender and upholder of national unity and the Communist Party which could mobilize mass support. Thus although there was a temporary accommodation with America when it pressured Holland to give up West Irian, it soon petered out. Sukarno, meanwhile, had accepted Soviet and East European military aid. Indeed a degree of competition emerged between the two superpowers over cultivating the support of Indonesia.[19]

As Sukarno became more militant as a Third World leader he began to lean more to the Chinese side as the Sino–Soviet conflict unfolded. Sukarno's claims as a nationalist and anti-imperialist leader coalesced in his belligerent response to the proposal to establish Malaysia, triggered by a revolt in Brunei in December 1962. The armed confrontation (or *Konfrontasi*) that was countered by British and Commonwealth troops threatened to further subdivide Southeast Asia as Sukarno responded by creating 'the axis of Djakarta–Phnom Penh–Hanoi–Peking–Pyongyang'.[20] Others identified a more modest but more sinister Sino–Indonesian axis. Close links were also established between the Indonesian and Chinese communist parties. This in turn heightened tensions between the Indonesian army on the one side and the communists and Sukarno on the other. In the event an abortive coup attempt took place on 1 October 1965 which resulted in the death of six generals. Troops under the leadership of Major General Suharto overcame the coup forces within two days. Whether or not the Chinese were involved in the coup, their influence in the country was eliminated and the limitation of their capacity to exercise power cruelly exposed as many tens of thousands of ethnic Chinese as well as alleged communists were killed. President Sukarno was finally removed from power in 1966 and General Suharto as the new leader was able to bring confrontation to an end. The following year the new relations with Malaysia were to form the core of the newly established ASEAN. This was immediately denounced by both Peking and Hanoi as a proto-imperialist organization. The divisions in the communist world had combined to cause losses for both the Soviet and Chinese sides. But these events also demonstrated the extent to which the fortunes of the external powers could be determined by the interplay of domestic forces in the smaller regional powers.

Sino–Soviet relations deteriorated still further during the Cultural Revolution that began in China in 1965–66. This also prevented them from joining forces to assist Vietnam. The Chinese had rejected

Soviet overtures to this effect as Mao suspected that the ultimate Soviet purpose was to broker a deal with the United States to the detriment of China. Rejecting Soviet requests for an air corridor and for use of Chinese bases in the south, the Chinese reluctantly agreed to allow Soviet military aid to be sent through Chinese territory by train. Soviet military assistance soon exceeded that of the Chinese in both quantity and quality. In fact it was essential for Hanoi in combatting American air power. By this stage the Soviet Union had begun to upgrade its military forces to the north of China. A security treaty was signed with the Mongolian People's Republic in 1966 that led to the stationing of Soviet forces in the south of the country. In 1967 China began to match the Soviet build up in quantity if not quality. In 1968 the Chinese took fright at the Soviet invasion of Czechoslovakia and the proclamation of the Brezhnev Doctrine that allowed the Soviet Union the right to intervene in a socialist state to 'safeguard the revolution'. Interestingly, the North Vietnamese supported the Soviet rather than the Chinese position, while North Korea did not commit itself.

In March 1969 the Chinese instigated a limited conflict on one of the disputed riverine islands. After unsuccessful attempts to open negotiations, victorious Soviet sorties into Xinjiang and hints about a possible Soviet surgical nuclear strike eventually led to a meeting at Beijing airport between the Soviet Premier Kosygin and Zhou Enlai in September, as the former returned from the funeral of Ho Chi Minh that both had attended in Hanoi. That diffused the immediate crisis.[21] The Chinese had sought to convince the Soviet Union that the PRC could be credibly defended on the basis of self reliance. The Soviet side feared that an uncontrolled China could open a second front in addition to the main front in Europe. It additionally attempted to persuade the West that they shared a joint interest in restraining China and it continued to drop broad hints that it was contemplating a strike against Chinese nuclear targets. It was only then that Kissinger and President Nixon were alerted to the possible implications for the United States. The Sino–Soviet conflict had finally reached the point where the changes it had wrought to the fundamentals of the central balance of power during the Cold War became clear.

THE SECOND INDO-CHINA WAR

This war arose from the perception in Washington that a communist victory in the South, building upon the earlier victory in North

Vietnam, would work to the advantage of its global adversary and that it would lead to the fall of the rest of Southeast Asia to the enormous disadvantage of the West. Back in April 1954 President Eisenhower had claimed that all Southeast Asia was like a row of dominoes. If you knocked over the first one, what would happen to the last one was 'the certainty that it would go over very quickly'.[22]

In the late 1950s Hanoi reactivated the war through insurgency in the South, that consisted initially in a systematic campaign to assassinate local officials. The regime in the South, led by the Catholic Ngo Dinh Diem and his brother Ngo Dinh Nhu, had a narrow base of social support and was destined never to succeed in generating a South Vietnamese nationalist ethos. Certainly they lacked the national authority of Ho Chi Minh and the communist movement that he led. The Diem regime was ineffective and it faced opposition from different social groups it tried to suppress. In December 1960 the establishment of the National Front for the Liberation of South Vietnam (NLF) marked an important stage in the development of the armed struggle. The incoming Kennedy Administration regarded the struggle as aggression from the North that initially was blamed on Moscow and then attributed to Beijing. The administration took the view that the Chinese had to be shown that wars of national liberation could be stopped and that the United States had to show its allies and friends in the Third World in particular that it stood by its commitments. It was this kind of thinking that realists were to criticize for its failure to distinguish peripheral from vital interests – even before American liberals attacked the moral basis for prosecuting the war.

The regime in the South was ineffective in carrying out the economic and socio-political programmes recommended by American advisers. The American government, however, persuaded itself that, in the words of Defense Secretary McNamara in June 1962 after his visit to Vietnam, 'every quantitive measurement we have shows we're winning this war'. In one of his last press conferences President Kennedy declared:

> Our goal is a stable government there, carrying on a struggle to maintain its national independence. We believe strongly in that.... In my opinion for us to withdraw from that effort would mean a collapse not only of South Vietnam but Southeast Asia. So we are going to stay there.[23]

Not long afterwards Diem and his brother were killed in a military coup of which the US government had prior knowledge. Three weeks later, in November 1963, President Kennedy was assassinated and Lyndon Johnson became president. Under his direction, the United States armed forces replaced the South Vietnamese army as the main combat troops. The attempt to compel the North to negotiate through a graduated escalation of bombing backfired. The United States misunderstood the commitment of the communists to the nationalist cause and that bombing, as shown by the bombing of Nazi Germany in the Second World War, would stiffen resistance, especially of a dictatorship. In 1968 as a result of the Tet Offensive and its impact within the United States President Johnson decided that he could continue no longer. By that stage the United States had 525,000 troops in Vietnam. It took another five years before an agreement was reached with North Vietnam on American withdrawal and a political settlement, and a further two years before the final American humiliation as the northern army reunified Vietnam by force in April 1975. By that stage, however, the Sino–American rapprochement had long destroyed the original American rationale for containing China in Vietnam.

The war had also embroiled the other two weaker countries of Indo-China, Laos and Cambodia, whose neutrality had supposedly been established by the Geneva Agreements. Indeed that of Laos had been reconfirmed by an additional Geneva conference in 1962. Of the two, Laos had developed less of a national identity or statehood. Its fortunes were very much the by-play of external forces. The main figures and even elements of the military were dependent upon external patrons within the region and at times even beyond the region. The most powerful politically and militarily were the Pathet Lao who were very much, in effect, a provincial branch of the Vietnamese communists. Although other regional interests were also engaged, it was in keeping with Hanoi's strategic perspectives that its interests should predominate especially as the supply routes to the South (the Ho Chi Minh Trail) ran through Laos. Consequently, the victory of the communist forces there followed closely on the tails of those in Vietnam.

Although Vietnamese interests were broadly similar in Cambodia, through which the Ho Chi Minh Trail also ran, politically Cambodia was more developed and nationally more coherent than Laos. One of the keystones of Cambodian nationalism was resentment against the Vietnamese for having encroached upon their once strong and extensive kingdom. The Mekong Delta of South Vietnam was once Cambodian land and there were still ethnic Khmers resident there. But events in Cambodia too were shaped by the war in

Vietnam. Prince Sihanouk manoeuvred to retain neutrality for his country by conceding territorial access to the Viet Cong, which served as the pretext for his overthrow in 1970 by a rightist military coup which set up a fragile and oppressive administration. The Vietnamese communists then acted to crush the Cambodian army so enabling the extremist indigenous Khmer Rouge to expand its power, ultimately seizing Phnom Penh in 1975.

The second Indo-China war is usually considered to be an unmitigated disaster for the United States. It was America's first defeat in a major war and the repercussions of the failure still resonate at home more than twenty-five years later as a constraint against committing American troops to foreign combat. The war also resulted in a sense of America's relative decline, especially as the Soviet Union, after its experience in the Cuban missile crisis, had taken the opportunity to narrow substantially the gap with the United States in nuclear and conventional power. But the extent of the damage can be exaggerated. Although SEATO was shown to be a broken reed and (unlike in the Korean War) the European allies stayed at home, regional allies such as Australia, New Zealand, the Philippines, South Korea and Thailand did contribute forces in one form or another. Arguably, the United States also missed opportunities to exploit the Sino–Soviet rift, but the war divided the two communist powers still further even though they both had to assist the North. There can be little doubt that the conflict took on a momentum of its own as its original objectives were overtaken by the mechanics of prosecuting the war. The roots of the Vietcong insurgency were traced to Moscow and by 1964 they were located in Beijing,[24] but by 1965 Moscow assistance was being sought to put pressure on Hanoi and by 1966 tacit understandings were reached with the Chinese on how to limit the war from escalating into a Sino–American one.[25] In the end the larger strategic purposes of the war got lost altogether as Washington aligned with Beijing and pursued détente with Moscow.

A positive lesson was soon learned from the war: that American resources were not unlimited. A chastened President Nixon announced in Guam in July 1969 a new security doctrine for the United States in Asia. Henceforth its allies would be expected to do the bulk of the ground fighting while the Americans would contribute with their navy and air force from off-shore as well as with military supplies and military training. Within the region it can be argued that the defeat in Vietnam marked the beginning of gnawing uncertainties about the durability of American capacity and will to deploy countervailing power when needed. Yet as seen from the perspective of the 1990s it is difficult to point to long term damage to American interests in the Asia-Pacific. No dominoes fell beyond Indo-China and most of America's allies prospered, leaving America still as the dominant force in the region, while a socialist Vietnam embraced free market economics.

The impact elsewhere in Pacific Asia

The acute polarities of the Cold War ensured that the status quo in Northeast Asia was not challenged during the 1950s and 1960s. The stalemate of the Korean War had resulted in a local settlement that was endorsed by the great powers. No matter that both North and South regarded it as no more than provisional neither could challenge the division of the country without the support of the external powers. Since that division did not challenge their interests sufficiently to warrant a resumption of the war a stand-off ensued that was directly comparable to the one between East and West in Europe. The North was able to sustain its independence by taking advantage of the Sino–Soviet rift, but each had too much to lose by challenging the status quo to allow its interests to be tied to the North's war chariot. For its part the South did not have its confidence in the American commitment tested until the changes wrought by the Sino–American rapprochement and its own economic revival. That left North and South to focus on domestic reconstruction amid the costs of sustaining a high degree of military preparedness. Although both were dictatorships, the communist North was tighter and more pervasive in its control of the society and economy as its leader, Kim Il-Sung, consolidated its grip. The South Korean dictator, Syngman Rhee, by contrast, had to allow for parliamentary politics. His attempts to subvert them eventually brought him down after student disturbances in 1960. A brief period of rule by a democratically elected government that was badly divided and ineffective was ended by a military coup a year later, which brought Park Chung Hee to power for the next eighteen years.

Japan's position as the key nodal point of American strategy and economic concerns in the Asia-Pacific was not seriously challenged by either the Soviet Union or China. As part of its policy of accommodation towards the West in 1955–56 the Soviet Union initiated talks with Japan too. This culminated in mutual recognition and in Japan's entry to the United Nations. But no agreement was reached on the group of four islands adjacent to Hokaido still occupied by the Soviet Union. Consequently, they were unable to agree upon a peace settlement. This left Japan firmly in the American camp. Although the Japanese found ways to trade with the PRC (contrary to the American embargo) that too did not affect the country's international position. By focusing upon economic development Japan was able to emerge by the end of the 1960s as one of the world's leading economic powers.

There were few vital interests at stake for the two superpowers in Southeast Asia. This was also largely true for the two major regional powers, China and Japan. Under these less restrictive circumstances, the more fluid geopolitical conditions of Southeast Asia allowed for a greater degree of change to take place. As we saw in the previous chapter, the states of Southeast Asia, with the exception of Thailand, had all experienced European colonial rule. That, together with the manner of their emancipation, had a profound effect upon their subsequent identities as states. These identities in turn shaped both their domestic politics and their foreign relations. Indeed the two have been closely linked from the perspective of international politics. The internal and external politics of the states of Southeast Asia were closely inter-linked. Whether considering the treatment of an ethnic minority such as the Chinese, or assessing the importance of Islam as a political influence, or indeed even examining the question of the territorial claims of states, it is not always clear whether the external dimensions are derived from the domestic political arena or *vice versa*. It should also be recognized that although the major external powers in this period may not have identified vital interests for which they were prepared to fight major wars, this did not mean that they lacked interest in the region. Indeed at times they even showed a willingness to intervene in support of territorial claims and of disaffected élite groups. With these broad considerations in mind, the international history of each of the main states will be surveyed briefly.

The Philippines

As previously noted, the Philippines has been described as 'being simultaneously a kind of detached bit of [Latin America] an East Asian offshore island, the occasional and uncertain champion of an embryonic community of Southeast Asian states, and indubitably a part of the Malay world'.[26] The central pillar in its foreign relations continued to be the manifold connection with the United States which, in addition to the alliance and the military bases, also included pervasive American commerce and culture. Filipino troops were deployed in Vietnam and American airfields were used, albeit not for bombing. The sense of dependence has also evoked a certain anti-American rhetoric in Filipino nationalism and a concurrent search for ways to assert a Southeast Asian identity and to find endorsement within the region for such an identity. Essentially the Philippines has been self-absorbed with its own problems such as the continued rumblings of the Huk insurgency, and the discontent of the Muslim minority in the south, centred on the island of Mindanao. But the overwhelming problem has stemmed from a political system that has been strong on the rhetoric of democracy and weak on orderly governance, which consequently has been unable or unwilling to address the economic, social and administrative difficulties that have existed since independence. Its relations with its Southeast Asian neighbours have been somewhat guarded despite institutionalized regional links, notably that of the Association of Southeast Asian Nations, but also the two ill-fated regional associations that preceded it. In addition to the degree of distance from its neighbours caused by their separate identities and the Filipino ties with the United States, the Philippines' claim to Sabah which was incorporated within the Malaysian Federation created problems too, even though it was not pursued with much vigour.

Thailand

On the whole Thailand is more homogenous than most of the other Southeast Asian states with around 90 per cent of the population identifying themselves as ethnic T'ais, as Buddhists and as T'ai speakers. The traditional concern with the threat from Burma abated in the post independence period as the Burmese state became tied down by its various domestic insurgencies. But Thailand has been troubled to the east. There has been periodic fear of subversion through T'ai speaking Laos in the 1950s and 1960s partly because of suspected Chinese influence through their road building activities in the north and partly through a Vietnamese inspired communization of Laos. Accordingly, the Thais supported the so-called right-wing Lao leaders and they felt vindicated when their suspicions that the 1962 Geneva Agreement on Laos would work out in favour of the Vietnamese were confirmed. Part of the problem from a Thai perspective was the vulnerability of their adjacent northeast provinces which were relatively neglected. Meanwhile traditional

Thai–Khmer animosities were exacerbated by complaints about the way in which Khmer and Thai minorities were treated in each other's countries. Essentially, Thai governments thought of Cambodia as an unreliable buffer against Vietnam. To the south, the Malay speaking areas of Thailand's Kra peninsula have posed problems less because of possible separatism than as a base for insurgency and cross border smuggling. Here there has been more cooperation with Malaysia to quell the troubles rather than the eruption of discord over possible irredentism. The alliance with the United States was crucial as much for the Thai military in enhancing its domestic political primacy as in sustaining Thailand's international position. But it has been an alliance that served Thai interests too; and it proved to be no barrier to Thailand's active pursuit of schemes for regional inter-governmental cooperation.

Malaysia

Malaysia, whose official religion is constitutionally defined as Islam, has been troubled by its ethnic mix, which even after the expulsion of Singapore in 1965 (see p. 70), was made up of some 45 per cent Malay, 35 per cent Chinese, 10 per cent Indian and a further 10 per cent from elsewhere. It was formed as a Federation in 1963 to include the two states of Sarawak and Sabah in northern Borneo, Singapore, and peninsula Malaya itself. Brunei was originally proposed as a member, but in the end it did not join. The Federation was seen as a means of divesting remaining British colonial possessions in Borneo and using them to counterbalance the Chinese population of Singapore. Its formation brought to a head a number of factors that have been central to Malaysia's domestic and international concerns. The communal problems between Malays and Chinese are both domestic and external issues of great complexity. As elsewhere in the region, the Chinese are resented both because of their command over much of the commerce and because of their preservation of their distinctive ways of life with their ties to the Chinese homeland. They are also regarded as the beneficiaries of the colonial era. As Muslims, the Malays are subject to the twin pressures of asserting their Islamic faith and of temporising it in order to accommodate the Chinese and Indians in their midst. Even the Islamic world in Malaysia is divided between the more tolerant and those of a more fundamentalist persuasion. Not surprisingly, communal conflict has been a continual spectre and indeed in 1969 when the establishment Alliance Party, incorporating members of both communities, did less well in the elections than expected, severe rioting broke out. The subsequent regrouping of the 'grand coalition' implemented a 'New Economic Policy' which allocated a greater share of the nation's wealth to the Malays whose cultural heritage was to be better protected and whose advancement was to underpin political dominance with economic control. These events had an extensive impact upon the region, as they drew attention both to the inability of Chinese governments in either Beijing or Taipei to protect the Overseas Chinese and to their economic significance in each of the countries in the region.

Similarly, the challenge of a more assertive Islam within the Malay community may be seen as simultaneously a domestic matter for the less fundamentalist UMNO leadership and as a regional and/or international one that affected the wider world of Malay culture especially after the 1967 Arab–Israeli War and Israeli control of the holy places. In fact pan-Malay solidarity (with anti-Chinese undertones) had been briefly fanned in 1963 with the short lived formation of Maphilindo – an acronym comprising Malaya, the Philippines and Indonesia. But its development was aborted by the establishment of Malaysia only a few weeks later. The two initial challenges to its legitimacy, by the Philippines and Indonesia respectively, may have abated rapidly, but they too may be seen as illustrative of wider problems. The Philippines' claim to Sabah has been a continual reminder that Malaysia's territorial integrity cannot be taken for granted. The Indonesian denunciation of Malaysia as a neo-colonial entity and its political, economic and military confrontation (*Konfrontasi*) of the Federation from 1963 to 1966 highlighted contradictory elements in the Malaysian international posture. Its defence and economic interests placed it within the Western camp, but its changing regional interests and domestic pre-dispositions involved a degree of unease with that situation. Hence Malaysia sought membership of the Non-Aligned Movement not long after.

Ethnic tension resulted in the expulsion of Singapore from the Federation within two years. The question of regional identity arose towards the end of *Konfrontasi* in late 1965 when the Malaysian government began to cultivate relations with Indonesia and to distance itself from Britain despite the latter having defended the Federation along with Australia and New Zealand military. Yet at the same time, the Malaysian government made a number of gestures favourable to the United States. Kuala Lumpur, for example, was the only Asian capital that President Johnson visited in 1966 that was not a co-belligerent in Vietnam. As against that, however, there were countervailing regional associations notably those that led to the establishment of the Association of Southeast Asian Nations (ASEAN) in 1967. Signifying a new understanding between Malaysia and Indonesia its five member governments committed themselves to strengthening their economic and social stability so as to prevent external interference and to accept the temporary character of foreign bases which were not to be used to interfere with other states in the region.

Indonesia

Indonesia, which is made up of more than 13,000 islands, of which 1,000 are inhabited, has been subject to a sense of weakness and vulnerability arising from the social and geographical fragmentation and to a sense of what Michael Leifer has called an 'entitlement' to play a leading role in the management of regional order in Southeast Asia.[27] In the first decade after independence the state successfully overcame challenges to its integrity. In particular, in 1958 it overcame an armed revolt based on several major islands that had a degree of assistance from external forces including the United States. The vociferous objection to external interference that has been a marked feature of successive Indonesian governments should not obscure the fact that American diplomatic pressure was instrumental ultimately in gaining independence from the Dutch in 1949 and in recovering what came to be called Irian Jaya (the former Dutch New Guinea). In both instances it proved possible to use Cold War factors to Indonesian advantage. The circumstances of the first occasion were discussed in the previous chapter. The Irian Jaya case was facilitated in part 'by Sukarno's ability to use Soviet arms transfers to persuade the government of the United States of the political utility of persuading, in turn, the Netherlands government to revise its adamant opposition to transferring the territory to Indonesia'.[28]

In Indonesia too there was a close correspondence between domestic and external policies. The period of parliamentary democracy 1950–59 saw a commitment to an 'independent and active' foreign policy which involved non-alignment as part of a policy designed to cater to a national mood that was still shaped by the experience of the national revolution or struggle for independence. But it also 'served as a way of sustaining domestic priorities designed to overcome economic, social and administrative shortcomings'.[29] However, it was with the advent of the period of 'guided democracy' under the leadership of President Sukarno that the linkage became even more evident. Sukarno balanced two incompatible coalitions, first, with the more conservative armed forces, and second, with the Communist Party (PKI). The former provided physical power and the latter a mass base. Their incompatibility led to the avoidance of taking critical decisions on domestic policy. Foreign policy issues which evoked a nationalist response had the great virtue of providing Sukarno with 'great freedom of political manoeuvre without arousing domestic discord'.[30] His confrontationalist style against the West, depicted as the 'old established forces' ever anxious to thwart and obstruct the 'new emerging forces' such as Indonesia, were most evident in the campaign to acquire West Irian (Irian Jaya) from the Dutch and in the armed confrontation with Malaysia as a creature of neo-colonialism after its creation in 1963.

With the collapse of guided democracy after the abortive coup of 1965, the government of General Suharto established a new domestic order that soon found expression in a different approach to foreign policy. While still upholding the long standing goals of abjuring military alliances and asserting pre-eminence in the affairs of the Southeast Asian region, the new government abandoned the leftist style rhetoric of Sukarno for a growing association with the Western industrialized states. Relations with Beijing immediately soured as it was openly accused of being implicated in the 1965 coup. This accentuated the impression of a new pro-Western tilt that was only slightly mollified by the retention of correct relations with the Soviet Union. The ending of the confrontation with Malaysia resulted in a situation in which the five governments of Southeast Asia who were interested in regional cooperation were sufficiently like-minded to combine that with the exercise of reconciliation with Indonesia. Thus on 8 August 1967 in Bangkok the Association of Southeast Nations (ASEAN) comprising Indonesia, Malaysia, Singapore, Thailand and the Philippines came into being. Since the last two were allied to the United States and were involved in the American war effort in Vietnam, which was then at its height, and in order to minimize communist and non-aligned possible suspicions about its orientation, the main emphasis was placed on ASEAN's role of facilitating cooperation in economic, social and cultural matters. The goal of encouraging peace and stability in the region was given less public attention, but it was still uppermost in mind. The extent to which this was done, however, did reflect long standing Indonesian perspectives. Thus the members committed themselves to strengthen the economic and social stability of the region and to preserve their national identities and security from 'external interference in any form and manifestation'. They also affirmed the temporary character of foreign bases that could remain only with 'expressed concurrence' of the host countries and with the proviso that they did not subvert countries within the region.[31]

Singapore

As a city state made up predominantly of ethnic Chinese, Singapore was acutely conscious, under its leader, Lee Kuan Yew, of its vulnerability given its geopolitical location between Malaysia and Indonesia. This was particularly true after its expulsion from the Malaysian Federation in August 1965. It had reason to fear both Sukarno's *Konfrontasi* and the profuse expressions of pan-Malay solidarity after its end. Accordingly, it welcomed both the formation of ASEAN in 1967 and the decision to form the Five Power Defence Arrangements by the British Conservative government on its coming to power in 1970, by way of recompense for the British decision to retreat militarily from east of Suez. The agreement committed Britain, Australia and New Zealand to maintain a modest defence presence in both Malaysia and Singapore. Singapore has sometimes taken high profile positions that would not always be welcome to its vastly larger neighbours as a way of securing their proper respect. Moreover, unlike perhaps either Malaysia or Indonesia, Singapore has a geostrategic interest in encouraging rather than discouraging the presence of external great powers in the seas of the region. Such is the Singaporean concern about being absorbed by its neighbours that its defence posture has been likened to that of a poisonous shrimp that draws attention to itself by its brilliance as a warning to potential predators about the terrible pains that would follow from swallowing it.

This period of bipolarity began with an assertive American attempt to consolidate the containment of communism in East Asia and ended with the United States in a more chastened mood after its travails in Vietnam. The heady days of the Eisenhower and Kennedy Administrations interpreted every gain by a supposedly monolithic international communist movement as something to be denied in principle rather than to be responded to in terms of variable geopolitical significance. But one of the first decisions of the Nixon presidency in 1969 was to limit American military interventions in

East Asia to air and naval power alone. Meanwhile the Sino–Soviet rift which the West had anticipated in the late 1940s and early 1950s duly took place, but the West was ill placed to exploit it until after the debacle in Vietnam, when Kissinger and Nixon appreciated the geopolitical significance of the rift. Meanwhile a stalemate developed in Northeast Asia while in Southeast Asia the United States got bogged down in Vietnam. As China turned inwards during the Cultural Revolution the other Southeast Asian states were able, after the fall of Indonesia's President Sukarno, to contain their differences and various disputes by establishing a regional association. Although more modest in its scope, the more pragmatic orientation of ASEAN ensured a longer and more effective life span than the more trumpeted declarations of Asian and African solidarity as epitomized by the Bandung Conference. However, the established bipolar character of containment in Asia had run its course as the deeper significance of the emergence of China as a separate centre of power was to emerge in the course of the pending Sino–American rapprochement.

NOTES AND REFERENCES

1 Gordon H. Chang, *Friends and Enemies: The United States, China, and the Soviet Union, 1948–1972* (Stanford: Stanford University Press, 1990); and John Lewis Gaddis, *The United States and the End of the Cold War: Implications, Reconsiderations, Provocations* (Oxford: Oxford University Press, 1992).

2 Donald S. Zagoria, *Vietnam Triangle: Moscow, Peking, Hanoi* (New York: Pegasus, 1967).

3 Much of this is captured in a book written at the end of the period under review. See, Milton Osborne, *Region of Revolt, Focus on Southeast Asia* (Australia: Pergamon Press, 1970).

4 See George F. Kennan, *Memoirs 1950–1963* (New York: Pantheon Books 1983) pp. 58–59; and Hans J. Morganthau, *A New Foreign Policy for the United States* (New York: Praeger, 1969) pp. 129–56.

5 For an account that draws a sharp distinction between Soviet economic relations with Asian communist countries and the majority of the other East Asian countries see A. Hewett and Herbert S. Levine (eds) 'The Soviet Union's Economic Relations in Asia' in Donald S. Zagoria, *Soviet Policy in East Asia* (A Council on Foreign Relations Book, New Haven and London: Yale University Press, 1982) pp. 201–28.

6 For an authoritative account of Kennan's ideas see John Lewis Gaddis, *Strategies of Containment* (Oxford: Oxford University Press, 1982) Chapters 2 and 3.

7 Cited in Stephen E. Ambrose, *The Rise to Globalism, American Foreign Policy Since 1938* (London: Penguin, sixth revised edition, 1991) pp. 142–43.

8 This account draws upon Gaddis, (*ibid.*) Chapter 4 and the quotations are from pp. 98 and 103 respectively.

9 Martin Borthwick, *Pacific Century* (Boulder: Westview Press, 1992) p. 394.

10 Gaddis, *Strategies of Containment* (*op. cit.*) Chapters 5 and 6. The quotation from Ridgway is on p. 195.

11 This and the following paragraph have benefited from the excellent analysis by Thomas E. Stolper, *China, Taiwan and the Off-Shore Islands* (New York: M. E. Sharpe, 1985).

12 These were, respect for territorial integrity and sovereignty; non-aggression; non-interference in internal affairs; equality and mutual benefit; and peaceful co-existence.

13 For accounts see, G. H. Jansen, *Nonalignment and the Afro–Asian States* (New York: Praeger, 1966); George McT. Kahin, *The Asian–African Conference* (Ithaca: Cornell University Press, 1956); and Peter Lyon, *Neutralism* (Leicester: University of Leicester Press, 1963).

14 Stephen A. Fitzgerald, *China and the Overseas Chinese: A Study of Peking's Changing Policy* (Cambridge: Cambridge University Press, 1973).

15 For accounts of Chinese policies in Southeast Asia see Jay Taylor, *China and Southeast Asia: Peking's Relations with Revolutionary Movements* (New York: Praeger, expanded and updated, 1976); and Melvin Gurtov, *China and Southeast Asia – The Politics of Survival* (Lexington: D. C. Heath & Co., 1971).

16 This account relies strongly on Stolper (*op. cit.*) Chapter VIII.

17 The advent of new archival material and the significance of new perspectives since the end of the Cold War, have deepened knowledge of the Sino–Soviet conflict. The most notable book to have been published so far is Sergei N. Goncharov, John W. Lewis & Xue Litai, *Uncertain Partners: Stalin, Mao and the Korean War* (Stanford: Stanford University Press, 1993) which has transformed understanding of the establishment of the Sino–Soviet alliance and the beginnings of the Korean War. Nevertheless the best books that treat the breakdown of the relationship remain Donald S. Zagoria, *The Sino–Soviet Conflict 1956–1961* (Princeton: Princeton University Press, 1962) and John Gittings, *Survey of the Sino–Soviet Dispute* (Oxford: Oxford University Press, 1969).

18 For the most complete account of China's development of nuclear weapons see John Wilson Lewis and Xue Litai, *China Builds the Bomb* (Stanford: Stanford University Press, 1988).

19 See Michael Leifer, *Indonesia's Foreign Policy* (London: George Allen & Unwin, for the Royal International Institute of International Affairs, 1983) pp. 45–53.

20 (*ibid.*) p. 105.

21 For detailed accounts and analysis see Thomas Robinson, *The Sino–Soviet Border Dispute* (Santa Monica: The Rand Corporation, 1970); and Gerald Segal, *Defending China* (Oxford: Oxford University Press, 1985) Chapter 10.

22 See note 7.

23 Cited in Ambrose (*op. cit.*) pp. 208–9.

24 Gaddis, *Strategies of Containment* (*op. cit.*) pp. 249–50.

25 See the discussion in Allen S. Whiting, *The Chinese Calculus of Deterrence* (Ann Arbor: University of Michigan Press, 1975).
26 Peter Lyon, *War and Peace in South-East Asia* (London: Oxford University Press, for The Royal Institute of International Affairs, 1969), p. 46.
27 Michael Leifer, *Indonesia's Foreign Policy* (*op. cit.*) p. xiv.
28 (*ibid.*) pp. 67–68.
29 Leifer, *Indonesia's Foreign Policy*, (*op. cit.*) p. 29.
30 (*ibid.*) p. 55.
31 For further readings on Indonesia see Franklin B. Weinstein, *Indonesian Foreign Policy and the Dilemma of Dependence* (Ithaca: Cornell University Press, 1976); Michael Leifer, *Indonesia's Foreign Policy* (*op. cit.*); J. A. C. Mackie, *Konfrontasi: The Indonesia–Malaysia Dispute 1963–1966* (Kuala Lumpur: Oxford University Press, 1974); and Peter Polumka, *Indonesia's Future and South-East Asia* (London: Internal Institute for Strategic Studies, Adelphi Papers No. 104, 1974).

3 The period of tripolarity, 1971–89

The structure of the international system during the period between 1971–89 has often been depicted as a strategic triangle comprising the United States, the Soviet Union and China. There is some merit in this view, but it should not be exaggerated.[1] China did not carry the same strategic weight as the other two and its impact on global configurations of power was still quite limited. The essentials of the Cold War between Moscow and Washington and the centrality of the strategic balance between the two superpowers and their allies remained in place. The principal change that occurred was that China became more openly recognized as a complicating factor in the conduct of American–Soviet relations especially in East Asia where its influence was more evident. Henry Kissinger's surprise visit to Beijing in July 1971, which may be said to have formally ushered in this new phase in international politics, did not suddenly elevate China to superpower status. Unlike either of the super-powers, China's military reach continued to be limited to areas adjacent to its land borders. It lagged far behind in military technology and its economy was not yet of global significance. What gave a new salience to China's significance was the strategic weight the Soviet Union had gained as a result of its sustained military build-up while the United States had been bogged down in Vietnam. Now that the Soviet Union had 'caught up' with the United States the China factor acquired a new importance.

China's international strategic importance stemmed, first, from the fact that alone among the other countries in the world it claimed to be able to defend itself from either of the superpowers, who in turn had gone to great lengths to contain Chinese power; and second, from its independent diplomatic stance as demonstrated by its shift from alliance with the Soviet Union to revolutionary isolationism and now to an alignment with the United States. China

also benefited from its geographical location and its perceived potential. But China's elevation to the diplomacy of tripolarity also stemmed from the importance the two superpowers accorded the country
in their conduct of relations with each other. That, however, did not
alter the fact that the dominant strategic relationship in world affairs
was still that of the United States and the Soviet Union. The key
pillars of the Cold War remained in place throughout this period
and these emanated from the confrontation in Europe where the
Chinese impact was not great.[2] The Soviet leaders regarded themselves as representatives of the fellow superpower with whom the
Americans had to deal over serious issues. As Brezhnev once put it,
Nixon went 'to Peking for banquets but to Moscow to do business'.[3]

Each of the parties to the strategic triangle perceived it differently
and changed their policies over time. The Chinese, whose principal
foreign policy concerns to date could be described as seeking to
manoeuvre between the two superpowers in order to preserve
China's independence, opened to America in order better to contain
the Soviet Union. Later, however, the Chinese shifted to a more
independent position as the Soviet threat declined and as the
Reagan Administration no longer seemed to need the Chinese coun-
ter-weight as much as its predecessors. Kissinger and Nixon, as the
architects of the new structure of international relations, saw it less
as a means of bringing unrelenting pressure on one party by the
other two than as a means of bringing about an equilibrium in which
the Soviet leaders would see it to be in their interests to act with
restraint.[4] Their successors, however, argued as to whether it would
be possible to rein in a Soviet Union that had not acted with
'restraint' by supplying sophisticated weaponry to China – what
became known as playing the 'China card'. The issue was finally
settled by the Reagan Administration's huge military build-up that
made the Chinese role almost redundant.[5] The Soviet leaders, who
had less room for manoeuvre in the triangle than the other two,
first emphasized their significance to the Americans as a fellow
superpower, only later to vent their spleen on the Chinese as
extreme 'anti-Soviets' who had got the Americans on their side, and
finally to end up in a position in which they sought to cultivate
relations with the Chinese partly in order to limit American unilateralism.[6]

Even within the Asia-Pacific the effect of tripolarity was not to
change the fundamental pattern of alliances involving the United
States and the Soviet Union, but rather to change the position and
relations of China. Thus American alliances with South Korea,

Japan, the Philippines, Thailand, etc., all held, as did the Soviet alliances with Mongolia, North Korea and North Vietnam (soon to be a reunified Vietnam). Even the one American international alliance that was ended – that with Taiwan – was soon renewed through domestic American legislation in the form of the Taiwan Relations Act. As against that, China's relations in the region changed radically, notably in Southeast Asia where relations were soon established with former adversaries Malaysia, the Philippines and Thailand only to deteriorate rapidly with its former ally Vietnam. Moreover, the underlying strategic enmity between the United States and the Soviet Union was complicated in the Asia-Pacific by a Sino–Soviet conflict that was particularly intense in the 1970s and whose influence was still apparent for much of the 1980s.

The period of tripolarity may be divided roughly into two: from 1971 until 1979, when the United States still sought détente with the Soviet Union and when Sino–Soviet relations continued to be marked by deep enmity; and from 1980 to 1989, which was characterized initially by greater enmity between the United States and the Soviet Union and a slow improvement in Sino–Soviet relations, and by the late 1980s ended in a more balanced relations between the three powers, culminating in the normalization of Sino–Soviet relations and the ending of the Cold War. As seen from the more mechanistic view of the strategic triangle, the United States was favoured by the 'pivot' position during the first period as it alone enjoyed good relations with the other two who in turn sought to cultivate Washington against the other rival. But it was principally China who became the 'pivot' in the second period as it benefited from the deterioration of relations between the other two and was accordingly cultivated by them. However, tripolarity was only one of the elements that shaped relations between the three great powers. Other factors must also be taken into account, such as strategic developments, questions of ideology, changes in the domestic political circumstances in each of their societies and the impact of developments elsewhere. Nevertheless the periodization also accords with other important developments. The year 1979 was a turning point in many ways as it was the year in which China launched its brief incursion into Vietnam, and the Soviet Union later invaded Afghanistan, which led the United States to adopt a more confrontationist policy towards the Soviet Union. It was also the year in which China's new policies of economic reform and openness began to take shape and in which the United States and China commenced a new period of normalized relations.

TRIPOLARITY PHASE I: 1971–79, THE PROBLEMS OF DÉTENTE

Tripolarity, according to its chief exponent, Henry Kissinger, was meant not only to serve American interests, but also to promote the goal of equilibrium among the main powers and thus serve the general interest. The United States seemingly enjoyed the key position of the 'pivot', as it could deal directly with the other two while they in turn froze each other out in bitter confrontation.

But the immediate effect of Henry Kissinger's visit to Beijing in July 1971 was to serve China's interest by accelerating the return of the People's Republic of China to full participatory membership of the international community. That autumn the UN General Assembly voted overwhelmingly to expel the Republic of China (i.e. Taiwan) and replace it with the PRC. The general trend of improving state relations with the PRC reached a high tide as nearly all states rushed to normalize relations with Beijing. But the startling diplomatic success of the Americans in establishing a strategic alignment with the Chinese, according to Kissinger's own account, was followed not by immediate conciliatory moves by the Soviet Union, but by Moscow's encouragement of India to act boldly in facilitating the break up of Pakistan, a staunch ally of the PRC. After signing a treaty with the Soviet Union in August 1971 the Indian government assisted the rebellion in East Pakistan in seceding and in establishing the state of Bangladesh. According to Kissinger, only American pressure (including the so-called 'tilt to Pakistan') prevented India, with Soviet connivance, from proceeding to capture the whole of Kashmir and in the process destroying the remaining Pakistani army and leading to the dismemberment of West Pakistan. That in turn would have left China vulnerable and it could possibly have undermined the Nixon/Kissinger initiative to establish a new and necessary balance of power.[7] It is clear even from this self-serving account that the opening to China did not automatically result in more 'restrained Soviet behaviour' and it also pointed up that the weakness of China could make it a liability for the United States under certain circumstances as well as an asset under others.

In fact, from the outset each of the powers not only understood tripolarity differently but they also experienced the pressures of tripolarity in different ways. This arose in part from the lack of symmetry among the three powers and in part because of the ways in which domestic factors interacted with the external pressures. Thus China's relative weakness made it court the United States in the first place against the perceived threat of the Soviet Union. But ideological rivalry with the Soviet Union, which went to the heart of the legitimacy of Mao and his Cultural Revolution, intensified his hostility towards the country and, at least in the eyes of his Soviet adversaries, precluded any prospect of an accommodation until after his death. Thus for most of the 1970s China's leaders sought in vain to establish an international coalition to confront the Soviet Union and openly derided the American development of détente with the Soviet Union as appeasement. The Soviet leaders were so persuaded that Mao personally was at the heart of Chinese hostility towards them that they put out feelers towards the Chinese after his death in 1976. In the event it was not until Deng Xiaoping had gained the ascendancy in Beijing in late 1978 and jettisoned much of Mao's ideological legacy that China's leaders were in a position to explore the prospects for improved relations.

The Soviet leaders during this period focused almost entirely on their relations with the United States with whom they felt that a broad strategic parity had been achieved that was only marginally affected by the Chinese factor. As long as the Soviet leaders thought that the United States sought détente and stability they concluded that the Americans would resist Chinese efforts to transform the dynamics of tripolarity into an anti-Soviet united front. Only once the United States abandoned détente in President Carter's last year did the Soviet leaders believe that Washington had combined with Beijing against them. In other words even then the Soviet leaders saw tripolarity as a function of bipolar relations between Moscow and Washington. It was not until 1982, when the Soviet Union was bogged down in Afghanistan and demonstrably in a weakening position compared to the United States which was engaged in a rapid military build up, that the Soviet leaders responded positively to Chinese earlier initiatives to improve relations.

The United States leaders, and Henry Kissinger in particular, consciously sought to exploit the dynamics of triangular diplomacy. Yet it is not easy to identify what specific tangible gains the United States achieved in its dealings with the Soviet Union either in the arms control negotiations or in the attempts to constrain Soviet activism in the Third World. Indeed, it can be argued that Soviet activism was in part activated by concern about the China factor. Furthermore it has been argued persuasively that the intensification of the Soviet military build up to the north of China in the middle 1970s threatened American strategic interests too.[8] Moreover, during the Nixon and Ford Administrations when Kissinger played a major role in shaping foreign policy, the American efforts to consolidate détente with the Soviet Union were made at the expense of exciting suspicion among China's leaders.

Following the departure of Kissinger in 1976 the main effect of tripolarity seemed to be to excite divisions among American decision makers. The Carter Administration consciously sought to pursue a more idealist foreign policy, but it felt the pressure of tripolarity through divisions within the administration about whether or not to use the threat of arming China as a means of restraining aggressive Soviet behaviour. The arguments between Secretary of State Vance and National Security Adviser Brzezinski were continued into the next administration, as exemplified by the contrast between Secretary of State Haig and his successor, Shultz. Haig went so far as to argue that China 'may be the most important country in the world' for American security interests.[9] For Shultz, China was little more than an important regional power, albeit of great potential, that was constrained by its communist system and, as far as Asia was concerned, for him 'the centrepiece has always been Japan'.[10] The issue was finally settled as a result of the changing balance of power in favour of the United States which had the effect of reducing China's potential strategic significance.

The regional impact

The transformation of China's position in the central balance between the United States and the Soviet Union may have had less impact on the global bipolar system than previously thought, but it certainly had an immediate effect on the Asia-Pacific region. From being a target for American containment policies China had become a partner in alignment with the United States. Moreover the Sino–Soviet enmity that was hitherto confined to the ideological realm and to direct bilateral confrontations was now to become more readily apparent in the region as a whole. Given the significance of China for all the countries in the region, the political, security and economic consequences were both immediate and far reaching.

The first to feel the impact was Taiwan. Hitherto it had been one of the cornerstones of American global strategy. It was at the centre of the American containment strategy in Asia and in particular of the confrontation with Chinese communism. By the Chinese, too, Taiwan had been regarded as of key significance in America's geopolitical strategy and as one of the critical points from which an invasion of the mainland might have been launched. Henceforth in the perspective of Beijing Taiwan returned to being a problem of sovereignty and Chinese unity: it was important but not a pressing issue that threatened the survival of the state and it was at best a secondary problem in Sino–American relations. Its significance had changed as the Sino–American international geopolitical alignment had changed. This was perhaps demonstrated by the famous Shanghai Communique of February 1972 signed by US President Nixon and the PRC Premier Zhou Enlai which, as Kissinger rightly claimed, 'was not about Taiwan or bilateral exchanges, but about international order'.[11] Interestingly, the terms of the communique were to allow America alone of all the Western countries to maintain full diplomatic relations and a security treaty with Taiwan while simultaneously maintaining a quasi-embassy in Beijing. Even when relations were normalized between Washington and Beijing in January 1979 Washington was still able to insist on its interest in a peaceful resolution of the Beijing–Taipei dispute and on its intention to continue to sell arms to the island. Although the United States had to abrogate its defence treaty with Taiwan (technically, the Republic of China) the Taiwan Relations Act of the US Congress that was signed by the president in April 1979 committed the US to maintain a capacity to 'resist any resort to force . . . that would jeopardise the security . . . of the people on Taiwan'. Much as this was resented by Beijing it did not stop the Chinese leaders from cultivating the United States as a strategic partner nor in seeking to deepen economic and other relations with it.

The Taiwan issue had in effect become a bilateral issue between the peoples on both sides of the Taiwan Straits with the United States as the guarantor that the issue should not be settled by force. The formal position of the PRC did not change until relations were normalized in January 1979. At that point the Beijing leaders dropped their harsh threat to 'liberate' Taiwan in favour of a milder offer of 're-unification' to be based on the granting of what on paper was a considerable degree of autonomy. The threat to use force was retained, according to Deng Xiaoping, lest the island ally itself with the Soviet Union, declare independence, or prolong matters unduly. The government in Taipei rejected the blandishments of Beijing, as it was buttressed by Taiwan's economic success and promises of American support. Little changed until the second half of the 1980s when the development of economic ties across the Straits and the beginnings of democracy on the island introduced important new factors into cross-Straits relations.

Japan too reacted smartly to the dramatic news of the American opening to China by accelerating its own moves to normalize relations with its giant neighbour. But it was not before the Japanese had replaced the relatively right-wing Eishiro Sato, who had links with the Kuomintang in Taiwan, with Kakuei Tanaka as prime minister, that the Chinese agreed to establish diplomatic relations in September 1972. The American *démarche* came as a shock to the Japanese, and another soon followed with a major change in American economic policy: surcharging imports and ending the trade of dollars at a fixed price for gold. It was, to say the least, disconcerting for a country that had hitherto been regarded as America's most important ally in Asia to find that its democratic friend, economic partner and strategic associate had suddenly sought an alignment with communist China, Japan's giant neighbour and, until that point, their joint antagonist, without even informing Tokyo in advance. Indeed such was the fascination of China for Henry Kissinger that Mao 'went so far as to advise [him] to make sure that when he visited Asia [he] spend as much time in Tokyo as in Peking'.[12] It was as if Mao and Zhou Enlai appreciated the significance of the US alliance with Japan as a constraint upon the Soviet Union and as the bedrock of strategic stability in East Asia better than Nixon and Kissinger. Indeed, according to Kissinger the Chinese leaders never sought to play off Japan and the US against each other.[13]

Japan therefore was able to develop relations with the PRC without encountering international pressures or constraints except for those emanating from the Soviet Union. Thus Japan normalized relations with the PRC amid a piece of creative diplomacy by which it was able to maintain diplomatic relations with Taiwan in all but name.[14] The PRC, like its predecessor the ROC, waived aside potential claims to reparations then estimated to be worth $50 billion.[15] Disputes about the sovereignty of the Senkaku (or in Chinese, Diao Yu Tai) Islands were put aside by joint agreement and within three years agreements were reached about fishing, navigation and communication matters as both sides deepened their economic relations.

Until 1978 Sino–Japanese relations were conducted almost entirely as simply bilateral matters, sheltering as they did under the Japanese security alliance with the United States that the Chinese too regarded as a stabilizing factor. The issue that raised larger regional and international questions was the signing of a peace treaty. The Soviet Union too was anxious to sign such a treaty with Japan and at the same time it was concerned by Chinese attempts to persuade Japan to sign a treaty that *inter alia* expressed opposition to 'hegemony' which was widely regarded as a Chinese code word for the Soviet Union. However, Soviet–Japanese negotiations broke down on Soviet refusal to acknowledge even the legitimacy of the Japanese right to dispute ownership of the four islands to the north of Japan. Soviet diplomacy was judged to be overbearing and that paved the way for the Chinese to obtain Japanese agreement, in August 1978, to sign a Treaty of Peace and Friendship with them instead. To assuage Japanese sentiments the Chinese agreed that opposition to hegemony should be mentioned in the preamble rather than be dealt with as a separate clause. They also accepted the wording that the treaty was not directed against any third party.

It was nevertheless the Soviet factor that brought Sino–Japanese relations back into the maelstrom of international and regional politics. In the Soviet perception the United States had already adopted a more pronounced anti-Soviet position in the course of the visit to China in May 1978 by Z. Brzezinski, President Carter's National Security Adviser,[16] and now the Sino–Japanese treaty contributed to the Soviet sense of isolation and encirclement. In the view of the Soviet leaders they were now confronted in East Asia by an alignment of the most populous, the most successful economically and the most powerful states (i.e. China, Japan and the United States). That may well have played a part in the Soviet decision to support Vietnam in its conquest of Cambodia in late 1978 and in its own invasion of Afghanistan a year later. The Sino–Japanese treaty also contributed to emboldening the Chinese to mount their attack on Vietnam in early 1979. Whether or not Japan's leaders appreciated the larger significance of their treaty with the PRC, Sino–Japanese relations necessarily were a part of the international dimensions of the Asia-Pacific region and could not be seen or understood primarily through the prism of bilateral relations, important though they were for both countries. Nevertheless Sino–Japanese relations always had dimensions that could only be understood in a bilateral context.[17]

Interestingly, the situation on the Korean peninsula was not greatly altered by the change in Sino–American relations. The North felt that its capacity to pursue an independent course had been considerably limited as it saw its two giant neighbours and allies separately seek détente with its principal enemy the United States. In 1972 it made a gesture towards opening talks with the South and began to purchase industrial plants and other forms of advanced technology from the smaller capitalist countries. However, little came of these cautious beginnings and the North was left in default of loan repayments to a number of countries. It was only in the latter half of the 1980s that the impact of the Gorbachev changes in the Soviet Union and the primacy of economics in China's foreign policy began to make a difference to the international dimensions of the Korean divide between North and South.

The 1970s were marked by the North's worse relations with the Soviet Union than with China. Although the Soviet Union no longer sought to control the North it nevertheless sought to constrain it from possible adventurous acts that might embarrass the Soviet Union in its relations with the United States, in what was still one of the world's most dangerous trouble spots. Unlike in the case of Vietnam, the opportunity to recruit North Korea to the Soviet side because of China's alleged 'defection' to America simply did not arise. The Koreans did not regard the Chinese as a long standing historical threat to independence, nor could the Soviet Union assist the North in achieving nationalist aims of unification without considerable risks to its own national security interests. On the contrary, these Soviet concerns led its leaders to dilute their support for the North's claim to be the only sovereign body with the legitimate right to rule the whole of the Korean peninsula. Instead they suggested to the North that the model of the two Germanys should be applied to Korea.

The Chinese, by contrast, quickly apologized for the excesses of the Cultural Revolution, and Zhou Enlai's visit in 1970 assured Kim of Chinese acceptance of the sole legitimacy of the North. At that point he shared the Northern view that the danger of Japanese militarism was once again evident. China's new relations with the United States that began only a year later entailed a certain cooling of relations. The two allies also began to differ on the alleged menace of Japan and by 1978 the Chinese signed a treaty with Japan. Nevertheless the North continued to tilt towards China without cutting off links with the Soviet Union. This may be seen from the North's criticism of the Vietnamese invasion of Cambodia and its corresponding silence about the Chinese attack on Vietnam. Not surprisingly, in this period the Chinese rather than the Soviets were the principal suppliers of weaponry to the North.[18]

The South was principally concerned about the depth and durability of the American defence commitment in Korea. Indeed that had been a primary consideration in the deployment of 50,000 combat troops to fight in South Vietnam in response to President Johnson's request for international support for the American war effort. The Nixon and Ford Administrations were careful to give assurances of continued support to South Korea after the opening

to China and in the course of the stages of the American withdrawal
from South Vietnam, culminating in the final debacle of 1975. However, the anxieties that were raised the following year by the
incoming Carter Administration because of the campaign pledge to
withdraw American forces from South Korea were not completely
assuaged even though President Carter was soon persuaded to
change his mind.[19] These considerations were not a function of
tripolarity, but rather arose from the impact on the United States
of its disastrous experience in Vietnam and from different assessments of Soviet behaviour. In other words the Korean situation
continued to be dominated by the Cold War considerations associated with the bipolar system even though that system itself had
weakened. The reason for the persistence of the stalemate stemmed
from the mutual hostilities of North and South supported by the
external powers rather than primarily from the external powers
themselves.

The impact of the Sino–American *rapprochement* and the emergence of tripolarity was immediate and far reaching in Southeast
Asia. America's new relations with China, coupled with the pursuit
of détente with the Soviet Union, removed the last vestiges of the
original strategic purposes for American intervention in Vietnam.
The potential success of the North could no longer be seen as a
victory by proxy for the geopolitical interests of the Chinese communists. Nevertheless the American process of withdrawal was prolonged, principally because of the perceived need to withdraw 'with
honour' in order to sustain America's credibility as an ally and to
assuage domestic forces. To this end the United States sought to use
the linkage with the Soviet Union to bring pressure to bear upon
North Vietnam and to persuade the Soviet Union that it should act
with restraint in international affairs if détente were to work as a
basis for international order. In the event the negotiations with the
North dragged on in a context in which it was by no means apparent
that Moscow could dictate to Hanoi or that Hanoi could determine
Soviet reactions.

Meanwhile the repercussions of the Sino–American alignment
were bringing about new divisions and realignments in Indo-China
that were to culminate in the third Indo-China war. The new challenges from the changes in the region's international environment
had the effect of transforming the Association of Southeast Asian
Nations (ASEAN) into a more cohesive diplomatic community.
These changes must be set within a wider context than that of the
emergence of tripolarity alone. The British had decided in January

1968 to accelerate the timetable of their military disengagement
from East of Suez. Three months later a Soviet naval flotilla made
its first appearance in the Indian Ocean – soon to be seen as the
harbinger of a more active Soviet naval presence in this part of
the world. In March that year after the Tet Offensive by the Vietnamese communists President Johnson's decision not to seek re-
election and to pursue a solution by negotiation was seen as a
decisive turning point in acknowledging the limits of American
power. This was confirmed when, to the manifest unease of
America's Asian allies, the recently elected President Nixon stated
in Guam in July 1969 that the United States was no longer prepared
to undertake principal combat roles in their defence. The American
opening to China was seen therefore as indicating a new role in the
region for China. It also was to pave the way for introducing
the Sino–Soviet conflict as an additional interposition in the region.

The impact of these changes was deepest in Indo-China. This
was not immediately apparent as China's leaders sought to assuage
Vietnamese fears of Chinese betrayal. Chinese aid continued to
flow and Chinese diplomatic support for North Vietnam remained
formally correct. But the North Vietnamese, who were already
reliant upon the Soviet Union for the supply of advanced weaponry,
had reason to fear Chinese attempts to subordinate Vietnamese
interests to their own, and consequently leaned still further towards
the Soviet side. In January 1973 the Americans and the North
Vietnamese finally signed agreements in Paris that confirmed the
American final military withdrawals. Two years later in April 1975
the North swiftly overran a demoralized South. Meanwhile the
Chinese took the opportunity in 1974 to seize by force the remaining
part of the Paracel Islands occupied by the South. These islands in
the South China Sea are claimed by both China and Vietnam and the
Chinese opportunistic seizure further added to the growing enmity
between Hanoi and Beijing that was still largely concealed behind
a veil of diplomatic niceties. However, the American debacle in
Indo-China exacerbated Chinese fears of a Soviet attempt to fill the
vacuum left by the departing US forces.

The critical point of division between China and Vietnam centred
upon Cambodia. April 1975 also witnessed the final victory of the
Khmer Rouge in their capture of Phnom Penh from the forces of
Lon Nol whose pro-Western army had ousted Prince Sihanouk five
years earlier. The virulent anti-Vietnamese nationalism of the
Khmer Rouge served Chinese interests as it served to deny Vietnam
the opportunity of dominating the whole of Indo-China. But the

prospects of finding a basis of accommodation between the competing parties did not materialize as the Khmer Rouge initiated a series of provocative assaults along the borders with Vietnam. These in turn heightened Vietnamese fears about Chinese attempts to limit their independence. Emboldened by their closer links with the Soviet Union, the government in Hanoi, which had experienced difficulties in imposing a command economy upon the South, took measures in 1978 to encourage the ethnic Chinese (who as elsewhere in Southeast Asia dominated much of the local commerce) to leave. There also emerged a conjunction of interests between the Soviet desire to constrain China and the Vietnamese security objectives of removing the Khmer Rouge challenge and defying Chinese attempts to prevent the Vietnamese from asserting their claims to exercise special influence over Indo-China as a whole.

By the end of 1978 the international, regional and local lines of conflict combined to bring about the third Indo-China war. Backed by membership of COMECON in June and by a formal friendship treaty with the Soviet Union in November, the Vietnamese invaded Cambodia on 25 December, captured Phnom Penh on 7 January and imposed a regime of their choice. The Khmer Rouge forces retreated as guerillas to hideouts primarily near the borders with Thailand. The Chinese, having signed a treaty with Japan in the summer and after agreeing to normalize relations with the United States in December 1978, followed up with visits by Deng Xiaoping himself to both Washington and Tokyo in which he vowed to 'teach Vietnam a lesson'. Despite obtaining less than enthusiastic backing the Chinese launched an attack on 17 February 1979 into North Vietnam, ostensibly because of border violations. Three weeks later the Chinese troops were withdrawn after inflicting considerable damage, but not before their limitations as a fighting force had been exposed by the Vietnamese. This then resulted in a stalemate that lasted ten years, in which an internationally isolated Vietnam was dependent upon the Soviet Union to sustain its dominant position in Cambodia while being confronted on the margins by resistance forces that enjoyed international legitimacy and the support of China, the United States, and the ASEAN countries.[20]

The impact of these international and regional changes to the security environment of the ASEAN countries was to facilitate their emergence as a more cohesive diplomatic body after first highlighting some of their different security perspectives. Their first response to the new international position of China illustrated these divisions. In 1971, under pressure from the US State Department to resist the

PRC's claim to the China seat at the United Nations, the Philippines acquiesced in the interests of its American alliance; Thailand and even non-aligned Indonesia abstained; but Malaysia and Singapore voted in favour of the PRC. Singapore was concerned about the sentiments of its majority community; and the Malaysian government sought to find an accommodation with Beijing so as 'to demonstrate to the country's resident Chinese community and to its insurgent communist party that its legitimacy was recognized and endorsed by its counterpart in Beijing'.[21] In fact this was the origin of the initiative to declare Southeast Asia a Zone of Peace, Freedom and Neutrality (ZOPFAN). As first conceived, Malaysia sought formal neutralization to be guaranteed by the external powers including the PRC. But at Indonesian insistence all reference to external guarantees was removed and the resulting declaration of November 1971 specifically called for recognition and respect for a ZOPFAN that would be 'free from any form or manner of interference by outside powers'.[22]

In 1974 Malaysia became the first ASEAN country to recognize the PRC. Thailand and the Philippines followed suit a year later but not until after the victories of the revolutionaries in Cambodia and Vietnam. Indeed the victories fundamentally changed the regional security environment of ASEAN. The American debacle in Vietnam raised doubts about its residuary security role in Southeast Asia at a time when the relatively conservative governments of ASEAN suddenly found themselves directly confronted by triumphant revolutionary regimes to the north. In response a summit was held in February 1976 that sought to affirm the purpose of the Association as a body primarily concerned with internal security and of its vision for attainment of a regional order that emphasized the peaceful settlement of disputes. It held out the prospect of the socialist Indo-Chinese states becoming associated with ASEAN through a Treaty of Amity and Cooperation.

As the new lines of conflict emerged between Cambodia and Vietnam, China and Vietnam and China and the Soviet Union, the ASEAN countries found themselves being courted in 1978 by the two sets of disputants. Vietnam's invasion and occupation of Cambodia proved to be the turning point. By imposing by force on a recalcitrant neighbour a government of their own choosing, the Vietnamese violated a fundamental tenet that held ASEAN together. But perhaps more to the point, they challenged the immediate national security interests of Thailand. As the front-line state, Thailand's interests predominated in shaping the ASEAN response. However, they did not entirely override the long standing tendency among ASEAN members, especially Malaysia and Indonesia, to regard China as the long term threat to the region and to see Vietnam as something of a buffer against the spread of Chinese influence. Thus the ASEAN response was to avoid condemning Vietnam while at the same time refusing to accept the legitimacy of the new government in Phnom Penh. Accordingly, recognition continued to be granted to the previous government and state of the Khmer Rouge – regardless of the latter's gruesome record.

The result was a situation in which Thailand forged in effect an alliance with China alongside its existing formal alliance with the United States that emboldened it to confront Vietnam by helping the Chinese, in particular, to assist the remnant Khmer Rouge and other resistance forces lodged in sanctuaries along the porous Thai border with Cambodia. Vietnam aided by the Soviet Union maintained an army of occupation in Cambodia that was able to provide relative security for its puppet government to build a degree of administrative effectiveness. However, Vietnam was unable to wipe out the resistance forces without risking a potentially wider conflict with Thailand. Meanwhile ASEAN played an effective diplomatic role in orchestrating the isolation of Vietnam, especially at the United Nations. ASEAN lacked the necessary military muscle or corporate solidarity to change the stalemate. For example, a resolute Vietnam saw no reason to respond sympathetically to Malaysian and Indonesian attempts to draw it into a diplomatic settlement. The stalemate was only broken ten years after the initial invasion when the Soviet Union was no longer able to continue to supply Vietnam with the matériel it needed to prosecute the war and underpin its economy.

TRIPOLARITY PHASE II: 1980–89, FROM CONFRONTATION TO THE END OF THE COLD WAR

The Soviet invasion of Afghanistan at the end of 1979 ended whatever remaining interest the Carter Administration still had in détente. The President's complaint that his opposite in the Kremlin had 'lied' to him was symptomatic of the view that the Soviet Union was not a responsible treaty partner. As a result, in his last year as President, Carter initiated a significant re-building of American military power that was to be carried to great lengths by his successor President Reagan, with whom the policy was to be identified. The deterioration in relations with the Soviet Union also had an effect on American policy towards China. President Carter authorized the export to China of 'non lethal' military equipment including advanced computers and other high technology products.[23]

From a Soviet perspective the politics of the strategic triangle had already changed more than a year earlier when in May 1978 Carter's National Security Adviser, Z. Brzezinski, had openly indicated an American tilt towards China.[24] But the American response to Afghanistan was such as to persuade the Soviet leaders that it was no longer a question of triangular politics but a growing direct confrontation of the Soviet Union by the United States.[25] The Soviet position in the Asia-Pacific had worsened considerably. It was faced by a hostile coalition of Japan, China and the United States, with the latter now embarked on a huge military build up. Additionally its major ally, Vietnam, was also isolated and required considerable economic and military support. Lacking also in extensive economic relations in the region, as well as being diplomatically isolated because of the double effect of the invasions of Cambodia and Afghanistan, the Soviet Union possessed only military power with which to advance its interests. Having become bogged down in Afghanistan and its ally stalemated in Cambodia there was no clear avenue open to the Soviet leaders to translate their military power into political advantage, especially as the United States had embarked on a course of rapid military build up. The opportunities for reaching new understandings on the basis of détente had gone.

As perhaps the most skilful practitioners of realpolitik, the Chinese sensed the Soviet predicament at an early stage.[26] In April 1979 the Chinese proposed the resumption of talks with the Soviet Union, ostensibly in accordance with the terms of the long defunct thirty-year treaty of 1950. Having consolidated their relations with the United States, the Chinese may have been emboldened by the lack of a Soviet move to defend the Vietnamese ally when it was under attack from themselves. The Chinese initiative may also have been a portent of the Chinese diplomacy of seeking a favourable and peaceful international environment in which to pursue the priorities of domestic economic development. Ideology was ceasing to be a problem between the two sides as the Chinese had begun to dismantle much of Mao's ideological legacy. Sino–Soviet talks began in September, but were then suspended by the Chinese after the Soviet invasion of Afghanistan. However, the domestic economic imperatives in China were such that there was a steady push to improve relations with the Soviet Union. Before long a succession of cultural, scientific and other kinds of delegations visited each country. Trade began to pick up. The Soviet Union had responded in kind in 1981 and in March 1982 Brezhnev delivered a speech in Tashkent aimed primarily at a Chinese audience in which he stated for the first time in nearly twenty years that in the view of the Kremlin China was a socialist country.[27]

From the perspective of China's leaders and Deng Xiaoping in particular, the new opening to the Soviet Union was important as it reduced tension and perhaps added some leverage to China's dealings with the United States. But it was the relationship with America that was vital. America was the key to the opening of China to the international economy; it was still the centre and powerhouse of high technology in the world; and its forces provided the kind of strategic stability in the Asia-Pacific that had proved beneficial to China. The declaration of an 'independent foreign policy' at the CCP Congress in September 1982 should not be taken at face value. It did not mean that China had placed itself in the middle ground between the two superpowers. China still tilted strongly towards the United States on the important strategic questions. Thus throughout the 1980s the American intelligence monitoring facility for observing Soviet missile tests in Central Asia remained in place in Xinjiang. The PRC and the US continued to pursue parallel policies in Cambodia and Afghanistan where they each supported the resistance forces and kept up the pressure on Vietnam and the Soviet Union respectively. To be sure, irritations grew in Sino–American relations. The Taiwan issue was a problem in the first two years of the Reagan Administration and the Americans were displeased by Chinese criticisms of American behaviour in the Middle East and Central America, but the Chinese were more circumspect closer to home.[28]

In fact by the end of 1982 the pattern of triangular relations began to change because of changes in the underlying distribution of power between the protagonists rather than because of any mechanistic properties of the triangle itself. The huge American military build up coupled with the Soviet adverse strategic position was the key. As noted earlier, George Shultz, who replaced Alexander Haig as the American Secretary of State in August 1982, reflected some of the implications of this by according Japan a higher priority in US policies in Asia. Essentially, the US no longer needed China in order to deal with the Soviet strategic challenge. Interestingly, Deng Xiaoping was careful to insist that there could be no consummation of Sino–Soviet relations before the Soviets had made the concession of removing the three famous 'obstacles' – ending Soviet

support for Vietnam in Cambodia, withdrawing the Soviet occupation forces from Afghanistan, and reducing the Soviet military
threat on the Chinese border. These obstacles did not prevent distinct improvements in Sino–Soviet relations in the course of the
decade, but they did signify to the Americans that the Chinese were
not in danger of re-aligning with the Soviet Union. Meanwhile
the Reagan Administration had retreated from Reagan's declared
intention of restoring state relations with Taiwan during the election
campaign. But it withstood Chinese threats to downgrade relations
over the question of advanced arms sales to Taiwan. Nevertheless a
new *modus vivendi* was reached between Washington and Beijing
after the Americans agreed to increase high-tech transfers to China.
In practice, however, the Americans had begun to downgrade
China's significance in the management of strategic relations with
the Soviet Union.[29]

The unravelling of the Cold War and the end of the 'triangle'

The economic stagnation of the Soviet Union had become evident
even before Brezhnev's death, but the full scale of the problem did
not become clear until the accession of Gorbachev in 1985. The
Soviet economy was declining and the general living conditions were
deteriorating so as to resemble those of a Third World rather than an
advanced industrial country. The economy had been badly skewed in
favour of the military. Gorbachev and his team of reformers recognized that there was a foreign policy dimension to this sorry state
of affairs and initiated a new policy under the guise of 'new thinking'
that sought to reverse the excessive reliance that had been put upon
military force.[30]

   It soon became evident that Gorbachev's first foreign policy
priority was to manage relations with the West. In fact the new
Soviet approach seemed to be to disentangle itself from costly
regional conflicts in the Third World so as to focus more clearly on
bilateral security issues with the United States. In the process China
was becoming marginalized in the management of security relations
between the two superpowers. Thus China played little or no part
in the negotiations that led to Soviet consent in the Intermediate
Nuclear Force (INF) agreement of December 1987 to eliminate all
of its SS-20 missiles, including those in Asia. Similarly, China was
not a party to the international agreement of 1988 by which the
Soviet Union pledged to withdraw all its armed forces from Afghanistan. Yet China was a major beneficiary of both.[31]

In two major speeches in Vladivostok in 1986 and Krasnayorsk in 1988 Gorbachev addressed a number of Chinese concerns. He accepted in principle the Chinese claim that their riverine borders in Northeast Asia followed the middle of the main channel (the Thalweg Principle) rather than along the Chinese bank as had previously been asserted since Tsarist times. He also promised unilaterally to withdraw some Soviet forces from Mongolia and Afghanistan and to negotiate a reduction of forces along the Sino–Soviet border. Additionally, he pledged to withdraw from Cam Ranh Bay, but he argued that that should be tied to an American withdrawal from Subic Bay in the Philippines. More to the point, from a Chinese perspective, Gorbachev began to cut Soviet assistance to Vietnam after having indicated that he would not allow Soviet obligations to that country to stand in the way of his larger objective of improving relations with China. By late 1988 he had agreed to press Vietnam to withdraw unconditionally from Cambodia and announced the unilateral reduction of more than a quarter of a million Soviet troops from Asia. The Vietnamese then declared that all their forces would be withdrawn from Cambodia by September 1989 irrespective of a Cambodian settlement. This paved the way for what was termed the 'normalization' of Sino–Soviet relations through a visit to Beijing by Gorbachev himself in May 1989. As an indication as to how great the change in strategic relations had become the American side positively welcomed the event, as was symbolized by a visit to Beijing by President Bush himself three months earlier. The Sino–Soviet summit which was overshadowed by the Tiananmen demonstrations did nothing to harm Sino–American relations. It took place at a time of improved Soviet–American relations and neither the Chinese nor the Soviet leaders wanted to put at risk their respective relations with the United States.[32]

At that point the impact of huge domestic upheavals took over. The unprecedented demonstrations in Tiananmen Square that culminated in the massacre of civilians by the Chinese People's Liberation Army on 4 June not only threw Sino–American relations into crisis, but they also appalled Gorbachev and prevented any further substantive developments in Sino–Soviet relations. These events were followed in the autumn by the sudden collapse of the communist regimes in Eastern Europe starting with East Germany and the breach of the Berlin Wall which has been taken as the symbolic event that marked the end of the Cold War. Collectively, these events also signified the final end of the strategic triangle. The apparent collapse of Sino–American relations was not accompanied by an improvement in Sino–Soviet relations and, in any case, the United States and the Soviet Union had embarked on a closer relationship based on entirely new terms by which the Americans lent their support to Gorbachev and his reform programme while he in turn ceased to oppose American foreign policy initiatives. In short the Cold War between the two superpowers was over.

The regional impact

The Korean peninsula at first experienced a heightening of tension in the early 1980s before the accession of Gorbachev changed the course of Soviet policy. From 1985 onwards the impact of the Soviet 'new thinking' coupled with the priority the Chinese gave to economics paved the way for the transformation of the foreign relations of the two Koreas. By the time of the end of the Cold War South Korea had successfully developed its 'northern policy' of cultivating relations with China and the Soviet Union, and it was clearly only a matter of time before full recognition and diplomatic relations would be established. Although that in itself would not necessarily bring about a settlement of the Korean question, it would disengage it from the conflict of the superpowers.

Such an outcome was far from obvious in the early 1980s. The continued build up of Soviet naval power in the Pacific had accentuated the importance of its nuclear strategic forces in the Sea of Okhotsk, targeted on the United States, and the means to defend them with advanced weaponry. This in turn raised concern in the American forces in the Far East and in South Korea. That was the context in which the South acquired advanced military aircraft from the US. The North, possessing only the relatively obsolescent Chinese aircraft and troubled by China's relations with the United States, turned to the Soviet Union. At that point the more conservative Chernenko had succeeded Andropov as the Soviet leader. During his brief rule he presided over a cooling of relations with China that was marked *inter alia* by gaining access to North Korean ports for the Soviet Pacific Fleet and for establishing rights to overfly Korean territory, thus gaining better intelligence about Manchuria. The Soviet Union also supplied North Korea with more advanced aircraft and related weapons systems. The breakthrough in their relations was symbolized by Kim Il-Sung's first official visit to Moscow for more than twenty years in May 1984.[33]

With the accession of Gorbachev in March 1985 the pattern began to change. The commitment to reform at home and the development of a foreign policy based on 'new thinking' inclined the Soviet Union to find ways of disengaging from regional conflicts, to reach arms control agreements with the United States and to improve relations with China. This immediately reduced the scope of North Korea to play off its two giant allies against each other. The Chinese meanwhile had begun to develop economic relations with the South by using the route through Hong Kong. By 1987 their indirect trade was valued at three times that of China's trade with the North. The Soviet Union too had indicated an interest in cultivating ties with the South. To the dismay of the North both attended the 1988 Olympic Games in Seoul.

Unlike the situation at the end of the 1960s, the South Korean economy now far outshone that of the North. In 1984 the GDP of the South stood at US$83.2 billion, more than double that of the North's US$39.9 billion.[34] Constrained by the reduction of support from its two giant neighbours and confronted by a South whose economy was technologically more advanced and whose rate of growth continued to outstrip its own, the North attempted in a small way to open its own economy to the capitalist world along lines pioneered by the Chinese. But it found its options severely circumscribed as it both refused to reform its domestic economy and was unable to pay outstanding debts to Western countries remaining from its last attempt to acquire Western technology more than a decade earlier in 1973–74. Thus the impact of the changed relations between the superpowers and of China's economic based foreign policy was to reduce the significance of the Korean peninsula in the management of global strategic relations. This in turn left the North as an isolated Stalinist state at a disadvantage with the South which by this stage had become one of East Asia's 'little tigers' – a Newly Industrializing Country (NIC). These conditions paved the way for the beginning of a dialogue between the two Koreas. But the basis of the divide between the two as sole claimants for legitimacy for Korea as a whole remained.

Japan was little affected either by the decline or the re-emergence of détente. Unlike the West Europeans, the Japanese neither attempted to pursue a separate path of improved relations with the Soviet Union, nor did they entertain the same kind of concerns about the reliability of the American security guarantee. The Japanese public opposition in 1982 to the Soviet deployment of SS-20s in the Far East had less to do with any fears about the possible 'de-coupling' of the United States from Japan and 'had more to do with hurt national pride at having been left out of East–West arms deliberations'.[35] This was illustrative of those countries that were separately allied to the United States, among whom Japan was primary, who having consolidated their new statehood and attained considerable economic success, went on to develop a sense of patriotic pride and a national assertiveness that found expression in a degree of resentment against what were regarded as the overbearing demands of the United States. From the American point of view it was considered only proper that these countries should shoulder more of the defence burden under these more propitious circumstances. Hence Japan came under increasing pressure from the United States. Japan did indeed become more active in using economic and diplomatic instruments that in many ways paralleled American strategic policies and by the end of the 1980s Japan had agreed to undertake responsibility for protecting the seas within a thousand mile radius of Tokyo. But part of the problem was that unlike NATO there was no regional security arrangement that bound the various allies with the United States in a common approach to the region. Consequently, anything that went beyond Japan's immediate security concerns as understood in Tokyo was in fact resisted.

Perhaps more than the United States, Japan had a special interest in promoting trade and economic development in Eastern Asia as a way of encouraging political stability. For reasons of geography the region was important for Japanese security in a way that was not true for the United States. As the constraints of bipolarity diminished it was to be expected that the differences in emphasis between the United States and Japan should become more evident. As we shall see, Japan was the most reluctant of the G-7 countries to apply sanctions against China after the Tiananmen killings and it was the first to rescind them.

As the significance of bipolarity declined long standing trading problems between Japan and the United States acquired more salience. The yawning trade gap in Japan's favour that continued to grow despite the oil shocks of the 1970s became a source of deepening recriminations between the two sides. Having encouraged the development of the Japanese economy during the Cold War period in part by allowing exceptionally favourable terms of trade that did not involve reciprocity, the United States throughout the 1980s was continually engaged in a vain struggle against some of its consequences. It was one thing for an American president to play down the issue during the period of high confrontation with the Soviet Union, but it was quite another when that confrontation began to abate in the second half of the 1980s. However, the full significance of the reduced tolerance of the United States was not to become clear until the Cold War was well and truly over.

The weakening of the significance of bipolarity set the context for a remarkable transformation of Taiwan. In the late 1980s it embarked upon the road of democratization at home and in developing economic relations with mainland China across the Straits (primarily through Hong Kong). This was the product of a particular combination of international, regional and domestic factors that in their own way illustrate the dynamic qualities of the interactions of international politics in the region. As we have seen, China's leaders had already perceived by the mid-1980s that the threat from the Soviet Union had abated and they had accordingly placed an even higher priority on economics in their foreign relations. This led to a remarkable growth in China's economic relations with South Korea – which, of course, had its own reasons for improving relations with the giant ally of North Korea. At the same time Hong Kong was developing ever closer economic ties with neighbouring Guangdong Province – a trend that was intensified by the Sino–British agreement in 1984 to revert sovereignty of the colony to China in 1997. Sino–American ties had settled considerably after the irritations of the early 1980s so that the Taiwan issue was no longer prominent on their agenda.

Taiwan had already reacted to some of these changes by agreeing to participate in several international institutions alongside the representatives of the PRC even though this required dropping the official name of the Republic of China. For example, its athletes participated in the 1984 Olympic Games under the rubric of 'Chinese Taipei'. That neatly by-passed the question as to whether it was a rival claimant to the legitimacy of the Chinese state or merely a Chinese province. These changes to the external environment of Taiwan coincided with domestic developments that made continuation of the *status quo* increasingly untenable. Kuomintang authoritarian rule was subject to increasing challenge from a growing middle class that was the product of the successful economic development of the island. There was a need for a generational change in many of the political institutions, notably the legislature, as many of the original mainlanders who came with Chiang Kai-shek in the late 1940s were incapacitated by advanced age. There was a perceived need to broaden the social bases of the ruling institutions by incorporating more of the local Taiwanese. The proclaimed positions that sustained Kuomintang rule were losing legitimacy and the absolutely negative response to the appeals from the mainland for greater contact across the Straits carried less support. Moreover there was a fear that Taiwan would lose its competitive economic position in the fast changing Asian–Pacific economy and miss out on the opportunities presented by the opening up of the Chinese economy. Fortunately for Taiwan, the respected Chiang Ching-kuo (Chiang Kai-shek's son and heir) was still at the helm to initiate the beginnings of the transition to democracy and the opening to China.[36]

International concerns in Southeast Asia centred primarily on the Cambodian question. Here too the developments that were later to make a settlement possible should be understood as flowing from the interactions of international, regional and local political developments. The new détente between the Soviet Union and the United States that was manifested by the arms control agreement of 1987 and the agreement by the Soviet Union in 1988 to withdraw from Afghanistan, the priority that Gorbachev attached to improving relations with China and the constraints that were imposed by his domestic reform agenda and the foreign policy based on 'new thinking', were incompatible with continuing to extend to Vietnam the economic and military assistance that alone made it possible for Vietnam to maintain forces of occupation in Cambodia. Meanwhile at its Sixth Party Congress in December 1986 Vietnam's leaders committed themselves to replace the conventional socialist economic model with a programme of Renovation (*Doi Moi*) as economic failure was damaging the legitimacy of the regime, but they still upheld their 'special' relations with Laos and Cambodia.[37] After the limits to Soviet aid were made clear in 1988, Vietnam announced in April 1989 that it would withdraw its forces from Cambodia in September. This effectively removed Cambodia from being a critical issue in either Soviet–American or Sino–Soviet relations. That, however, still left unresolved the competition between Vietnam and China for a balance of power in Indo-China favourable to their respective interests, which had found expression in their support for opposing sides in the Cambodian civil war. In 1987 and 1988 the Vietnamese attempted in vain to reach a negotiated settlement that would have excluded the Chinese and ostracized the Khmer Rouge (the faction that had enjoyed Chinese support as the most effective and most determined opponent of Vietnam). But it was not until the Vietnamese sought to make their peace with the Chinese in 1989 and 1990 and deferred to China's right to broker a deal among the indigenous Cambodian factions that the way was open for reaching a settlement. Vietnam had found that it 'could no longer reconcile imperative economic reforms with the preservation of its hegemony over Cambodia'.[38] This reduced the significance of Cambodia as a critical issue in regional affairs.

Although ASEAN was active as a diplomatic community in isolating Vietnam and in maintaining international support for the Cambodian resistance, it was not critical in determining the outcome of the conflict. Indonesia did join with France as co-chairman of an international conference on Cambodia which met first in July 1989 in Paris with the other ASEAN countries participating. But the arrangements for power sharing within Cambodia proved elusive at that stage. That problem could only be addressed after the contest between China and Vietnam had been settled in favour of the former. A final agreement on power sharing arrangements was not reached before the end of the Cold War.[39]

NOTES AND REFERENCES

1 Considerable differences exist in the scholarly literature about the character and significance of the strategic triangle. Compare, for example, Steven I. Levine, 'China's Foreign Policy in the Strategic Triangle', in June Dryer (ed.) *Chinese Defense and Foreign Policy* (New York: Paragon House, 1988), who tends to discount China's significance, with Thomas W. Robinson, 'On the Further Evolution of the Strategic Triangle', and Lowell Dittmer, 'The Strategic Triangle: a Critical Review', both in Ilpyomg Kim (ed.) *The Strategic Triangle: China, the United States and the Soviet Union* (New York: Paragon House, 1987). There have also been attempts to apply game theory or mechanistic principle to explain the operational dynamics of the triangle. See, for example, Gerald Segal, *The Great Power Triangle* (London: Macmillan, 1982); and Lowell Dittmer, 'The Strategic Triangle . . .' and his earlier, 'The Strategic Triangle: An Elementary Game of Theoretical Analysis', *World Politics* (July 1981) pp. 485–515. For a retrospective account of the complexities of the relationships see Robert Ross (ed.) *China, The United States, and The Soviet Union: Tripolarity and Policy Making in the Cold War* (New York and London: M. E. Sharpe, 1993).
2 See Lawrence Freedman, 'The Triangle in Western Europe' in Gerald Segal (ed.) *The China Factor: Peking and the Superpowers* (London: Croom Helm, 1982) pp. 105–25.
3 Henry Kissinger, *The White House Years* (London: Weidenfeld & Nicolson and Michael Joseph, 1979) p. 836.
4 Kissinger, *The White House Years*, p. 764.
5 Banning N. Garret and Bonnie S. Glaser, 'From Nixon to Reagan: China's Changing Role in American Strategy,' in Kenneth A. Oye *et al.* (eds) *Eagle Resurgent?: The Reagan Era in American Foreign Policy* (Boston: Little Brown, 1987).
6 Robert Legvold, 'Sino–Soviet Relations: The American Factor', in

Robert Ross (ed.) *China, The United States and the Soviet Union,* especially pp. 66–80.

7 See Kissinger's account of the Indo-Pakistan crisis in *The White House Years,* pp. 843–918, especially pp. 913–18.

8 Stephen Sestanovich, 'US Policy Toward the Soviet Union, 1970–1990: The Impact of China' in Robert Ross (ed.) *China, the United States, and the Soviet Union* especially pp. 134–35.

9 Alexander M. Haig Jr., *Caveat: Realism, Reagan, and Foreign Policy* (New York: Macmillan Publishing Co., 1984) p. 194.

10 George P. Shultz, *Turmoil and Triumph: My Years as Secretary of State* (New York: Charles Scribner's Sons, Macmillan Publishing Co., 1993) p. 173.

11 *The White House Years,* p. 1086.

12 *The White House Years,* p. 1089.

13 (*ibid.*) p. 1090.

14 David N. Rowe, *Informal 'Diplomatic Relations': The Case of Japan and the Republic of China, 1972–74* (Hamden: Shoe String Press, 1975).

15 Chae-Jin Lee, *China and Japan, New Economic Diplomacy* (Stanford: Hoover Institution Press, Stanford University, 1974) p. 10.

16 Robert Legvold, 'Sino–Soviet Relations: The American Factor', in Robert Ross (ed.) *China, the United States, and the Soviet Union,* pp. 69–70.

17 For the best account of these see Allen S. Whiting, *China Eyes Japan* (Berkeley: University of California Press, 1989). See also Laura Newby, *Sino–Japanese Relations: China's Perspective* (London: Routledge, for the Royal Institute of International Affairs, 1988).

18 For a clear account of the North's relations with its two giant neighbours see Ralph N. Clough, 'The Soviet Union and the Two Koreas' in Donald S. Zagoria (ed.) *Soviet Policy in East Asia* (New Haven: Yale University Press, A Council on Foreign Relations Book, 1982) pp. 175–200.

19 Nam Joo Hong, *America's Commitment to the Security of South Korea: The First Decade of the Nixon Doctrine* (Cambridge: Cambridge University Press, 1986).

20 For accounts of the origins and development of the third Indo-China war, see David W. P. Elliot (ed.) *The Third Indo-China Conflict* (Boulder: Westview Press, 1981); Grant Evans and Kevin Rowley, *Red Brotherhood at War* (London: Verso Books, 1984); Nayan Chanda, *Brother Enemy: The War After the War* (San Diego: Harcourt Brace Jovanovich, 1986); and Robert S. Ross, *The Indochina Tangle; China's Vietnam Policy, 1975–1979* (New York: Columbia University Press, 1988).

21 Michael Leifer, *ASEAN and the Security of South-East Asia* (London and New York: Routledge, 1989) p. 55.

22 (*ibid.*) pp. 147–50.

23 For details see Harry Harding, *A Fragile Relationship: The United States and China since 1972* (Washington DC: The Brookings Institution, 1992) pp. 91–94.

24 Legvold in Ross (ed.) *China, the United States and the Soviet Union* (*op. cit.*) pp. 69–70.

25 (*ibid.*) pp. 76–80.

26 Kissinger described them as 'the most unsentimental practitioners of

balance-of-power politics I have encountered'. *The White House Years* (*op. cit.*) pp. 1087–88.

27 For accounts of Sino–Soviet relations see Chi Su, 'The Strategic Triangle and China's Soviet Policy' in Ross (ed.) *China, the United States and the Soviet Union* (*op. cit.*) pp. 39–61; Gerald Segal, *Sino–Soviet Relations After Mao* (London: The International Institute of Strategic Studies, *Adelphi Paper* No. 202, 1985); Guocang Huan, 'Sino–Soviet Relations' in Yufan Hao and Guocang Huan (eds) *The Chinese View of the World* (New York: Pantheon Books, 1989); and Thomas G. Hart, *Sino–Soviet Relations: Re-Examining the Prospects for Normalization* (Aldershot: Gower Publishing Group, 1987).

28 For the best and most detailed account of Sino–American relations in this period that nevertheless tends to exaggerate the depths of the troughs see Harry Harding, *A Fragile Relationship* (*op. cit.*) Chapters 3–6.

29 Robert S. Ross, 'U.S. Policy Towards China: The Strategic Context and the Policy-Making Process' in Ross (ed.) *China, the United States, and the Soviet Union* (*op. cit.*) pp. 169–71.

30 For a compelling contemporary analysis see Sewern Bialer, *The Soviet Paradox: External Expansion, Internal Decline* (New York: Vintage Books, 1986).

31 See the accounts of the two sets of negotiations in *Strategic Survey 1987–88* and *Strategic Survey 1988–89* (London: International Institute of Strategic Studies, 1988 and 1989).

32 For accounts see Harding, *A Fragile Relationship* (*op. cit.*) pp. 174–80; Steven M. Goldstein, 'Diplomacy amid Protest: The Sino–Soviet Summit,' *Problems of Communism* (Vol. 38, September–October 1989) pp. 49–71; and Herbert J. Ellison, 'Soviet–Chinese Relations: The Experience of Two Decades,' in Ross (ed.) *China, the United States and the Soviet Union* (*op. cit.*) pp. 93–121.

33 For accounts see Yufan Hao, 'China and the Korean Peninsula' in Yufan Hao and GuoCang Huan (eds.) *The Chinese View of the World* (New York: Pantheon Books, 1989) especially pp. 181–84; and, more generally, Gerald Segal, *The Soviet Union and the Pacific* (London: Unwin Hyman for the Royal Institute of International Affairs, 1990) Chapter 5; and Douglas T. Stuart (ed.) *Security Within the Pacific Rim* (Aldershot: Gower Publishing Group, for International Institute for Strategic Studies, 1987) see relevant chapters.

34 Yufan Hao, 'China and the Korean Peninsula' in Hao and Huan (*op. cit.*) p. 187.

35 Reinhard Drifte, 'Japan's Relations with the East Asia-Pacific Region', in Stuart (ed.) *Security Within the Asia Pacific Rim* (*op. cit.*) p. 26.

36 For accounts of the transformation of Taiwan see Peter R. Moody, *Political Change on Taiwan* (New York: Praeger, 1992); Simon Long, *Taiwan: China's Last Frontier* (London: Macmillan, 1991); Tun-jen Cheng and Stephen Haggard (eds), *Political Change in Taiwan* (Boulder and London: Lynne Rienner Publishers, 1992); and Denis Fred Simon and Michael Ying-mao Kau (eds) *Taiwan: Beyond the Economic Miracle* (London and New York: M. E. Sharpe, 1992).

37 Michael Leifer and John Phipps, *Vietnam and Doi Moi: Domestic and*

International Dimensions of Reform (London: Royal Institute of International Affairs Discussion Papers No. 35, June 1991).

38 Michael Leifer, 'Power-Sharing and Peacemaking in Cambodia?' in *SAIS REVIEW* (Winter/Spring 1992) p. 148. The analysis in this paragraph draws considerably from this article.

39 For a succinct account see Michael Leifer, *Dictionary of the Modern Politics of South-East Asia* (London: Routledge, 1995) pp. 12–14.

Part II
The policies of the great powers

The foreign policies of the major powers have contributed greatly to shaping the international politics of the Asia-Pacific. This is especially true of the United States which has dominated the region since 1945 by its military and economic power. The United States and the Soviet Union (until its demise and replacement by Russia), as the two superpowers, determined much of the structure of international politics as a whole and, therefore, the external environment of the region. As integral members of the region they also contributed to its development in their own right. Since the nineteenth century when Russia and the United States consolidated their presences on the northwestern and eastern shores of the Pacific Ocean respectively, they have been active members of the Asia-Pacific region which in turn has contributed to enlarging the scope of their identities and focus of operations as states. Although the extent of their engagement and commitments in the region may have varied over time, total withdrawal or neglect has never been a practicable option. For the United States in particular, East Asia has been seen as the only major economic and strategic powerhouse to rival Europe in importance. Correspondingly, it has also been regarded as a source of threat at the opposite extremity of a shared ocean.

In contrast to the two global powers, China and Japan have been essentially regional powers although they have exercised considerable influence on international politics beyond their region. It was only in the nineteenth century that they were actively brought into the wider world of international politics first as objects of Western interest, but later as active subjects in their own right. Without yet achieving the global reach and international significance of the two superpowers both China and Japan, in their different ways, have sought to exercise influence in areas far beyond the domains of the Asia-Pacific and they have sought to make their voices heard on the major international questions of the day. But it is within the Asia-Pacific that their power and influence has tended to be exercised. All the other states in the region have found it necessary to take into account their likely reactions when formulating policies of external significance.

The international dimensions of regional politics in the Asia-Pacific have been largely shaped by how each of the four major powers has defined its interests and identified friends and foes. The ways in which their governments have understood the interactions between their global concerns and their regional interests have largely shaped the patterns of international alignments and conflicts in the Asia-Pacific. Of particular importance is how the United States and the Soviet Union – as the two superpowers – understood how local issues and conflicts affected their management of the central global balance of power between them. Paradoxically, since the end of the Cold War the American difficulties in establishing international priorities through which to calculate and manage divergent interests within the Asia-Pacific have created new uncertainties in the international politics of the region.

It has been suggested that the impact of the two superpowers should be regarded as a kind of 'overlay' that was introduced from the outside by these two powers to blanket existing local problems and conflicts within the regime.[1] Such a view tends to underplay the dynamic quality of the interactions between the two arenas of politics. Each tended to interact with and shape the other. Not only did the 'external' powers intervene competitively in local conflicts and define the issues and combatants in terms of the larger international divide between them, but local élites tended to seek their external patronage and present themselves to their putative patrons in terms that would make it difficult for them to resist. It was not so much that the major powers imposed their external frames of reference upon local disputants in such a way as to camouflage and distort them, but rather that local élites would present themselves and their concerns in terms chosen by the external powers. Indeed their survival often depended on persuading the external power of its obligations to support them even at the expense of the interests of the external power itself. This involved penetrating the domestic political arena of that power so as to be able to bring pressure to bear upon the government of the day. Consider for example, Taipei's relations with Washington or Hanoi's with Moscow as offering instances where the lesser ally was able at times to exercise surprising influence over the policy of the superior.

Greater powers could also be manipulated in other ways. Such was the case of North Korea's relations with its two giant neighbours during the Cold War. For a long period the North exploited the differences between them to its own advantage. Despite his military and economic dependence upon the two great powers Kim Il-Sung was able to purge their supporters from his ranks and to create a myth about himself and his country's independence that was at total variance with the truth of his reliance upon China and the Soviet Union. A different example is provided by the way in which Indonesia's leaders successfully utilized American pressure upon the Dutch to obtain independence in 1949 and again over a decade later to acquire former Dutch New Guinea (or Irian Jaya).

Furthermore it should be appreciated that both the local and international arenas of politics were being affected by corresponding modernizing trends associated with international economics, statehood, health, technology, communications and the building of modern armed forces and so on. Consequently, both arenas were becoming enmeshed with each other in ways that transcended the immediate concerns of power politics. This became evident after the Sino–American *rapprochement* in the early 1970s that breached the hitherto impenetrable divide between communism and liberal democracy and paved the way for demonstrating that the economies of the capitalist states of East Asia were outperforming their socialist neighbours.

In addition to developing policies towards the region that were derived from the imperatives of the international structure of bipolarity and the operations of the central balance of power, each of the major powers also approached the region with its own perspectives and in accordance with its own distinctive styles of foreign policy making. These in turn may be said to stem from their particular historical experiences as nation-states and their forms of government. The historical experiences of the particular states have contributed to the ways in which successive leaders have understood the international identities of their respective countries and the character of their country's relations with the outside world. The forms of their particular systems of governments will have determined the processes by which they made and implemented foreign policy.

The historical experiences and the forms of government of each of the four major powers could hardly have differed more from each other. The United States, as a country of recent historical vintage made up of immigrants who declared their state into exist-

ence and whose written constitution and the legal edifices and institutions built around it continues to be the basic reference point in
affirming its identity, stands as a particular contrast to Japan whose
claims to a unique identity of people, culture and territory go back
into the mists of time. Both claim adherence to capitalism and
democracy, but their respective systems vary enormously and are a
source for both cooperation and conflict. Yet these two can be
contrasted with China, 'a civilization pretending to be a state',[2]
which has a continuous history stretching back several thousand
years and which is still adapting to the forced encounter with modernity that began 150 years ago. The Soviet Union/Russia is altogether different: a Eurasian state that grew out of the small state of
Muscovy on the periphery of the European state system to establish
dominion over the vast wastelands of Siberia right up to the northern
Pacific. Although the economies of both China and the Soviet
Union/Russia were organized along the lines of socialist command
economies and despite their being ruled by communist parties their
patterns of rule differed and their emergence from the Cold War
order has varied greatly.

NOTES AND REFERENCES

1 Barry Buzan, *People, States and Fear: An Agenda for International Security in the Post-Cold War Era* (Brighton: Harvester Wheatsheaf, 2nd
   edition, 1990) pp. 219–12.
2 Lucian W. Pye, 'China: Erratic State, Frustrated Society', *Foreign Affairs*
   (Fall 1990) p. 58.

4 The United States and the Asia-Pacific

The conduct of American foreign policy towards the Asia-Pacific since 1945 has been shaped by the complex interplay between global priorities and regional interests. As the world's leading power in the second half of the twentieth century, the United States has tended to cast its policies in terms of global visions and strategies. The significance attached to East Asia should be considered not only in terms of the historical evolution of American relations with that part of the world, but rather it should be understood with reference to its place within the broader international context of America's foreign relations. Relations with particular regions and countries may have their own distinctive features, but ultimately, the extent of the American engagement has been determined by the place allotted to them within the larger scope of American priorities as a whole.

American policies in the immediate aftermath of the Second World War were shaped by the desire to build a better world, formed in part by the perceived lessons of that war and of what had led up to it. The war itself was seen as an integral whole. In the words of President F. D. Roosevelt it was 'a single world conflict that required a global strategy of self defence'.[1] The war brought to the fore the tension in the balance of priorities to be attached to the Atlantic and Pacific dimensions of America's geopolitical interests that has continued ever since. Even though the Atlanticists won the day then, and in the persons of Dean Acheson and George Kennan they continued to shape priorities after the war, the global significance of East Asia was not overlooked. To the surprise of Churchill, Roosevelt insisted in 1943 on China being elevated to one of the 'Big Five' in the future United Nations. After the war Japan figured prominently in the State Department's thinking for global economic reconstruction and as one of the centres that the emerging policy of containment had to defend.[2]

THE DOMESTIC SOURCES

The determination of American global and regional strategies derive from domestic as well as international factors. The former include the influence of ideas about American identity and purpose and the impact of the divergent influences on foreign policy that derive from the diffusion of political power within the country.

As many have noted, the sense of 'American exceptionalism' that is central to American views of their country's identity has had a profound effect on United States dealings with the world outside.[3] The idea that by virtue of its special claims as a nation founded on the basis of liberty the United States exercises particular responsibilities to act as a beacon to others, or indeed, more actively, to uphold and to promote liberty elsewhere, has had a marked effect on its foreign relations. Realists of the distinction of Hans Morganthau and Henry Kissinger have noted with disapproval how this has resulted both in a tendency to retreat into an isolationism that deliberately avoids 'entanglement' (to use President Washington's loaded term) with the flawed old world of European power politics, and a tendency to engage in an undifferentiated globalism that in the name of idealist principles seeks to make the world a better place in the American image.[4] Others have argued that American foreign policy has exhibited a tension between its professed ideals and its general balance of power principle of preventing the emergence of a centre able to exercise a predominance of power in either Western Europe or Eastern Asia.[5] Still others have drawn attention to ideological elements that have sustained American attitudes towards other countries, such as a sense of superiority, race consciousness and democratization.[6] Related, but different, forms of analysis focus on cultural dimensions of American foreign policy particularly as they contrast with those in Asia.[7]

In practice American policy towards East Asia has been characterized by contradictions and inconsistencies. But it is clear particularly in retrospect that American ideals, however imperfectly applied, contributed to the development of myths about the conduct of relations especially with China, Japan and the Philippines that have had a profound influence on the conduct of policy. Since most of the rest of Asia was subject to European colonial rule until after the Pacific War, the United States had few opportunities to develop relations there let alone cultivate myths about those countries. American policies towards China in the nineteenth and first half of the twentieth century have been suffused with self-serving myths to the effect that they were imbued with noble purposes of upholding the Chinese state against external aggression and of transforming it for the good – i.e. in the direction of Christianity, the free market and democracy. The reality was much more complex, with America involved in great power politics and its business people engaged in commerce – perhaps not too dissimilar from the more self avowedly imperialist Britain.[8] American policy towards Japan in the 1930s did not reflect Theodore Roosevelt's principle that his country would necessarily oppose any who would be 'top dog' in Asia. Isolationism was applied in Pacific Asia as it was in Atlantic Europe. American pious rhetoric about self determination and democratization was in conflict with the reality of imperial rule in the Philippines after its acquisition in 1898. Although a process of self determination was begun early on and a date was set for the attainment of independence in the mid-1930s, the actual context was one that was imbued with neo-colonialism.[9] Nevertheless the ideals and the myths to which they gave rise were important elements in the conduct of American policies towards these countries in the second half of the twentieth century.

The impact of the actual process of American foreign policy making and implementation have contributed to shaping policy in a number of ways. As the American separation of powers is more complete than in the European parliamentary systems, American presidents have to share power with legislators who tend to have narrower policy agendas. Moreover the legislature (i.e. the Congress) is able to make independent contributions to foreign relations – often to the dismay of the executive. For example, it is in Congress that the more isolationist and protectionist tendencies have been traditionally evident, most famously in the rejection of America's participation in the League of Nations despite the role of President Wilson as one of its chief architects. In the early 1950s Congress also served as the base for McCarthyism, which undoubtedly deepened the ideological chasm of the early stages of the Cold War; and Congress has been the focus in the latter part of the twentieth century for the promotion of protectionist interests that have complicated still further the conduct of relations with Japan. Interestingly, Congress has also been the main fulcrum for the advancement of idealist impulses such as those associated with human rights.

Given that the president, unlike British prime ministers, for example, cannot command majorities in the legislature, he has had to exercise powers of persuasion that have resulted in both what Americans have called pork-barrel politics (offering or withholding Federal favours to Congressional districts) and in reaching over the heads of Congress to appeal directly to the American people. The former has tended to distort policy by making provisions for special interests and the latter has often given policy statements a populist and, at times, a crusading character. The tendency of American presidents to appeal to their people in broad crusading terms can be seen in the way the key doctrine of containment was articulated by President Truman in the apocalyptic terms of universalist rhetoric rather than the more graduated terms of its progenitor, George Kennan.[10]

The diffusion of political power in the American political system and the apparent, and often real, discontinuities between successive presidents, has frequently accentuated inter-bureaucratic rivalries and pitted the interests of incoming presidents against established networks of bureaucracy, Congress and others in Washington. It was concern with the convergence of interests between elements in the Department of Defense, Congress and the defence related industries that caused President Eisenhower to warn his fellow Americans shortly before leaving office in 1959 against the dangers of what he called 'the military industrial complex'. In the case of President Nixon and his principal foreign policy lieutenant, Henry Kissinger, this led to the cultivation of secret so-called 'back channels' in order to circumvent the conventional diplomatic and Congressional processes. Kissinger subsequently complained about the legalism and bureaucratism inherent in the conduct of America's foreign relations which he believed frustrated the practice of foreign policy according to the true national interest and in line with the principles of the balance of power.[11] Although no government with its attendant ministries and bureaucracies can be said to be entirely monolithic or free from the problems of 'bureaucratic politics', the American political system provides an environment that is more conducive for its operation than most.[12] The principal effect on relations with Asia has been to accentuate the difficulties of Asian governments in discerning the key elements of policy among the different voices often articulated in Washington.

More than in most democracies, American foreign policy making has allowed considerable room for the influence of public opinion. Perhaps the clearest examples can be drawn from the Vietnam War.

It was the loss of public support for further escalation as shown in opinion polls and in the results of the New Hampshire primary that led President Johnson, in March 1968, to announce the end of that policy and his refusal to stand for election for a second term. Interestingly, the available evidence at the time of his announcement showed that the North Vietnamese and their Vietcong allies had been crushed by the military response to their Tet Offensive. Thereafter it became an article of faith in Washington that the United States would not be able to engage in *prolonged* warfare because it would not be supported by public opinion.[13]

Interest groups also tend to exercise more influence on American foreign relations than is generally true of other democracies. The business or corporate sector has traditionally exercised influence both in the sense of advocating particular policies and in the more high-minded purpose of supplying leading personnel from the private sector to hold high positions in the public bureaucracy.[14] At different times businessmen have successfully pressed their special concerns and/or ideological outlooks on the conduct of American policy in Asia. Thus business interests contributed to the 'Open Door' policies of the last decade of the nineteenth century and to the virulent anti-communism that informed policy towards the People's Republic of China in the first twenty years of its existence.[15] More recently, they were apparently influential in persuading President Clinton to disassociate his concern for human rights from his decision to renew the Most Favoured Nation treatment to China by which its exports to the US were subject to the same tariffs as the lowest offered to others.

Neither the tradition of American idealism nor the process of its foreign policy making allow for the conduct of diplomacy in the often secret, unemotional, and professional way traditionally associated with Europe. Not surprisingly, it has often disappointed realists for whom 'the proper sphere of foreign policy' is the 'middle ground of subtle distinctions, complex choices, and precarious manipulations'.[16] Since 1945 (and indeed for the hundred years before that) American policies towards the Asia-Pacific in general and some of its key countries, such as China or Japan in particular, have not been conducted in such measured ways. It is only by reference to these complex domestic factors as well as the external influences that it is possible to understand the evolution of American relations with the region since 1945.

CONTAINMENT IN THE ASIA-PACIFIC

The doctrine of containment was fashioned primarily with the Soviet Union and Soviet communism in mind. Its origins were in Europe and indeed it was in Europe where its principles were best applied and where its ultimate purpose of bringing about the collapse of the communist system was eventually achieved. But since containment was expressed in moral and universal terms it evoked a Manichean view of a world divided between two opposing systems that soon became the reality in Europe where the 'iron curtain' sharply demarcated borders separating the two camps. It was an approach to understanding the world that came to be broadly accepted in the United States. Thus, despite the Vietnam debacle and the soul searching to which it gave rise, American public opinion supported the long term policy of opposition to the Soviet Union.

As it was a way of understanding the world rather than a strategy that related means to ends, containment in practice encompassed a number of different strategies in the course of the forty-odd years in which it served as the fundamental basis for American foreign policy.

Being a universal doctrine, containment was extended from Europe to the Asia-Pacific, but with very different results. Being more diverse, the Asia-Pacific could not be divided by a tangible iron curtain that separated two tightly bound sets of military alliance systems buttressed by competing ideologies, socio-economic and political systems. Yet it was in Asia that the United States fought the two major wars of containment which ended by almost undermining the cohesion of American society. It was in Asia that the United States had to balance some of the contradictions of containment such as propping up dictatorial and fragile regimes in the name of upholding democracy against communism, or expending enormous costs in areas of relatively low strategic priorities in terms of America's global position so as to demonstrate commitment to allies, only to see this allow the principal adversary (the Soviet Union) to improve its strategic standing as a result. Yet by the end of the Cold War containment in Asia could nevertheless be described as a success: America has remained the predominant power; all its allies (with the exception of South Vietnam) have consolidated their statehood and prospered economically; and even its adversaries (or former adversaries) have embraced the market economy. To be sure many problems remain and new ones have emerged – not least the difficulties in understanding the post Cold

War situation and in devising a coherent and consistent strategy for
the new era.

The beginning

American thinking about the new order after the Second World
War was built upon the Atlantic Charter of 1941. This distinguished
between the 'aggressor nations' (Germany, Japan and Italy) who
were to be permanently disarmed and the 'peace loving nations'
who would gradually reduce their force levels. The key element in
the American vision of the post war order was that the main allies
(including the Soviet Union) who fought the war against the
aggressors would work together to create a better world. At this
stage President Roosevelt envisaged that China would become the
major power in Asia as it was revitalized through close association
with the United States. In 1944 a series of international conferences
was held under the American aegis to forge agreement for the new
character of the post war world. These led to the establishment of
the United Nations and to the creation of a liberal, international,
economic and financial system named after the location of the conference at Bretton Woods. Conferences were also held on the subjects of food and agriculture and on the way to provide relief and
rehabilitation. At this stage if there were a degree of friction it was
with Britain (rather than the Soviet Union) since, as part of his
'four freedoms' which underpinned the American vision, Roosevelt
expected the Europeans to allow their colonies to proceed towards
self determination and independence. This was anathema to Churchill, who made it clear with specific reference to Hong Kong that
'nothing would be taken away from England without war'.[17] He also
distrusted the American idealist approach to Stalin – preferring
instead to deal with him on the basis of traditional power politics.
Although the American expectations of a new cooperative international order were soon dashed by the Cold War, important
elements of this idealist vision remained to shape future developments of international relations including the Asia-Pacific region.

The ending of the war in the Pacific, however, provided evidence
of how in practice American idealism was tempeied by considerations of power. At Yalta in February 1945 Roosevelt's behaviour
was in the mould of classic colonial big power practices. Not only
did he make secret concessions to Stalin at China's expense by
agreeing to allow the Soviet Union exclusive rights in Manchuria
(including the use of a naval base) despite the absence of Chinese

representation there, but he also undertook to persuade Chiang Kai-shek to accept them. Having made these concessions in order to get the Soviet Union to join in the war against Japan, and indeed having agreed at Yalta that the Soviet Union would be one of the four occupying powers, the United States in the end defeated Japan largely by its own efforts (including the use of the atom bomb) and in effect denied the Soviet Union a significant role in the occupation of Japan.

Considerations of power could also be expressed in the language of idealism and universalism. Not long after China was plunged into civil war in 1946, the new American president declared in effect the beginning of the policy of containment in what became known from March 1947 as the Truman Doctrine. In taking over from a weakened Britain the support of Greece and Turkey so as to halt a possible Soviet advance on the Mediterranean, Truman explained American purposes in the universal terms of a policy 'to support free peoples who are resisting attempted subjugation by armed minorities or by outside pressures'. He depicted the new state of the world as a struggle between two ways of life and that America was obliged to defend democracy from its oppressive enemy. This was of course the language of morality rather than of strategy. Arguably the two coincided in Europe, but in Asia matters were less clear cut.

The United States had tried but failed to mediate in the Chinese civil war and it became clear that China would not play the role in the post war international order as originally conceived in Washington. Attention in the State Department was already shifting to the desirability of rehabilitating the Japanese economy as part of the general programme of reconstructing the economies of Western Europe. This was less a Cold War issue than a matter of averting a damaging world wide recession threatened by the enormous imbalance between American exports to the rest of the world and its imports. At the same time Japan, in contra-distinction to China, was seen as an economic centre with potential significance to alter the world balance of power. With regard to occupied Germany, the State Department began to argue in late 1946 to early 1947 in favour of replacing the policy of punishment with one of rehabilitation. The relaunching of the economies of Germany and Japan was seen as essential if 'the free areas of Europe and Asia' were to 'function vigorously and healthily'.[18] By mid-1947 the American occupation policy in Japan began to change emphasis from seeking to eliminate the vestiges of the past that were associated with militarism and the capacity to prepare for war, towards encouraging economic development and political stability. The constitution that had been developed by the Americans with its famous Article Nine that renounced war was modified in practice to allow for what were called 'Self Defence Forces'. The huge economic conglomerates, the *zaibatsus*, such as Toshiba and Mitsubishi began to be discreetly encouraged; and the forces of the left found the policies of the American occupation distinctly less friendly.[19]

American policy in Southeast Asia in the early years after the war was torn between promoting the independence of colonies from their European masters and recognizing the need to avoid undermining fragile European allies. At the same time its treatment of its own colony of the Philippines hardly served as an edifying model as to how independence should be granted. The United States moved rapidly to grant independence to the Philippines in 1946, but it did so on terms that were favourable to American economic interests. For example, American firms were granted 'equal rights' with Filipinos in the exploitation of the natural resources of the country. Furthermore American strategic interests were protected the following year by the Military Bases Agreement by which the United States leased for 99 years twenty-three bases with full jurisdiction.[20] With regard to Indonesia the United States took the view that the Dutch could not sustain their rule there by force, however successful they might be in the short term. Moreover by late 1948 the United States was less concerned about the fragility of Holland itself. After the Indonesian Republicans had defeated the armed challenge of the radical and communist forces in Madiun in September 1948 the United States needed little persuasion to support the Indonesian nationalists. American pressure was successfully applied to persuade the Dutch to concede independence in 1949.[21] In Indo-China, however, the United States did not put similar pressure on the French. The problem from an American perspective was that the effective nationalist resistance to the French was led by the communist Vietminh.

Elsewhere in East Asia the United States had made no preparations for the future of Korea after the defeat of Japan, beyond some vague ideas about placing the country under an international trusteeship. In the event a hastily contrived agreement was reached with the Russians that for the purposes of occupation the peninsula be divided between them at the 38th parallel. The Red Army stopped at the parallel in early August 1945 even though it was nearly a month before the first American contingent arrived. This indicated that at this point neither side regarded Korea as of great strategic significance. With great difficulty the Americans tried to build a democratic state in the South under the leadership of the autocratic Syngman Rhee. In 1947 the US referred the matter to the United Nations who supervized elections in the South. The North refused to accept the UN role. Syngman Rhee was duly elected, the Republic of Korea was inaugurated in August 1948 and he proceeded to consolidate his rule through a ruthless dictatorship. In September 1948 the Democratic People's Republic of Korea was established in the North after a series of communist style elections that had begun almost two years earlier. The last Soviet forces were withdrawn in March 1949 and the Americans, whose armed forces were still over-stretched after the massive demobilization at the end of the Second World War, followed suit in June. Despite some misgivings in the Pentagon and the State Department as to what had been done in the American name, it was felt that the best had been made of a bad job.[22]

Even the communist victory in China in October 1949 was not seen entirely within the prism of the Cold War and containment. The theme of the American government's White Paper was that the communist success was the result of deep seated upheavals within the country. It hardly fitted the purpose of the Truman Doctrine of supporting 'free peoples who are resisting attempted subjugation by armed minorities or by outside pressures'. In his letter of transmittal to Congress, Acheson seemingly contradicted his department's argument, by asserting that China had come under the control of the Kremlin. But that representation was part of a larger purpose, or strategy, of seeking to bring about a split between the two communist giants by playing on Chinese nationalist sentiments. It was envisaged that the historical legacy of Russian imperialism combined with the Soviet incapacity to meet Chinese needs of external economic support would lead to a rift. Such thinking at this stage implied a more flexible approach than that ordinarily associated with containment. Indeed the American government was even prepared to contemplate the conquest of Taiwan and the defeat of Chiang Kai-shek and his remnant forces by the Chinese communists. There was also the prospect that the United States would recognize the People's Republic of China before long.[23] Acheson also played on the theme of Sino–Soviet national differences in his speech of 12 January 1950 while Mao Zedong was negotiating a new partnership in Moscow.[24]

American strategy in the Asia-Pacific at this stage in January 1950 as outlined by Truman and Acheson envisaged a perimeter defence stretching from the Aleutian Islands in the north, reaching through Japan and the Philippines down to Australia and New Zealand in the south, but excluding Korea. These were the areas of the highest priority.[25] Acheson did not altogether ignore South Korea, however, as he argued that its defence would be based on collective security through the United Nations.[26] Moreover, Cold War calculations were very much in evidence in American approaches towards the region even if not yet expressed in terms of containment. For example, despite misgivings, the United States recognized the fragile and less than independent Indo-Chinese states as 'independent states within the French Union' both because it sought to bolster the French government itself and because it feared the consequences for the rest of Southeast Asia of a communist victory by Ho Chi Minh especially after the victory of the communists in China.[27]

It was the attack of North Korea upon the South on 25 June 1950 that brought the full application of containment to the Asia-Pacific. The attack provided the point at which American global and regional perspectives were joined. The end of the Berlin blockade in May 1949 was thought to have stabilized matters in Europe, but since then the Soviet Union had broken the American monopoly by testing an atomic bomb (in August) and the Chinese communists had declared their victory in October. Notwithstanding Acheson's attempts to sow dissension between them, Mao and Stalin concluded their treaty of alliance in February 1950. The surprise attack was seen as a turning point, 'Communism has passed beyond the use of subversion to conquer independent nations and will now use armed invasion and war'.[28] Within two days of the invasion Truman ordered American air and naval forces into action in Korea and announced that the navy would be interposed between Taiwan and the Chinese mainland. He also sent American military advisers to assist the French war in Indo-China.

In effect the strategy of the maritime defensive perimeter which distinguished between greater and lesser priorities was cast aside in favour of the containment strategy of seeking to deny the communist forces any further advances wherever they might occur. Although sound strategic reasons could have been advanced for denying the North victory in Korea in order to safeguard Japan and for denying Taiwan to the communist Chinese in order to secure American naval predominance in the West Pacific, these were not the reasons given for the American intervention. The key document that defined American strategy for containment was NSC-68 which had been submitted to President Truman and formally approved by him in September 1950. In the words of its principal architect, 'the under-lying conflict ... were (*sic*) far more fundamental than disagree-ments over specific interests, *inter alia*, control over geography, ports, oceans, raw materials, or even respect, prestige, renown or position in the eyes of history ... the contest was not one of competition over specific national interests; it had an absolute ideological quality about it, which, from the Soviet side, did not permit compromise'.[29]

The adoption of NSC-68 led to a massive increase in American defence spending rising from $13.1 billion in 1950 to $22.5 billion and then $44.0 billion in 1951 and 1952 respectively.[30] It also acceler-ated the supply of direct American assistance to the French forces fighting the Vietminh in Indo-China. But as far as the conduct of the Korean War was concerned, after the Chinese intervention destroyed the hopes of total victory over the North, containment resulted in a rather minimalist strategy of seeking to restore the *status quo ante*, lest to do more might provoke the enlargement of the conflict into a third world war. A more flexibly conceived national strategy might have suggested different options.[31] The immediate effect of the Korean War and the strategy of containment was an attempt to draw a demarcation line between the countries controlled by the communists and the rest of the Asia-Pacific. This included the attempt to establish an economic embargo against China even more severe than the one that applied against the Soviet Union.

THE APPLICATION OF CONTAINMENT: NORTHEAST ASIA

If the American intervention in the Korean War was the first instance of the application of containment in the Asia-Pacific, the thinking that underlay the doctrine also shaped the conduct of the war. American war aims were limited in the sense that they did not want to widen the war to attack mainland China lest they draw in the Soviet Union and precipitate a world war. This was an objec-tive shared by the other side, so that all sides combined to keep secret American bombing of Manchuria and Soviet piloting of many of the fighter jets on the communist side. The aim was to punish aggression but not to roll back communism. An early indication of this was Truman's refusal to accept MacArthur's suggestion that a contingent of nationalist troops be included in the allied forces. To be sure, when the opportunity presented itself after the sweeping victory of the Inchon landings, Washington pressed ahead towards the border with China in order to take over the North. But following the Chinese intervention the United States objectives were confined to restoring the *status quo ante*. The Korean War indeed was seen at the time as America's first limited war and as such it embodied the concept of containment.[32]

The Korean War gave further impetus to the policy of reconstruction in Japan. It accelerated the drive towards ending the occupation, signing a peace treaty and establishing a military alliance. Japan would gain full independence, in return for establishing a small 'self defence' army and for signing a ten year (renewable) agreement allowing the continuance of American bases in Japan and Okinawa. The Peace Treaty provided the occasion for the US to conclude separate treaties with the Philippines, and trilaterally with Australia and New Zealand. Ostensibly they sought reassurance against a resurgence by Japan. The details of reparations were left to be settled at a later stage, but the Americans made it clear to disappointed allies that these would have to be tempered so as not to cripple the country. John Foster Dulles, the leading American negotiator, pointed out to the Japanese Prime Minister, Yoshida 'the great utility of the reparations clause in creating employment in Japan through processing foreign materials'.[33] Of the Asian countries, India and Burma refused to attend the peace conference in San Francisco in September 1951 and neither of the two claimants to represent China was invited. The Soviet Union attended, but withdrew and did not sign. Although the Treaty left it to an independent Japan to decide with which China it would deal, political opinion within the United States made it clear that recognition of communist China would be unacceptable. The famous letter handed by Yoshida to the American ambassador on 24 December 1951 (i.e. before Japan had technically become sovereign) stated that Japan would conclude a treaty with Nationalist China.

Japan, it was clear, was to become the core base of America's arc of containment in the Asia-Pacific. The Americans provided military security and facilitated the economic reconstruction of the country. Boosted by the Korean War the Japanese economy benefited from access to American loans and to the American market while protecting Japanese industries at home. As Dulles had predicted, Japanese industry also profited from the forms of reparations in Southeast Asia. The Americans also went to great lengths to cement ties with Japan and to squash latent and not so latent neutralist tendencies. Thus as Secretary of State, Dulles was also instrumental in persuading the Japanese to reject the Soviet offer of a peace treaty in 1956. The Soviet Union had offered to settle the dispute over four islands to the north of Japan, seized at the end of the war as notionally part of the Kurile chain, by ceding claims to sovereignty over the two closest to Hokkaido. Dulles said that if Japan were to recognize the Soviet title to the other two islands the United States would ask that Okinawa be confirmed as American territory. He feared that the Japanese might be tempted by Soviet blandishments to separate Japan from the United States by going on to offer the country some kind of neutral status.[34] In 1960, despite considerable domestic opposition, the Japanese government signed a Security Treaty with the United States. But such was the intensity of the dissent that President Eisenhower cancelled a projected visit to mark the occasion.

The election of President Eisenhower had brought in an administration determined to take a more assertive approach towards the communists as opposed to the earlier policy of containment which was regarded as too passive. At the same time it was determined to reduce military spending and to translate America's nuclear superiority into effective diplomatic gains. This gave rise to the 'New Look' strategy. The first instance of this approach in the Asia-Pacific was the use of the threat of atomic weapons to end the awful military stalemate and bring the prolonged armistice negotiations in Korea to a rapid conclusion in 1953.[35] The armistice also highlighted the difficulties of the United States in dealing with recalcitrant allies in whose interests, presumably, containment was carried out. The Syngman Rhee government (regarded by many inside and outside the American government as a nasty dictatorship) was opposed to it and was only bought off by promises of aid and by a treaty-based guarantee of its military security by the United States. None of America's other allies wished to be associated with the treaty.

The issue of Taiwan raised more complex problems. At stake was not so much the American commitment to the defence of Taiwan island itself, but some of the islands just off-shore from the mainland. These above all symbolized for Chiang Kai-shek his indissoluble link to the mainland over which he claimed rightful title and to which he was vowed to return to vanquish the communists. As these islands were less readily defensible they were a thorn in the side of the Americans, who in the end came to prefer an arrangement by which Taiwan might be fully separated from China proper. In the course of the first off-shore island crisis in 1954–55 the Americans persuaded the nationalists to withdraw from the more northerly Ta

Chen (or Da Zhen) groups of islands, but the Nationalists dug in their heels over Quemoy and Matsu, which were immediately opposite Taiwan by the coast of Fujian Province. Although Washington regarded the islands as inconsequential in themselves, their continued possession was seen as vital to Nationalist morale. In March 1955 the Eisenhower Administration publicly and privately raised the prospect of using atomic bombs against China. This led Beijing to decide to develop an independent nuclear capability.[36] Eventually the matter was diffused by China's Premier Zhou Enlai's offer to negotiate, which he made while attending the first Asian–African conference in Bandung in April 1955. The crisis as a whole had the effect of confirming the reluctance of America's other allies in the Asia-Pacific from joining it in signing a mutual defence treaty with the Republic of China (i.e. Taiwan). Consequently, the United States alone signed a Mutual Defence Treaty with the Republic of China in December 1954.

As far as China itself was concerned, the Eisenhower Administration continued the policy of containment and isolation. The Geneva Agreements for Indo-China of 1954 were regarded as a set back for the West rather than a basis on which new relations could be developed. A publicly hostile stance that refused to acknowledge conciliatory gestures by Zhou Enlai in 1955 and 1956, on the grounds of high principled opposition to international communism, was privately explained as being designed to wean China away from the Soviet Union. Picking up on the approach of Acheson in the first nine months after the victory of the Chinese communists in 1949, Dulles claimed to be driving a wedge between the two communist giants by making the Chinese demand economic and strategic assistance from the Russians that were beyond the capacity and will of the Soviet Union to give.[37] Thus from 1956 to 1960 the Eisenhower Administration evinced a readiness to develop contacts and explore the prospects for negotiations with the Soviet Union that it specifically denied the Chinese. The Soviet invasion of Hungary in 1956 and its initiation of a crisis over Berlin in 1958 did little to erase the view in Washington, evoked by Khrushchev's speeches of 1956 that denounced Stalin and called for a new spirit of peaceful coexistence, that the Soviet leader was a potential partner for negotiations. Notwithstanding Zhou Enlai's conciliatory gestures continued through into 1956, Dulles took a tough line of rejecting contact through, for example, the exchange of journalists. Indeed in a speech in early 1957 in San Francisco he denounced the Chinese communists for still being puppets of the Russians when the American intelligence agencies knew that this was very far from the truth.

The second off-shore island crisis of 1958 once again raised the issue in Washington of whether their defence was integral to the defence of Taiwan. Once again the conclusion was that the islands could not be given up without undermining the morale and hence the survival of the nationalist regime. Once again the possible use of nuclear weapons against the mainland was openly discussed in Washington. In the event the Chinese side 'blinked first' and the crisis came off the boil. It has been persuasively argued that as a result of the diplomacy of the Korean War and the conduct of the two off-shore island crises the American and communist Chinese governments developed a pattern of interactions that suggested they had come to understand how to conduct their hostile relations in ways that would not lead to war.[38] But as in the earlier Truman Administration, and in the Kennedy and Johnson Administrations that were to follow, the Chinese communists were regarded as the primary instigators of what was seen as Vietnamese communist aggression in Indo-China.

These developments took place within a context in which American strategic thinking was responding to the changing circumstances of Soviet nuclear power and the strategic equation between the two superpowers. As the Soviet Union acquired missiles in the late 1950s capable of hitting continental USA so the rationale of 'massive retaliation' and limited nuclear warfare lost credibility as instruments for American foreign policy. Moreover as the futility of a nuclear war became apparent, American thinking turned to how to meet the challenge of a variety of possible communist points of expansion from local wars to wars of national liberation in what was later called the Third World. The former was to lead to the strategy of flexible response as articulated by the Kennedy Administration. The latter resulted in a Third World strategy that was designed to enhance 'nation-building' and to stop the seemingly invincible communist guerilla strategy through 'counter-insurgency warfare'.[39]

Indeed, with the advent of the Kennedy Administration, the Chinese communists under Mao's leadership were seen as more dangerous foes than the Russians. Especially after the Cuban missile crisis when détente was developed with the Soviet Union, the Chinese communists were regarded as still being led by first generation revolutionaries who were imbued with a fanaticism that was not susceptible to rational counter-argument. Their Soviet equivalents, however, being the third generation of leaders since the revolution, were thought to be more 'rational'. Moreover, the Soviet Union was said to have learned from experience that its conventional and nuclear military forces could not hope to prevail against the United States without bringing about the annihilation of both sides. Accordingly, it was thought to be prepared to reach understandings with the United States. The Chinese, by contrast, according to the Kennedy Administration, had still to learn that their people's war strategy was not invincible.

By this time, however, it was no longer a question of driving wedges between Moscow and Beijing, it was rather an issue for the Kennedy of the 'new frontier' (who according to his inaugural address was willing to 'pay any price, bear any burden ... in the defence of liberty') of winning the decisive battle against communist guerila warfare and thus winning the Cold War. At this time American military academies altered their curricula to focus on what was called 'counter insurgency warfare' with Mao's writings forming important texts. Kennedy averred to a French official in 1963: 'The Chinese are perfectly prepared, because of their lower value of human life to lose hundreds of millions [of people] if necessary ... to carry out their militant and aggressive policies.'[40] After the Cuban missile crisis Kennedy went so far as to instruct his special ambassador to sound out Khrushchev about his views on destroying China's incipient nuclear facilities.[41] Indeed much of the point of the 1963 Test Ban Treaty was to suggest that Washington and Moscow would work together to prevent the proliferation of nuclear weapons. In other words they would cooperate to try to prevent China from becoming a nuclear power. By this time the idea of the wedge as a means to wean China away from the Soviet Union was no longer uppermost in the minds of administration officials. Ironically, of course, this was at the high point of the Sino–Soviet split, and it seemed as if the Americans shared the Soviet view of the Chinese. Interestingly, the American and Soviet leaders simultaneously sided with India against China in their brief border war of October–November 1962 (i.e. immediately after the Cuban missile crisis).

In one sense President Kennedy had modified the American view of the Chinese communist claim to represent Chinese sovereignty. He no longer accepted the fiction that Taiwan represented all of China. His administration, however, wanted the communist Chinese state 'to modify its aggressive stance and behaviour and recognize *de facto* the existence of an independent Taiwan'.[42] Since that had become the core issue dividing the PRC and the USA, both in the sense of challenging the unity of the state and in the strategic sense of the island being a point from which attacks against the mainland could be launched, it could be construed as even more challenging than the previous position, which simply preferred one version of China to the other. By the time of the accession of President Kennedy the number of states recognizing communist as opposed to Nationalist China was increasing and was due to increase still further as more Third World countries achieved independence. Consequently, it was purely a question of time before the communists would prevail in terms of numbers and gain recognition at the United Nations instead of the Nationalists. Accordingly, the new Kennedy position threatened to remove that prospect. The fact that Chiang Kai-shek on Taiwan objected even more strongly meant that Kennedy's approach did not become official policy. But, not surprisingly, the Chinese communists regarded Kennedy as even more dangerous than his predecessor. Indeed they dubbed him the 'tiger with a smiling face'. The view of the Chinese communists as the ultimate menace was so deep rooted among Kennedy's people that in 1965 Dean Rusk attacked an article by the Chinese Defence Minister Lin Biao on the people's war as a Chinese version of Hitler's *Mein Kampf*. In fact, far from being an exhortation to expansion the article indicated that the Chinese would not intervene in the Vietnam War and that it advised Hanoi to scale down its conduct.[43]

Both the Kennedy and Johnson Administrations were committed to a view of the world that was still recognizably the one that underpinned NSC-68 of ten to fifteen years earlier. Namely that the communist challenge was universal and that it had to be met in the spirit of a zero-sum game, that a victory for one side was necessarily a loss for the other. Consequently, were the US to sustain the 'loss' of a small and distant country such as Vietnam the credibility of all its commitments would be undermined. As Secretary of State Dean Rusk put it in 1965, 'the integrity of the US commitment is the principal pillar of peace throughout the world. If that commitment becomes unreliable the communist world would draw conclusions that would lead to our ruin and almost certainly to a catastrophic war'.[44] This was to be the primary reason advanced for the American intervention in Vietnam, but initially it was explained as necessary to stop the Chinese communists who were said to be behind the Vietnamese communists.

By 1966 American attitudes towards how best to deal with communist China were beginning to change. In 1965 a tied vote in the

UN General Assembly on the question of who represented China meant that for the first time the Americans failed to obtain a majority in favour of the Nationalists on Taiwan. The Senate Foreign Relations Committee held hearings on China in 1966 and the establishment China experts favoured a change to 'containment without isolation'. Although the administration was still worried by a possible backlash because of the public's presumed residual sense of grievance over the 'loss of China', attitudes changed there too. Anxious to avoid a Chinese intervention on the Korean model the administration limited its escalations in Vietnam so as not to provoke the Chinese. This had the effect of providing a *modus vivendi* between the two sides despite the ferocity of the rhetoric directed against each other.[45] Nixon's famous *Foreign Affairs* article of October 1967 which held out the prospect for a new relationship with China was not considered to be highly exceptional at the time.

In other words by 1966–67 American attitudes towards China had developed significantly. The wisdom of seeking to isolate a state with a quarter of the world's population, that since its nuclear test of October 1964 had become a nuclear power and that was clearly an independent actor of some significance on the world stage, no longer made sense, especially as it had quite evidently broken away from the Soviet Union. This did not mean that containment was no longer applicable as the country was still perceived as a dangerous adversary in Asia and as a fomenter of revolution elsewhere in the Third World.

THE APPLICATION OF CONTAINMENT: SOUTHEAST ASIA

American historical relations with Southeast Asia were largely confined to the Philippines to which it granted independence of a kind in 1946. Even the final settlement of the Pacific War in this part of the Asia-Pacific was left primarily to the European allies – essentially the British – who restored their colonial rule. Britain, however, moved speedily to concede demands for Burmese and Indian independence. Britain and France also gave in to American pressure for the international rehabilitation of Thailand, a war time ally of Japan. Yet the American impulse to press the Europeans to grant independence was tempered by the need to avoid undermining the prestige and standing of the fragile governments at home in Europe. General De Gaulle pronounced upon the significance of the issue in August 1946: 'United with the overseas territories which she opened to civilization, France is a great power. Without these territories she would be in danger of no longer being one.'[46] The Americans in fact stood gingerly aside until their approach became infused with Cold War thinking. It was the fear of communism that drew the United States into active engagement in the area.

The British attempt to crush the communists in the course of the Malayan Emergency that began in June 1948 was watched with concern. But what gave rise to alarm was the French struggle with the Vietminh in Indo-China particularly after the communist success in China in 1949 which opened the Sino–Vietnamese border to a massive influx of Chinese military assistance. Unlike Indonesia, where there was a non-communist authority to whom the Americans pressed the Dutch to concede, the main nationalist movement in Indo-China was the communist dominated Vietminh. With considerable misgivings the Americans and also the British recognized the French imposed government of the Emperor Bao Dai as one of the associated states of the French Union that was set up in November 1949, and tried in vain to persuade the French to concede more to Bao Dai so as to establish him with some nationalist credentials. After the (communist) Democratic Republic of Vietnam gained the recognition first of the PRC and then of the USSR in January 1950, the American definition of the significance of Indo-China grew, as did their readiness to be committed there.

First the State Department in February 1950 and then the Joint Chiefs of Staff in April of that year sounded the alarm as to the possible consequences of the fall of Indo-China to the communists. They anticipated that Burma and Thailand would also succumb, to be followed by Malaya and the whole of Southeast Asia. That would jeopardize the American defence perimeter, allow the Chinese and the Soviets access to resources that could change the balance of power, and by denying Asian markets and materials to Japan could damage its relations with the United States.[47] Here lay the origins of the domino theory, beloved of Eisenhower and his successors, that if Vietnam fell so would all the rest. Although the Southeast Asian mainland was still not seen as sufficiently important in terms of stretched American global commitments to justify direct intervention, economic assistance was extended to the French in May. The outbreak of the Korean War in June 1950 provided the rationale for sending military as well as economic aid to the French. The latter steadily increased until by 1954 the United States was paying for more than 80 per cent of the French war effort.

The Geneva Conference of 1954 that settled the first Indo-China war was regarded by Dulles as a defeat for the West. The partition of Vietnam meant not only the establishment of a new communist state in Asia, but one that was the most powerful among the four Indo-Chinese states. The Conference had also brought out into the open Anglo–American differences on how to treat communist China. Within two months the United States took steps to bolster the security of the region against further communist gains, by the Manila Treaty of September 1954, that led to the establishment of the Southeast Asia Treaty Organization (SEATO). Despite its obvious weaknesses in having failed to elicit Asian support beyond Thailand, the Philippines and Pakistan (to whom the United States was already closely linked) and in obligating its members to a less than binding military commitment to each other's defence, it provided a mechanism for extending a commitment to Cambodia, Laos and South Vietnam without their assuming treaty obligations themselves. It served the American purpose of enhancing its deterrent position in Southeast Asia without committing it to increasing its military deployments. Southeast Asia continued to be regarded as a region of lesser strategic priority.[48]

During the remainder of the 1950s the United States sent military advisers to Laos, South Vietnam and Thailand. Existing military missions in the Philippines and elsewhere were enlarged. Lacking in sympathy for Asian neutralism or non-alignment, the Eisenhower Administration tended to regard these manifestations of Asian nationalism as helpful to the communist menace. Indonesia used this concern adroitly in eliciting American pressure on the Dutch to relinquish West Irian which they eventually did in 1963. Previously, the United States had become involved in regional revolts in Indonesia in 1958 as Dulles was persuaded that they were rebelling against growing communist influence in Jakarta. But on being informed that the Indonesian army which was putting down the rebellion was staunchly anti-communist Dulles quickly changed tack.[49]

North Vietnam began its attempt to reunify the country through unleashing guerilla warfare in the South and through the formation of the National Liberation Front of South Vietnam in 1960. This involved the development of a supply route that went south, first via Laos and later included Cambodia – the so-called Ho Chi Minh Trail. The situation of its eastern uplands gave strategic significance to Laos, as competing external patrons sought to uphold their candidates for control of its government. As Eisenhower prepared to leave office he strongly recommended to the incoming Kennedy that he take a stand on Laos as it was the linchpin domino. Its fall to communism would be followed by Cambodia, South Vietnam and probably Thailand and Burma.[50] The critical juncture in Laos was reached in 1961: a civil war had broken out and the side of the neutralists and Pathet Lao (who were virtually an adjunct of the Vietnamese communists) were being supplied by Soviet airlifts while the rightists were backed by Thailand and the CIA. Being reluctant to intervene after the American Cuban debacle at the Bay of Pigs, it was only the following year, in May 1962, after the despatch of 6,000 marines to neighbouring Thailand, that the United States was able to secure an agreement at a conference convened in Geneva for the formal neutralization of the country and the withdrawal of all foreign troops. Laotian neutrality was ostensibly preserved, but in practice several thousand Vietnamese military personnel remained, ensuring that the trail to South Vietnam would be kept open.[51]

Imbued with the activist approach symbolized by the evocation of the myth of the 'new frontier', the Kennedy Administration developed a theory of modernization and nation building that together with counter-insurgency warfare was directed towards defeating the communist strategy of revolutionary guerilla wars or wars of national liberation that both Moscow and Beijing were pledged to support. This was seen as fitting in with the new general strategic doctrine of flexible response which was regarded as more credible than that of massive retaliation, given that the Soviet Union was thought to have acquired the capability to strike continental America with nuclear weapons. Consequently, the Kennedy Administration placed much emphasis on political reform in the South as well as in seeking to build up the South Vietnamese army. Dissatisfied with the authoritarian style of President Diem, the United States encouraged his overthrow. But his assassination on 1 November 1963 led to a succession of coups by generals which had the effect of undermining such little authority as had been enjoyed by the unlamented Diem. America was in effect faced with the choice of cutting its losses and reconciling itself to the eventual victory of the communists or becoming more deeply and directly involved in the fighting. Kennedy himself was assassinated later that November. He had prevaricated over the choice and his former associates were divided as to which path he would have chosen.

His successor President Johnson decided to intervene with combat troops and in March 1965 he began a sustained bombing campaign against the North with the morale of the South very much in mind.

Ironically in view of the later anti-war movement, the American commitment at this juncture enjoyed considerable public support. Moreover it was principally the realists, such as Walter Lippmann and Hans Morganthau, who opposed the war at this stage as a dereliction of American strategic priorities. As in Korea, the Americans sought to limit the war, but this time that meant avoiding a military confrontation with China as well as with the Soviet Union. As a result it was decided not to invade North Vietnam, nor to bomb southern China. The American strategy was geared to graduated escalation by which the bombing of the North was increased in intensity step by step. Meanwhile ground forces in the South were increased rapidly in the vain hope of pressing Hanoi to concede that it could not win so as to negotiate a settlement that would guarantee the survival of the South. Within three years American forces had been increased to nearly 550,000.

The war showed no signs of coming to a conclusion, much of it was televised and beamed into people's homes. It became unpopular and the discontent it evoked tended to merge with America's domestic woes, leading to major riots in several cities. A foreign policy could not for long be sustained against such domestic opposition. Thus it was the communist Tet Offensive at the end of January 1968 that proved the turning point. Although their urban uprising was eventually crushed, the early communist successes in the main cities including Saigon that were shown on television suggested that the American task was hopeless. President Johnson turned down a request from his commander in the field, General Westmoreland, for an additional 200,000 troops and announced in March 1968 after the New Hampshire primary that he was calling a halt to the bombing and that he would not seek a new term in office. This in effect brought to an end the stage of containment when the United States acted as if its resources were limitless and as if it could oppose the further expansion of communist power wherever it might arise.

President Johnson's legacy in foreign affairs included not only the huge Vietnam problem, but also, and importantly, a strained but working relationship with the Soviet Union. Building upon the momentum of the 1963 Test Ban Treaty, various other arms control agreements were agreed, including the 1968 Nuclear Non-Proliferation Treaty. Despite their differences, both superpowers in the end sought to restrain their allies in the Middle East War of 1967; and Johnson acquiesced in the Soviet invasion of Czechoslovakia even as he sought to limit Soviet pressure on the more independent communist countries, Romania and Yugoslavia. Johnson had even tried to elicit Soviet help in reaching agreement with Vietnam during the course of his summit meeting with the Soviet Premier Kosygin in Glassboro in June 1967. Johnson claimed to be following a two track policy of thwarting communist aggression in Vietnam on the one hand and showing on the other that 'there was an alternative to confrontation' through the creation of 'a climate in which nations of the East and West could begin cooperating to find solutions to their worst problems'.[52] The Chinese were not a party to the latter. Indeed they thought, not entirely without reason, that such cooperation that did exist in American relations with the Soviet Union was directed against them.

AMERICAN POLICY IN ASIA DURING THE PERIOD OF TRIPOLARITY

The advent of President Nixon and his close foreign affairs collaborator Henry Kissinger, brought fresh perspectives to what they regarded as the problem of managing global order. Nixon soon accepted that great as American power still was – indeed no other country disposed of remotely comparable military, economic or technological resources – it could no longer seek to dictate the character of international order by its efforts alone. The first practical indication of the new approach was Nixon's informal briefing to the press during a stopover in Guam in July 1969. In what became known as the Nixon Doctrine he pledged to maintain all existing treaty commitments and the shield of nuclear deterrence, but called upon any victim of other types of aggression to assume the responsibility for providing manpower for its own defence, while the United States would provide training, weapons and off-shore assistance through air and sea forces. This provided the rationale for the 'Vietnamization' of the war – i.e. the withdrawal of American ground troops and their replacement by the forces of the South Vietnamese army. However, this was not thought of as a simple withdrawal, such as when the French finally called it a day and withdrew from Algeria. The American withdrawal was considered within the larger context of America's global strategic responsibilities. It was thought essential that America's credibility as a provider of security and international order should not be undermined by a defeat at the periphery of superpower contention where it had committed so much force, treasure and prestige – hence the concept of 'peace with honour'. The Nixon Administration claimed that the Doctrine provided a new kind of flexibility that was absent from earlier doctrines of containment. Others, however, noted what seemed to be a contradiction between maintaining the same commitments as before while providing fewer capabilities with which to meet them.[53]

The China factor

The China factor came into view early in the Nixon Administration. According to Kissinger it was the 1969 Sino–Soviet border conflict and the attendant Soviet soundings as to how America would react in the event of a Soviet attack upon China's nuclear installations that first alerted Washington to the strategic significance of China for the United States and the vision of international order. This prompted the secret diplomacy that finally resulted in Henry Kissinger's path-breaking visit to Beijing in July 1971. Kissinger regarded the end of 1969 as the beginning of the triangular diplomacy with the communist world. As he later explained, 'We moved toward China not to expiate liberal guilt over our China policy of the late 1940s but to shape a global equilibrium.'[54]

Kissinger's visit to Beijing in July 1971 was arranged in secret through the good offices of Pakistan. The immediate response of the shocked Soviet leadership, according to Kissinger, was to sign a treaty of friendship with India on 9 August 1971. This was at a time when the Pakistani army was engaged in the suppression of widespread civil unrest in East Pakistan where a momentum was building up for secession. In Kissinger's view the treaty and the subsequent Indian assistance to the secession of Bangladesh was an opportunity for the Soviet Union 'to demonstrate Chinese impotence and to humiliate a friend of both China and the United States'.[55] As if to demonstrate that the score had been evened somewhat, it was on the day after the signing of the treaty with India that President Brezhnev issued the formal invitation to President Nixon for a summit meeting in Moscow in May or June 1972 (i.e. after the Beijing summit due in February). The United States then sent a naval task force to the Gulf of Bengal as part of its famous so-called tilt towards Pakistan. According to Kissinger, Zhou Enlai joined him in believing that the United States had indeed saved West Pakistan.[56]

The episode may be seen as setting the tone for what was later called US–Chinese 'parallelism'. Within a context of complementary local, regional and global interests, the two states acted separately, but in the knowledge of the other's actions, to support a joint ally –

in this case Pakistan. But the episode also masked a fundamental difference between the two sides that was to haunt the development of their relations and to cause divisions within subsequent American administrations. Mao and Zhou Enlai sought a united front against the Soviet Union and therefore wanted the United States to take an unyielding confrontationist approach towards it. Nixon and Kissinger, however, still sought détente with the Soviet Union in order to draw it into their vision of global equilibrium.

By virtue of China's relative weakness and vulnerability to Soviet military power, questions of national security were uppermost among the concerns of China's leaders. They came to suspect that Kissinger's interest in détente would encourage him to concede too much to the Soviet Union and that the result would be some kind of superpower condominium. Moreover, as the weaker power, China was always in danger of being used as a tactical pawn by the United States to 'buy' agreements with the Soviet Union at China's expense. By the mid 1970s after SALT I, the Vladivostok Agreement of December 1974, grain sales, technology transfer and the Helsinki Accords of mid-1975, Mao complained that Washington had 'stood on China's shoulders' to reach agreements with Moscow.[57]

In the aftermath of the Kissinger and Nixon visits, Mao and Zhou Enlai abandoned their opposition to America's alliances in the Asia-Pacific. Thus Mao came to appreciate the significance of the Tokyo–Washington axis and even chided Kissinger at one point for not spending as much time in Tokyo as he did in Beijing. Mao and Zhou Enlai also tacitly supported the US military presence in the Philippines, Thailand and even South Korea. Moreover, although they could not say so publicly, the two Chinese leaders also shared an interest with Washington in seeking to forestall a humiliating US exit from Vietnam. The formula on Taiwan in the Shanghai Communique of 1972, whereby the United States avoided taking a position on the status of Taiwan, satisfied Mao to the extent that he had subordinated the Taiwan issue to larger strategic concerns. Indeed alone of all the countries in the world the United States for most of the 1970s was able to maintain its embassy for China in Taipei and continue its security treaty with Taiwan as the Republic of China while its leaders enjoyed close relations with those in Beijing.

Despite Nixon's initial apprehensions his opening to China and his subsequent visit evoked a mood of euphoria in the United States. The reaction of America's Asian allies was positive, but more guarded. Japan felt subject to two Nixon shocks. The first was that it had not been informed in advance let alone consulted about the *rapprochement* with China; and the second was the almost simultaneous announcement of the withdrawal of the US dollar from the gold standard. American unilateralism on matters of such intrinsic importance to its most significant Asian ally was profoundly unsettling. But at least the way was open for Japan to develop its own relations with China. Essentially the United States left its allies to make their own adjustments to China although it assured them of the continuation of its existing commitments.

Triangular diplomacy

The triangular policy of Nixon and Kissinger that also characterized the brief Ford Administration (in which Kissinger was Secretary of State) was predicated on avoiding taking sides and on maintaining good relations with both the Soviet Union and China so as to promote the vision of an international order by which all the major powers would agree to act with restraint and not challenge the *status quo* by resort to violence either directly or indirectly. Since the Soviet Union was the only other true global power, the main thrust of the policy was directed towards it. Triangular diplomacy, from the American perspective, was primarily directed at restraining the Soviet Union, because China's global reach was limited and the likelihood of it re-engaging with its former ally (at least in this period) was remote. Building on relations of adversarial partnership with the Soviet Union begun by Kennedy and Johnson, Nixon and Kissinger espoused a policy of détente, by which they hoped to persuade the Soviet leadership of their common interest in basing international order on the balance of power – or to use Kissinger's phrase, 'global equilibrium'. Central to this policy was the doctrine of linkage, according to which all major events should be seen as interconnected. It meant that progress in one area of interest to the US, say Vietnam, could be made conditional on progress in another area of interest to the Soviet Union, say the Middle East, trade, or arms limitation. Above all it was meant to induce the Soviet Union to act with 'restraint'. In other words the Soviet Union was not to sponsor the further expansion of communism. This could be seen as but another version of containment.

There were several problems with this strategy. For example, certain of these areas, such as arms control, may have had an intrinsic importance in themselves that should not have been made conditional on other matters. Similarly, it gave rise to a tendency to see the world as still dominated by the two superpowers even though both Nixon and Kissinger were on record as seeing the emergence of a more complex multipolar world. Perhaps, more damagingly, such an approach called for carefully calibrated policies that could not be sustained given the diffusion of power within the American political process. By 1974, for example, the administration's capacity to use trade with the Soviet Union for linkage purposes was constrained by the Jackson–Vanik amendment that required the Soviet Union to allow open emigration as a condition for normalizing trade. Opposition in Congress and in the State Department constrained Kissinger from acting as he would have wished over Angola in 1975. Moreover, the Kissinger approach antagonized the liberals, on the one hand, with its ill-concealed disdain for their moral concerns and, on the other hand, it simultaneously opened itself to criticism from the right for institutionalizing a process by which the Soviet Union made gains while the United States accepted a less than superior strategic position.

The immediate issue for the United States for the duration of the Nixon Administration, however, was to manage the withdrawal from Vietnam with 'honour'. In the event an agreement for a cease-fire and for the withdrawal of the remaining American forces was reached with Hanoi in January 1973 after both sides had failed to achieve a decisive advantage in the war. The agreement also called for the return and accounting of prisoners (an issue that subsequently was to be an obstacle to the normalization of American relations with Vietnam for more than twenty years), continuation of American military and economic aid to the South, whose political future was to be left to be settled by elections and, finally, an American offer of economic assistance to the North. According to Kissinger the American constraint on Hanoi was the recourse to bombing, but once this was denied by Congress and once Nixon had become enfeebled by Watergate, the way was open for Hanoi to attack the South with impunity.[58] Be that as it may, the Northern offensive in March 1975 succeeded rapidly and Saigon fell on 29 April amid ignominious scenes as the last American helicopters fled the embassy. American forces had been withdrawn two years earlier, but the trauma of defeat was deep and long-lasting especially at home.

In the Asia-Pacific, however, the impact of the American debacle was less severe. To be sure both Cambodia and Laos also fell to communist forces. Although it was not known at the time the former were fanatically anti-Vietnamese, and no other dominoes fell. Thailand endured as did the other pro-Western states of Southeast Asia and the American position in the Western Pacific was little affected. Indeed nearly ten years before, communism had been eliminated from Indonesia. Arguably the Soviet Union, as the principal supporter and arms supplier of Vietnam, benefited. It had taken the opportunity of the American concentration on the Vietnam War to augment its naval capabilities and its Pacific Fleet, which had become the largest in the Soviet Navy, and gave the Soviet Union a significant capacity to project force in the region.[59] But in the process it brought into play its conflict with China and the incipient conflict between China and Vietnam which had been revived from 1971 – albeit behind the scenes. Thus despite its humiliation in 1975 and its virtual military disengagement from Southeast Asia (except for its important bases in the Philippines), by virtue of the third Indo-China war that began in Cambodia in 1978/79 and the Soviet invasion of Afghanistan in December 1979, the United States in the end did not have to pay a significant price in the region for its failings.

The Carter Administration

By this stage President Carter was in office. His administration's early initiatives in Asia did not inspire confidence in its strategic sense of purpose. Although the Carter Administration sought to apply tripolarity in a different way from the two previous administrations who stood accused of abandoning American values, it failed to develop a clear sense of priorities that could be understood by its two major communist interlocutors. Arising out of the Soviet obligations to observe human rights that were incurred by the Helsinki Agreements of 1975, the Carter Administration emphasized human rights issues in the conduct of relations with the Soviet Union. That antagonized the Soviet leaders who saw it as a ploy to undermine their government and it delayed progress in negotiating further arms limitation agreements until it was too late. Additionally, the administration agonized openly about whether to treat the two communist giants equally and about whether to play the 'China card' by supplying China with arms and by deepening relations whenever the Soviet Union was judged to have behaved aggressively. Unlike Moscow, Beijing was not required to show greater respect for human rights, but to their intense embarrassment, some of the governments of America's Asian allies were not spared. More disquieting was the early insistence on removing the 50,000 American troops still based in South Korea, even though President

Carter was soon dissuaded from such a unilateral and potentially destabilizing exercise. Sending an emissary to Vietnam to initiate diplomatic contact was seen within the region as reflecting a domestic American agenda of purging guilt about policy towards the erstwhile enemy, rather than being the result of a newly thought out strategy. With a new and not fully settled leadership in Beijing that sought an unyielding approach to the Soviet Union rather than making compromises on Taiwan, the visit there by Secretary of State Vance in August 1977 to explore the prospects for normalizing relations did not proceed well.[60]

The sharpening of tensions between China and Vietnam in 1978 brought to a head incipient divisions in the Carter Administration between those led by the National Security Adviser, Z. Brzezinski, who sought a more confrontationist approach towards the Soviet Union and who also favoured closer relations with China, and those, headed by Secretary of State C. Vance, who sought to renew détente with the Soviet Union and to maintain an even balance between the two. Although there was agreement about the desirability of normalizing relations with China, there were also those who wanted to normalize relations with Vietnam. Meanwhile the administration encouraged Japan in August 1978 to sign a peace and friendship treaty with China despite the anti-hegemony clause (which was generally seen as aimed at the Soviet Union). Soviet attempts to intimidate Japan had backfired. As the tension deepened between China and Vietnam and its Soviet ally, the Carter Administration found in Deng Xiaoping (who had just consolidated his supremacy) a leader who was willing to make the necessary compromises to establish full diplomatic relations with China. This also meant in effect the end of attempts to establish diplomatic relations with Vietnam.

The normalization of relations with China involved ending official relations with Taiwan, withdrawing remaining troops and terminating the security treaty. But an understanding was reached that whereas Beijing would not renounce the use of force, the United States would continue to sell arms to Taiwan. This was followed up in April 1979 by American domestic legislation, known as the Taiwan Relations Act, that was enacted against Carter's wishes, obliging the executive to regard any use of force against Taiwan as a threat to the security of the western Pacific and as of 'great concern' to the US.[61]

The establishment of formal diplomatic relations with the PRC was followed in January by a highly successful visit by the Chinese leader Deng Xiaoping to the United States, in the course of which he openly vowed to 'teach Vietnam a lesson' for its invasion of Cambodia in December 1978 with Soviet support. An embarrassed Carter Administration neither supported nor fully and openly opposed Deng. The limited Chinese incursion into Vietnam of February–March 1979 was followed by an unofficial alignment with Washington. In April 1979 China accepted the installation in Xinjiang of electronic listening devices to monitor Soviet rocketry, that had been displaced by the Khomeni revolution in Iran. In January 1980 Defense Secretary Brown visited Beijing in the aftermath of the Soviet invasion of Afghanistan and began a policy of exporting to China advanced military technology of a non-lethal character. Before the year was out China and the United States had established 'parallel' policies on Cambodia and Afghanistan. As separate allies of both Thailand and Pakistan they supported them in different ways and also supplied arms to the Cambodian and Afghani resistance fighters operating with the assistance of the two respective allies. The two also worked together to deny the Cambodian seat at the UN to the Vietnamese installed government in Phnom Penh and to isolate Vietnam both economically and politically. More broadly at this time 'on issue after issue – from the unity of NATO to the strengthening of the Association of Southeast Asian Nations – Peking's position came to resemble those of the United States'.[62]

The Reagan Administration

The accession of the Reagan Administration did not fundamentally change the coordinated 'parallel' policies pursued with China with regard to Cambodia and Afghanistan, but nevertheless the character of Sino–American relations changed. Several factors accounted for this. President Reagan himself offended Beijing by his early rhetoric that called for upgrading American relations with Taiwan. Perhaps more importantly, the Reagan strategy of a massive rebuilding of American nuclear and conventional forces coupled with a more robust approach to the Soviet Union meant that by the summer of 1982 Washington no longer put so much emphasis on tripolarity as a means for restraining Soviet behaviour. If China had become less important to the United States China had also gained a greater degree of diplomatic manoeuvre as it had less cause to fear Soviet aggression. Additionally, with the Soviet Union bogged down in Afghanistan, the Chinese could afford to take the 'sting' out of relations with the Soviet Union. Consequently the Chinese began to move to what they called at the Twelfth Communist Party Congress in September 1982 an 'independent foreign policy' according to which China would 'never attach itself to a big power or a group of powers'.

A series of incidents took place by which the Chinese sought to test the character of the American commitment to them. This brought out the last conflict within an American administration about the significance of the China card. On this occasion it was Secretary of State Alexander Haig who argued about the intrinsic strategic significance of China for the United States against a more general trend to devalue China's significance as both a trading and strategic partner. His replacement by George Shultz in June 1982 brought about a more sober reassessment of the significance of China. It was thought that China was decades away from becoming a global power and that in view of the different cultures and strategic perspectives Shultz warned in March 1983 that Sino–American relations would inevitably be characterized by 'frustrations and problems'. Pride of place in American policy should belong to Japan. Henceforth China loomed smaller in American strategic calculations than at any time since the original *rapprochement* more than ten years earlier.[63] Interestingly, as mutual expectations were reduced, the United States developed its best working relations with China in the remaining years of the Reagan presidency. To be sure there was American disquiet about Chinese arms sales to Iran and Iraq in the course of their war, but essentially their 'parallel' partnership over Cambodia and Afghanistan continued until the 1988/89 agreements with the Soviet Union brought the issues to an end as matters of global concern. Moreover, trade and other relations with China developed well despite the differences between the two societies. Indeed popular opinion within the United States chose to believe that the economic reforms in China were leading the country in a more liberal direction.

American relations with its formal allies in the 1970s and 1980s underwent important changes despite the fact that the United States remained the fundamental provider of regional security. Although the Nixon Doctrine and the subsequent American debacle in Vietnam raised doubts about the extent to which the United States would be prepared to intervene militarily to uphold its commitments, on the whole these doubts did not give rise to major problems. These arose largely in response to the growing economic power of first, and most notably, Japan and then of the other Pacific Rim countries that by the mid-1980s came to be regarded as Newly Industrialising Countries or Economies (NICs or NIEs). In many respects their economic achievements may be regarded as a product of the success of America's post war policies. By having provided military security, investment and privileged access to the domestic American market without demanding equal reciprocity, successive American administrations had provided them with unusually favourable opportunities to develop.

Three problems arose with Japan after its rapid economic growth elevated it to the world's third (or perhaps second) largest economy in the early 1970s. First, from the late 1960s Japan developed a large and growing trade surplus with the United States, and as it grew so did American discontent. Second, the United States became dissatisfied with Japan as a 'free-rider' and demanded that it contribute more to regional security. Third, Japan began to recognize that in some respects its interests diverged from those of its American ally and with the growth of the Japanese economy came a sense of pride and self assertiveness that tended to resent American pressure to accommodate what were seen as particular American rather than common concerns. In many ways these problems were exacerbated in the 1980s as a result not only of the huge American trade deficit, but also of the massive budget deficit that arose from the Reagan Administration's vast expenditure on defence. A good part of the latter was financed by Japanese investment.

Two decades of constant trade friction were capped in 1987 by the American imposition of trade sanctions for the first time. In fact, as both sides recognized, their two giant economies were interdependent, but the one was conscious of its vulnerability as a resource-poor country whose interests did not always coincide with its long term protector, and the other felt that it could no longer sustain a vast trade imbalance that was felt to have been obtained through unfair practices, especially since the American economy had lost its hegemonic character. These problems were exacerbated by the cultural divide between the two countries.[64] Their incipient conflict was contained, however, by their overriding interest in not challenging the basis of their security alliance and by recognition of the mutual dependence of their economies. As long as the Cold War lasted it served to prevent recurrent disputes from escalating to challenge the fundamental ties between the two allies.

THE END OF THE COLD WAR AND AFTER

The end of the Cold War may have been seen as a triumph for the United States and the values it espoused, but in bringing to an end forty years of the policies of containment the American government was left without any clear guidelines for understanding the new era, let alone with a sense of purpose and a coherent strategy around which to organize its foreign policies. At first, especially as America seemed to be leading the world community as a whole in condemnation of the Iraqi invasion of Kuwait, President Bush enthused about the emergence of 'a new world order' based on 'a new partnership of nations ... whose goals are to increase democracy, increase prosperity, increase the peace, and reduce arms'.[65] The phrase 'new world order' soon assumed an ironic twist in the chaotic aftermath of the Gulf War, but the rhetoric concerning the spreading of democracy and the free market found new expression in the Clinton Administration as its National Security Adviser Anthony Lake advanced the doctrine of 'enlargement' as a core concept for a foreign policy that would assist the spread of these Western practices. It was as if the end of the Cold War was akin to the end of a major international war that facilitated the establishment by the victors of a new international order as at the Congress of Vienna in 1815 or at the conclusion of the two world wars earlier this century.

Although the West and the United States may be said to have won the Cold War, it would have been more accurate to suggest that the Soviet Union and communism had lost. To be sure the United States had not been inactive and it had played a critical role in facilitating settlements of long standing regional conflicts that had been integral to the Cold War in the late 1980s, a role that was continued into the early 1990s with its significance in the ending of the Cambodian conflict in 1991. Yet it soon became apparent that uncertainty and self questioning rather than the exultation of victory more accurately conveyed the American mood. Without the priorities imposed by opposition to Soviet communism and its alleged expansion there was no longer an agreed basis for harnessing domestic affairs to serve long term foreign policy goals. Moreover, in the absence of a global sense of strategic priorities it became more difficult to identify the relative significance of different regions in the world. Amid these new uncertainties domestic forces acting primarily through Congress began to impinge more on foreign policy, both in the parochial sense of strengthening the pressure for protectionism and in the idealist sense of calling for greater priority to be given to promoting human rights and democracy in the world.

The new approaches by the United States raised particular problems in the conduct of relations in the Asia-Pacific. First, unlike the situation in Europe and the Soviet Union, the communist states of North Korea, Vietnam and above all China survived the ending of the Cold War and they regarded the American rhetoric about the new world order and the enlargement of the scope of democracy as aimed at undermining their political systems. This was especially true of China in the years immediately following the killings of demonstrators near Tiananmen on 4 June 1989. Additionally, the new American rhetoric aroused hostile reactions from previously friendly regimes who had become more nationalistically assertive as a result of the exceptional economic performances of their economies. Second, the startling economic dynamism of East and Southeast Asia had deepened the region's significance for the American economy far beyond that of trans-Atlantic trade. Now that the strategic overlay of confronting the Soviet Union had disappeared the United States was less willing to tolerate what it regarded as unfair trade practices that had resulted in huge trade deficits with East Asia and Japan in particular. Moreover, the United States had to decide whether to continue with the series of bilateral treaty relationships that had hitherto characterized its formal relations in the area or whether to change tack in favour of multilateral arrangements. More broadly, new questions arose about the significance of American security commitments in the region and the corresponding force deployments.

In response to calls from Congress the Pentagon published in the spring of 1990 a major review of the strategic future in the Asia-Pacific. Although it still regarded the Soviet Union as a military threat, the review stressed that in the future America's role would be as the 'regional balancer, honest broker, and ultimate security guarantor'. It added that if the Soviet threat were to decline substantially, the American military presence would continue to check the 'expansionist regional aspirations' of 'second tier' states. The review also noted that the American forces in the Pacific were needed for responding rapidly to crises elsewhere such as the Middle East. Nevertheless the review stated that about 10,000 out of a deployment of about 110,000 troops would be withdrawn within a five year period and it implied that if the strategic environment continued to improve in the region more substantial withdrawals would take place.[66] In 1992 another strategic review foreshadowed plans to reduce US deployments in East Asia still further, but in February 1995 Assistant Secretary of Defense for International Security, Joseph S. Nye, sought to reassure Asian governments that a new official report held that the cut-backs resulting from the end of the

Cold War had finished and 'no further changes in war fighting capability [were] currently planned'.[67]

American allies and friends in the region, however, were not fully reassured about the commitment to retain sufficient military force deployed in the Asia-Pacific. They recognized that irresistible pressures for further withdrawals could arise within the US. Moreover, they were concerned about the extent to which the United States would 'check' regional expansionism in practice. The United States had already indicated to the Philippines in the 1980s that their treaty did not extend to the latter's claims in the South China Sea where the littoral Southeast Asian states fear China's creeping assertiveness. Moreover, the United States decided to withdraw altogether from its bases in the Philippines when the agreement over them expired in 1991. This was occasioned partly by the enormous damage inflicted by the volcanic eruption of Mt Pinatubo on Clark Airfield, but it was spurred by the long and bitter negotiations with the Filipino government which under nationalist pressures demanded payments and conditions that the US was not prepared to meet in the new era. Singapore hastened to provide the use of certain limited facilities but not as an effective replacement. Yet despite repeated official American pledges to retain the current force level deployments in the region, many friendly governments feared that perhaps within ten years American domestic pressures would lead to their recall. Interestingly, Thailand, America's long term ally in the region, turned down an American request to establish off-shore supply depots to be used in the event of emergencies in the region and in the Gulf. The Thais explained that this might be opposed on nationalistic grounds and besides it might give offence to the Chinese. As for the security role of American forces, it was recognized that this might forestall the emergence of a regional hegemony and possible great power rivalry between China and Japan, but it was openly doubted whether force would be used in regional conflicts beyond Korea and possibly Taiwan.[68]

After a certain degree of hesitation the United States eventually embraced the concept of *multilateralism* as a complement to its series of bilateral ties. Recognizing the concern to find means of drawing China into more regular patterns of cooperation and security discourse in the region the United States provided encouragement at the Post Ministerial Meeting of ASEAN in Manila in July 1992 for the development of a new multilateral organization. This eventually bore fruit with the establishment of the ASEAN Regional Forum (ARF) that held its inaugural meeting in Singapore in July

1993. Although essentially a consultative body, ARF, which includes the major states of the Asia-Pacific and most of the East Asian states, is seen as an important body for incorporating China within multilateral approaches in the hope that it would develop as a 'good citizen of international society' as it inevitably grows in power.

On the occasion of his first visit to South Korea and Japan in the summer of 1993 President Clinton articulated a vision of an Asian–Pacific community that would buttress the region's economic significance. Seeing the Asia-Pacific Economic Cooperation Forum (APEC) as the only available inter-governmental institution President Clinton took the opportunity of its scheduled ministerial meeting in Seattle in November 1993 to enhance its significance by convening a summit meeting of member states. Clinton depicted an emerging Asian–Pacific community that would unite on free trade issues and develop ever closer ties. The occasion also provided an opportunity for him to meet the President of China and Deng Xiaoping's designated successor, Jiang Zemin, so as to improve the rather acrimonious atmosphere between the two great states of the region. But the difficulties of sustaining the purpose underlining the vision of community soon surfaced as in succeeding months the United States found itself in dispute with many of the states of East Asia about trade and human rights matters. As for APEC itself, it was not at all clear that this essentially consultative organization could bear the more proactive demands which the American government sought to make of it. But at the next meeting in November 1994 in Bogor, Indonesia, it was agreed to set a deadline for the development of free trade among member states for the year 2010 for the industrialized economies and 2020 for the developing economies. However, APEC had yet to develop an effective secretariat capable of transforming the broader purposes into specific blueprints for action.[69] Despite attempts to talk up APEC as a community, there was clearly a long way to go before that could be translated into reality. Nevertheless American leadership had given a new sense of direction to APEC, but it remained to be seen in view of the many demands made upon the American government and the many differences of interest within the region whether American leadership could be sustained.

The conduct of relations with China raised a variety of major problems that involved balancing conflicting goals and differences between the legislative and executive branches of government. There was the constant difficulty of gauging its significance as a power after the end of the strategic triangle, especially as its sustained high economic growth rates and economic impact within the region brought it more sharply into focus as the rising power in the Asia-Pacific and perhaps in the larger world. The revulsion against the Tiananmen killings of 4 June 1989, coupled with the collapse of communism elsewhere and the long term social implications of China's economic reforms persuaded many within the United States that China's communist system could not endure, and that it was America's duty to assist in its passing. Two approaches emerged. One called for encouraging gradual change through a process of constructive engagement, by which first, a dialogue would be continued with China's leaders to prevent a new isolation of the country and to encourage the more reform minded leaders, and second, economic interactions would be continued so as to encourage entrepreneurs and the rise of a new middle class which would gradually push the country towards democracy. The other approach called for the maintenance of sanctions and the exercise of political and economic pressure to uphold human rights and carry out political reform.

President Bush adopted the first approach and Congress espoused the second. Under pressure from Congress, where human rights groups had finally begun to lobby against China in the late 1980s, President Bush imposed sanctions against the Chinese government in the immediate aftermath of Tiananmen. These involved ending meetings between leaders, cutting off military ties and the sale of military related technology, and suspending official financial assistance. Almost immediately, Bush countered his own sanctions by secretly sending a senior official to Beijing and repeating the exercise a few months later. Alarmed by what he regarded as the spiralling downwards of Sino–American relations, Bush took various measures to limit the damage amid strong Congressional criticism. Eventually, there were responses from the Chinese side. But the domestic conflict within the United States soon centred on the MFN issue (Most Favoured Nation – that is, the terms of trade offered to any other state). The renewal of MFN which was due in 1990 became possible in part because there was not the same kind of consensus about the suspension of trade as there was about the suspension of loans and military assistance. Not only were business groups opposed to this, but even others who favoured exerting pressure on China were not prepared to go so far. The final step in improving relations was signified by President Bush's meeting with the Chinese Foreign Minister in Washington in November, after his abstention in the UN

Security Council allowed the passage of a resolution to enable the use of force against Iraq.

That still left Sino–American relations in a fragile condition. There was continued opposition in the US to China's repressive political system and the constant violations of human rights. The Bush and Clinton Administrations constantly chafed at what they saw as Chinese violations of norms and rules concerning the proliferation of weapons of mass destruction and the export of missiles. The Chinese side was also placed under constant pressure for not observing proper trade practices, acting illegally, not protecting copyright and so on. The Chinese tended to react angrily to what was regarded as interference in internal affairs and to unequal treatment. The difficulties were compounded by differences over trading questions. American statistics showed a huge trade deficit as their trade grew, reaching in 1993 $23 billion and in 1994 $30 billion (second only to Japan). The Chinese figures showed a different story of almost balanced trade. While the Bush Administration sought to open up the Chinese market, Congressional critics sought to withhold the renewal of MFN. A practice developed by which Congress would vote against renewal only to be vetoed by the president who was confident that there would not be a majority to override him.[70]

With the advent of President Clinton in January 1993 there was a conjunction of a Democratic President and a Democratic majority in both houses of Congress allowing a different approach to be tried, based on executive action. The President set the Chinese specific criteria for improving their observance of human rights if MFN were to be renewed. Meanwhile despite the growth of trade between them, Sino–American relations worsened as the Americans not only condemned the Chinese on human rights issues, but also accused them of nuclear proliferation, violating commitments to uphold the Missile Technology Control Regime and exporting weapons of mass destruction. Indeed at one point a Chinese ship, the *Yinhe*, was tracked to the Gulf on the charge that it was carrying ingredients for chemical weapons to Iran only to be found in the end to be carrying no such cargo.[71] But in May 1994 when the deadline was due on the MFN issue it was Clinton who backed down even though he acknowledged that the Chinese side had not met his conditions. Business pressure was intense, as was the proposition that many American jobs might be lost, but Clinton was also swayed by the importance of not alienating the Chinese government at a time when its cooperation was sought on Korea. Moreover, America's allies in Asia were anxious about the destabilizing consequences of a breakdown in Sino–American relations. In the event Clinton's *volte-face* did not give rise to great problems with Congress.

Yet Sino–American relations did not greatly improve as the American side was still concerned about China's failings as a trade partner and its failure to meet the minimum conditions for accession to the GATT. American demands were resented by the Chinese side. Negotiations between the two tended to be characterized by public acrimony and by a tendency to reach agreements only at the very last minute. The two sides also differed over Taiwan, which America was obliged by the Taiwan Relations Act to protect. But over and beyond the particularities at stake the conduct of America's relations with China were bedevilled by the incompatibilities of their respective political cultures and by the suspicion that China's emergence as an independent great power would necessarily challenge deep seated American interests. These problems were compounded by the inconsistencies of President Clinton himself and the lack of cohesive decision making on foreign affairs in general that characterized the Clinton Administration.[72] Moreover it seemed as if every issue that Washington regarded as a matter of international principles or norms found the US and the PRC on opposite sides. If many within the foreign policy élite in Washington saw the handling of relations with China as evidence of the Clinton Administration's maladroitness, the view in Beijing was altogether different. By 1995 many of the foreign policy élite in Beijing concluded that a determined effort to contain China's rise to greatness could be detected as a consistent strand running through the apparently disconnected agencies of the different branches of government and the media in the United States.

Many of the American problems with Japan acquired greater salience as the exigencies of the Cold War disappeared. Trade issues in particular loomed larger especially in the American perspective. As the American trade deficit with Japan continued to grow from $46.2 billion in 1985 to $49.1 billion in 1989 and then to $64 billion in 1993 the American government became dissatisfied with the previous approaches that demanded the removal of trade barriers and negotiating voluntary quotas on Japanese exports. Congress in particular reacted to public opinion surveys in 1989 showing that Americans felt that Japanese economic power was a greater threat to the United States than Soviet military power. Two approaches were debated and in time the United States tried each in turn. The first called for opening the Japanese home markets to construct a 'level playing field' and the second demanded a results-oriented policy of managed trade that targeted particular trade balances or market shares of nominated sectors.

President Bush opted for the first. In launching the Strategic Impediments Initiative in 1989–90 the Bush Administration initiated what has been called, 'the most intrusive and sweeping effort by one sovereign country to alter the economic policies and business practices of another'.[73] The Japanese soon responded by arguing that the problems stemmed in part from American structural deficiencies. In the end a two-way agreement was reached, but not before nationalist sentiments were further inflamed on both sides. However, American fears of the alleged dangers of Japanese investment in their country (which was always less than that of Britain) abated as the Japanese recession that began in 1991/92 caused much of that investment to be withdrawn. President Clinton's Administration has tried the managed trade approach, the effectiveness or otherwise of which has yet to be ascertained. But the effect of these trade disputes was to make it more difficult to reach agreements and understandings on other issues.

The security partnership has been damaged by difficulties in establishing co-development and co-production of advanced weapon systems and by continued disagreements over the free-rider issue. The problem in demanding ever greater financial contributions from Japan for American force deployments is that it might heighten resentment in both countries of the image of Americans as hired mercenaries. The tardiness with which Japan agreed to contribute to the initial Western effort in imposing sanctions against Iraq in the summer of 1990 was somewhat mitigated by the alacrity with which the Kaifu government announced its $9 billion contribution to Operation Desert Storm. But even this was qualified and it evoked American criticism about Japan's unwillingness to share the human and political risks.[74]

Although still close, Japanese and American security perspectives in the Asia-Pacific coincide less in the post Cold War era. The question of Japan's territorial dispute with Russia over the four northern islands is no longer seen by the United States as linked with the former strategic objective of containing the Soviet Union. For its part Japan has not shared the high regard that America has given to the domestic regeneration of Russia and it has not invested capital there on a commensurate scale. Japan is less concerned by political repression in China and has fewer reservations about incorporating it in the region's economic system. From a longer term perspective Japan may fear China's great power ambitions and may feel uncertain about the durability and willingness of the commitment to contain them. Meanwhile Japan has finally begun the process of allowing the stationing abroad of members of its Self Defence Forces, but only under UN auspices and so far in strictly non-combatant roles. Japan is approaching the point at which it will have satisfied the credentials to become a permanent member of the UN Security Council and the United States will have to decide upon the character of its relations with an increasingly more assertive and independent Japan.

American policy towards the two Koreas is shaped by global as well as regional concerns. It is the prospect of the acquisition of nuclear weapons by the North and the implications that would have for further nuclear proliferation in Northeast Asia and in the Third World that gives a global dimension to what would otherwise be the regional issue of unravelling the last vestige of the Cold War. This gave rise to tortuous and inconsistent diplomacy by the United States and by the Clinton Administration especially. It was partly a question of divided counsel in Washington and partly the difficulty of matching the regional and global priorities.

By 1991 the Americans had confirmed their suspicions about the nuclear facilities being developed by the North and demanded that it submit to inspections by the International Atomic Energy Agency. It eventually agreed but only after President Bush had removed all remaining nuclear warheads from the South at the insistence of the South. President Bush was then subject to criticism in Washington for having given away his main bargaining chip for nothing. In the event IAEA inspections took place in 1992 and evidence was found that some nuclear facilities had been used for purposes other than had been admitted. The North then refused to allow mutual inspections as previously agreed with the South. There then followed a long series of stonewalling by the North and prolonged talks between the North and the US amid talk of sanctions and other threats. The Clinton Administration in particular appeared to take determined stands only to fail to carry them through. It also reversed itself on a number of tactical issues about the negotiations. But after the visit to Pyongyang in May 1994 by former President Carter it appeared that new progress was possible. Even the death of Kim Il-Sung in July did not bring the new negotiating process to a halt.

A complex agreement was eventually agreed on 13 August 1994, by which Pyongyang agreed in effect to give up over a five-year period its suspected capability to develop nuclear weapons in return for an American commitment to satisfy its more immediate energy needs with oil supplies to the value of $5 billion, and arrange for the provision of two new light-water reactors and other high-tech products. The United States also undertook to normalize diplomatic relations and reduce barriers to trade and investment. Although it was appreciated that the agreement could unravel during the complex process of its enactment the agreement was hailed as a breakthrough and it had the effect of diffusing the immediate crisis.[75] But two long term difficulties would require astute diplomacy. One problem centred on the fragility of the North and the role of the South. The South is keen to supply the two reactors as part of its general agenda of establishing economic influence over the North with a view to developing a gradual process of reunification. The North, however, seeks to bolster its own standing by reaching independent arrangements with the United States at the expense of the South. The other problem stemmed from the uncertainties inherent in the relationship between the US and the PRC. As the principal major powers engaged in Korea a deterioration in their relations could unsettle the immediate external setting that made the agreement possible in the first instance. Nevertheless there is an expectation that the agreement should hold as it manifestly serves the interests of the principal parties.

The much criticized and inconsistent American diplomacy over Korea especially under President Clinton should not be regarded as simply a feature of his general diplomacy, but it must be understood within the constraints that applied in this context. The unilateral use of force was ruled out because of the uncertainties of success and the dangers of unleashing a wider war. The application of sanctions by the United Nations would have required the consent and active participation of China. This was unlikely in view of Chinese fears of the possible consequences of the probable collapse of the North. Meanwhile by the application of pressure and by leaving the Chinese little alternative but to use such influence as they possess in Pyongyang, the United States was able to show that the North had not 'got away with it' and that this was not an easy option for other mavericks to acquire nuclear weapons.

Despite initial hesitation President Clinton attempted to provide leadership in the region as a whole by convening a summit for the annual meeting of the Asia-Pacific Economic Cooperation (APEC) forum in November 1993 with a view to transforming it into a more formal free trade area. Given its consultative character, the well known reservations of ASEAN to being marginalized by the combined economic interests of the US and Japan, and the difficulties of coping with the enormous diversities of the economies of the member states, little could be expected in the short run. But as against that the initiative was widely welcomed as a means of keeping the United States directly engaged in the region. Problems arose, however, as the Clinton Administration soon picked quarrels with its Asian partners on trade and human rights questions that were perceived as challenges to their respective domestic, political and economic orders. That in turn raised questions about the seriousness of the American commitment to the region as articulated by President Clinton.

By way of conclusion it may be noted that as a Pacific power, the United States cannot but be engaged in the region. But the primary question is whether there will continue to be sufficient domestic support in America to sustain a role as the 'regional balancer' and guarantor of stability that was envisaged in the 1990 and 1995 Pentagon reports and as desired by its friends and allies in the region. This in turn raises the question as to whether the inconsistencies of the Clinton Administration reflect deeper problems of the diffusion of power in the American political system that militate against the development of a coherent foreign policy especially in the post Cold War era. Two issues about American leadership are of particular concern in the region. First, for how long will the American public continue to underwrite the security of allies whom it regards as unfair trade competitors. Second, how will America accommodate the rise of Chinese power. The first issue will determine how soon and in what way Japan may strike out on its own and the second will shape Chinese behaviour in the region in the immediate future. More generally, the American response to these challenges will shape the future balance of power in the Asia-Pacific.

NOTES AND REFERENCES

1 Cited in James C. Thomson, Jr., Peter W. Stanley and John Curtis Perry, *Sentimental Imperialists: The American Experience in East Asia* (New York: Harper & Row, 1981) p. 192.
2 For the accounts of Acheson, see Ronald L. McGlothlen, *Controlling the Waves: Dean Acheson and US Foreign Policy in Asia* (New York: W. W. Norton & Co. 1993) pp. 26–40; and for those of Kennan see John Lewis Gaddis, *Strategies of Containment* (Oxford: Oxford University Press, 1982) pp. 76–79.
3 For a sustained, if unsympathetic, account see Christopher Coker, *Reflections on American Foreign Policy Since 1949*, (London: Pinter Publishers Ltd, 1989).
4 See Hans J. Morganthau, *A New Foreign Policy for the United States*

(London: Pall Mall Press, 1969) p. 15; and more generally, Henry Kissinger, *Diplomacy* (New York: Simon & Schuster, 1994) which contrasts unfavourably American idealism with traditional European statecraft.

5 See for example, Bernard H. Gordon, *New Directions for American Policy in Asia* (London and New York: Routledge, 1990) p. 7; and President Theodore Roosevelt who in 1903 stated that America must oppose any who would be 'top dog' in Asia, cited in Lau Teik Soon and Leo Suryadinata (eds) *Moving into the Pacific Century: The Changing Regional Order* (Oxford: Heinemann, 1988) p. 3. See also John Lewis Gaddis, 'The Modern World: World War I to 1984' in Michael P. Hamilton (ed.) *American Character and Foreign Policy* (Grand Rapids: William B. Eerdmans Publishing Co., 1986) p. 38.

6 Michael H. Hunt, *Ideology and U.S. Foreign Policy* (New Haven: Yale University Press, 1987).

7 Perhaps the most notable writer on this theme is Akira Iriye. See in particular Iriye (ed.) *Mutual Images: Essays in American–Japanese Relations* (Cambridge, Mass.: Harvard University Press, 1975). See also Warren I. Cohen, *America's Response to China: A History of Sino–American Relations* (New York: Columbia University Press, third edition, 1990).

8 See W. I. Cohen (*op. cit.*) Michael H. Hunt, *The Making of a Special Relationship: The United States and China to 1914* (New York: Columbia University Press, 1983); and John K. Fairbank, *The United States and China* (Cambridge, Mass.: Harvard University Press, fourth edition, 1983).

9 Thomson *et al. Sentimental Imperialists* (*op. cit.*) Chapter 8, pp. 106–33.

10 Gaddis, *Strategies of Containment* (*op. cit.*) especially pp. 51–53.

11 There are many examples in his *White House Years* and *Years of Upheaval* (London: Weidenfeld & Nicolson and Michael Joseph, 1979 and 1982 respectively). But his discussion of the opening to China brings out very well his irritation with the bureaucratic ways of the State Department in outlining agendas based on long established issues and in determining their priorities through institutional bargaining. These he felt obstructed the diplomacy based on changes in the balance of power. Consequently, his secret diplomacy tended to bypass the State Department altogether. See *The White House Years*, Chapter XVIII, pp. 684–732.

12 The classic, but perhaps exaggerated and much disputed account, is that of Graham T. Allison, *Essence of Decision: Explaining the Cuban Missile Crisis* (Boston: Little Brown, 1971).

13 For general accounts of the significance of public opinion see James N. Rosenau, *Public Opinion and Foreign Policy: An Operational Formulation* (New York: Random House, 1961) Chapter 4. See also, Charles W. Kegley, Jr. and Eugene R. Wittkopf, *American Foreign Policy: Pattern and Process* (New York: St Martin's Press, 1991) Chapter 9. For a more historical survey see Melvin Small, 'Public Opinion' in Hogan *et al. Explaining the History of American Foreign Relations* (Cambridge: Cambridge University Press, 1991) pp. 165–76.

14 Michael J. Hogan, 'Corporatism' in Hogan *et al. Explaining the history of American Foreign Relations* (*op. cit.*) pp. 226–36.

15 Thomas J. McCormack, *China Market: American Quest for Informal Empire 1893–1901* (Chicago: Chicago University Press, 1967); and Stanley Bachrack, *The Committee of One Million: 'China Lobby' Politics 1953–1971* (New York: Columbia University Press, 1976).

16 Morganthau, *A New Foreign Policy . . .* (*op. cit.*) p. 15.

17 William R. Louis, *Imperialism at Bay* (Oxford: Oxford University Press, 1978) p. 285.

18 Dean Acheson, *Present at the Creation* (New York: W.W. Norton & Co. 1969 – reissued 1987) p. 229. For the broader significance attached to Japan see John Lewis Gaddis, *Strategies of Containment* (Oxford: Oxford University Press, 1982) Chapter 3; and Ronald L. McGlothlen, *Controlling the Waves: Dean Acheson and US Foreign Policy in Asia* (New York: W. W. Norton & Co., 1993) Chapter 2.

19 W. G. Beasley, *The Modern History of Japan* (London: Pall Mall, third edition, 1981).

20 For a critical account see Frank H. Golay, *The Philippines, Public Policy and National Economic Development* (Ithaca: Cornell University Press, 1961).

21 Michael Leifer, *Indonesia's Foreign Policy* (London: George Allen & Unwin, 1983) pp. 19–26.

22 For a critical account see Bruce Cummings, *The Origins of the Korean War* 2 vols (Princeton: Princeton University Press, 1990). For a careful historian's analysis see Peter Lowe, *The Origins of the Korean War* (London: Longman, 1986). On the demobilization see, John Lewis Gaddis, *Strategies of Containment* (Oxford: Oxford University Press, 1982), p. 23.

23 Nancy Bernkopf Tucker, *Patterns in the Dust: Chinese-American Relations and the Recognition Controversy* (New York: Columbia University Press, 1983).

24 For an account of the impact of the speech on Mao and Stalin see Sergei N. Goncharov, John W. Lewis and Xue Litai, *Uncertain Partners: Stalin, Mao, and the Korean War* (Stanford: Stanford University Press, 1993) pp. 101–4.

25 As Kissinger has pointed out these were the precise terms which General Douglas MacArthur, then Commander of America's Pacific Forces, had used in public in March 1949 to define the 'line of defense'. *Diplomacy* (*op. cit.*) p. 475.

26 Bruce Cummings, *The Origins of the Korean War* 2 Vols (Princeton: Princeton University Press, 1990), Vol. 2, pp. 423–28 argues that it was understood by all concerned that South Korea was included in the defence perimeter. Michael Schaller, *Douglas MacArthur: The Far Eastern General* (Oxford: Oxford University Press, 1989) pp. 161, 163, 172: and John Merril, *Korea: The Peninsular Origins of the War* (Newark: University of Delaware Press, 1989) pp. 166–67 argue to the contrary that Korea was excluded. Goncharov *et al. Uncertain Partners* (*op. cit.*) pp. 141–42 present evidence that the North Koreans told the Soviets in the Spring of 1950 that the Americans would not intervene, but that Stalin was not altogether convinced.

27 Evelyn Colbert, *Southeast Asia in International Politics 1941–1956* (Ithaca: Cornell University Press, 1977) pp. 204–8.
28 Truman statement of 27 June 1950 cited in *ibid.* p. 477.
29 Paul H. Nitze, 'Grand Strategy Then and Now: NSC-68 and its Lessons for the Future', *Strategic Review* Vol. 22, No. 1, Winter 1994, pp. 16–17.
30 'Appendix' in Gaddis, *Strategies of Containment* (*op. cit.*) p. 359, where he gives the percentages of GNP allocated to defence for the three years as 4.6, 6.9 and 12.7 respectively.
31 Kissinger argues the case very strongly in his *Diplomacy* (*op. cit.*) Chapter 19.
32 David Rees, *Korea: The Limited War* (London: Hamish Hamilton, 1964). For recent accounts of the war see, Max Hastings, *The Korean War* (London: Michael Joseph, 1987); and Jon Halliday and Bruce Cummings, *Korea: The Unknown War* (London: Viking Penguin, 1988).
33 Acheson, (*op. cit.*) p. 544.
34 Kimura Hiroshi and K. O. Sarkisov, 'Japan and the Soviet Role in East Asia' in Warren I. Cohen and Akira Iriye (eds) *The Great Powers in Asia 1953–1960* (New York: Columbia University Press, 1990) pp. 165–67.
35 Although the Americans thought that the threat had been instrumental in effecting an agreement Chinese researchers forty years later have tended to play down its significance. See Rosemary Foot, 'Nuclear Coercion and the ending of the Korean Conflict', *International Security*, vol. 13, no. 3, Winter 1988/89; and Zhang Shu Guang, *Deterrence and Strategic Culture: Chinese–American Confrontations, 1949–1958* (Ithaca: Cornell University Press, 1992) p. 133.
36 Nancy Bernkopf Tucker, *Taiwan, Hong Kong, and the United States: Uncertain Friendships* (New York: Twayne Publishers, Macmillan Publishing Co., 1994) p. 41.
37 Gordon H. Chang, *Friends and Enemies: The United States, China, and the Soviet Union, 1948–1972* (Stanford: Stanford University Press, 1990).
38 J. H. Kalicki, *The Pattern of Sino–American Crises: Political-Military Interactions in the 1950s* (Cambridge: Cambridge University Press, 1975).
39 For a succinct and skilful analysis of the evolution of American strategic thinking see Robert S. Litwak, *Detente and the Nixon Doctrine* (Cambridge: Cambridge University Press, 1984) Chapter 1, 'America as the Night-Watchman State 1947–1968', pp. 11–47.
40 Cited by Walter LaFeber, *The American Age: US Foreign Policy at Home and Abroad 1750 to the Present* (New York: W. W. Norton & Co. second edition, 1994) p. 593.
41 *ibid.* p. 593. The irony of this should be noted since it was precisely the prospect of such an exercise by the Soviet Union that was to alert Kissinger and Nixon six years later to the advantages to the United States of preventing such an exercise.
42 W. W. Rostow, cited in Gaddis, *Strategies of Containment* (*op. cit.*) p. 231.
43 Harry Harding and Melvin Gurtov, *The Purge of Luo Jui-ch'ing: The Politics of Chinese Strategic Planning* (Santa Monica: Rand Corporation R-548–PR, 1971).
44 Gaddis, *Strategies of Containment* (*op. cit.*) p. 240.
45 Allen S. Whiting, *The Chinese Calculus of Deterrence* (Ann Arbor: University of Michigan Press, 1975) pp. 170–95.

46 Cited in Evelyn Colbert, *Southeast Asia . . . (op. cit.)* p. 205.
47 Colbert, *Southeast Asia . . . (op. cit.)* p. 204.
48 Gary R. Hess, 'The American Search for Stability in Southeast Asia: The SEATO Structure of Containment' in Cohen and Iriye, *The Great Powers . . . (op. cit.)* pp. 272–95 and Colbert *Southeast Asia . . . (op. cit.)* Chapter 11.
49 Michael Leifer, *Indonesia's Foreign Policy (op. cit.)* pp. 50–51.
50 Dwight D. Eisenhower, *Waging Peace: The White House Years, 1956–1961* (New York: Doubleday, 1965) p. 607.
51 For a succinct analysis see Michael Leifer, *The Foreign Relations of New States* (Melbourne: Longman Australia, 1974) pp. 79–80. See also Kissinger, *Diplomacy (op. cit.)* pp. 645–47 for an argument that America could have intervened successfully with a relatively small force to have stopped the war in South Vietnam from erupting at an early stage, but it was prevented from doing so by a mixture of misplaced idealism and the remoteness of the country in American consciousness.
52 Lyndon B. Johnson, *The Vantage Point: Perspectives of the Presidency 1963–1969* (New York: Holt, Reinhart and Winston, 1971).
53 See the discussion in Litwak, *Detente and the Nixon Doctrine (op. cit.)* Chapters 3 and 4.
54 Henry Kissinger, *The White House Years* (London: Weidenfeld and Nicolson and Michael Joseph, 1979) p. 192. See also Chapter VI for his account of the 'First Steps Toward China'.
55 Kissinger, *The White House Years (op. cit.)* p. 867.
56 *ibid.* p. 913.
57 Michel Oksenberg, 'A Decade of Sino–American Relations', *Foreign Affairs*, vol. 61, no. 1, Fall 1982, p. 180.
58 See Chapter 27 in Henry Kissinger, *Diplomacy* (London: Simon & Schuster, 1994) pp. 674–702 and p. 692 in particular.
59 For a balanced discussion of the strengths and weaknesses of the Soviet position see Paul F. Langer, 'Soviet Military Power in Asia' in Donald Zagoria (ed.) *Soviet Policy in East Asia* (New Haven: Yale University Press, for the Council on Foreign Relations, 1982) pp. 255–82.
60 Oksenberg, 'A Decade . . .' *(op. cit.)* p. 183.
61 Harry Harding, *A Fragile Relationship: The United States and China Since 1972* (Washington, DC: The Brookings Institution, 1992) p. 86 and more generally, Chapter 3. See also Tucker, *Taiwan, Hong Kong and the United States . . . (op. cit.)* pp. 132–40.
62 *ibid.* p. 94.
63 *ibid.* p. 136.
64 For a discussion of the latter point see Bernard K. Gordon, *Political Protectionism in the Pacific* (London: IISS, Adelphi Paper, 228, Spring 1988). For divergent views of US–Japanese relations on these matters see, Kathleen Newland (ed.) *The International Relations of Japan* (Basingstoke: Macmillan, 1990); Takeshi Inoguchi and Daniel I. Okamoto (eds) *The Political Economy of Japan* vol. 2 (Stanford: Stanford University Press, 1988), Edward J. Lincoln, *Japan's Unequal Trade* (Washington DC: The Brookings Institution, 1990); and Roger Buckley, *US–Japan Alliance Diplomacy 1945–1990* (Cambridge: Cambridge University Press, 1992).

65 Address to the UN General Assembly 8 October 1990, cited in Kissinger, *Diplomacy* (*op. cit.*) p. 804–5.
66 US Department of Defense, 'A Strategic Framework for the Asian Pacific Rim: Looking towards the 21st Century' (Washington, DC: April 1990).
67 *International Herald Tribune* 28 February 1995.
68 For extensive discussion of American security dilemmas in the late 1980s see, William Tow, *Encountering the Dominant Player: US Extended Deterrence Strategy in the Asia-Pacific* (New York: Columbia University Press, 1991). For analyses of the early 1990s see, the articles on America and Asia by Robert A. Scalapino, Bernard K. Gordon and Stephen W. Bosworth in the *Foreign Affairs* series, 'America and the World' for 1989/90, 1990/91 and 1991/92 respectively (Vols 69/1, 70/1 and 71/1).
69 John McBeth and V. G. Kulkarni, 'APEC: Charting the Future', *Far Eastern Economic Review* (*FEER*), 24 November 1994, pp. 14–15.
70 For a detailed account up to the end of 1990 see Robert S. Ross, 'National Security, Human Rights, and Domestic Politics: The Bush Administration and China' in Kenneth A. Oye *et al.* (eds) *Eagle in New World: American Grand Strategy in the Post-Cold War Era* (New York: HarperCollins, 1992). For a carefully considered account of Sino–American relations during the course of the Bush presidency see Harding, *A Fragile Relationship* (*op. cit.*) Chapter 8, 'Deadlock'.
71 Nayan Chanda, 'Drifting Apart', *FEER*, 26 August 1993, pp. 10–11.
72 Harry Harding, 'Asia Policy to the Brink,' *Foreign Policy*, No. 96, Fall 1994, pp. 57–74.
73 Mike M. Mochizuki, 'To Change or to Contain: Dilemmas of American Policy Towards Japan' in Oye *et al.* (eds) *Eagle in a New World* (*op. cit.*) p. 344.
74 See Mochizuki (*op. cit.*) pp. 348–53.
75 The main points of the diplomacy over the North Korean 'bomb' can be followed in the successive issues of *Strategic Survey* (London: IISS) beginning with issue 1991–92. For an account of the agreement see Nigel Holloway and Shim Jae Hoon, 'North Korea: The Price of Peace', *FEER*, 25 August 1994, pp. 14–15.

5 The Soviet Union/Russia and the Asia-Pacific

The Soviet Union and the new Russia will be treated together, but in sequence. If the Soviet Union was a global power the new Russia is more of a regional power. The demise of the Soviet Union in 1991 and its replacement by Russia have fundamentally changed the character of the relations between the Eurasian state and the countries of the Asia-Pacific, as has indeed happened even more strikingly elsewhere in the world. In addition to the loss of the capabilities of a superpower, another significant change was the abandonment of communism and the concomitant claim to lead a world wide communist movement. Nevertheless there are important continuities. First, it is important to recognize that despite its universalist communist pretensions, a Russian imprint on Soviet conduct was always evident even though its depth may have been disputed.[1] Second, and by the same token, the Soviet legacy is evident in many respects even as the leaders of the new Russia grope towards a different future. Importantly, the new Russia has been regarded internationally in some respects as the heir of the Soviet Union. For example, it assumed without question the Soviet permanent seat on the UN Security Council. And, like the Soviet Union before it, the new Russia still aspires to be recognized as a global power alongside the United States. In this respect Russia still disposes of a nuclear arsenal of superpower dimensions and its military industries can still produce advanced weapons systems.

The new Russia has also inherited the borders of the former Soviet Union, except of course, where these were taken over by the new states formed from the old Soviet Republics. In the Asia-Pacific, broadly defined, these include the five Asian Central Republics of Turkmenistan, Uzbekistan, Tajikistan, Kyrgyzstan and Kazakhstan. The last three together with Russia share a border with China's Xinjiang Autonomous Region and accordingly impinge directly on the narrower definition of the Asia-Pacific used in this book. All five states are members of the Commonwealth of Independent States (CIS) with Russia as the key member. Those bordering China negotiate remaining border issues collectively, which in practice tends to mean that the new Russia has succeeded to most of the old border and territorial disputes of the former Soviet Union which the union itself had inherited from Tsarist Russia.

Despite the loss of vast tracts of lands to the former Soviet Republics, Russia is still the world's largest state, stretching across the vast Eurasian landmass from the Baltic to the Pacific. In that respect both the Soviet Union and Russia have tended to regard the Far East as an outpost, a point of vulnerability to be defended, rather than a gateway to the Asia-Pacific – even though the rhetoric of presidents Gorbachev and Yeltsin may have suggested otherwise.

The conduct of Soviet policy towards the Asia-Pacific since 1945 has been shaped by the competing priorities of global, regional and domestic security and ideological concerns. Ideological concerns, as understood here, do not refer only to the doctrinal matters of Marxism–Leninism, but rather to the practical consequences at home and abroad that arose from the claim by successive Soviet leaders to be at the head of a world wide communist movement. Global issues centred primarily on the strategic relationship with the United States and regional ones focused primarily upon China, Japan, Korea and Vietnam.

Domestic concerns about the region arose largely as a consequence of the vast geographical expanse of the Soviet Union. This has contributed to a sense of insecurity, at one level, about the thinly populated Russian Far East that was supplied by the Trans-Siberian Railway and by sea via the Indian Ocean, both of which were vulnerable to interdiction in war time. Indeed it was the tyranny of distance that caused the Russian explorers and traders to retreat from northern California in the first half of the nineteenth century and for the government to sell Alaska to the United States in 1867.[2] The wars fought with Japan in the first half of the twentieth century for dominance in Korea, Manchuria and inner Asia established a linkage between defeat abroad and upheaval at home and they also came to illustrate the strategic necessity of avoiding having to fight a war on two fronts. That historical legacy combined with the Soviet goal of matching and perhaps exceeding the United States in military terms as a fellow superpower found expression in an over-militarized approach in the Far East.

At perhaps deeper levels the distant Russian outposts in the Far

East illustrated ambiguities about the sense of identity of this vast Eurasian state. The uneasy suspension between East Asia and Western Europe has led Russian people, as Dostoevsky noted, to be regarded as Europeans in Asia and as Asiatics in Europe.[3] It has been argued persuasively that 'the Soviet far east is an extension of European Russia into Asia'.[4] Although three-quarters of the Soviet Union lay in Asia and about 30 per cent of the Soviet population lived in its Asian lands, the Soviet Union neither considered itself nor was it considered by others to be Asian. It was not invited to the first Asian–African conference in Bandung in 1955, nor did it evince any desire to attend. When it sought to attend the abortive follow-up conference ten years later in Algeria, it did so mainly in order to spike the guns of its Chinese adversaries. At most, Soviets and Russians have thought of themselves as Eurasians. Any Asian identity that was claimed was done for political advantage, as for example when Stalin greeted a visiting Japanese foreign minister in 1941 with the toast: 'You are an Asiatic, so am I.'[5] The Soviet Union has been rightly described as 'a power in East Asia but not an East Asian power'.[6] Pacific Russia has not been integrated into the region. With the exception of the decade of the special relationship with China in the 1950s the economic links with East Asia have been of minimal significance. Since the break with China, trade with Pacific Asia has averaged at between 5 to 10 per cent of Soviet total trade, and with the exception of the Asian communist countries Soviet trade accounted for a negligible proportion of that of individual Asian countries.[7] The absence of significant economic and political intercourse with the countries of the region meant that once the conflict with China emerged in the 1960s Soviet policy in East Asia became excessively reliant on military means.

IDEOLOGICAL AND INSTITUTIONAL INFLUENCES ON POLICY

The Soviet Union came into existence as a result of the Bolshevik Revolution and despite its many changes it bore the marks of its birthright until its demise nearly seventy-five years later. Perhaps the most important of these was the absolute rule by the highly centralized communist party that was subject to no state law and was constrained only by its evolving customary practices and legitimized by its ideology. The party's role in principle was to construct the socio-economic basis for socialism and communism at home and to promote the expansion of other revolutions abroad. In practice, however, the legacy of Lenin – the founding father – was ambiguous as the revolution had bequeathed a state as well as a new international movement. Very early on, by the Treaty of Brest Litovsk of 1918, it was decided to put the interests of preserving the nascent state before the prospects of extending the revolution. Moreover, after the civil war and the defeat of the allied intervention in 1921 it was argued that the revolutionary state could co-exist with the hostile capitalist states which encircled it because of the implacable rivalries between them. In other words, the Leninist legacy in foreign affairs was ambiguous in at least two respects: first, the Soviet leadership being in command of both party and state was charged with promoting revolution abroad through leading foreign communist parties whose interests at critical moments could be sacrificed for those of the Soviet state; and second, the state leaders were enjoined to exploit divisions between other states in order to ensure the survival of the Soviet Union and co-exist with them while simultaneously seeking to undermine them through their communist parties.[8]

A further legacy from the Leninist era was a view of the relations of the Soviet communist party state with the nationalist movements in the colonies and semi-colonies of Asia and, by extension, Africa. Seen as the weak link of imperialism, it was the Soviet obligation to assist their struggles for independence even though they might be led by representatives of their upper and middle classes, as this was seen as weakening the metropolitan capitalist states and hastening the revolutionary process there. In addition to giving rise to another layer of ambiguity in adjusting the priorities of immediate Soviet state interests and those of the independence movements, it also raised problems of adjusting both those interests to those of communist parties in Asia. Thus even Lenin found it expedient to turn a blind eye to the persecution of local communists in order to cultivate relations with Kemal Ataturk the radical nationalist leader of Turkey.[9]

Adam Ulam, perhaps the most notable Western interpreter of Soviet foreign policy, has argued that some of the very qualities that brought the Bolsheviks to power also served to handicap them:

> Extreme suspiciousness of every movement and every government not fully sharing their ideology and an underestimation of the staying power of Western countries, and a view of international politics as consisting mainly of the clash of economic and military interests.[10]

With the advent of Stalin, these traits were emphasized still further. Under his personal dictatorship the doctrine of 'socialism in one country' that had emerged earlier to deal with the disappointment of the failure of revolutions elsewhere in Europe was now interpreted as requiring the total subordination of communist parties everywhere to the needs of the Soviet state whose security interests were defined exclusively in accordance with the astute but paranoid outlook of one man. But not even he was able to dominate the Chinese Communist Party, so that the incipient contradiction of seeking both to encourage and to control the Chinese comrades remained to haunt both him and his successors after the Second World War. 'Socialism in one country' acquired an even more autarchic character when, through his programme of forced collectivization of agriculture and national industrialization, begun under the First Five Year Plan in 1928, Stalin also created an economic system that clearly cut off the Soviet Union from the international (capitalist) economy. Moreover the terror and the climate of distrust that it nurtured at home had a corresponding effect in heightening suspicion of the outside world.

As applied to foreign policy, Stalin consistently argued that the Soviet Union faced an encirclement by capitalist powers with whom war at some stage was inevitable and yet that in the short term it was possible to live in peaceful co-existence with these powers by taking advantage of their irresolvable rivalries. This left it open to the Soviet leader to make temporary alliances and to practice balance of power politics. This in fact characterized his policies in the 1930s, which culminated in the Nazi–Soviet Pact in 1939. The war time alliance with Britain and America did not lead Stalin to share Roosevelt's internationalist outlook. And, as the conferences of Teheran and Yalta were to show, what Stalin practised was traditional power politics in order to promote the survival and development of Soviet goals as he understood them. Thus in East Asia he sought the restitution of Russian borders and privileges going back to the nineteenth century and the establishment of buffer zones around the Soviet Union that he could dominate.

The countries of East Europe and North Korea emerged as communist states closely modelled on and tightly controlled by the Soviet Union – in practice by Stalin. In theory the socialist camp was bound by the principles of socialist internationalism – allegedly a higher form of relationship than obtained between the Western allies. Tito's Yugoslavia refused to accept Stalin's control and was expelled from the camp in 1948. It went on to develop a form of nationalist communism that was to complicate the Soviet Union's relations with its East European satellites thereafter. With the establishment of a communist regime in China an even greater challenge was posed to Soviet control of the socialist camp. The Soviet leadership of the socialist camp and the international communist movement, it is clear, was both a source of strength and of weakness. Under Stalin's leadership it provided strategic depth and a source of inspiration that communism could spread under a single banner and thus face the future with confidence, especially as the Soviet form of industrialization had supposedly been vindicated by the triumph of the war against Germany. At the same time leadership of the communist world carried the seeds of weakness as the Soviet Union was necessarily obliged to maintain the new communist regimes and underwrite their security while all the time being vulnerable to the emergence of nationalist challenges that could question the authority and the universal validity of that leadership which was expressed in ideological terms. Even the great Stalin had been challenged by Tito. As was to be seen it was one thing for him to shrug off the challenge, but that was to be beyond his successors in the end. The ideological challenge that China was to present augmented those of strategy, politics and other points of difference. Stalin's successors were also to find the price of leadership of the socialist camp was the need to tend to the demands of far flung members such as Vietnam and Cuba in ways that did not always accord with their sense of Soviet interests. Moreover, as many have pointed out, it was easier to have relations with non-communist India than communist China and easier to manage a neutral buffer state like Finland than a fellow communist one such as Poland, Hungary or Czechoslovakia.

With the death of Stalin, no one man was able thereafter to exercise total dominance over the Soviet party and state and it became possible to identify different interests and personalities exercising influence over policy. Indeed, bureaucratic interests became sufficiently evident for scholars to speculate about the extent to which policy making was subject to bargaining between the major organizations of state.[11] Although first Khrushchev and then Brezhnev were the principal leaders in their day, the ouster of the first in 1964 by his erstwhile colleagues and the general conservatism of the latter suggested more of an oligarchy. Meanwhile the diversity of Soviet industrial society became more evident. Although remaining a dictatorship the Soviet Union gradually acquired authoritarian as opposed to totalitarian characteristics. The machinery of political repression was still in operation, but debates and differences of opinion were more freely aired and in time a more subtle view of international relations gradually took root.[12] By the same process ideology lost its vitality and cohesiveness, while still remaining the core of legitimacy for the rule of the Communist Party of the Soviet Union (CPSU).[13]

By the end of the Brezhnev era Soviet foreign policy had become greatly militarized in the sense that as its economy stagnated and the appeal of ideology declined, much of the exercise of Soviet foreign relations depended on the direct or indirect use of armed force. That was the only arena in which the Soviet Union could be counted as a superpower rival to the United States. Doubtless that contributed to the growing influence of the military in Soviet life where the military industrial complex is now said to have accounted for 40 per cent of the Soviet GDP. But this did not mean that the military had come to dominate decision making or that the communist party had lost its grip on the leadership.[14]

With the accession of Gorbachev in 1985 and his reformist agenda, foreign policy came to reflect more the domestic priorities of those reforms which were in turn a reaction to the deep seated systemic crisis prevalent in the Soviet Union. At the same time, by seeking cooperation with the international community, Gorbachev and the new personnel whom he had advanced sought to encourage the process of open reform at home. By initiating the processes of demilitarization and de-ideologization in the interests of domestic reform he initiated policies that led to the acceptance of asymmetrical arms control agreements and the withdrawal of Soviet forces and support from regional conflicts elsewhere.[15] They also contributed to endorsing the principle of self determination, even for socialist states, that led to the collapse of communism in Eastern Europe and the independence of the Baltic States. These developments have generally been seen as the result of restructuring from above rather than the response to unstoppable pressures from below. Yet in turn the reforms unleashed a plurality and confusion of forces that accelerated the process of disintegration. Perhaps the key problem was that the economic reform at home only succeeded in undermining the existing inefficient but functioning economic system, with the result that the only domestic return for the policies of demilitarization and closer integration with the Western world was economic chaos and the loss of support from potential domestic constituencies. By the summer of 1991 time had run out for both Gorbachev and the Soviet Union. The result in the Far East of the general process of demilitarization and disintegration was to emasculate Russia as a significant great power in the Asia-Pacific.

STALIN'S POWER POLITICS IN EAST ASIA, 1945–53

The terms of the Yalta Agreements of February 1945 made clear Stalin's fundamental security objectives in the Far East. By seeking to retain effective control over Outer Mongolia (the Mongolian People's Republic), restore the rights and territories lost to Japan in 1904 and re-establish the extra-territorial rights exercised by Tsarist Russia in Manchuria, Stalin aimed at enlarging the buffer zone on the Soviet periphery and having access to warm water ports. As he explained to the Nationalist Chinese foreign minister who had come to negotiate a treaty of friendship and alliance later that summer, 'in the past, Russia wanted an alliance with Japan in order to break up China. Now we want an alliance with China to curb Japan'.[16] Before the treaty was signed on 14 August, the United States had dropped the atom bomb on Hiroshima that in effect obviated the American need for the Soviet intervention on which the agreement to Stalin's terms had been based. Stalin hastily declared war on Japan and launched a rapid offensive against the Japanese forces in Manchuria and Korea. This not only ensured Soviet control of Manchuria, but it also guaranteed Soviet dominance of Korea north of the 38th parallel as agreed with the United States earlier in August 1945.[17]

At the end of the Pacific War Chiang Kai-shek's government sought an alliance with Moscow principally to ensure Soviet recognition and to limit the cooperation between Soviet and Chinese communist forces in Manchuria. At this point Stalin calculated that the communists could not win a civil war with the nationalists and he was greatly concerned about the implications for Soviet national interests from the American commitment to the nationalists. Indeed part of his reason for establishing a buffer zone across northern China was to make provision against a China that would be linked to America in ways envisaged by Roosevelt's war time planners. Hence he urged Mao to put aside armed struggle and enter a coalition government with Chiang Kai-shek. It was not until the Autumn of 1947 when the military position shifted in favour of the Chinese communists that Stalin accepted Mao's claims that the communists would win and that the Americans would not be able to stop them. Indeed in January 1948 when Stalin made his famous admission to Milovan Djilas that he had been proved wrong by the

Chinese communists, he also noted that China was different from Greece, where America, 'the strongest state in the world' would never let the communists win.[18]

Stalin's calculations took into account the global balance and especially the situation in Europe. He refused to recognize the Democratic Republic of Vietnam as proclaimed by Ho Chi Minh in September 1945. Even though Ho had proved to be a trustworthy agent of the Comintern, Stalin's European priorities made him assign a higher importance to helping the communists in France gain entry into the coalition government. With the outbreak of the Cold War Stalin insisted that the East European states reject the offer of Marshall Aid. The ever suspicious Stalin began to tighten his personal dominance of the 'socialist camp' in Europe through extensive purges of so-called 'cosmopolitans' and others. This was also related to the confrontation with Tito and his expulsion from the socialist camp. Mao and the Chinese could not be treated in the same way. China was simply too big and the independent national character of its revolution as led by Mao was too well established.

This did not mean, however, granting the Chinese communists a free hand. After the establishment of the People's Republic of China in October 1949 Mao went to Moscow to negotiate a new treaty of alliance. He arrived on 16 December and he did not return to Chinese soil until 27 February 1950. In the two months of hard bargaining Stalin succeeded in holding on to most of the gains he had claimed at Yalta and in the 1945 treaty with the nationalist government. But he also had to accept the burden of agreeing to come to China's assistance in the event of an attack by Japan 'or any state allied with her and thus being in a state of war'. The latter qualification was to prove its importance in the Korean War and other Sino–American military engagements. Stalin may have disappointed his new Chinese allies with the paltriness of his economic assistance limited to the value of $300 million spread over five years, but he pleased them with his secret military assistance.[19]

Stalin greatly embarrassed Mao by insisting on an 'Additional Agreement' by which the Chinese had to agree to forbid citizens from third countries from residing or undertaking any economic activities in Manchuria or Xinjiang. Apparently, Stalin had in mind to insist on the exclusion of Americans in particular from all parts of China, but eventually he settled for these bordering provinces, the effect of which was to limit any foreign economic influence there to the Soviet Union alone. The only precedents for this were the unequal treaties of the imperialist era. The Chinese leaders had to swallow this bitter pill the day after they, together with Stalin, had repudiated Acheson's accusations that Stalin had special designs on these territories. The pill was not sweetened by the inclusion of the Soviet Far East and Central Asia in the zones denied to third parties as that ban was already in place. No wonder the protocol was kept secret for forty years. Mao's bitterness was apparent when in 1958 he referred to these provinces as Soviet colonies.[20]

As for broader Asian concerns, Stalin was keen to designate China as having primary responsibility for the further expansion of communism there without at the same time conceding that Mao had made independent contributions of universal significance to the treasure house of Marxism–Leninism. In this way China could be a kind of buffer to absorb such retaliation as the Americans might choose to carry out without Stalin conceding to Mao a leading role (albeit of a lesser kind) in the international communist movement. This was signalled in the order in which the two communist giants recognized the Democratic Republic of Vietnam in January 1950. China was first on 18 January and the Soviet Union followed almost two weeks later. During this time of course Mao was still in Moscow. Interestingly, Ho Chi Minh visited Moscow while Mao was there but Kim Il-Sung did not.

'Throughout the early postwar years, Kim was wholly dependent on Moscow, and North Korea can be justly called a Soviet satellite.'[21] The Soviet Union also extended more military aid to the North in the late 1940s and early 1950s than to Mao's armed forces during the same period. Despite the good personal relations between the Chinese and North Korean leaders, the lead-up to the war was determined almost exclusively by Stalin and Kim until a few months before the attack by the North. Kim had been pressing Stalin as early as 1949 for permission to unify the country by force. Attempts to ignite a takeover of the South by guerilla warfare had failed. But Kim nevertheless hoped for a successful uprising once his troops had broken through the defences of the South. He claimed that a swift victory would ensue. Stalin, however, was concerned with the wider picture. He once told Kim that 'the Americans will never agree to be thrown out of [Korea and] lose their reputation as a great power'. But Stalin did not dismiss the possibility and consulted Mao. After all it was China, in Stalin's calculations, that would have to bear the brunt of any failures. Apparently, Mao first thought that the Americans would intervene only to backtrack on this view later. In any event Stalin continued to prevaricate. When Kim visited him in April Stalin stressed his preoccupation with the situation in the West and urged him to consult Mao as he had 'a good understanding of Oriental matters'. In effect Stalin had consented subject to Mao's approval. But Mao had been manoeuvred into a situation where he could not disapprove. Having obtained Stalin's promise of support for an invasion of Taiwan, Mao could hardly warn against the prospect of American intervention in Korea without inviting Stalin to draw similar conclusions about Taiwan. According to Chinese scholars, Mao, not surprisingly, urged Kim to rely upon guerilla warfare.[22] But Kim followed his own course with Soviet assistance.

Stalin's objectives were mixed: locally, he hoped to expand his buffer zone in Asia. From a regional perspective, by dominating the Korean peninsula he could expect to bring pressure to bear upon Japan that would limit its utility to the United States; moreover, he could also expect to widen the rift between Mao and the United States. Indeed were Kim to fail, as indeed was the case, China and America could be expected to be engaged in hostilities which would thereby draw a line between them. From a more global strategic perspective America was bound to become more engaged in Asia – hopefully at the expense of its engagement in Europe – whether as a result of a humiliating loss or as a result of taking on a commitment in Korea. On the face of it the calculating Stalin had everything to gain and nothing to lose whatever the outcome.

In the event Stalin's gains were mixed. The reaction of the Western allies in Europe – the key geopolitical centre between East and West – was to consolidate the newly established NATO with an integrated command structure. Moreover, the American intervention led to a huge rearmament programme enabling the United States to be engaged militarily in Asia without reducing its deployments in Europe. Japan became even more tightly locked into the American alliance network. China, however, became more estranged from the United States and, in Stalin's terms, more trustworthy. But China had also proved itself in war to be a great power in its own right and it was a China whose leaders had acquired new grievances against the Soviet Union. Right to the end Soviet interests were put ahead of those of China even in Korea where the terms for beginning truce negotiations in 1951 as initiated by Moscow included neither the issue of Taiwan nor China's entry into the UN.[23] It has been suggested that in his last year Stalin began to soften his confrontationist approach in Europe and to recognize that the newly independent post colonial states were a new factor in world politics.[24]

His death in March 1953 left the issue to be explored by his successors.

PEACEFUL CO-EXISTENCE AND THE ASIA-PACIFIC, 1953–71

The policies of Stalin's successors towards the Asia-Pacific can only be understood within the context of Moscow's larger concerns. The death of the great tyrant meant that the harsher aspects of Soviet totalitarian rule had to be relaxed both at home and within the socialist camp. It meant too that China could no longer be circumscribed within the confines of limited economic assistance and the Korean stalemate. Beyond that the Soviet advances in nuclear weaponry and the means of delivery were narrowing the gap with the United States and thereby leading to a situation in which understandings had to be reached if a disastrous nuclear war were to be averted. Further afield the significance of the newly emerging Third World countries was gradually making itself felt.

The response of the Soviet leaders to these challenges may be subsumed within the concept of peaceful co-existence. As re-defined by Khrushchev it went beyond the terms set out by Lenin and Stalin to mean a long term policy based on the recognition that the advent of the nuclear balance of terror ruled out the notion of a war between the socialist and capitalist camps, let alone the thesis that such a war was inevitable. Since the antagonism between the two camps remained this called for a precarious combination of conflict and cooperation. It also meant that the Soviet Union would have to ensure that it achieved strategic parity with the United States so as to allow the momentum of what was termed 'the correlation of forces' (i.e. the sum total of economic, military and political factors) to work out in favour of the Soviet side. In other words peaceful co-existence meant peaceful competition. Moreover, that was understood to operate not only between the two camps, but also within the capitalist countries where it was argued that a peaceful transition to communist rule would now be feasible under the new conditions. Clearly the promotion of violent revolution in the countries of the West risked undermining the prospect of developing peaceful competitive relations with their governments.

Within the socialist camp peaceful co-existence, as understood by the Soviet leaders, meant that its members could enjoy considerable autonomy under Soviet leadership. In practice, however, the upheavals in Poland and Hungary in 1956 and in Czechoslovakia in

1968 showed that this was an elusive formula to follow and only Soviet intervention or the threat of intervention kept the integrity of the camp intact. Socialist internationalism was interpreted as allowing the Soviet Union to intervene to uphold the essence of the fruits of socialism as understood by its leaders. But the corollary was that the Soviet Union had to expend precious economic resources in support of these countries. Those that were beyond the effective reach of Soviet military intervention such as Cuba, Vietnam or North Korea were able to use the concept of socialist internationalism to obtain material assistance and security guarantees.

As applied to the Third World the new approach allowed the Soviet Union to promote itself as the 'natural ally' of those countries whose leaders professed to be opposed to imperialism and the West as well as to promote wars of national liberation against colonial rulers. This was soon extended to mean that with Soviet support Third World countries under the right sort of revolutionary leadership could transform themselves in time into fully fledged socialist countries.

The three dimensions of peaceful co-existence were linked and may be seen as requiring precarious balances to be drawn in each sphere as well as between them. Matters were aggravated by the vehement opposition of the Chinese from the late 1950s onwards. Sensing that Khrushchev's attempts to establish a *modus vivendi* with the United States would require the subordination of their interests and aspirations to those of the Soviet Union, China's leaders and Mao in particular began by opposing his policies. But given the character of relations between communist states Mao soon raised their differences into an ideological dispute. He went on to accuse the Soviet leaders of turning their backs on Marxism–Leninism and becoming in effect 'New Tsars'. Mao used the same ideological critique to attack what he regarded as his domestic opponents so that the Cultural Revolution that began in 1966 was suffused with anti-Sovietism. By 1969 armed conflict took place on their borders and amid ill concealed threats of a possible Soviet attack upon China's nuclear installations Beijing opened its doors to Washington, thus fulfilling one of Moscow's worst nightmares.

The immediate response of an uneasy collective leadership to Stalin's death was to agree to the armistice in Korea and to continue to put greatest emphasis upon their European strategic interests. Consequently during the Geneva Conference in June 1954 they joined with the Chinese in pressuring Ho Chi Minh to accept the division of the country at the 17th parallel principally because the Soviet Union was keen to support the then French government which was opposed to West German entry into the European Defence Community. But now the Soviet leaders had to deal with a more assertive China. After the Conference the Chinese Premier, Zhou Enlai, toured Eastern Europe (hitherto a strict Soviet preserve) in a manner befitting a leader of an independent major power. From there he visited India and Burma and together with their leaders declared the Five Principles of Peaceful Coexistence which from a Soviet point of view either implied a kind of 'Asia for Asians' approach that excluded them or a claim that the Chinese could make independent ideological innovations of universal significance without reference to them.

In September Khrushchev, the First Secretary of the CPSU and the effective if not unchallengeable leader, headed a delegation to China. As his own, perhaps self-serving, account showed it was an uneasy occasion in which mutual distrust was evident behind the scenes, but withheld from public view.[25] All the Soviet special privileges in China – the last of the old imperialist style foreign concessions – came to an end, including Port Arthur (Lushun) and Dairen (Dalian) despite the 1950 agreement, reaffirmed in 1952, that the withdrawal would await a peace treaty with Japan. Agreements were also reached to extend Soviet economic assistance to China, which, together with earlier agreements, were to provide the basis on which Chinese industrialization could take off. The divisions and uncertainties in the Kremlin had certainly increased China's leverage.

However, Sino–Soviet divisions were apparent in Asia. While the Chinese pursued their own course at Bandung, the Soviet leaders cultivated separate relations with India. In February 1955 a substantial aid agreement was reached and in June Prime Minister Nehru was lavishly received in Moscow. Unlike the Chinese, the Soviets could offer significant aid to Third World countries and also show that they could compete in this area with the United States. At the end of the year Khrushchev visited India where he sided with his hosts over Kashmir. Pakistan, which had formally allied itself with the United States, was told that relations could improve when it returned to an 'independent' policy. The Soviet Union was building 'influence by intervening in a regional quarrel on behalf of the party engaged in struggle against "imperialism and its lackeys" '.[26] But it was also establishing a separate and close relationship with a big Asian power other than China.

The year 1955 was a year of substantial thawing of Soviet external relations. In addition to developing new policies towards Third World countries, a naval base was evacuated in Finland, Soviet troops withdrawn from Austria and the neutralization of the country within the Western economic framework was agreed. More remarkably, the Soviet leaders made their peace with Tito on bended knee. However, as the Geneva Conference of the big four demonstrated, only the 'atmospherics', but not the substance of East–West relations had improved.[27] An exploration of relations with Japan was begun that culminated in a joint declaration in October 1956, marking the restoration of diplomatic relations and stipulating *inter alia* that two of the four disputed islands would be returned to Japan upon conclusion of a peace treaty.[28] The underlying Soviet objective was to weaken Japan's ties with the United States. Interestingly, in subsequent years Soviet leaders went so far as to deny the existence of a territorial dispute. It was not until the accession of Gorbachev that the issue was once again openly recognized.

The culmination of the thaw was Khrushchev's enunciation of a new doctrine of peaceful co-existence and his denunciation of Stalin at the Twentieth CPSU Congress in February 1956. As we have seen, these moves were to prove explosive in their consequences, at first within Eastern Europe and then later in relations with China. Although Sino–Soviet differences were apparent at the conference of the ruling communist parties convened in Moscow in 1957, the somewhat chastened Khrushchev promised to assist the Chinese in the development of an atomic bomb. The promise was rescinded in 1959. In 1958 Khrushchev floated the idea of holding a summit meeting on the Middle East to which he suggested that India be invited without even mentioning China. After a visit to China the idea was dropped. The Chinese later charged Khrushchev with failing to support them during the Taiwan off-shore island crisis of 1958 until the high danger mark had passed. In 1959 as Khrushchev was preparing to visit President Eisenhower trouble erupted on the Sino–Indian border and, to the chagrin of the Chinese, Khrushchev had a statement of regret issued in which both sides were treated as equals, rather than following the customary practice of siding with a fellow socialist country. In April 1960 the Chinese finally went public with their complaints and accusations.

This brought out into the open the fact that Soviet policy in the Asia-Pacific was designed not only to counter the American policy of containment, but also to compete for influence with China. During the 1950s and the early 1960s the North Koreans and the

Vietnamese took care to avoid taking sides while sympathizing in practice with the Chinese. Much as they needed access to the more advanced Soviet weaponry their interests required a harder rather than a softer line to be taken with Washington. Khrushchev, for his part, did not want any crisis or confrontation that might be caused by what he regarded as their intransigence or belligerence, to damage his approach to Washington. Consequently, Khrushchev's reaction to the Laos crisis of 1961/62 was to wash his hands of Indo-China. It was only after his ouster in 1964 that the new Soviet leaders returned. In fact Premier Kosygin was visiting Hanoi in February 1965 when the Americans began to bomb the country.

The American intervention in Vietnam worked out well for the Soviet Union. In strategic terms it engulfed the United States in a massive outpouring of resources that weakened it both at home and abroad. It provided a breathing space for the Soviet Union to catch up with America in nuclear weaponry and in the development of its navy. In diplomatic terms the Soviet Union gained from the American difficulties with its allies and from the condemnation of the non-aligned. It also gained from being solicited for its good offices to negotiate a settlement. Although it was unable to win over the Chinese for 'united action' in Vietnam, in a curious way the Soviet Union benefited from that too. Since it alone could provide the advanced weaponry necessary to counter the US bombing the Chinese could be painted into a corner, accused of putting their own interests ahead of their responsibilities to Vietnam. And no amount of Chinese rhetoric could dispel the Vietnamese doubts that Mao reached an understanding with the Americans that they would not extend the war to China, before unleashing the Cultural Revolution at home. Interestingly, it was the same reassurance that the Americans would keep the war limited that enabled the Soviet Union to benefit at so little cost to itself.

As far as non-communist Asia was concerned, the Soviet leaders continued and deepened their support for India which became perhaps the best ally of the Soviet Union. The new Soviet leaders manoeuvred cleverly in the 1965 war between India and Pakistan. They helped India shrug off the rather clumsy ultimatum from China and were able to offer their good offices to both sides in brokering the Tashkent Agreement the following year. Khrushchev also attempted to cultivate relations with Indonesia. President Sukarno visited Moscow in 1956 and Khrushchev reciprocated in 1960. Considerable arms were sold and Moscow lent its support to Sukarno's campaign to obtain West Irian from the Dutch. In the event Sukarno may be said to have used the Soviet support and weaponry to elicit sufficient American pressure on the Dutch to yield. When the Sino–Soviet conflict surfaced it suited Sukarno to side with the Chinese on ideological grounds and this was confirmed when he initiated the campaign of *Konfrontasi* against the establishment of Malaysia in 1963. The Soviet Union had to accept the 'loss' of a country which at one point it had supplied with amounts of advanced weaponry that in the non-communist world were exceeded only by Egypt and India.[29] The Soviet leaders were to draw quiet satisfaction from the failure of the 1965 coup, the demise of the pro-Chinese Communist Party of Indonesia (PKI) – notwithstanding the bloody massacre of hundreds of thousands of their members and of local ethnic Chinese – and the side-lining of Sukarno himself. Thereafter the Soviet leaders tried to develop business-like relations with Singapore, Malaysia itself and Suharto's Indonesia. But the Soviet role was minor as it was not significant economically and these countries were essentially pro-Western, as became clear with the negative Soviet response to the formation of ASEAN in 1967. Nevertheless it served President Suharto's claims to be non-aligned to have relations with the Soviet Union, even though in practice that did little to affect the fundamental pro-Western stance of his government.

It may be worth noting that with regard to Japan the Soviet Union did little to encourage its government to loosen ties with the United States. The possible concession on the disputed islands that was envisaged in 1956 receded from view as Soviet leaders began to insist that the matter had been settled and that there was nothing to discuss. Instead Soviet statements tended to take a threatening tone especially as its Pacific fleet gained in substance. It is nevertheless important to recognize that its deployments had as much to do with the strategic relationship with the United States as it had with regional issues.[30]

The launching of the Cultural Revolution in 1966 seems to have been taken by the Soviet leaders as requiring a military response. A defence treaty was signed with the Mongolian People's Republic leading initially to the stationing there of two Soviet divisions and air support forces in 1967. By 1970 the number of Soviet ground divisions opposite China grew to thirty-three from the eighteen deployed in 1965.[31] Soviet diplomats sounded out how the West might respond to a Soviet strike against China's nuclear facilities. The Chinese initiated hostilities on the riverine border in March 1969 to which the Soviet Union responded with superior force three weeks later. But it was not until a successful incursion by a Soviet column took place in Xinjiang that the Chinese eventually agreed to begin talks. In 1969 Brezhnev also launched a scheme for establishing a collective security system in Asia. But this was seen as so obviously directed against China that not even India responded positively. Soviet pressure, however, proved in the end to be counterproductive as it brought about precisely what had been feared all along in Moscow – a *rapprochement* between Beijing and Washington.

THE IMPACT OF TRIPOLARITY, 1971–89

It is important to recognize at the outset that at 'a fundamental level, Soviet perceptions of the triangle turned out to be far more a function of the state of US–Soviet relations than perceptions of US–Soviet relations were a creature of the triangle'.[32] In other words, important though China was, the central concern of Soviet foreign policy remained the United States. This was obviously true of the larger international strategic situation and of relations in such crucial areas as Europe and the Middle East. But even here, until Sino–Soviet relations began to improve from about 1980 onwards the Soviet leaders were anxious lest the heretical and implacable Chinese should adversely influence American attitudes towards détente. It has also been argued that an unstated reason for the Soviet Union to retain something of a numerical advantage in some of the categories of weapons agreed with the Americans in the Strategic Arms Limitation Talks was to cope with the nascent and growing Chinese nuclear capabilities.[33] From a Soviet perspective the significance of China during the period of tripolarity may be seen in two separate phases: in the course of the first phase that lasted until 1979 the Chinese were regarded as the main source of anti-Soviet hostility seeking to push the United States from the path of détente towards confrontation; in the second phase from 1980 until about 1987/88 the role was reversed as Washington was cast in the role of seeking to restrain Beijing from reaching an accommodation with Moscow.[34]

Whatever the case elsewhere, the relations with China and the impact of tripolarity were at the heart of Soviet policy in the Asia-Pacific. Indeed the first Soviet response to Kissinger's surprise visit to Beijing in July 1971 was to bolster the Indian position and show up the underlying weakness of China in its incapacity to assist its Pakistani ally during its hour of need as the civil conflict in East

Pakistan threatened to dismember the country. A treaty was signed with India in August obliging the two parties to consult in the event of war. Although Kosygin urged Mrs Gandhi not to intervene, the Soviet Union rushed substantial quantities of arms and gave unstinted support to India in the United Nations when it overran East Pakistan in December. The United States then claimed to have saved West Pakistan by sending a carrier force to the Bay of Bengal. The Pakistani Prime Minister Z. Bhutto then visited Moscow in March 1972 to normalize relations, leading to the Simla Agreement of July 1972 by which the Soviet Union persuaded India and Pakistan to re-establish relations. The realities of Soviet power had prevailed over the Sino–American arraignment and even their ally Pakistan had to defer to Soviet power to extricate itself from the threat of further dismemberment.[35] From a longer term perspective the Soviet leaders hoped that the alliance with India would serve their larger purpose of containing China. But it is generally thought that 1971 was the high-point of Indo-Soviet relations. Thereafter relations remained close, but India proved reluctant to align itself fully with subsequent Soviet policy in the region.

The Soviet approach to Japan that on the face of it looked promising in the early 1970s was to end badly from the Soviet point of view. Far from being able to build on the détente established with the United States and on the Japanese desire to maintain equidistance between China and the Soviet Union, coupled with a Japanese interest in exploring the commercial possibilities of investing in Siberia, the Soviet leaders succeeded only in alienating Tokyo and in driving it towards closer relations with Beijing while cementing its ties with Washington. Following the normalization of relations between Tokyo and Beijing in September 1972, Japanese Prime Minister Tanaka visited Moscow the following year – the first such high level visit for seventeen years. While Brezhnev pressed for the joint development of Siberia Tanaka pressed for the return of the 'Northern Territories'. The resulting communique was ambiguous at best but it did call for further negotiations towards a peace treaty (which by implication would have to deal with the issue in one way or another). By the time these were initiated Moscow had objected, in February 1975, to the mention of an 'anti-hegemony' clause in the proposed peace treaty between China and Japan. Soviet leaders continued their objections and also proposed that a treaty of good neighbourliness be signed with them in lieu of a peace treaty – thereby shelving the territorial issue, the existence of which Foreign Minister Gromyko was denying by the summer.

In an attempt to employ coercive diplomacy the Soviet Union began to increase the movements of its much enhanced air and naval forces to the north of Hokkaido. Even at this point the Japanese Foreign Minister, Miyazawa, sought to restore some flexibility in the Japanese relationship with its two giant neighbours by criticizing Chinese visitors in July 1976 for commenting adversely on the Soviet refusal to return the territories. This brought him even more openly into the Sino–Soviet cross fire. By this point the Soviet side had been emboldened by the 1975 Helsinki Agreements which ratified the Soviet–imposed borders in Eastern Europe. Other matters soon intervened including the defection of a Soviet pilot with his highly secret MIG-25 and the Soviet unilateral extension of its territorial waters by 200 miles, thus deepening the territorial and fisheries disputes with Japan. Meanwhile the Soviet side had raised so many difficulties over the question of Japanese cooperation in the exploitation of resources in Siberia that Japanese companies lost interest. In the end the Soviet side sought to compel the Japanese to drop their insistence on a peace treaty in favour of a treaty of good neighbourliness. Amid military exercises in the 'Northern Territories' on an unprecedented scale Moscow warned Japan against signing a peace treaty with China. Japanese public opinion, never well disposed towards the Soviet Union, became distinctly hostile and under pressure from the United States the Japanese government duly signed the Treaty of Peace and Friendship with China on 12 August 1978. Far from manoeuvring cleverly to take advantage of the differences that existed between the other three great powers of the Asia-Pacific, Soviet diplomacy and heavy handed attempts to use its new found military power in the region only brought them together. By the end of 1978 the Soviet Union faced a hostile alignment of China, the United States and Japan.[36]

Various explanations have been advanced for the peculiar rigidity of the Soviet treatment of Japan. Some have argued that the obsessive Soviet anxieties about China blinded their leaders to the possibilities of flexible manoeuvre.[37] Others have argued that the problem lay in the deep seated feelings of hostility and resentment in Russian attitudes towards Japan which saw concessions in terms of a loss of prestige, rather than as an opportunity to strike a bargain.[38] It has also been suggested that beginning in the early 1970s the Kurile Island chain acquired a new strategic significance as a critical line of defence to protect the Soviet submarine-based second strike capability that was located in the Sea of Okhotsk.[39] Perhaps it was a mix of all three combined with a Soviet desire to have a clear *quid pro quo* in the sense of tangibly separating Japan from the United States in the 1950s or from China in the 1970s.

The Soviet tendency in the 1970s to use its greater military power and especially its naval forces to promote and establish regimes to its liking in parts of Africa and the Middle East had contributed to the souring of relations with the United States and to the decay of détente. That had doubtless weakened the position of those such as Secretary of State Vance in the Carter Administration who stressed the importance of reaching arms control agreements with the Soviet Union and maintaining a policy of even-handedness between it and China. In the Soviet view it was the visit to China by the American National Security Adviser Z. Brzezinski in May 1978 that marked the turning point towards the hardline approach favoured by China.[40] By this stage it was clear that Sino–Vietnamese relations had substantially deteriorated as the Chinese had publicly accused the Vietnamese of seeking regional hegemony and the Vietnamese had encouraged tens of thousands of ethnic Chinese to leave. The Soviet response was to heighten the differences and assist Vietnam in its plans to force out the troublesome Chinese-supported Khmer Rouge government from Cambodia and impose an alternative more to their liking. In June Vietnam was admitted to the Moscow dominated Council for Mutual Economic Assistance (CMEA or Comecon) and in November a treaty was signed similar to that signed with India before its attack upon East Pakistan.

As if to demonstrate contempt for Chinese power despite the normalization of Sino–American relations announced on 16 December 1978, Vietnamese forces armed by the Soviet Union invaded Cambodia on 25 December driving the Khmer Rouge to enclaves near the Thai border. Following a successful tour of the United States Deng Xiaoping ordered an attack upon Vietnam in February 1979. Although from a strictly military point of view the war went badly for the Chinese and could be said to have vindicated the military prowess of Vietnam and its backer the Soviet Union, from a strategic point of view the Chinese rammed home a geopolitical message that made the military costs acceptable to them. It soon became apparent that the international and diplomatic consequences were disastrous for the Soviet Union especially in the Asia-Pacific. Vietnam became as much a liability as a strategic asset. Although the Soviet navy gained access to the former American bases in Vietnam, the Soviet Union and its ally were effectively isolated in the region. Continued Chinese pressure was allied to an economic embargo orchestrated by the United States and Japan and by a diplomatic campaign led by the ASEAN countries that ostracized Vietnam internationally and denied legitimacy to the regime it had imposed in Cambodia. The final blow was the Soviet intervention in Afghanistan in December 1979 in which Soviet forces enabled their beleaguered candidate to take over power only to face the prolonged resistance of the Afghani Mojehadin. By 1980 the Soviet Union faced in effect a hostile coalition of all the countries in the Asia-Pacific save Vietnam and the indeterminate North Korea. Even India was less than supportive.

Paradoxically, the Soviet nadir in the early 1980s proved to be a turning point. Relations with the Chinese began to improve. As the Chinese reacted to a change in the balance of forces, with the Soviet Union bogged down and isolated and the United States set on the path of rearmament and determined opposition to the Soviet Union, the Chinese were ready to distance themselves from the US and explore openings to Moscow. This was assisted by the Chinese appreciation of the depth of the economic difficulties in the Soviet Union and by ideological changes associated with the Chinese reforms begun in December 1978 that involved the abandonment of the Maoist ideology of class struggle. New difficulties had also emerged in Sino–American relations. Brezhnev made a few moves to improve relations and left a legacy on which his successors could build.[41]

The main breakthrough occurred under the leadership of Gorbachev. But the higher priority that Soviet leaders habitually attached to relations with the West was evident as Gorbachev turned to the Asia-Pacific only in 1986. In two keynote speeches in Vladivostok in July 1986 and Krasnayorsk in September 1988 Gorbachev in effect acknowledged that past Soviet policy had been a series of costly failures. Seeing the normalization of relations with China as the key to developing better relations in East Asia and to participating in the economic dynamism of the region, Gorbachev made a series of unilateral concessions to the Chinese. These included accepting the Chinese argument that their river borders followed the centre of the main current rather than the line of the Chinese bank (the ostensible cause of the 1969 conflict) and making unilateral troop withdrawals from Mongolia and the Russian far east. Initially, he sought to maintain ties with the Asian communist states, but the Chinese insisted that the Soviet Union withdraw from Afghanistan and above all stop its military assistance to Vietnam, as well as cutting back still further its force levels to the north of China as preconditions for normalization. Finally in 1988 under severe economic pressure at home and from the Americans abroad Gorbachev withdrew from these 'gains' of the late 1970s and early 1980s. The road then opened for Gorbachev's visit to Beijing in May 1989 to normalize relations. The visit itself was overshadowed by the demonstrations in Tiananmen Square, but nevertheless a deal was struck over Cambodia which endorsed a trend that was already evident of the winding down of Soviet aid to Vietnam. In the event the suppression of the students in Beijing a month later opened yet a new gulf between the Soviet and Chinese leaders. Although both sides maintained·correct relations at the state level, the collapse of communism in Eastern Europe further widened the divide between the two sides.[42]

Gorbachev also sought to open the Soviet far east to the economies of the Asia-Pacific, to develop multilateral approaches to addressing security problems and to improve relations with the countries of ASEAN. The Soviet Union squared the circle in the Security Council of avoiding offending either the ASEAN countries or its ally Vietnam, by ensuring that it was not party to the settlement of the Cambodian conflict. Gorbachev, however, failed to address the question of Japan's claims to the Northern Territories until his domestic position was so weak that his 1991 visit to Tokyo failed in its basic objectives of establishing good relations despite the signing of some fifteen agreements. While Gorbachev felt that the territorial issue could only be negotiated once Japan had agreed to join with its Western partners in granting aid and favourable terms for the conduct of economic relations, his Japanese hosts held on to the view that nothing could be done before the territorial issue was settled. Moreover, the Soviet far east lacked the necessary infrastructure of communications, appropriate institutions, etc. to appeal to Japanese companies or to enable the Soviet Union to participate actively in the economic affairs of the region. Having withdrawn its military assistance to Vietnam and having offered no support to its ally in its military engagement with the Chinese over the Spratlys in 1988, the Soviet Union shrunk to insignificance in Southeast Asia. The only clear return for Gorbachev's policies in the Asia-Pacific was the cultivation of relations with South Korea. Unable and unwilling to continue supporting the economy and military of the North, Gorbachev responded to the *Nord Politik* of the South. Unlike the other countries of the region, the South had very good reasons to cultivate economic ties with the Soviet Union. It was a blow to the North and diminished the security threat and, correspondingly, it enhanced the legitimacy and the freedom of diplomatic manoeuvre of the South. These developments led to the normalization of relations as the two presidents met in the United States in June 1991.[43]

THE RE-EMERGENCE OF RUSSIA

The abortive coup by the hardliners that brought about the final disintegration of the Soviet Union, the fall of Gorbachev and the rise of Yeltsin not only ended communist power but it brought into being a Russian Federation and fourteen other republics. The new Russia soon descended into chaos as it struggled along the difficult road of transition towards marketization and a greater degree of democracy. Its foreign policy became very much a product of domestic weakness as it sought to obtain favourable loans from the West amid attempts to assert authority over the newly established republics – the so-called new abroad. The misery and the growing lawlessness of much of Russian social life also sparked a revival of Russian nationalist sentiments. Indeed Russian domestic weakness was to be used in several cases as a diplomatic bargaining counter. For example, the demands for Western economic assistance were predicated precisely upon the greater danger to its nascent democracy and embryonic market forces if that aid were to be denied. Similarly, Russian resistance to conceding territory to others was now explained by reference to the difficulties of the central government in meeting localist and nationalist objections.

Curiously, the collapse of European communism and the disintegration of the Soviet Union has facilitated a marked improvement in Sino–Russian relations. Whatever the private misgivings in Beijing about Gorbachev's role in the fall of communism in Europe and the Soviet Union, it suited both Beijing and Moscow to put aside ideological differences and develop still further their correct relations. This pattern was followed after the accession of President Yeltsin, even though the fall of Leninism in the socialist motherland has increased the pressure on the communist regime in China. High level visits have been exchanged, 97 per cent of their borders have been settled by agreement leaving only two or three riverine islands in dispute. Economic relations have continued to grow so that in 1993 China ranked as Russia's second most important trading partner. With their military rivalry ostensibly behind them, China has bought advanced aircraft and hired hundreds of Russian experts made redundant from the Soviet military industries to work in upgrading Chinese military production. In some ways the pattern of the 1950s has been reversed as the Russians now wish to learn from the Chinese experience of economic reforms. However, the historical and cultural differences allied to the residual geopolitical differences between these two great continental countries imbued with proud nationalist passions will necessarily limit the quality of their partnership.

For the time being Russia is a participant in many of the regional institutions of the Asia-Pacific such as the PECC, ARF, etc. but its effective influence is confined to Northeast Asia. If before it was Soviet strength that was a barrier to making the necessary territorial concessions to Japan, in the 1990s it is domestic weakness and opposition within its far east region that prevents the Russian government from reaching a satisfactory compromise. It remains to be seen whether under the new circumstances a Japan that is undergoing domestic changes and seeking to become a permanent member of the UN Security Council may display a new flexibility by, for example, accepting a Russian concession over the territories at the end rather than at the beginning of a process of accommodation. Russia may also wish to show that its views and interests should not be neglected by displaying a capacity to influence events on the Korean peninsula. Russia may also have a role to play in the establishment of any multilateral approaches towards enhancing regional security. But in the long run Russia will emerge from the margins only once its domestic situation becomes less chaotic. Thus it is unlikely to become a major power in the region again before the next century.

NOTES AND REFERENCES

1 For a discussion with reference to differing schools of thought see Alexander Dallin, 'The Domestic Sources of Soviet Foreign Policy' in Seweryn Bialer (ed.) *The Domestic Context of Soviet Foreign Policy* (Boulder: Westview Press, 1981) pp. 335–408 and in particular pp. 354–56.

2 For a brief account of the latter see Segal, *The Soviet Union and the Pacific* (London: Unwin Hyman Ltd, 1990) pp. 15–23.

3 Cited in John J. Stephan, 'Asia in the Soviet Conception' in Donald S. Zagoria (ed.) *Soviet Policy in East Asia* (New Haven: Yale University Press, 1982) p. 35.

4 Malcolm Mackintosh, 'Soviet Attitudes Towards East Asia' in Gerald Segal (ed.) *The Soviet Union and East Asia* (London: Heinemann, 1983) p. 7.

5 Stephan, 'Asia in the Soviet Conception' in Zagoria (*op. cit.*) p. 36.

6 Gerald Segal (ed.) *The Soviet Union and East Asia* (*op. cit.*) p. 1.

7 A. Herbert and Herbert S. Levine (eds) 'The Soviet Union's Economic Relations in Asia' in Donald S. Zagoria (ed.), *Soviet Policy in East Asia* (*op. cit.*) p. 202 – see also the chapter as a whole pp. 201–28; and Gerald Segal, *The Soviet Union and the Pacific* (*op. cit.*) p. 136 – see also his chapter 'The Economic dimension' pp. 136–85.

8 Among the many accounts that may be usefully consulted see Adam Ulam, *Expansion and Coexistence: Soviet Foreign Policy, 1917–73* (New York: Praeger, second edition, third printing, 1976) Chapters II and III, pp. 31–125; and Alfred G. Meyer, *Leninism* (Cambridge: Harvard University Press, 1957).

9 Helene Carrere d'Encausse and Stuart R. Schram, *Marxism in Asia* (London: Allen Lane, The Penguin Press, 1969) pp. 40–41.

10 Adam Ulam, *Expansion and Coexistence. . .* (*op. cit.*) p. 22.

11 See in particular G. H. Skilling and F. Griffiths, *Interest Groups in Soviet Politics* (Princeton: Princeton University Press, 1971); Erik P. Hoffmann and Frederic J. Fleron, Jr. (eds.) *The Conduct of Soviet Foreign Policy* (Chicago: Aldine/Atherton, 1971); Seweryn Bialer (ed.) *The Domestic Context of Soviet Foreign Policy* (*op. cit.*); and Jiri Valenta and William Potter, *Soviet Decision-Making for National Security* (London: Allen & Unwin, 1984).

12 Margot Light, *The Soviet Theory of International Relations* (Brighton: Wheatsheaf Books Ltd, 1988) and Allen Lynch, *The Soviet Study of International Relations* (Cambridge: Cambridge University Press, 1987).

13 See the general argument of Joseph L. Nogee and Robert H. Donaldson, *Soviet Foreign Policy Since World War II* (Oxford: Pergamon Press, 1988) Chapters 2 and 3, pp. 10–62.

14 Michael MccGwire, *Military Objectives in Soviet Foreign Policy* (Washington DC: Brookings, 1987).

15 Michael MccGwire, *Perestroika and National Security* (Washington DC: Brookings, 1991).

16 *ibid.* p. 3.

17 Max Hastings, *The Korean War* (London: Pan Books, 1988) pp. 15–16.

18 *ibid.* p. 24.

19 For contemporary evidence of Chinese disappointment see John Gittings, 'The origins of Chinese Foreign Policy' in David Horowitz (ed.), *Containment and Revolution* (Boston, M.A.: Beacon Press, 1967) pp. 207–8. For an account (based on Chinese materials recently made available) of the extensive military assistance following Liu Shaoqi's secret visit to Moscow in August 1949 that was increased still further after Mao's visit, see Chen Jian, *China's Road to the Korean War* (New York: Columbia University Press, 1994) pp. 77 and 84. Chen also states that these new materials suggest that China's leaders were eminently satisfied with the character and volume of all Soviet aid. He found no evidence of disappointment. But it should be noted that this is based on selective research materials gleaned from Chinese researchers rather than from first hand access to the Chinese archives.

20 For a fascinating and detailed account of the negotiations and the attitudes of both sides see Goncharov, Lewis and Xue (*op. cit.*) Chapters 3 and 4, pp. 76–129. For the quote by Mao see Stuart R. Schram (ed.) *Mao Tse-tung Unrehearsed* (London: Penguin Books, 1974) pp. 101–2.

21 Goncharov *et al.* (*op. cit.*), p. 131. The subsequent account of Moscow's role in the Korean War relies heavily on their Chapters 5 and 6.
22 Hao Yufan and Zhai Zhihai, 'China's Decision to Enter the Korean War: History Revisited', *The China Quarterly* No. 121, March 1990.
23 Ulam, *Expansion and Coexistence* (*op. cit.*) pp. 533–34.
24 Marshall D. Shulman, *Stalin's Foreign Policy Reappraised* (Cambridge: Harvard University Press, 1963). For a conflicting view see Robert C. Tucker, *The Soviet Political Mind* (New York: W. W. Norton, revised. 1973).
25 *Khrushchev Remembers*, translated by Strobe Talbot (London: First Sphere Books, 1971) Chapter 18, pp. 424–40; and Volume 2 (London: Penguin Books, 1977) Chapter 11, pp. 282–343.
26 Nogee and Donaldson (*op. cit.*) p. 180.
27 *ibid*, pp. 114–17. See also Ulam, *Expansion and Co-existence* (*op. cit.*) pp. 566–69.
28 For a detailed examination of the history and complexity of the competing claims to what the Japanese call the 'northern territories' or 'islands', see John J. Stephan, *The Kurile Islands: Russo–Japanese Frontier in the Pacific* (Oxford: Clarendon Press, 1974).
29 Michael Leifer, *Indonesia's Foreign Policy* (London: George Allen & Unwin, 1983) pp. 62–69.
30 Paul F. Langer, 'Soviet Military Power in Asia' in Zagoria, *Soviet Policy in East Asia* (*op. cit.*) p. 258.
31 Lawrence Freedman, 'The Military Dimension of Soviet Policy' in Segal (ed.) *The Soviet Union in East Asia* (*op. cit.*) p. 93.
32 Robert Legvold, 'Sino–Soviet Relations: The US Factor' in Robert S. Ross (ed.) *China, The United States, and the Soviet Union: Tripolarity and Policy Making in the Cold War* (New York: M. E. Sharpe, 1993) p. 78.
33 Adam Ulam, *Dangerous Relations: The Soviet Union in World Politics 1970–1982* (Oxford: Oxford University Press, 1983) pp. 75–77 and 245–47.
34 Legvold (*op. cit.*) p. 76.
35 This account has drawn on Robert H. Donaldson, *Soviet Policy Towards India: Ideology and Strategy* (Cambridge: Harvard University Press, 1974) especially pp. 225–34.
36 For a detailed account of the relevant Soviet–Japanese diplomacy see Fuji Kamiya, 'The Northern Territories: 130 Years of Japanese Talks with Czarist Russia and the Soviet Union' in Zagoria, *The Soviet Union in East Asia* (*op. cit.*) especially pp. 134–45.
37 This is a point made repeatedly by Adam Ulam. See, for example, *Dangerous Relations* (*op. cit.*) pp. 153 and 245–46.
38 Jonathan Haslam, 'The Pattern of Soviet Relations Since World War II' in T. Hasegawa, J. Haslam and A. Kuchins (eds) *Russia and Japan: An Unresolved Dilemma Between Distant Neighbours* (Berkeley: University of California, 1993).
39 See, for example, Michael McGwire, 'A New Trend in Soviet Naval Developments', *International Defense Review* Vol. 13, No. 5, June 1980. This has been disputed by Haslam (note 36).
40 Legvold (*op. cit.*) pp. 69–70.

41 For an account of the specific steps taken to improve relations see Gerald Segal, *Sino–Soviet Relations After Mao* (London: IISS Adelphi Paper 202, 1985).

42 For a comprehensive account of the lead up to the summit with Deng Xiaoping see Steven M. Goldstein, 'Diplomacy Amid Protest: The Sino–Soviet Summit', *Problems of Communism* (September–October 1989). For an account of policy towards China in the Gorbachev years see Charles E. Ziegler, *Foreign Policy and East Asia: Learning and Adaptation in the Gorbachev Era* (Cambridge: Cambridge University Press, 1993); and for an account of policy towards Southeast Asia see Leszek Buszynski, *Gorbachev and Southeast Asia* (London: Routledge, 1992). For a broader evaluation see Robert A. Scalapino, 'Russia's Role in Asia: Trends and Prospects', in *Russia and Japan (op. cit.)*.

43 For details see Amy Rauenhorst Goldman, 'The Dynamics of a New Asia: The Politics of Russian–Korean Relations', *Russia and Japan (op. cit.)* pp. 243–75; and Ziegler, *Foreign Policy and East Asia (op. cit.)* Chapter 6, pp. 108–27.

6 China and the Asia-Pacific

If the United States and the Soviet Union (until its replacement by the less significant Russia) may be described as global powers with a regional interest in the Asia-Pacific, China may be understood as a regional power with global influence.[1] China's principal security interests are largely concentrated in the Asia-Pacific and its capacity to project power is limited in the main to that region. But the most important threats to its security as perceived by successive Chinese leaders came from one or other of the superpowers and for the first forty years of its existence the PRC treated its security problems within the region as a function of its relations with the two superpowers. The predominance of the superpowers in the Chinese perspective necessarily gave China's regional concerns a global orientation. Indeed in the 1980s it was persuasively argued that China did not even have a regional policy as such.[2] It is only since the end of the Cold War that China's leaders have developed policies which recognize that the future security and prosperity of their country requires the cultivation of close relations with the Asia-Pacific as a whole. This regional orientation does not mean that China's leaders have ceased to think of their country in global terms, but it is a recognition of the centrality of the region to the Chinese economy and of the importance of the fast growing Chinese economy to the region itself. Since the Asia-Pacific region is regarded not only as a major economic centre alongside those of Europe and North America, but also as an engine of growth for the world economy as a whole, China's growing weight within the region serves to enhance its global significance too. However, China's emergence as a rising power has raised new problems for its smaller neighbours in the region as to how best to accommodate it while preserving their independence.

In addition to the strategic factors, China's claims to be considered as a power of global significance arise perhaps most strongly from its historical legacy of centrality. But these claims have also been enhanced by the international recognition they have received. China is the only Third World country to be one of the Permanent Five (P5) members of the UN Security Council. By virtue of the country's size and independent revolutionary achievements China was the only serious rival to the Soviet Union's leadership of the international communist movement. Finally, China's home grown distinction of being the world's most populous country, the heir to one of the world's great civilizations, with a history of continuous statehood reaching back for more than two thousand years has been recognized in the special respect accorded it by diplomatic envoys from throughout the world. As a result China's leaders have tended to claim a leading global role which their country's capabilities do not yet allow them to exercise. The leaders of the PRC have consistently argued that they have a right to be heard on every major problem in the world. It has been argued with some justice that 'without first having acquired the reach of a global power, China acts as if it has already become a world power'.[3]

China's conduct within the Asia-Pacific must be understood against the backcloth of a complex series of factors including its historical legacy, its projection of a multiple international identity and its search for modernity and great power status, as well as the series of interactions with the superpowers and neighbouring countries. China's international relations must be seen as inherently dynamic and unsettled as they reflect the imperatives of domestic renewal and the yearning to achieve genuine standing as a country of the first rank in terms of cultural and scientific achievement as well as in economics and power politics. Meanwhile China's leaders think of their country as one that has yet to recover from the consequences of the humiliations visited upon it by the imperialists in the hundred years from the 1840s to the 1940s. Thus even as China has become increasingly integrated with the international economy and indeed within the Asia-Pacific region, these old grievances continue to be of current significance.

From a geographical point of view China extends beyond the confines of the Asia-Pacific as followed in this book. China not only faces the Pacific, but it also looks into inner Asia and borders on the Indian subcontinent. In fact traditionally China has been a continental power. The centre of gravity of China was inland. Historically it has always been threatened by conquest from the north. Until the advent of the Europeans China had not been challenged from the sea. Despite the fact that considerable commerce took place and that the danger of piracy was ever present, the Chinese authorities traditionally thought of the sea as a barrier rather than a gateway. China, the Central Kingdom, was described as the land 'within the four seas'. Indeed the Chinese authorities found it difficult to understand at first that the conquering Westerners who had come by sea in the nineteenth century nominally to seek trade were fundamentally different from foreigners from central Asia who also sought trading privileges.[4] One of the problems that contemporary Chinese are experiencing is having to shift from a continental to a maritime orientation. In other words it can be argued that, despite China's traditional dominance of East Asia, it is only in the contemporary period that China is becoming a full member of the Asia-Pacific.

THE IMPRINT OF HISTORY

Contrary to the myth of a timeless, unchanging imperial system China's international history is varied and offers a number of different models for contemporary Chinese. Michael Hunt has drawn attention to at least two imperial styles and to what he has called 'a multiplicity of traditions'. These have involved

> virtual political hegemony and cultural supremacy over much of Asia as well as repeated subjugation and internecine strife. They hold up many models of statecraft, from the lofty imperial style to shrewd Machiavellian cunning. They teach the use of brute force, of trade and cultural exchange, of secret diplomacy and alliances, of compromise and even collaboration with conquerors.[5]

All of these except perhaps the first and the last have been on display in one form or another in the international behaviour of the People's Republic of China.

Indeed much of the PRC's approach to the outside world may be seen as an attempt to recapture the past glory which in the views of its leaders had been mercilessly destroyed by the West and by Japan in the course of China's century of shame and humiliation from the 1840s to the 1940s. This yearning for greatness should not necessarily be seen as a drive to expand aggressively at the expense of others. Rather it should be understood as a desire to re-establish China's stature as a centre of civilization which until modern times was superior in terms of culture and technology. The modern world challenged China not only in terms of power, but also in terms of civilization. Accordingly, it was not enough for the Chinese simply to try to catch up with Western military technology, but their society had to be transformed. This has set up a tension between seeking to modernize so as to be sufficiently strong and prosperous in order to prevent a repetition of the humiliating defeats of the nineteenth century, and striving to preserve a distinct Chinese cultural identity. The first calls for integrating with the modern foreign world and the second demands resistance to its alleged malevolent external influences. The tension finds expression in China's attachment to a fierce sense of independence that has made the PRC such a difficult ally down the years. In many ways this relates to anxieties of the Qing and even of the previous dynasty about the possible destabilizing effects upon Chinese society and ways of thought that contact with foreigners and foreign societies might engender. This, of course, has been even truer for the communist leadership of the PRC.

The definition of China's sovereign territory is also associated with the problem of interpreting the legacy from the past. The PRC, like the republic before it, was established both as a break from the past and as a successor to that past. Although new revolutionary beginnings were proclaimed in domestic and foreign affairs, China's sovereign territory was defined in terms of succession to the Qing. This raised ambiguities about claims to certain territories. In 1936 Mao Zedong (in company with leading Chinese nationalists) went so far as to lay claim to the Mongolian People's Republic and called a former tributary state, Korea, a former Chinese colony and proceeded to claim that the Mohammedan and Tibetan peoples would join a future Chinese federation. Tibet at that point was technically under Chinese suzerainty although in practice independent.[6] The more extravagant claims were dropped from the formal agenda after the establishment of the PRC in 1949. Henceforth there was no question of self determination being applied to any of the people living within the then designated Chinese territory or indeed to people in territories claimed to be Chinese, such as Taiwan or Hong Kong. In time it led to the assertion that all the diverse ethnic peoples who lived within China's borders belonged to the 'Chinese family' and had always done so. This had the effect of claiming that members of the same ethnicity who lived on one side of the border were regarded as Chinese and on the other side as alien. It had strange consequences for the writing of earlier history as wars between Chinese armies and nomadic outsiders now had to be treated on many occasions as civil wars.[7] Since all of its borders were said to be the product of unequal treaties imposed by the imperialists, not only did they all have to be re-negotiated, but questions arose as to whether the Chinese might subsequently lay claims to 'lost lands'. In 1964 Mao deliberately raised the spectre of claiming vast tracts of eastern Siberia in the course of the dispute with the Soviet Union.[8]

More generally, there are traditions regarding the conduct of foreign relations that have left their imprint on contemporary practice. Prominent among these is the practice of centrality – being the 'central actor in international dealings, with considerable autonomy'. The Qing characteristically dealt with different peoples in disparate ways using separate bureaucracies. No conceivable links existed between the Qing's southern neighbours and those to the north, so that Qing China 'had no natural allies and no permanent enemies, but a complex of mutually separable relationships with its neighbours'.[9] In the century of 'shame and humiliation' China's leaders found themselves confronting the foreign powers in effect as a group. Accordingly, China's leaders have sought to regain the freedom for manoeuvre and initiative by dealing with foreign powers individually rather than as a unit. In fact the PRC may be said to have displayed a remarkable aptitude as the weaker power in upholding independence by the politics of manoeuvre between the two superpowers. Strange as it may have seemed in the West, one of the abiding fears of Mao and his successors from the 1960s until the demise of the Soviet Union in 1991 was that the two superpowers might establish a condominium. At the same time Chinese traditions of rewarding materially the bearers of tribute and lesser rulers who acknowledged their legitimizing majesty have found parallels in modern times as the PRC has acted (albeit not consistently) as a benefactor of lesser states and clients.[10]

The historical experience of the communist-led revolution and the impact of Mao's strategic thinking, which used to loom large in accounts of underlying influences that shaped the conduct of China's foreign policy, loom less large from the perspective of the 1990s. But it would be a mistake to overlook them altogether, especially as for the first fifteen years of economic reform and openness China's foreign policy was still determined in the last resort by Deng Xiaoping and fellow founding fathers of the party, the army and the state. As long as communist party rule continues in China its historical experiences will necessarily be influential. Ideology may not carry the same weight that it once did, but it cannot be disavowed and it still finds expression in the residual but persistent need to somehow differentiate 'socialist' China from the external 'capitalist' world. The United Front may no longer dominate Chinese approaches to international relationships, but aspects of its approach may still be seen in policies towards Hong Kong and Taiwan 'compatriots' and even towards 'overseas Chinese'. The influence of Mao's doctrines of people's war may have declined in the armed forces and, since the end of the threat from the north, they are no longer important as a deterrent factor. Nevertheless as long as the Chinese armies lag behind the modernity of others, Mao's doctrines will not be completely abandoned and the experience of triumphing in the revolution against superior and more modern forces will still contribute to the self confidence of China's rulers.

Historical cultural influences have shaped Chinese foreign policy making in several ways. As in the past, foreign relations in general have been regarded as extraordinarily sensitive and have been subjected to tight central control. Indeed decision making has been dominated first by Mao Zedong and then by Deng Xiaoping. Although Deng has not exercised the total dominance of his predecessor, he has nevertheless made the key decisions on the most important issues. As a result of the economic reforms and the policy of openness since 1978 the number of groups and institutions involved in foreign relations has greatly expanded and it is possible to identify a growing influence being exercised by discrete groups such as the military, economic and regional interests, and perhaps even élite opinion as registered by experts.[11] Nevertheless Mao and Deng have exercised personal power almost like latter day emperors. Indeed it can be argued that they have enjoyed still greater power as they have been less restrained by custom and ritual. This has facilitated the PRC's remarkable capacity to change alliances and move in new directions.

As presented by China's leaders, the transformations that have taken place in their foreign relations are nothing more than wise adaptations to changing international circumstances. The external world has always been portrayed as being in flux. Far from damaging the standing of a leader the adaptability works to enhance the esteem with which his statesmanship is held. The moral tone of Chinese insistence on principles reflects a political culture that has long prized 'ethics more than the law, moral consensus more than judicial process and benevolent government more than checks and balances'.[12] In contrast with the Western penchant for the legalist approach the Chinese prefer more broadly worded agreements that leave ambiguities for time to solve. Despite their formal adherence to Marxism–Leninism, China's leaders' views of international relations have been state centred and concerned with behaviour and relationships rather than with underlying socio-economic structures. The critical question that has determined Chinese views of a given state has tended to centre on its relations with China and its stance towards China's principal enemy. Until the end of the Cold War this largely depended on China's relations with Washington and Moscow. Since these could change quickly and abruptly, Chinese behaviour towards other countries could seem puzzling and Machiavellian. However, as seen from China's point of view, its leaders were acting responsibly and morally. Indeed most of Chinese 'principled' pronouncements on world affairs invoke a moral tone, with pretensions to moral leadership. Alongside this has been a suspicion of entangling alliances and of multilateral commitments that, in binding China, are regarded as restricting its capacity for independent manoeuvre. As many have noted, even when China's leaders championed the cause of the Third World they stood aloof rather than join any Third World international groups.[13]

Finally, these experiences may explain the extraordinary tenacity with which China's leaders have held on to the Western traditional sense of inviolable sovereignty. But it is also important to recognize that the Leninist tradition and the lessons of the revolutionary warfare that brought the communists to power also made them the most astute practitioners of balance of power politics. They perceived this not just in the classical Western sense of calculating the distribution of power and acting accordingly. Nor did they quite follow the Soviet way of seeking to identify the correlation of forces that purported to take into account more than just the straightforward military factors. Rather they tended to understand power relations as a dynamic process in which it was important to appreciate the momentum of change. Thus they described the precise change of balance in Soviet–American relations on the eve of their famous *rapprochement* with the United States in 1971 as the Soviet Union being on the offence and the United States on the defence (*Sugong Meishou*).

THE PRC'S RELATIONS IN THE ASIA-PACIFIC

The unification of China under a new and vigorous government was bound to present problems of adjustment to the countries of the Asia-Pacific. It was not clear how its historical assertions of centrality would be addressed in the very different modern world. Similarly there was uncertainty as to how particular disputes over territory and borders as well as the legacy of the colonial era would be handled. How would the new China relate to the newly independent states and their regimes? What would be the relations between the new China and the overseas Chinese? These more particular concerns became inextricably linked for the first forty years after 1949 by the impact of the Cold War and by China's changing conflictual relations with the two global powers. The end of the Cold War has raised new issues about adapting to China's economic integration within the region and its rising power at a time of increasing doubts about the durability of the American military commitment to East Asia. The evolution of the relations with the Asia-Pacific are best treated chronologically in order to demonstrate the significance of China's relations with the two superpowers.

Opposition to the United States, 1949–69

The alliance with the Soviet Union, 1950–58

The alliance, the details of which were outlined in the previous chapter, tied the PRC in an uneasy dependence on the Soviet Union. Born of necessity and joined under conditions of distrust, the alliance provided Mao with a security treaty against an attack by the United States, in return for which he had to recognize the independence of Mongolia and to concede a whole set of special privileges for the Soviet Union in Manchuria and Xinjiang, more extensive even than had been exacted by the Tsars. Such hopes that the PRC leaders may have entertained about conquering Taiwan were shattered by the American decision to protect the island immediately upon hearing of the attack by North Korea upon the South. Having been manoeuvred into agreeing to Kim Il-Sung's plans to annex the South by force Mao found that he had to intervene to support the North once the American-led UN forces crossed into the North and approached the Chinese border. He prevailed over doubting colleagues on the grounds that the incipient challenge to China's security and the survival of the revolution had to be met. That, together with the economic embargo announced by Truman at the same time as the decision to protect Taiwan, placed China in the forefront of the Cold War in Asia as the main target for American isolation and containment – a situation that was to last for the next twenty years.

The Korean War proved to be the first modern war in which Chinese armies had been able to withstand the might of Western forces with superior fire power. That not only enhanced the PRC's prestige as a great power, but it endorsed its arrival as a regional power of considerable potency. This became evident after Stalin's death had paved the way for reaching an armistice agreement in Korea that then led to the convening of the Geneva Conference from April to July 1954 on both Korea and Indo-China. The PRC played a major role at the Conference. By this time, the Chinese detected a more relaxed international climate and were keen to encourage it so as to be able to focus upon their own programme of industrialization. The death of Stalin had brought forth a weaker Soviet leadership that not only gave up the special privileges exacted by Stalin, but was willing to provide the PRC with sufficient economic assistance to launch the First Five Year Plan. Consequently, the Chinese at Geneva put pressure on the Vietnamese communists to withdraw from considerable areas they had occupied in the South, back to the 17th parallel, and to allow Laos and Cambodia to become neutral. The Vietnamese communists neither forgot nor forgave the Chinese for forcing them to yield so as to enable a potentially viable anti-communist state to emerge in the South. They saw it as part of a long standing historical tendency of the Chinese to demand deference from them and to prevent them from attaining their rightful dominance of what came to be called Indo-China.

Moreover, the seeds of the territorial dispute with Vietnam and others over the sets of islands in the South China Sea were sown early in the 1950s and it became clear that when it came to the question of sovereign claims the composition or strength of the government concerned made little difference. In May 1950 a reported remark by President Quirino of the Philippines about the dangers to his country's security that would arise from the occupation of the Spratlys by 'an enemy', was angrily denounced in Beijing which then took the opportunity to assert its claims. A more formal claim was put forward in 1951 by Zhou Enlai to all four major sets of islands in the South China Sea in response to the draft Peace Treaty with Japan. The Vietnamese delegation, represented by the Bao Dai government, at the San Francisco Peace Conference to which neither of the Chinese governments was invited, took the opportunity to state Vietnam's claims to the Paracel and the Spratly Islands.[14] Little of substance happened at this time especially as the Chinese side lacked the capacity to enforce its claims.

As elsewhere, the PRC also softened its approach to Japan. Jettisoning its earlier calls upon the Japanese Communist Party to confront the Americans, the PRC responded to Prime Minister

Yoshida's interest in resuming economic ties in a small way in 1952. A Sino–Soviet joint approach in October 1954 raised the tempo to allow also for people-to-people diplomacy. But unlike the Soviet Union, the PRC was unable to press ahead towards normalization because of Tokyo's recognition of Taipei. And it was that link that was publicized by the first ever visit to Taiwan by a Japanese Prime Minister, Kishi Nobusuke, in the different atmosphere of 1957 that led to a downgrading of relations the following year.

The PRC's new stance was also reflected in its approach to the newly independent states of Asia. In the first flush of the victory of the revolution Mao had claimed that two years after achieving independence the people of India were still living 'under the yoke of imperialism and its collaborators'.[15] By 1951 that approach had been set aside and in 1954 the PRC signed a treaty about Tibet with India, the preamble to which listed rules for international conduct that were later to be proclaimed as the Five Principles of Peaceful Co-existence.[16] The more moderate approach caused the Colombo powers to invite China to the first Asian–African Conference that was held in Bandung, Indonesia in April 1955. Meanwhile Beijing had begun to praise the virtues of neutralism in Asia. Zhou Enlai cultivated the delegates from the other twenty-eight countries in Bandung including representatives of America's allies such as the Philippines, Thailand and Pakistan. He had a major impact on Prince Sihanouk and subsequent Cambodian foreign policy by convincing him that non-alignment offered the best safeguard for Cambodia's security against neighbouring historical antagonists, both of whom were allied to the United States.[17]

It would have required more than Zhou Enlai's moderation, welcome as it was, to assuage concerns about China within Southeast Asia. It was noted that the earlier revolutionary approach was downplayed rather than abandoned. The Chinese had earlier broadcast their support for communist insurgencies in Southeast Asia, and their new tendency to argue that state relations were separate from communist party relations if anything only served to accentuate the suspicions of many of their neighbours. A further set of problems arose from the position of the so-called overseas Chinese who generally dominated commercial activities in Southeast Asia. Their cultural and often familial ties to China often excited suspicion, which China's patrimonial attitude as expressed from time to time did little to dispel. In 1954 the PRC redefined citizenship within its new constitution as a result of which Chinese living abroad were no longer automatically regarded as citizens of the PRC. They were encouraged to choose either local nationality or that of the PRC. If the latter, they were forbidden to participate in local politics. A practical example of the new policy was the treaty signed with Indonesia in April 1955, after the Bandung Conference. Ethnic Chinese residents of Indonesia who had not acquired citizenship were given the right to choose between the two nationalities within two years. But domestic opposition delayed ratification of the treaty for years and discriminatory legislation was nevertheless passed in 1958.[18]

Ethnic Chinese were subject to much local animosity arising out of their dominant positions in the local economies, a sentiment that was fuelled by nationalist resentment at their role during the colonial era. They were also vulnerable to rapacious officials. The advent of the PRC raised suspicions about their fundamental loyalties. The PRC leaders were not always sensitive to their predicament as from time to time they tended to refer to them all as fellow descendants of the Yellow Emperor, yet as the patrimonial power the PRC was often at a loss to help them. Matters were not helped by the fact that some of the local insurgent communist party membership such as that of Malaya was made up primarily of ethnic Chinese. Thus upon independence in 1957 the Federal government of Malaya concluded a defence treaty with Britain and shunned polite noises from Beijing. Nevertheless it carefully avoided establishing military ties with the United States and it stayed out of SEATO. Neither Thailand nor the Philippines were persuaded to open relations with Beijing. Yet the main effort of Beijing during the Bandung years was directed towards the vain attempt to persuade these countries to forgo their alliances with the West in favour of better relations with their fellow Asians in Beijing.[19] Perhaps China's best relationship in Southeast Asia in this period was with Burma. It was the first regional state to establish diplomatic relations and its foreign policy adhered closely to the practice of non-alignment.

The Chinese moderate approach began to change in 1957 in large part because the United States had not responded positively to the PRC overtures. These had not been entirely disingenuous as the Chinese had probed American reactions over the Taiwan issue in 1954 by occupying some of the islands south of Shanghai leading to the so-called first off-shore island crisis. It was diffused dramatically by Zhou Enlai's diplomacy in Bandung, but the resultant Sino–American ambassadorial meetings in Geneva soon ended in stalemate because of the impasse over Taiwan. Meanwhile the American response to the Geneva Conference had been to tighten up its series of alliances including the Manila Treaty and a security pact with Taiwan (technically, the Republic of China). In fact part of the reason for the PRC's pressure on the off-shore islands was to warn off other governments from participating in the pact. The American readiness to deal with Moscow was not matched by a similar attitude toward Beijing. In 1957 the PRC reacted angrily to the news of the American deployment of nuclear tipped missiles on Taiwan. The change was also caused by the deterioration in Sino–Soviet relations arising out of Khrushchev's handling of de-Stalinization, what was regarded as his mismanagement of Eastern Europe and his readiness to compromise with the United States, when Mao in particular felt that it was necessary to take a sharp approach. Despite these differences the Soviet Union agreed in late 1957 to assist the PRC in developing nuclear weapons.

By 1958 the strains in Sino–Soviet relations came to a head in part because of Mao's anxieties about his country's psychological as well as material dependency on the Soviet Union combined with the deep seated differences over international strategy.[20] In April Khrushchev had proposed negotiating a nuclear test ban with the Americans that aroused Chinese resentment at this apparent move against their acquiring a nuclear capability. At a crucial meeting in the summer Mao summarily rejected Khrushchev's suggestion to establish a joint fleet together with joint naval and air communications facilities in China.[21] Not long after that meeting Mao initiated the second off-shore island crisis by bombarding Quemoy in the apparent expectation of forcing the Taiwan garrison to surrender 'without an American response, thereby demonstrating to Khrushchev Peking's resolve, Washington's impotence, and Moscow's irrelevance'.[22] But Mao had to back down, having in the process cemented the American commitment to the off-shore islands as well as Taiwan itself. This had the effect of 'freezing' the situation until Sino–American relations were normalized twenty years later.

Self reliance and opposition to both superpowers, 1959–69

Sino–Soviet relations on the whole continued to deteriorate. An exasperated Khrushchev withdrew the offer of nuclear assistance in 1959 and in 1960 finally withdrew altogether the Soviet experts who had been assisting in China's development. The latter was timed to inflict maximum damage as China was suffering from one of the greatest man inflicted famines in history as a consequence of the Mao inspired Great Leap Forward. Although Mao withdrew from the forefront of policy making for a while, he began to make his return in 1962 not only with renewed emphasis on radicalism and self reliance, but with a claim that the Soviet leaders had abandoned the true path of socialism in favour of revisionism – a danger, as Mao was soon to make clear, that in his view existed in China too. This meant in effect that in Mao's opinion there was no room for compromise either at home or abroad. Not all his colleagues agreed, but Mao's views prevailed and were to culminate in the destructive Cultural Revolution. What had happened in the Soviet Union, in Mao's view could happen in China too. The link between domestic foes and the external threat therefore was even more insidious and dangerous in the Soviet case as it reached into all sections of the Communist Party. The domestic groups that were linked to the American threat were the intellectuals and former capitalists who by comparison were more easily dealt with as outsiders to the citadel of power. For Mao the Soviet problem went beyond the issue of its approach to the United States.[23]

Despite Beijing's militant rhetoric, its responses to developments in Southeast Asia in the late 1950s and early 1960s suggested a preference for cautious diplomacy over revolutionary violence.[24] This was true of China's responses to what it regarded as adverse developments in the domestic security arrangements and/or diplomacy of Laos, Cambodia, Thailand and Burma, where its principal goal was to dissuade countries from pursuing policies hostile to itself, particularly in association with the United States.[25] The approach to India, however, was different. As a major regional power which was a leader of the non-alignment movement and one of the most prominent leaders of the Third World it challenged the Chinese confrontationist approach to the two superpowers. Nehru's close association with the arch 'revisionist' Tito only made matters worse from Mao's point of view. The Tibetan uprising in March 1959 led to the Dalai Lama's flight to India and disputes about the border led to small scale fighting later that year. Khrushchev did not side publicly with China as was his duty towards a fellow socialist state. This paved the way for a more intensive border war in 1962 when in response to India's 'forward policy' in what was then called the North Eastern Frontier Agency the Chinese, claiming to 'teach India a lesson', inflicted a humiliating defeat upon the Indian army. This contrasted with relatively generous border agreements that China reached with Burma and Nepal. Indeed China found it easier to establish enduring relationships with smaller avowedly neutralist countries such as Burma and Cambodia. The effect of the war was to damage India's international prestige, to seal a close relationship between India and the Soviet Union and to deepen Sino–Pakistani ties.[26]

The rise of Sukarno in Indonesia and his effective dominance over foreign policy provided the opportunity for the PRC to develop a relationship that had seemed to be going badly awry only a year earlier. In 1959 the Chinese had protested angrily at the way in which the Indonesian army carried out a government decree that in effect prohibited Chinese people from engaging in retail trade outside the main cities. The Chinese went so far as to arrange the shipment of tens of thousands of them to China. At one point the Chinese Foreign Minister was said to have warned his Indonesian counterpart, who had come to Beijing to settle matters by diplomacy, that 'if Indonesia did not rescind its anti-Chinese measures, Peking would call on the Singapore Chinese to launch a trade boycott to bring Indonesia economically to its knees'.[27] In the event, mindful of a possible Soviet interest in exploiting the issue as Khrushchev visited Jakarta in February 1960, the PRC backed down. Only to find that it was fortunate in the rise of Sukarno. Given his emphasis on the significance of the so called new emerging forces, the relatively conservative image of the Soviet Union that emerged from the public polemics of the Sino–Soviet dispute made Sukarno favour China after the success of the West Irian campaign in late 1962 and the onset of his campaign of confrontation with Malaysia in early 1963. When Sukarno withdrew in pique from the United Nations in 1965 and threatened to establish an alternative body he found a ready response in Beijing.

From a Chinese perspective all went well until the abortive coup of 1965. The Indonesian army claimed that the PRC was implicated. Members of the Indonesian Communist Party and ethnic Chinese were then slaughtered in their hundreds of thousands, as the PRC was powerless to help them. The new order of General Suharto had no place for relations with China and amid the early chaos of the Cultural Revolution all relations were severed in 1967. As suddenly as warm relations were begun so they were ended. The volatility of apparent ideological partnerships in the Third World stemmed from the highly personalistic character of many of their governments, as the Chinese discovered from their dealings in Africa in attempts to replace the Soviet Union as the true supporter of anti-imperialism and national liberation.

Relations with Japan remained of a different order. There was a residual sense of guilt in Japan about its conduct in the war in China, especially as many regarded China as an important source in the development of Japanese culture and there were elements within Japan that did not wish to be cut off from China. Additionally, certain business interests sought economic relations. The PRC was interested not only in weakening the American trade embargo, but also in developing wider relations with Japan in the hope of weakening its ties with Taiwan and the United States. In 1962 the semi official Memorandum Trade Agreement was signed in Beijing. In 1964 Mao, in an interview with Japanese journalists, caused considerable anger in Moscow as he declared that the Southern Kuriles along with many other territories had been unjustly acquired by the Soviet Union. This was at a point when Mao had developed a view that the smaller and medium capitalist countries belonged to a special intermediate zone between the two superpowers, implying that they should find common cause with China. France, under the presidency of De Gaulle, recognized the PRC in 1964. But Mao was unable to make a similar breakthrough with Japan and in the end little came of his initiative.[28]

Mao's central concerns lay with asserting self reliance and opposing the two superpowers, whom he argued tended to collude against China even though their interests were fundamentally antagonistic. At the heart of their collusion in his view was their opposition to China's acquisition of nuclear weapons. China's first nuclear test took place in October 1964 and for a time it alarmed both the Soviet Union and the United States. Mao was so exercised by the threat of war from the north as well as from the east that he ordered, at tremendous cost, that a third front of defence and military related industries be developed in the mountainous redoubt of Sichuan deep in the interior.[29] However, the American intervention in Vietnam which had been prompted initially by concerns to contain China and to disprove the effectiveness of Maoist revolutionary warfare proved to be a turning point. The United States, seeking to limit the war to prevent a rerun of the Korean War, did not invade the North, but confined its ground fighting to the South and attacked the North only from the air and the sea. This meant that the Soviet Union as well as China was drawn in to helping the defence of a fellow socialist country. But far from bringing the two communist giants together the war divided them still further as Mao rejected the Soviet proposal for united action. Meanwhile a tacit understanding was reached with the United States that its forces would not invade the North or attack China and that China would not directly enter the war. That understanding had been reached in part as a result of the Chinese demonstration of discrete commitment by helping to arm the North Vietnamese and by the visible, but unpublicized, deployment of Chinese troops in the North.[30] Once convinced that there would not be a repeat of Korea, Mao unleashed the Cultural Revolution which was designed to sweep away his domestic Soviet style 'revisionist' opponents and establish new revolutionary political culture for the country. The spill over into foreign affairs was disastrous in the short term as it alienated many of the Asian countries that previously had been cultivated on geopolitical grounds, including Burma, Cambodia and North Korea.

Alarmed by the new militancy of the Chinese and perhaps also responding to Mao's 1964 challenge to Moscow on the territorial issue, the Soviet Union began to upgrade its armed forces along the lengthy border with China. Perhaps mindful of the claims on Mongolia' that Mao had raised with Khrushchev in 1954, despite having recognized its independence four years earlier, the Soviet Union signed a defence treaty with Mongolia in 1966 and by the following year had stationed several divisions there. The growing tension and pressure from the militarily superior Soviet forces led the Chinese to attack one of the disputed islands in the Ussuri River on the Manchurian border in March 1969. The Soviet response, which involved penetrations across the border into Xinjiang, eventually compelled the Chinese to negotiate in September.[31]

At this time Soviet officials began to sound out discreetly how the West might react if the Soviet Union were to attack China's nuclear installations. The high stakes that Mao had been playing in confronting both the superpowers had finally reached the ultimate crisis. The various attempts to find counter-weights in the Third World and among the smaller capitalist powers had failed. The attempts to signal to the United States in the autumn of 1968 that the PRC wished to resume the dialogue in the wake of the Soviet invasion of Czechoslovakia had gone unheeded. From that point, however, the PRC broke away from its self inflicted isolationist stance to encourage a new wave of diplomatic recognition by many countries including those from the West. It was not until 1969, as a result of the fighting, that President Nixon and his National Security Adviser Kissinger responded. Meanwhile if Beijing had been pleased by the Nixon Doctrine, acknowledging that the United States would no longer commit land forces to fight wars in Asia, it was less pleased by the US–Japan agreement about the reversion of Okinawa that included Japanese claims that its security interests extended to South Korea and Taiwan.

The management of tripolarity, 1970–89

The tilt to America to counter Soviet encirclement, 1970–81

The Sino–American *rapprochement* which constituted a watershed in the Cold War involved several understandings and agreements of global, regional and more local consequence. From a global perspective it loosened still further the bonds of bipolarity by adding a tripolar dimension. Although China was not a global power it did affect the global balance. China had gained American support against (Soviet) 'hegemony' and had elicited a promise that Washington would not collude with Moscow against Beijing. Beyond that the PRC's international standing was enhanced when in October 1971 it took over the China seat at the United Nations including that as a permanent member of the Security Council. The American proposal to allow for a dual membership including the ROC (i.e. Taiwan) was defeated. At a regional level the Chinese reached an understanding about Japan that made them appreciate that the retention of the American security treaty with Japan was preferable from their point of view to a Japan that in fending for itself might experience a resurgence of the very militarism that the Chinese professed to fear. At the same time Mao and Zhou indicated to Nixon and Kissinger that they did not threaten Japan or South Korea. The Taiwan issue became localized in the sense that up until then it had been at the centre of the Sino–American confrontation and one of the key points of the geostrategic line of containment. As specified in the Shanghai Communique signed by Nixon and Zhou in February 1972, the Americans in effect agreed to 'one China but not now' and the Chinese in effect acquiesced in a continued American diplomatic and military presence on the island at least for the time being.[32] The visit by Nixon to Beijing had a wider symbolic significance. It was striking that there was no question of Mao visiting Washington and it was as if a powerful barbarian leader was making amends for previous hostility by deferring to the emperor in Beijing.

At the same time China's role within the region was transformed. It now looked forward to developing relations with all of the allies of America and the West who had hitherto been parties to security treaties of which the PRC had been the target. The axis of conflict had changed. The principal one in the region had become that between China and the Soviet Union although that operated within a global framework that continued to centre on the United States and the Soviet Union.

However, unlike the PRC's relations with most of the countries in the world its relations with its pro-Western neighbours that involved immediate local and regional security issues took longer to normalize. They had been divided over the UN vote on China's membership, but the PRC sought to improve relations with all of them.[33] The slight delay with Japan was of China's doing, essentially to make a point about Taiwan. Not only had Prime Minister Sato signed the Okinawa Agreement extending Japan's security interests to include South Korea and Taiwan, but he had personally shown public partiality to the nationalist government there. Consequently, the Chinese delayed allowing the Japanese to establish diplomatic relations until they acquired a different prime minister. After the accession of Tanaka in 1972 relations were speedily normalized.

Elsewhere in Pacific Asia matters moved more slowly. The North Vietnamese understandably felt betrayed. Ten years later the Vietnamese Foreign Minister Nguyen Co Thach said that Mao had told his Prime Minister Phan Van Dong that

> his broom was not long enough to sweep Taiwan clean and ours was not long enough to get the Americans out of South Vietnam. He wanted to halt reunification and force us to recognize the puppet regime in the South. He had sacrificed Vietnam for the sake of the United States.[34]

Not for the first time did the Vietnamese communists feel that their interests were being sold out in the interests of their great power neighbour. Not surprisingly, they turned even more strikingly to the Soviet Union. But just as the PRC could not at this point disavow the Vietnamese struggle without losing prestige and credibility, so the North Vietnamese could not afford openly to repudiate the PRC. Only in 1974, after the Paris Agreements, but before enforced unification, when the Chinese acquired by force that part of the Paracel island group held by the South, was some of the bitterness of the North made public.

The ASEAN countries were slow to respond to China's new international position and to its more positive appraisal of their Association. Not only was there the long standing problem of the overseas Chinese, but they still distrusted China for its links with the communist insurgents in their countries. As late as 1 October 1974, the PRC's National Day, Zhou Enlai gave pride of place to communist leaders from Southeast Asia.[35] Moreover, the Chinese continued to allow broadcasts by insurgent communist parties such as the 'Voice of the Malayan Revolution' to emanate from Yunnan province. The pressures from the Cultural Revolution were still fresh and the memory of China's long historical shadow had far from faded. The fact that China's best relations in Southeast Asia had been based on a kind of deference from the relatively small and vulnerable, neutral Burma and Sihanouk's Cambodia hardly commended it in the eyes of the ASEAN countries. The PRC had been loud in its condemnation of ASEAN as an agent of the imperialist West until 1968 and although Beijing changed its declaratory approach two years later, it was still regarded with suspicion. The Malaysian and Indonesian political and military élites in particular saw the PRC as the long term threat to their country's independence. When eventually recognition came it was out of self interest, rather than because of any change in the configurations of great power relations. The ASEAN countries may be said to have benefited from these, in the nature of things. Thus in 1974 the Malaysian government recognized the PRC in the expectation that this would be of assistance in handling problems with the relatively large ethnic Chinese community that accounted for 35 per cent of the population. The Philippines followed suit over a year later, while also extending relations to the Soviet Union, thereby demonstrating a symbolic even-handedness rather than acquiescence in the Chinese approach. Thailand also extended recognition in 1975, mainly because of the communist Vietnamese success and the need to find a counterbalance now that the Americans were on their way out of Vietnam. Indonesia, however, refused to follow suit as the PRC was still held responsible for the coup of 1965 and the armed forces were resistant to any PRC diplomatic presence that might complicate their lucrative arrangements with the local Chinese businesses. As a predominantly ethnic Chinese city, located between Malaysia and Indonesia, Singapore prudently announced that it would not recognize the PRC before Indonesia. But Prime Minister Lee Kuan Yew nevertheless visited Beijing in 1976.[36]

The communist victories in Indo-China and America's final ignominious departure from Saigon in April 1975 brought to the fore the Sino–Soviet conflict as the principal great power conflict in Southeast Asia. The Chinese became increasingly shrill in their warnings to the countries of the area about letting in the Soviet wolf through the back door as the American tiger was leaving through the front. Earlier Chinese worries that Kissinger, in Mao's phrase, was 'climbing on [China's] shoulders to reach Moscow', were now tinged with alarm. Not only was the Chinese alignment with the United States being used in order to establish détente with the Soviet Union, but in the Chinese view the Americans and the Europeans were making concessions to the Russians by, for example, recognizing the borders the Soviet Union had imposed in Eastern Europe. The Chinese feared that this would leave them even more exposed to Soviet power as indicated perhaps by their over vigorous pronouncements that China was secure and that it was the West that was in danger. In any event by 1977 a pattern had emerged by which China was in an alignment with the United States and was the principal supporter of the anti-Vietnamese Khmer Rouge regime in Cambodia, while the reunified Vietnam exercised dominance over Laos and was backed by the Soviet Union.

By 1978 matters had reached the stage by which the Vietnamese and the Chinese were competing for the support of the ASEAN states. Vietnam reversed its earlier hostility to ASEAN and then its Zone of Peace proposal for regional order; and the Chinese, for their part, claimed to have watered down their support for the local communist parties and implied that the only reason for supporting them at all was fear that the alternative was to have them sponsored by Vietnam and the Soviet Union whose aggressive ambitions knew no bounds. In the Spring the Vietnamese began to 'encourage' the resident ethnic Chinese to leave in hundreds of thousands amid rumours of an impending war. They not only fled northwards to China, but when that route was closed they embarked on often unseaworthy boats across the South China Sea. Many perished and many ended up in adjacent countries as unwanted refugees. Not only did this deepen Sino–Vietnamese enmity, but it also touched on the raw nerves of the overseas Chinese question that affected the ASEAN countries as well as China. Meanwhile the cross border attacks by the ultra-nationalist Khmer Rouge into Vietnam, in particular, eventually caused the latter to attack Cambodia and impose by force a regime to its liking in late January 1979.[37] The Chinese government had long objected to what they regarded as attempts by Vietnam to assert dominance over the whole of Indo-China especially with the backing of a hostile superpower. But the anger of China's leaders was intensified by the perception of Vietnamese ingratitude for extensive Chinese assistance over nearly thirty years.[38]

The Vietnamese invasion had been preceded by a hasty re-enforcement of power alignments by both sides. In May Carter's National Security Adviser, Brzezinski, visited Beijing and pleased his hosts with his much tougher approach to the Soviet Union than exhibited by Secretary of State Vance in August 1977. In June Vietnam was admitted to the Soviet dominated Council for Mutual Economic Assistance (CMEA). In August the Chinese, who had begun to complain about encirclement, at last reached agreement with Japan about a peace treaty that included a reference to anti-hegemonism (the key concept aimed at the Soviet Union). In early November Vietnam signed a treaty with the Soviet Union that was very similar to the Indo–Soviet treaty that was agreed prior to the Indian attack on what was then East Pakistan. Although earlier in the year the United States had been toying with the prospect of establishing relations with Vietnam, on 16 December the Chinese and American governments finally agreed to establish diplomatic relations. Taiwan, which had been the stumbling block hitherto, was settled in a way that ostensibly met Beijing's long standing terms involving the cessation of all official American relations, the abrogation of the Security Treaty and the withdrawal of all military personnel without the Chinese agreeing in turn to resolve the issue only by peaceful terms. The Chinese nevertheless accepted that the Americans were to continue to sell arms to Taiwan – albeit in a limited way that would eventually come to an end. The upshot was that Taiwan would continue to be able to defend itself against possible mainland attack for the foreseeable future and therefore it would be able to retain its *defacto* independence from Beijing. Although elements in the Beijing leadership were not happy with this aspect of the normalization agreement, Deng Xiaoping's insistence prevailed. He wanted to secure American acquiescence in his plan to 'teach Vietnam a lesson'.[39]

The Chinese duly attacked across the border with Vietnam in February and after five weeks in which they destroyed much of the infrastructure of the adjoining provinces they withdrew. The inadequacies of their forces and their military doctrine were badly exposed and they failed to divert Vietnamese forces from Cambodia. But the alternative, of acquiescing in Vietnam's destruction of a client regime and its assertion of dominance in Indo-China, would have damaged China's prestige, destroyed its great power pretensions and exposed it as something of a paper tiger before the Soviet Union and its proxy. Moreover the Chinese did in fact teach the Vietnamese a lesson in geopolitics in the sense that unlike their former adversaries, France and the United States, or indeed its then ally, the Soviet Union, China was a constant presence as a more powerful neighbour. In the event the United States led Japan in imposing an effective economic embargo on Vietnam and the ASEAN countries promoted an effective diplomatic opposition to Vietnam in the United Nations and the Third World. This was intensified after the Soviet invasion of Afghanistan in December 1979, which led to a tacit strategic partnership with the United States described euphemistically as the pursuit of parallel actions. Without publicity each in its own way was allied to the frontline states of Thailand and Pakistan respectively and each gave military assistance. Each in its own way supported the resistance fighters in Cambodia and Afghanistan and each supported the relevant international embargoes and diplomatic opposition.

Interestingly, it was at this point that the Chinese began to explore an opening to the Soviet Union. The first initiative was made in 1979 after their withdrawal from Vietnam when the Chinese called for talks that were neatly pegged to the expiry of their long defunct 1950 treaty. These were then put off because of the Soviet invasion of Afghanistan, but once the dust had settled somewhat in 1981 the Chinese again signalled that they sought to improve relations.[40] In the Chinese view the momentum of strategic advantage had begun to swing away from the Soviet Union and there was no longer the pressing need for the Chinese to tilt so heavily towards the Americans. The fact that the incoming Reagan Administration touched on a number of matters of great irritation to the Chinese accelerated the process by which the Chinese sought to distance themselves from the United States.

The independent foreign policy, 1982–89

The new policy was given added weight by being declared at the Twelfth Party Congress in September 1982. The General Secretary, Hu Yaobang, explained that henceforth China would follow an independent foreign policy in the conduct of its relations with the United States and the Soviet Union and that China would eschew alliances as these might limit the country's capacity to exercise independent initiatives and damage relations with third parties. The United States too was now said to behave in a hegemonic fashion and the Chinese reserved the right to criticize such actions in the Middle East, Central America and elsewhere. The new declaratory policy enabled the Chinese side once again to place itself at the forefront of Third World concerns and to assume a posture more congruent with its sense of international identity and dignity.

In practice China continued to pursue parallel political and military policies with the United States over Cambodia and Afghanistan. Moreover, the American intelligence facilities to monitor Soviet missile and related activities, which were transferred to Xinjiang from Iran after the fall of the Shah, continued to operate uninterruptedly throughout this period. Nevertheless the new policy of independence should not be dismissed as being of purely declaratory significance. It served three fundamental purposes: it provided a basis for gradually improving relations with the Soviet Union which substantially increased the Chinese sphere for independent manoeuvre. Second, it reflected the major ideological changes that had taken place in China, which defined economic development as the highest priority and repudiated Mao's emphasis on class struggle. Finally, the new policy more explicitly served the new approach by Deng Xiaoping that called for economic reform at home, and openness to the international economy abroad on the basis of adherence to communist party rule.

China's leaders tended to define their new approach in general and global terms rather than with specific reference to the Asia-Pacific region. But it was here that the policy came into effect. Thus in 1984 and 1985 as the Chinese determined that the prospects for a world war had finally receded, Deng Xiaoping singled out 'Peace and Development' as the 'two really great issues confronting the world today'. While noting that peace centred on East–West relations he suggested that development involved North–South relations and that the latter was the key. China, he said, would be truly non-aligned with regard to East–West relations where it would oppose hegemonic behaviour. In North–South relations, he claimed, China supported dialogue and encouraged South–South co-operation.[41] A further indication of the PRC's more relaxed view of its strategic environment was evident from the change in the strategic guidance given to the armed forces that took place in the spring of 1985. Instead of being instructed to prepare for an 'early, major, and nuclear war' the Chinese military were directed to focus their preparations for conducting local limited wars around China's borders as being the most likely form of conflict in the foreseeable future.[42]

In practice, however, China's policies were directed almost entirely towards the region. Sheltered from concern about the possible Soviet threat by the American determination, under the aegis of President Reagan, to face down the Soviet Union from a position of military strength, the Chinese were able to centre their foreign policy on economic development. The policies of seeking modernization through economic reform and opening to the international economy that were begun in December 1978 had profound international implications. Although they were temporarily eclipsed by the brief war with Vietnam, the international implications of the policies of modernization called for a greater interdependence with the international economy and the pursuit of policies of accommodation with the West and the East Asian market economies in particular.

Relations with the United States were unaffected by the openly stated policy of the newly appointed Secretary of State, George Shultz, to anchor America's policies in Asia on Japan rather than China as advocated by his predecessor, Alexander Haig. In fact Sino–American relations enjoyed perhaps their most constructive and trouble free period from the end of 1982 until the Tiananmen killings in 1989.[43] As for the Soviet Union, the question became not whether relations would improve, but rather when and under what terms they would be normalized. Deng insisted that that could only take place once the deployment of Soviet forces had been substantially scaled down in the north (including Mongolia), the intervention forces withdrawn from Afghanistan, and above all the Soviet support that enabled Vietnam to continue to occupy Cambodia had come to an end. Meanwhile Sino–Soviet trade began to pick up, border talks were resumed and exchanges of middle level officials occurred.

Against this background China's economic interests began to play an increasingly important role in the conduct of foreign policy and enhanced the significance of relations with countries of the Asia-Pacific. Not surprisingly, the relationship with Japan prospered, but perhaps not as much as might have been expected. Although relations were formally correct and both sides professed friendship and interdependence, there were elements of distrust, resentment and even fear that each side felt towards the other. The Chinese felt entitled to special treatment as they had renounced claims to reparations in 1972 and yet they complained that Japanese companies held back somewhat from investing in China and were less generous in transferring technology than say the Americans. They also found it unacceptable that certain senior Japanese officials from time to time denied the aggressiveness and brutality of Japan's armies during the Pacific War. Such occasions were used to warn against the re-emergence of militarism, i.e. the resurgence of a militarily powerful Japan. The Japanese in turn resented Chinese strictures and what they regarded as attempts to interfere in domestic Japanese politics.[44]

Economic interests were to the fore in the development for the first time of relations with South Korea from 1985 onwards. Initially operating through Hong Kong, economic ties expanded quickly and soon involved dealings between officials. The improvements in Sino–Soviet relations had reduced the capacity of North Korea to exercise countervailing pressure on China. In 1984 during the short reign of the more conservative and ailing Chernenko in the Soviet Union, in return for advanced weaponry Soviet surveillance planes were allowed access to Korean air space, the better to monitor China's forces, and Soviet ships visited North Korean ports. With the accession of Gorbachev these arrangements came to an end. By that point, however, the Chinese no longer felt obligated to the North, still less would they allow the North to exercise a veto on their relations with the South. By this time South Korea had begun a deliberate policy of cultivating the North's communist allies. China's economic centred policies enabled it to respond, thereby beginning the process of eroding the last remnants of the Cold War.

Similar interests and flexibility were in evidence as the Chinese on the mainland responded positively to the beginnings of economic relations initiated unofficially from Taiwan in the second half of the 1980s. Again these were directed through Hong Kong. By 1987 Taiwanese residents were allowed to visit the mainland. This in turn led to the development of what has been called 'Greater China' involving a complicated economic nexus that brought together the economies of Taiwan, Hong Kong and the Chinese provinces of Guangdong and Fujian.[45] The new approach by the Deng leadership had also facilitated the negotiation of an agreement in 1984 for the reversion of Hong Kong to Chinese sovereignty thirteen years later on terms that guaranteed the continuation of the Hong Kong way of life for a further fifty years. For China's leaders and Deng Xiaoping in particular the prize was the restoration of sovereignty over this prime symbol of the humiliation of their country in the nineteenth century. Although it was important to do so under conditions that would allow the territory to continue to be prosperous and stable so that it could continue to play a key role in the modernization of the country, Deng showed at one point in the negotiations that if necessary that could be sacrificed as long as the proper terms of sovereignty were not infringed.[46]

The economic imprint on China's foreign policy was also evident in Southeast Asia where the strategic configurations of Indo-China had precedence. Throughout most of the 1980s a stalemate had evolved on the Cambodian issue. Vietnam was unable to wipe out totally the forces resisting its military occupation of Cambodia, but they in turn were confined to bases operating along the border with Thailand and were incapable of dislodging the Vietnamese. The Chinese as the supporters of the Khmer Rouge (the principal resistant force) and the *de facto* allies of Thailand were also the diplomatic associates of the ASEAN states in their successful fostering of international diplomatic opposition to Vietnam. Although the Malaysian and Indonesian governments claimed to fear the longer term threat of China and saw Vietnam as a possible buffer to China, the Vietnamese proved to be too intransigent to respond positively to initiatives from these governments to display some flexibility. Consequently, the Chinese were able to take advantage of the situation to deepen economic ties with all the ASEAN countries, including the conduct of direct trade with Indonesia, despite the absence of diplomatic relations. This extended their relations beyond the Indo-Chinese issues.[47] Nevertheless residual problems remained about local unease concerning the rising power of China especially in the light of the historical legacy of claimed superiority. These included uncertainty about the character of the interlocking webs of loyalties of the ethnic Chinese and Beijing's claims upon them; conflicting claims to the Spratly Islands in the South China Sea; and more broadly, worries about the extent to which the leaders in Beijing understood the concerns of their neighbours and were willing to act with restraint.

It was the ending of tripolarity and of the Cold War that brought this period of Chinese foreign policy to an end. Gorbachev's fulfilment of the essentials of Deng Xiaoping's three preconditions for normalising relations paved the way for his visit to Beijing in May 1989. Instead of that turning out to be a triumph for Deng, it contributed to the greatest crisis of his rule. The subsequent killings in Tiananmen Square on 4 June ended the honeymoon with the West and changed China's international relations especially as this bloody event was followed only months later by the relatively bloodless ending of communist rule in Eastern Europe and the end of the Cold War itself.

REGIONALISM IN THE POST COLD WAR PERIOD, 1989–95

The end of the Cold War has provided the PRC with the opportunity for the first time to develop truly regional policies. No longer would these be determined by the perceived need to counter hostile moves by one or other of the superpowers. Instead they could be fashioned to serve the purposes of economic development. This prospect stemmed from the end of the lingering Soviet threat. For the first time in the forty-year history of the PRC and indeed for the first time since the Opium War 150 years earlier the Chinese heartland was no longer under threat from a superior modern force.

At the same time the end of tripolarity meant that China had also been regionalized by the change in global politics. The PRC's capacity to project force was relatively limited even within the context of the Asia-Pacific let alone beyond it. Moreover, the bulk of the country's foreign economic relations were conducted within the region. Yet Chinese strategic perspectives continued to be very much attuned to the global as well as to the regional situation. In the late 1980s Chinese strategists assumed that the capacity of the superpowers to dominate the international system would steadily decline and that bipolarity would be gradually replaced by multipolarity. They did not anticipate the collapse of the East European socialist systems and they were shocked by the disintegration of the Soviet Union. Instead of the Gulf War being protracted, the Chinese were startled by the awesome effectiveness of the high-tech weaponry of the American-led allies. It suggested that after all the United States had emerged as the only dominant global power.[48] Even though subsequent events were to show that American power was less effective than the victory over Iraq might have implied, China's leaders nevertheless felt exposed before the United States as there was no other power that they could hope to use as a balance or lever against the United States. The sense of exposure was in part due to the suddenness with which the relations with the United States had changed because of the Tiananmen killings of 4 June 1989.[49]

The immediate effect of the events surrounding the end of the Cold War from Tiananmen to the collapse of the Soviet Union just over two years later was to transform the definition of the main security threat by China's leaders. If earlier it had been primarily military henceforth it was primarily political. The key threat to China as seen by its leaders was to the survival of communist party rule. Very soon after Gorbachev's visit in May 1989 he came to be seen as a betrayer of communism in Eastern Europe, a threat to the survival of communism in the Soviet Union and an insidious danger to China where many were attracted by his more democratic approach. In many ways the threat posed by the Americans was even worse as access to the American market and technology were vital to China's economic development, yet its cultural and material attractions were inherently subversive of communism as was the American idealist desire to transform China, all summed up in the Chinese fear of 'peaceful evolution'. This was seen as a conscious policy designed to undermine communist rule by peaceful means through the introduction of capitalist and democratic norms. Prominent among the latter was the emphasis on Chinese failures to honour human rights. An added difficulty arose from the fact that the more conservative or leftist elements in the Chinese leadership used the general concern about peaceful evolution as a means to criticize the market oriented aspects of the economic reforms being pushed by Deng Xiaoping.[50]

These developments contributed to the Chinese emphasis upon cultivating better relations within the region. They reinforced the tendency to give the highest priority to the search for a peaceful international environment. Confining their misgivings about Gorbachev and subsequently Yeltsin to domestic audiences only, China's leaders pursued a diplomatically correct course towards Russia and the other members of the Commonwealth of Independent States (CIS) especially in Central Asia.[51] In part this was done to forestall Taiwan which had hoped to establish formal relations with these countries, but the principal reason would appear to be the interest in cultivating better relations with neighbours to safeguard stability, ease China's integration in the region, improve economic relations and circumvent American-led attempts to impose upon China the status of an international pariah. It fitted into a pattern in which China improved relations with all its immediate neighbours by displaying a flexibility on outstanding questions including borders. Agreements were reached not only with Russia and the new Central Asian republics, but also with others including, most notably, India. Bereft of its Soviet ally, India too sought better relations with China. Although neither government was prepared to concede to the other on their disputed borders, the Chinese took a more neutral position on the dispute between India and Pakistan over Kashmir and it no longer openly challenged Indian dominance of South Asia. In view of the new international and regional circumstances Indonesia finally agreed to restore diplomatic relations in 1990. President Suharto recognized the importance of dealing directly with the PRC if his country were to play a significant role in the region in accordance with its long held sense of entitlement.

An important dimension of China's new regionalism has been the relatively constructive role that it has played in helping to diffuse two of the long standing regional conflicts that for many years were linked to the wider confrontations between the great powers – Cambodia and Korea. Following the normalization of Sino–Soviet relations and the cessation of all Soviet aid to Vietnam, the Vietnamese leaders not only had to complete their military withdrawal from Cambodia in late 1989 as they had promised earlier, but they had to make their peace with the Chinese and defer to China's right to broker a deal among the indigenous Cambodian factions to include the participation of the notorious Khmer Rouge. The Supreme National Council comprising all the competing Cambodian factions met in Beijing with a Chinese representative as the only foreign observer. That paved the way for the Paris Agreements in October 1991 that duly led to the carrying out of elections in Cambodia under the auspices of the United Nations. The Chinese played an important, if unobtrusive role, especially in bringing pressure to bear upon the Khmer Rouge not to disrupt the peace process. Following the elections, however, the Chinese government has done little to assist in preventing the decline into chaos and civil war. It would appear that the Chinese interest is limited to preventing a regional rival from asserting dominance over Indo-China and that its interest does not extend at this point to establishing an order more to its liking. Beijing has tolerated the highly active role of the Cambodian People's Party in the Phnom Penh coalition as it is no longer an agent of Vietnam, and the Chinese communist leadership has no desire to see Vietnam collapse given its political system. Nevertheless the Chinese played an important role in delinking the Cambodian conflict from wider regional divisions and in contributing to the UN sponsored settlement – tenuous though that has turned out to be.

The other major regional conflict has been Korea. The Chinese have been praised by the Americans for their behind the scenes role in effecting the Geneva Accords of August and October 1994 between the United States and North Korea. But the Chinese interests on the Korean peninsula are mixed. The South has become an important economic partner that plays a significant role in the economies of the adjacent provinces of Shandong, Liaoning and Jilin. Although the Chinese are allied to the North they have refused to allow it to dictate their policies towards the South; in 1992 they formally recognized the South and, by indicating that they would not veto its entrance into the United Nations, they virtually compelled the North to join as well. Both actions caused anger in

Pyongyang. Even though the Chinese have become the sole suppliers of oil and food to the beleaguered North, they claim not to exercise significant influence over the regime there. The Chinese have openly declared their opposition to the nuclearization of the Korean peninsula, but have been unable to prevent the North from manufacturing weapons' grade plutonium. At the same time the Chinese do not wish the North to collapse. Consequently, the Chinese have ploughed a narrow farrow of opposing the use of force or the imposition of economic sanctions to compel the North to honour its obligations of allowing inspection of its nuclear power facilities by the International Atomic Energy Agency (IAEA) and of insisting upon a negotiated settlement. Ideally, the Chinese would like to see the North abandon its rigid Stalinism in favour of a path of economic reform on the Chinese model so as to ensure its survival and facilitate its recognition by Japan and the United States, to match the South's recognition by Russia and China. They fear, however, a collapse by the North that could destabilize the Korean peninsula and adversely affect China too.[52]

China has joined a number of the regional organizations. Since these are mainly of a consultative character they have not challenged fundamental Chinese concerns about autonomy, independence and sovereignty.[53] The main problem concerned the membership and status of Taiwan. Since the PRC would not accept any designation that suggested that Taiwan might be a sovereign state and the government in Taiwan refused any designation that implied that it was a subordinate province, compromise names had to be found. The breakthrough occurred with the Asia Development Bank (ADB) in 1986 after a three year wrangle in which the PRC had initially demanded the expulsion of Taiwan. The formula 'Taipei, China' was reluctantly accepted by both. In May 1988 the PRC joined the Pacific Economic Cooperation Council and the formula 'Chinese Taipei' was accepted. In 1991 the PRC, Hong Kong and Taiwan joined the Asia-Pacific Economic Cooperation (APEC) with the latter reverting to the ADB formula. In that year the Chinese foreign minister attended the opening of the ASEAN foreign ministers' conference as a guest of the host, Malaysia, and he also held separate private talks with the ASEAN counterparts. In 1993 China was a founder member of the ASEAN Regional Forum which focuses through dialogue explicitly upon security issues. Although these regional organizations are essentially consultative they have brought the PRC into more regular contact with multilateral gatherings in which a wide range of economic and even security matters are dealt with in such a manner as to familiarize different agencies and bureaucracies in Beijing with the concerns of their neighbours and the region as a whole. Together with the manifold economic ties that have been progressively established they contribute to anchoring the PRC in a multi-faceted interdependent set of relations within the region. As seen by weaker neighbours, that contributes to long term security and, as seen from Beijing, it enhances its economic relations within the Asia-Pacific which are crucial for the continuing growth of its economy. A further dimension of China's new found regionalism may be seen from the encouragement given to the different provinces of China to develop their own foreign economic relations with adjacent neighbours.[54]

As part of the new regionalism, the Chinese authorities finally disassociated themselves from the communist movements in Southeast Asia. They encouraged the Communist Party of Malaya to agree to a cease-fire in 1989 and in 1990 the Chinese Premier Li Peng told President Suharto that the Indonesian communist exiles in Beijing were not allowed to engage in politics. The Chinese government has sought to cultivate economic ties with the ASEAN countries as part of the larger strategy of economic development. The improved relations served the Chinese well in the immediate aftermath of Tiananmen. The ASEAN countries have become important allies in resisting Western pressure on human rights. Interestingly, the Chinese defend their position not so much from the communist perspective but, like their ASEAN friends, as a developing Asian country with different cultural values.

There are nevertheless conflictual dimensions to China's new regionalism. These may be characterized as long standing irredenta that are fuelled in part by the deeply felt mission to correct perceived historical injustices involving the interventions of the major powers and in part by the growing Chinese military capacity to impose a settlement. In the Chinese view that has been inculcated by the education of successive generations this century, these territories have historically been Chinese and others have encroached upon them during the period of Chinese weakness, and that far from being aggressive they have acted with restraint against neighbours who have gone so far as to erect installations and station armed forces on some of these islands. The principal points at issue are a series of islands disputed with maritime neighbours, possession of which would affect the distribution of maritime resources and the configuration of the strategic environment. Indeed if China's full claims in the South China Sea were to be enforced China would be left in virtual control of this major seaway between the Indian and Pacific Oceans and it would reach deep into the maritime heart of Southeast Asia. Important economic resources may also be at stake as the islands are alleged to command gas and oil reserves that are of increasing significance as the countries of the region require growing supplies of energy to service their fast growing economies. China in fact began to be a net importer of energy in 1994.

In the 1990s most attention has been focused on the Spratly Islands that are claimed as a whole or in part by China, Vietnam, Malaysia, Brunei, the Philippines and Taiwan (as the Republic of China on Taiwan). China, which has used force to impose its exclusive sovereign claims to the Paracel Islands against South Vietnam in 1974 and which also fought a military engagement with Vietnam in 1988, has perhaps the longest based historical claims. But some of the islands reach close to the shores of littoral countries and the latter exhibit apprehension as China's capacity to project force increases and as the Chinese presence in the area thickens. In 1995 a dispute arose over installations that the Chinese had built on Mischief Reef, which was also claimed by the Philippines and is less than 150 miles from the Filipino coast and more than 1, 000 miles from the most southerly Chinese island of Hainan. The Chinese have resisted regional solutions preferring instead to deal on a bilateral basis, suggesting that conflicting sovereign claims be put aside for the time being while the economic resources may be developed jointly. Some Chinese actions have belied the relative benevolence implied in their formal posture. Apparently targeting Vietnam in particular, the Chinese authorities granted exploration rights to an American company in a part of the South China Sea contested with Vietnam, with the promise to come to its defence if necessary. Amid evidence of a vigorous naval policy to assert an increasing presence in the seas around China, a new law was passed in Beijing in 1992 that formalized China's territorial claims and authorized its armed forces to protect them. China also disputes with Japan the sovereignty over a barren island south of the Okinawa chain, ownership of which would be important in determining the division of the maritime and sea-bed rights of the East China Sea. Division of other maritime rights are also disputed with South Korea, Japan and Vietnam.[55]

The way in which Beijing chooses to advance its claims to Hong Kong and Taiwan may also affect the stability of the region. Although the reversion of Hong Kong to Chinese sovereignty is subject to an international agreement reached with Britain in 1984 there is considerable uncertainty about the character of administration that Beijing will authorize.[56] Should that be seen to undermine Hong Kong's current role as an economic centre for both China and the region, profound doubts would then be raised about the extent to which China can be integrated into the region. The Taiwan issue is of graver significance. The closer economic ties that have been established across the Taiwan Straits since the mid-1980s have coincided with the development of democracy on the island. That has resulted in the emergence of an opposition party that seeks outright independence and in the shift of the ruling party to advocating dual recognition for Taipei and Beijing, along the lines of the earlier German precedent of accepting the existence of two separate governments, as a prelude to eventual unification once the mainland has caught up economically and politically with Taiwan. Beijing has hotly rejected both positions and has threatened the use of force to prevent them from being realised. The consequences of that would be dire indeed for the security of the region as a whole and possibly for China's continued economic engagement with the wider world.[57]

The process of economic reform and openness has been accompanied by an intensification of nationalistic sentiments particularly as communism has ceased to serve as a credible ideology. In some respects, as in dealing with the new countries of Central Asia, the enhanced nationalism has exuded sufficient self confidence to result in policies of restraint. But in others a harsher more abrasive quality is evident. In part this arose from the truculence of the response to Tiananmen and the perceived threat to the communist political system itself as China's leaders absorbed the shocks of the collapse of communism in Europe in 1989–91 and as they reacted to the sanctions imposed by the West. But in part it also arose from an appreciation of China's growing weight in international affairs that made possible the assertion of sovereignty over territories that had hitherto been out of reach for one reason or another. The result has been to pose Beijing with a series of dilemmas. Is it to assert territorial claims at the expense of good neighbourliness and risk the economic exchanges that have served the country so well? Is it to impose its will upon Hong Kong because of alleged trouble-making by the British and by subversive democrats, and risk both losing the economic benefits that the territory has brought and damaging China's international standing as a country with which to do business? Is it to use force against a more democratic Taiwan lest it break away for good and risk an enlarged armed conflict and cause the countries of the region to seek countervailing power? The answers to these questions may turn less on rational choice than on the dynamics of the political succession. The less disruptive that may be, the more likely it is that a self-confident leadership will emerge that would be able to pursue China's sovereign claims with moderation and with due regard to the wider issues that they encompass. The more difficult the succession the more likely a weak leadership would respond erratically and assertively to perceived challenges, especially if it were dependent upon the armed forces who are imbued with more virulent nationalist sentiments.

China is the rising power of the region. Historical experience of the rise of Germany in Europe or of Japan in Asia cautions that the appeasement of such powers is often fraught with danger. It by no means follows that the Chinese case will follow those precedents. China's economic interests are benefiting from a favourable international environment, and a regime that has staked its survival on continuing to improve the economic conditions of its people has even stronger incentives than most to avoid putting them in jeopardy. Moreover, as long as the United States retains its current military deployments in the Western Pacific it will serve as a mighty force for stability. But there is apprehension in the region that they might be withdrawn because of domestic budgetary pressures within the United States and perhaps because of a declining readiness to provide security for American trading adversaries. Even more to the point is concern as to whether there will be the political will in Washington to play the balancer role. Meanwhile Sino–American relations have become fraught with difficulties as nearly every issue which the Americans think embodies a principle of universal significance finds the US and the PRC on opposite sides. Thus the two major countries are divided on matters of human rights, nuclear proliferation, the sale of weapons of mass destruction, trade liberalization, democratization, self determination for Tibet and so on. The point has been reached where many Chinese leaders are convinced that the United States is deliberately obstructing China's rise to great power status.

Not a few observers foresee an emerging rivalry between China and Japan as the two great East Asian powers. Concerned about China's growing military might, the Japanese have demanded greater transparency regarding China's military spending and its military plans and strategy. In 1995 Japan took the unprecedented step of suspending some of its aid in response to a Chinese nuclear test. There is apprehension that if the Chinese were to continue to ignore

Japanese concerns they could end up by provoking Japan into assuming a more dynamic military and strategic role which is precisely what the Chinese profess to oppose.

CHINA'S FUTURE

Much depends on domestic developments within China, over which no outside power has control. The above analysis has considered some of the consequences that might follow the emergence of a confident and assertive leadership, but perhaps the most destabilizing outcome would be of a fragmented and chaotic country whose problems would inevitably spread to damage the region. In this sense the future of the region as well as China's future role within it could well turn on the evolution of the pending succession problems. China is moving into a new era of politics without the dominance of personal leaders of the extraordinary stature of Mao Zedong or Deng Xiaoping to which it has been accustomed during the first forty-five years since the establishment of the PRC. It is doing so without an institutionalized system for political succession and with a weak legal culture.

This is occurring at a time of fundamental change and challenge not only to the structure of the Chinese state, but to the character of China's culture and identity. The process of modernization has brought China to the point where its historical continentalism is shifting to acquire maritime characteristics. The centre of gravity of the state is moving from the traditional preoccupation with administrative controls from a unitary centre towards a more decentralized system based on indirect macro-economic management as befits the transition from a command to a market economy. Elsewhere federalism would be the obvious answer for a country of this size, but China lacks the legal culture for such an arrangement. In practice, however, the regions and provinces are acquiring more autonomy. Those that are adjacent to neighbouring countries are developing special foreign economic relations with them. Divisions have appeared between coastal and interior provinces, vast movements of people are taking place as peasants leave the land and as the coastal regions exercise a pull upon the interior.[58] Meanwhile vast problems of demography, environmental degradation and infrastructural weaknesses threaten to overwhelm the state's capacity to deal with them.[59] Communism has long lost its appeal and has long ceased to operate as a unifying ideology. Chinese nationalism alone commands general appeal. Whether or not this enormous process of transition can be accomplished peaceably will determine not only the future of China, but the future of the Asia-Pacific too.

By virtue of its size, history and potential China may be considered to be the most important country within the region that is capable of shaping its future security. Before the advent of the West and the forces of modernity China dominated East Asia less by force of arms than by the awe of its civilization, by the indirect means of what has been called the 'tribute system' and through manipulating differences between potentially hostile adversaries. The last 150 years may be seen as Chinese attempts to adjust to the impact of the West and to find ways to modernize. With the establishment of the People's Republic in 1949 it seemed as if the Communist Party-State had provided the answer. However, the last fifteen years of economic reform and opening to the international economy coupled with the collapse of communism elsewhere have raised afresh the question of the Chinese political identity and of its adaptation to the modern world.[60]

After fifteen years of economic reforms and opening to the international economy China, by the end of 1994, had leapt from being the world's thirtieth largest exporter in 1978, to becoming the tenth largest. Its economy had grown at an average of over 9 per cent a year and in each of the three years 1992–94 it had grown by 11–13 per cent. On the basis of purchasing power parity its economy ranked second only to that of the United States and, according to the World Bank, it was poised to become technically the world's largest economy in the year 2010.[61] With the demise of the Soviet threat China has been able to focus almost exclusively upon developing the economy in what its leaders regard as a largely tranquil international environment. As a result there has been a tendency to project forward the existing economic growth rates and to foresee China as the next emerging superpower.[62]

China, however, faces huge problems of adjustment that may very well greatly complicate its path to international greatness if not actually overwhelm it. Its vast population of 1,200 million, which will reach 1,300 million by the year 2000 (100 million more than initially targeted) poses immense problems. With 22 per cent of the world's population China has only 7 per cent of the world's arable land and 6 per cent of its usable water. The reforms have loosened central controls so that an estimated 150 million people have left the countryside to look for work in the cities and coastal regions.[63] The urban economy is threatened by the vast state owned enterprises as many of these run at a loss and are subsidized to the extent of a third of state budgeted expenditure. On the other hand they cannot be bankrupted for fear of the social consequences of throwing up to 100 million people out of work and denying them the welfare benefits that these enterprises provided. In the absence of an effective legal system and as a result of seeking to maintain the state and communist party structures while developing a market economy, corruption has spread to the extent that Jiang Zemin, the state and party leader, has warned that it could bring the regime down. The reforms have also weakened central controls and encouraged economic regionalism to the extent that central powers have been greatly weakened.[64] Caught half way between an administered command economy and a market based one, the regime has been unable to develop the institutions considered necessary to maintain effective macro-economic management of the economy. In the absence of effective controls and the collapse of communist ideology as a coherent public philosophy, public order is close to breaking down, crime is rampant and there is evidence of growing social unrest.[65] The environment that was greatly damaged in the previous period of socialist economics is being further degraded by the sheer magnitude of the uncontrolled economic growth that is taking place.[66]

If the large scale of these problems were not daunting enough, the regime also faces a problem of great proportions concerning political succession, the outcome of which may well determine whether China will emerge as the great power that many anticipate. The succession will be from the generation of the revolutionary founders of the party and the state to the generation of those skilled in obtaining patronage and in bureaucratic manoeuvre. It is epitomized in the contrast between Deng Xiaoping and his own chosen successor Jiang Zemin. The former holds no posts, but by virtue of his personal standing among the other 'founding fathers' and in the party and army high commands he is still the ultimate ruler.[67] Jiang Zemin, by contrast, is State President, General Secretary of the Party and Chairman of the Military Affairs Commission but commands the respect of few. Ostensibly China is headed for a period of collective leadership, but experience suggests that such a format rarely lasts. China is therefore headed for a period of great uncertainty in which the issue of political change will have to be addressed. The reversal of the reforms and of the policy of opening up to the international economy is generally considered to be unlikely, if not impossible. But that still leaves open a variety of possible alternatives, most of which would still pose problems for the region.[68]

China's growing international significance has been accompanied by a new sense of Chinese assertiveness that has taken a nationalistic form. In part this may be seen as a domestic response to the decaying appeal of communism as an ideology that has bound Chinese society together. But it also takes the form of a desire to re-establish sovereign control over 'lost' territories such as those in the South China Sea and Taiwan. Nationalistic sentiments are strikingly evident in many of the pronouncements of leaders of the Chinese armed forces whose strategic outlook is acquiring a more maritime orientation in keeping with the shift in China's security interests from the traditional continental concerns with inner Asia. Nevertheless China's new and growing capacity to project force at sea and more generally within the region should perhaps be regarded less as evidence of hostile intent and more as the corollary of its dynamic economic growth and its ambition to be regarded as a great power of the first rank.[69] China's growing strength troubles its neighbours and the extent to which the Chinese can demonstrate sensitivity to these concerns may well shape the character of security in the region in the years ahead. As was discussed earlier, this has already become a problem in Sino–Japanese relations, but perhaps the most important relationship will remain the difficult one with the United States.

NOTES AND REFERENCES

1 In a book written by Chinese scholars who had carried out research training in the United States the editors described their country as 'a regional power with global strategic significance and political influence'. Yufan Hao and Guocang Huan (eds) *The Chinese View of the World* (New York: Pantheon Books, 1989) p. xxix.
2 Steven Levine, 'China in Asia: The PRC as a Regional Power' in Harry Harding (ed.) *China's Foreign Policy in the 1980s* (New Haven: Yale University Press, 1984) p. 107.
3 Samuel S. Kim, 'China's International Organizational Behaviour' in Thomas W. Robinson and David Shambaugh (eds) *Chinese Foreign Policy: Theory and Practice* (Oxford: Clarendon Press, 1994) p. 417.
4 Jonathan D. Spence, *The Search for Modern China* (London: Hutchinson, 1990) pp. 162–64.
5 Michael H. Hunt, 'Chinese Foreign Relations in Historical Perspective' in Harry Harding, *China's Foreign Relations in the 1980s* (New Haven: Yale University Press, 1984) p. 10.
6 Edgar Snow, *Red Star Over China* (London: Pelican Books, revised and enlarged edition, 1972) pp. 128–29.

224   *The policies of the great powers*

Wang Gungwu, 'Pre-Modern History: Some Trends in Writing the History of the Song (10th-13th Centuries)' in Michael B. Yahuda (ed.) *New Directions in the Social Sciences and Humanities in China* (London: Macmillan Press, 1987) pp. 1–27.

8 John Gittings, *Survey of the Sino–Soviet Dispute* (London: Oxford University Press, 1968) pp. 166–67.

9 For this and the previous quotation see William C. Kirby, 'Traditions of Centrality, Authority and Management in modern China's Foreign Relations' in Thomas W. Robinson and David Shambaugh (eds) *Chinese Foreign Policy: Theory and Practice* (Oxford: Clarendon Press, 1994) p. 17.

10 Harry Harding, 'China's Co-operative Behaviour' in *ibid*. pp. 384–92.

11 See the discussions by Carol Lee Hamrin, 'Elite Politics and Foreign Relations' in Robinson and Shambaugh, *Chinese Foreign Policy* (*op. cit.*) pp. 70–112; and Kenneth Lieberthal, 'Domestic Politics and Foreign Policy' in Harding, *China's Foreign Relations in the 1980s* (*op. cit.*) pp. 43–70.

12 Wang Jisi, 'International Relations Theory and the Study of Chinese Foreign Policy: A Chinese Perspective' in Robinson and Shambaugh (*op. cit.*) p. 493.

13 This paragraph has drawn on Wang Jisi, (*ibid*.) pp. 481–505; Steven I. Levine, 'Perception and Ideology in Chinese Foreign Policy' in Robinson and Shambaugh (*op. cit.*) pp. 30–46; and Lucian Pye, *The Mandarin and the Cadre: China's Political Cultures* (Ann Arbor: Center for Chinese Studies, University of Michigan, 1988).

14 Chi-Kin Lo, *China's Policy Towards Territorial Disputes: The Case of the South China Sea Islands* (London: Routledge, 1989) pp. 27–28.

15 Michael B. Yahuda, *China's Role in World Affairs* (London: Croom Helm, 1978) pp. 47–48.

16 These were:

1 mutual respect for each other's territorial integrity and sovereignty;
2 non aggression;
3 non-interference in each other's internal affairs;
4 equality and mutual benefit;
5 peaceful co-existence.

It will be seen that these stress statism and that their vague terms apply best to relations between governments from divergent political systems. Not surprisingly, they have tended to be downplayed during the more revolutionary phases of Chinese foreign policy and to be highlighted during the more moderate ones. They have been revived during the 1990s as a way of deflecting the more intrusive of the post Cold War international norms, but it is doubtful how applicable they may be in the more interdependent world within which the PRC is seeking to integrate itself.

17 Michael Leifer, *Dictionary of the Modern Politics of South-East Asia* (London: Routledge, 1995) p. 211.

18 For a detailed account see Stephen Fitzgerald, *China and the Overseas Chinese* (Cambridge: Cambridge University Press, 1972).

19 Jay Taylor, *China and Southeast Asia: Peking's Relations with Revolution-*

ary Movements (New York: Praeger, 2nd edn. 1976) Chapter 5, pp. 251–372.

20 Steven M. Goldstein, 'Sino–Soviet Relations' in Robinson and Shambaugh (*op. cit.*) particularly pp. 237–44.

21 Allen S. Whiting, 'The Sino–Soviet Split', *Cambridge History of China Vol. 14*. (*op. cit.*) p. 493.

22 *ibid.* p. 499.

23 This theme is developed in Goldstein, 'Sino–Soviet Relations' (*op. cit.*). For a hard hitting account of Mao's approach and the problems it raised for China see Edward Friedman, 'Anti-Imperialism in Chinese Foreign Policy' in Samuel S. Kim (ed.) *China and the World: Chinese Foreign Relations in the Post-Cold War Era* (Boulder: Westview Press, 1994) pp. 60–74.

24 Whiting, 'The Sino–Soviet Split' (*op. cit.*) p. 502.

25 This is the argument of Melvin Gurtov, *China and Southeast Asia – The Politics of Survival* (Lexington: Heath Lexington Books, 1971).

26 For accounts see, Neville Maxwell, *India's China War* (London: Pelican, 1970); Alastair Lamb, *The China–India Border* (London: Oxford University Press, 1964); and Allen S. Whiting, *The Chinese Calculus of Deterrence*, (Michigan: University of Michigan Press, 1975).

27 Cited in Michael Leifer, *Indonesia's Foreign Policy* (London: George Allen & Unwin, 1983) p. 69.

28 Yahuda, *China's Role in World Affairs* (*op. cit.*) pp. 149–54.

29 Barry Naughton, 'The Third Front Defence: Industrialization in the Chinese Interior', *The China Quarterly* No. 115, September 1988, pp. 351–86.

30 Allen S. Whiting, *The Chinese Calculus of Deterrence* (Ann Arbor: University of Michigan Press, 1975) pp. 170–95. Interestingly, Hanoi made this charge after the 1979 war with China: see Ministry of Foreign Affairs, Socialist Republic of Vietnam, *The Truth About Vietnam–China Relations Over the Last Thirty Years* (Hanoi: Foreign Languages Press, 1979) p. 35.

31 For further detail and analysis on the above two paragraphs see Thomas W. Robinson, 'China Confronts the Soviet Union: Warfare and Diplomacy on China's Inner Asian Frontiers' in *The Cambridge History of China Vol. 15* (Cambridge: Cambridge University Press, 1991) pp. 218–301.

32 This paragraph draws on Jonathan D. Pollack, 'The Opening to America', *The Cambridge History of China Vol. 15* (*op. cit.*) pp. 423–25.

33 For an account of reactions in Southeast Asia see Taylor, *China and Southeast Asia . . .* (*op. cit.*) pp. 337–55.

34 *ibid.* p. 422.

35 Yahuda, *China's Role . . .* (*op. cit.*) p. 262.

36 For further details, see relevant *Southeast Asia Year Books* (Singapore: Institute of Southeast Asian Studies, 1974, 1975 and 1976) and *Asia Year Books* (Hong Kong: Far Eastern Economic Review, 1974, 1975 and 1976).

37 For extended analysis see Nayan Chanda, *Brother Enemy: The War After the War* (New York: Harcourt Brace Jovanovich, 1986); and Robert

S. Ross, *The Indo-China Tangle: China's Vietnam Policy, 1975–1979* (New York: Columbia University Press, 1988).

38 For Chinese and Vietnamese claims and counter-claims about the alleged perfidy of the other see Ministry of Foreign Affairs, *The Truth About Vietnam–Chinese Relations ... (op. cit.)*; and *On the Vietnamese Foreign Ministry's White Book Concerning Vietnam–China Relations* (Beijing: Foreign Language Press, 1979).

39 For details of the negotiations and of Sino–American relations at this time see Pollock, 'Opening to America' *(op. cit.)* pp. 435–56.

40 For an account of the gradual improvement in relations in the early 1980s see Gerald Segal, *Sino–Soviet Relations after Mao* (London: IISS/ Brassey's, Adelphi Paper No. 202, 1985).

41 Wang Jisi, 'A Chinese Perspective' *(op. cit.)* p. 486.

42 Paul H. B. Godwin, 'Force and Diplomacy: Chinese Security Policy in the Post-Cold War Era' in Kim, *China and the World (op. cit.)* p. 172.

43 Harry Harding, *A Fragile Relationship, The United States and China Since 1972* (Washington, DC: The Brookings Institution, 1992) Chapter 5 'Reconciliation', pp. 138–72.

44 For extended treatment see Allen S. Whiting, *China Eyes Japan* (Berkeley: University of California Press, 1989).

45 For detailed analysis of many of the relevant aspects see, *The China Quarterly*, 'Special Issue: Greater China' Issue No. 136, December 1993.

46 *ibid.* See also, Kevin Rafferty, *City on the Rocks* (London: Viking, 1989). On the negotiations see Robert Cottrell, *The End of Hong Kong* (London: John Murray, 1993).

47 For accounts of the economic relations see John Wong, *The Political Economy of Southeast Asia* (London: Macmillan Press, 1984); and Chia Siow-Yue and Cheng Bifan (eds) *ASEAN–China Economic Relations: Trends and Patterns* (Singapore: Institute of Southeast Asian Studies, 1987).

48 Godwin, 'Force and Diplomacy' *(op. cit.)* pp. 172–73.

49 See the account by Harding, *A Fragile Relationship (op. cit.)* Chapter 7, 'Crisis' pp. 215–46.

50 Richard Baum, *Burying Mao* (Princeton: Princeton University Press, 1994).

51 For an account of the adjustment of China's leaders to the changes in the Soviet Union/Russia see John W. Garver, 'The Chinese Communist Party and the Collapse of Soviet Communism', *The China Quarterly* Issue No. 133, March 1993, pp. 1–26. See also Lowell Dittmer, 'China and Russia: New Beginnings' in Kim (ed.) *China and the World (op. cit.)* pp. 94–112.

52 For a discussion of the problem of the North see Byung-joon Ahn, 'The Man Who Would be Kim', *Foreign Affairs* November/December 1994, pp. 94–108.

53 For an account of the various characteristics of Chinese behaviour in international organizations see Samuel S. Kim, 'China's International Organizational Behaviour' in Robinson and Shambaugh (eds) *(op. cit.)* pp. 401–34.

54 For an account of the different regional foreign relations that have emerged and of the centrifugal forces that have been encouraged as a

result see David S. G. Goodman and Gerald Segal (eds) *China Deconstructs* (London: Routledge, 1994).

55 For a detailed analysis of the legal dimensions see Jeanette Greenfield, *China's Practice in the Law of the Sea* (Oxford: Clarendon Press, 1992). For a political and strategic analysis see John W. Garver, 'China's Push Through the South China Sea: The Interaction of Bureaucratic and National Interests', *The China Quarterly* Issue No. 132, December 1992, pp. 999–1028.

56 for accounts of the relevant negotiations see Robert Cottrell, *The End of Hong Kong* (London: John Murray, 1993); and Percy Cradock, *Experiences of China* (John Murray, 1994).

57 For various assessments of these issues see Lin Zhiling and Thomas W. Robinson, (eds) *The Chinese and Their Future: Beijing, Taipei, and Hong Kong* (Washington, DC: American Enterprise Institute Press, 1992); and Robert Sutter (ed.) *Taiwan's Role in World Affairs* (Boulder: Westview Press, 1994).

58 For discussion of some of these developments see Gerald Segal, *China Changes Shape: Regionalism and Foreign Policy* (London: IISS/Brassey's, Adelphi Paper 287, March 1994); and David S. G. Goodman and Gerald Segal (eds) *China Deconstructs* (*op. cit.*).

59 Vaclav Smil, *China's Environmental Crisis* (Armonk: M. E. Sharpe, 1993). See also the discussion in Kenneth Lieberthal, *Governing China: From Revolution Through Reform* (New York: W. W. Norton, 1995) Part IV 'The Challenges Ahead', pp. 244–342.

60 For discussions of the identity issue see the various essays in 'The Living Tree: The Changing Meaning of Being Chinese Today' *Daedalus* Vol. 120, No. 2 of the Proceedings of the American Academy of Arts and Sciences, Spring 1991. See also, Lowell Dittmer and Samuel S. Kim, (eds) *China's Quest for National Identity* (Ithaca: Cornell University Press, 1993).

61 For a discussion of the various ways of assessing China's GDP per head see Robert Cottrell, 'China Survey' *The Economist* 18 March 1995, p. 9. He concluded that a more accurate estimate of purchasing power parity was about $2000 in 1994, 'which would credit China with an economy about the size of Germany's, but ranked by GDP would still be among the world's 30 or 40 poorest nations'.

62 See for example, Nicholas D. Kristof, 'The Rise of China', *Foreign Affairs* Vol. 72, No. 5, November–December 1993; and William Overholt, *China: The Next Superpower.*

63 On the latter see Dorothy J. Solinger, *China's Transients and the State: a Form of Civil Society?* (Hong Kong: Chinese University of Hong Kong, Hong Kong Institute of Pacific Studies, 1991).

64 On the possible fragmentation inherent in the new regionalism see Gerald Segal, *China Changes Shape: Regionalism and Foreign Policy* (London: IISS/Brassey's, Adelphi Paper 287, March 1994).

65 For evidence of social unrest see 'Quarterly Chronicle and Documentation' *The China Quarterly* No. 136 December 1993, pp. 1046–47. For an account of crime see Borke Bakken, 'Crime, Juvenile Delinquency and Deterrence Policy in China' *The Australian Journal of Chinese Affairs* No. 30, July 1993.

66 For a devastating account of the problem see Vaclav Smil, *China's Environmental Crisis* (*op. cit.*).

67 See 'Deng Xiaoping: An Assessment', *The China Quarterly* Special Issue, No. 135, September 1993 for accounts by seven specialists on different aspects of his leadership.

68 For a review of the main prospects see Harry Harding, 'China at the Crossroads: Conservatism, Reform or Decay' in *Asia's International Role . . . (op. cit.)* pp. 36–48.

69 David Shambaugh, 'Growing Strong: China's Challenge to Asian Security' *Survival* Vol. 36 No. 2, Summer 1994, pp. 43–59.

7 Japan and the Asia-Pacific

Since the early twentieth century Japan has been central to any conception of the Asia-Pacific as a region. In the build up to and during the Pacific War this found expression primarily in the abortive attempt to impose an economic empire by force.[1] Since 1945 Japan has emerged as the most dynamic economic centre of the region within a strategic and economic order established by the United States.

Japan is more than a regional power. Its economy is of global significance and geopolitically it is located at the junction of American, Russian and Chinese interests. For its part, Japan has been uncertain as to whether to regard itself as primarily a highly developed country that is part of the Western world as in the Trilateral Commission interacting with Europe and North America, or as still very much an Asian power that is wary of westernization and able in its own way to provide leadership to its Asian neighbours. In practice, however, Japan has played a relatively quiescent role in global affairs even where its own security interests may have been directly involved. This is largely a consequence of responsibility for its security having been assumed by the United States ever since its defeat in 1945. The relative quiescence has also been underpinned by domestic support for the principles of the 1947 'peace constitution' and by the pattern of domestic politics that emerged after the end of the American occupation in 1952. Only with the end of the Cold War did that pattern of Japanese domestic politics begin to change and in this new period Japan developed an international ambition that was expressed in a demand for a permanent seat on the Security Council of the United Nations that was significantly qualified by a refusal still to assume attendant military responsibilities.

Throughout the period of the Cold War, the United States in

effect guaranteed the security of Japan and maintained an international free trade order that allowed Japan to pursue its own narrow commercial interests. Japan resisted all American attempts to persuade it to participate in collective security schemes and avoided involvement in international strategic affairs. Indeed during the 1950s and 1960s Japan essentially followed the US lead in foreign affairs (while refusing to 'share responsibilities') and it was only in reaction to the 1971 'Nixon shocks' of failing to consult them on his opening to China and of his abrupt withdrawal of the US dollar from the gold standard that the Japanese began to develop a somewhat independent course. Even then the fundamental neo-mercantilist approach did not greatly change as Japanese foreign policy continued to be primarily reactive while seeking to avoid becoming embroiled in international conflicts.

The impact upon Japan of having most of its security responsibilities undertaken by the United States has been complex and many sided. Emerging out of the period of the US occupation that ended in 1952, the security arrangement that became central to American strategy in the Cold War era was first used by Prime Minister Yoshida Shigeru as a means by which Japan 'gave exclusive priority to pursuing economic recovery and maintaining political stability . . . [while deferring] indefinitely the task of preparing the Japanese people themselves for a return to the harsh realities of international politics'.[2] This set a course that became institutionalized. The neo-mercantilist policies initially adopted in the 1950s had profound effects upon the structure of domestic politics that in turn reinforced the character of those policies in dealing with the outside world.

The Yoshida approach in effect sought to reach an accommodation between those Japanese nationalists who found it demeaning for Japan to be confined to the status of dependency in security matters and those who adhered to the ethos of the 1947 'peace constitution' which pledged Japan to forswear war and the use or threat of force as an instrument of policy. Yoshida himself in later life came to regret the course that he had set. In 1963 nearly ten years after leaving office he wrote:

> For an independent Japan, which is among the first rank countries in economics, technology, and learning, to continue to be dependent on another country is a deformity (*katawa*) of the state. . . .
> I myself cannot escape responsibility for the use of the consti-

tution as a pretext (*tatemae*) for this way of conducting national policy.[3]

But the die was cast so that even thirty years later Japanese security was still dependent upon the United States without obliging Japan to reciprocate or to contribute to regional security.

Since the end of the Cold War the relationship between Japan and the United States has remained at the core of the security architecture of the Asia-Pacific, but it has been subject to new stresses and challenges. The demise of the Soviet threat and the greater salience of economic and domestic issues in American foreign policy has given a new edge to long standing problems in relations with Japan. The huge trade surpluses that Japan has enjoyed with the United States have become much more contentious as economic disputes have ceased to be counter-balanced by the cooperative dimension of the security problems of confronting the Soviet Union. A more nationalistically assertive Japan has resented American pressure to change its economic practices and to be more supportive of American leadership in world affairs even on issues fundamental to Japan such as the Gulf War of 1991 and the North Korean nuclear problem since 1993. Within Japan, however, these issues, the Gulf in particular, were seen less as problems that involved the country's national interests directly and more as matters that concerned relations with the United States.[4]

Japan's foreign relations have also been constrained by the legacy of the history of its aggression in the Asia-Pacific before 1945 with which it has yet to come to terms satisfactorily – at least in the eyes of many of the victims of that aggression especially in East Asia. Even those Japanese who adhere most strongly to the ethos of the 'peace constitution' have tended to see their country as a victim of the Pacific War rather than as its vicious perpetrator. They dwell in particular on the horrors of the atomic bombs dropped on Hiroshima and Nagasaki. In this respect they converge with more right-wing Japanese nationalists who play down the significance of Japanese aggression and war time atrocities often to the annoyance of neighbouring countries and to the embarrassment of Japanese prime ministers who have to demand the resignation of such people from the Cabinet.

Japan's neighbours have also professed concern about the possible re-emergence of Japanese militarism. Not only do they point to a failure to come to terms with its aggressive past, but they also note the speed with which Japan could transform itself into a country that could project overwhelming military power throughout the region. Due to its advanced technological capacities and its high levels of military spending Japan in 1990, it was claimed, possessed a military capability which 'must be rated first class in global, as well as regional, terms'.[5] Although certain inadequacies such as shortages of reserve forces and logistical weaknesses currently limit the exercise of Japanese power, it is believed in the region that these and other problems could be overcome very quickly indeed if the Japanese 'mood' were to change suddenly.

The possibility of such a transformation cannot be excluded because of the country's insularity and sense of vulnerability. Before the forceful advent of the West in the mid-nineteenth century Japanese history involved only limited interactions with others. The people of its four principal islands are remarkably homogeneous. Despite having emerged as a great trading and industrial country in the last 140 years Japan has retained a relative parochialism, but that has been coupled with a sense of vulnerability not only due to the possible threats of militarily superior powers, but also because of its lack of natural resources and its dependence upon external supplies. Despite having been perhaps the prime beneficiary of international order since the end of the Second World War the Japanese customarily think of the international environment as potentially threatening and prone to sudden upheavals. Their task has been to detect trends and accommodate themselves to them. Many see Japan's enhanced economic and political role within the region allied to its continuing neo-mercantilism and assertive nationalism as leading inexorably to a resurgence of militarism – especially if this were allied to a sharp change in the international environment that was adverse to Japan.[6]

Japanese perspectives, not surprisingly perhaps, do not encompass what to them would appear to be at best a far fetched notion that they may resume the militarist path of old. In delineating 'four Japanese scenarios for the future', the nearest the political scientist Takashi Inoguchi came to identifying what he called a *Pax Nipponica* was an economically dominant Japan that could act as the balancer in the power balance between the continental powers – rather like Britain in the nineteenth century. But even this role is predicated on what he regarded as the unlikely neutralization of nuclear weapons.[7] His own view about Japan's international role was more circumspect. Writing in 1993 he observed: 'At present, Japan's interests derive largely from its "search for an honourable place in the world community", from its apprehension of being isolated and from its genuine desire to make positive contributions to international security'. But too much should not be expected as 'Japan's historical legacy its weakly articulated vision of its international role and its feeble leadership will prevent it from taking up some responsibilities with vigour. These, however, are constraints that Japan will have to live with for the foreseeable future.'[8] There is therefore an abiding enigmatic quality to Japan's role in Asia as its history, economic significance and immediate military potential point to leadership capacities that are dormant, like a volcano that could nevertheless erupt if the pressures upon it were suddenly to change.

THE DOMESTIC SOURCES OF FOREIGN POLICY

The combination of highly activist neo-mercantilist economic policies and the generally cautious and reactive approach to the outside world that characterizes much of Japan's foreign policy may be said to be anchored in the structure of its government and politics. But at the same time that also draws upon deeply set ideas about Japan's identity and the legacy of Japanese history. The Japanese system of government has been characterized by continual rule by conservative parties (predominantly the Liberal Democratic Party – LDP – since its formation in 1955) in a triumvirate with the business community and above all the semi-autonomous bureaucratic ministries. The LDP has been notoriously factionalized, and the business community has been divided into four main groups. Nevertheless, especially in the 1950s and 1960s, a consensus prevailed on the necessity for reconstruction and high economic growth. This was achieved under the highly favourable external conditions provided by American hegemony, the general growth of the international economy and ready access to the American domestic market on a non-reciprocal basis.

The principal ministries involved in foreign relations included the Ministry of Foreign Affairs (MFA), the Ministry of International Trade and Industry (MITI), the Ministry of Finance (MoF) and the Ministry of Fisheries and Food (MAFF). Their interests often conflicted: MITI was primarily concerned with the promotion of Japanese economic interests based on its domestic industrial constituency; MoF was concerned with limiting budgetary expenditure; MAFF was concerned with defending farming and fishing interests and it benefited from an electoral system that was skewed in favour of farmers; and the MFA, bereft of an obvious domestic constituency, was in a relatively weak position as it sought to reconcile the domestic, not to say the parochial thrust of the external dimensions of Japan's interests, with the demands made upon Japan primarily by the United States.[9]

This resulted in a decision making process that was singularly effective in blocking most initiatives and that was simultaneously and paradoxically extremely well suited to adapting to changing circumstances. Various Japanese scholars have commented adversely on the powerful relationships that bind vested interests, bureaucrats and politicians in ways that dilute initiative: 'Reform efforts evaporate like drops of water on a hot griddle'. Moreover, their alliance is said to have 'closed Japan tight to the rest of the world'.[10] This system, however, has also proved remarkably capable in monitoring trends and when necessary adapting to changes. This was true, for example, of the two oil crises in the 1970s which left Japanese industry even more competitive as it became even more efficient in its use of energy; and, later, of the re-evaluation of the Yen in 1985 which accelerated the distribution of production capacity especially to Southeast Asia. But it is a system that gives rise to neo-mercantile practices rather than the provision of leadership or easy contribution to international public goods.[11]

Despite being the products of factional manoeuvrings that owe little to debates about public policy and still less to foreign affairs issues, Japanese prime ministers have been able to practice personal diplomacy and at times to provide leadership in foreign affairs. Japanese commentators have tended to credit each of their post war prime ministers with a distinctive personal approach that at times shaped policy in crucial ways.[12] While acknowledging the centrality of prime ministers in the Japanese foreign policy process outside observers tend to draw attention to the constraints that limit their capacity to exercise leadership.[13]

The effectiveness of these constraints must be understood against the backcloth of modern Japanese history and within the context of the conflicting systems of ideas that have shaped Japanese thinking about their role since 1945. The former inculcated the sense that as an outsider and a late developer Japan had to assess the international conditions set by the great powers and respond to them so as to best advantage Japan. The latter set up a tension between the pattern of ideas associated with the so-called 'peace constitution' by which the Japanese were pledged to renounce war forever, and the ideas associated with the security alliance with the United States. Japanese leaders were forever seeking to balance the two. Above all the 'lesson' of the last 150 years since this insular and self absorbed country was forcibly opened up to the Western world has been that the Japanese must be ever vigilant about the vulnerability of their country. As a state that became uniquely dependent upon trade, it has been concerned about securing supplies; and as an island chain of global geopolitical significance, Japan has been concerned about the shifting balance of forces between the great powers. As Kenneth Pyle has observed,

> since the Meiji Restoration, Japanese leaders have had a keen sensitivity to the forces controlling the international environment; they tried to operate in accord with these forces and use them to their own advantage. A shrewd politician grasped the 'trend of the times', adapted Japanese policy to these trends, and benefited from them.[14]

Historical forces, the character of the domestic political system and the strength of the appeal of the 'peace constitution' within Japan combined to intensify this reactive quality of Japanese foreign policy. The policy has not been without its successes and arguably it has served Japan well. The country has prospered and become an economic superpower without becoming embroiled in the many wars and armed conflicts that took place in the Asia-Pacific region. However, Japan's reactive neo-mercantilism and the parochial character of its intractable decision making processes has meant that external pressure alone has made it respond to the demands of international society about rules of trade. But as Japanese nationalistic pride has grown so has resentment grown at the pressure exerted by outsiders.

Yet it is the very growth of Japan's economic significance that has impacted adversely upon its partners and caused them to demand changes in Japanese practices. This is nowhere more evident than in the economic relations with its security benefactor and most important partner, the United States. Problems in the imbalance of trade which began in the 1970s have troubled the relationship and intensified as the Cold War came to an end. As American pressure increased the Japanese reaction continued to be one of reluctant adjustment. This has elicited a strong nationalist reaction typified by the famous 1989 book co-authored by the chairman of Sony entitled, *The Japan That Can Say 'No': The New US–Japan Relations Card*.[15] As is evident from the title, this is essentially a negative response rather than an alternative assertion of positive leadership.

Beginning in 1993–94, however, the Japanese political system responded to domestic and external changes that in large measure flowed from the ending of the Cold War, thereby commencing what many regard as a prolonged process of transformation. The Japanese Socialist Party could no longer sustain its cherished ideological positions and the Liberal Democratic Party finally split, spurred in part by voter dissatisfaction with its long running corruption scandals. This resulted in 1994 with the first non Liberal Democratic government for nearly forty years. It remains to be seen whether the projected electoral reforms will be carried out and much would then depend on whether that would set in tow a ripple effect that would contribute to systemic change. The Japanese economic miracle has been buttressed domestically by a conservative coalition of protected agriculture, organized business and a national bureaucracy imbued with economic nationalism. Externally it has flourished under the American security guarantee and an international economic order shaped however imperfectly by the United States. Japan is currently in a process of transition, the outcome of which may determine whether under the new conditions in the post Cold War period critical aspects of this nexus will change in any fundamental way. The only other source for profound change would be a major 'shock' from the outside that would once again remind the Japanese of their country's vulnerabilities and cause them to re-orientate their society as they have done before in modern history.

JAPAN'S RE-EMERGENCE UNDER AMERICAN HEGEMONY, 1945–70

There is considerable merit to the view that following the largely American occupation Japan has since 1952 focused on its own economic development and trade little troubled by considerations of security and foreign policy. This was a period of exceptional American power in international affairs and the Japanese benefited both from the security guarantee and the favourable external economic conditions provided by the United States. But such a view would be incomplete as it would overlook Japanese success in quite deliberately forging a foreign policy based on neo-mercantilism that enabled it to resist American demands that it play a greater role in regional security, especially on a collective basis. Thus Japan was able to conduct trade with the People's Republic of China, despite the American embargo, and to establish relations with the Soviet Union. At the same time the Japanese were able to take advantage of American initiatives on their behalf to re-establish economic ties with Southeast Asia. Consequently, by the end of this period Japan emerged not only as a major economic power second in size only to the United States, but it also began to exercise significant independent influence within the Asia-Pacific region.

The occupation was notable in its early years for the changes that it brought about in the constitution, local government, the judiciary, law, labour relations, land tenure and education. The principal objectives were to extirpate the influence of militarism and to advance democratization of Japanese society. From the point of view of foreign policy the most important change was the famous Chapter 9 in the constitution of 1947. In its original form it would have unambiguously pledged Japan to forswear the development of its own armed forces, but the final version qualified this somewhat by allowing for an interpretation which pegged that to the aim of an 'international peace based on justice and order'. That left open the prospect of preparing for defence against aggression as a legitimate option in an imperfect world.[16] The amendments were introduced to assuage the Japanese side, but by 1948 the American approach changed as the advent of the Cold War caused them to regard Japan as an ally to be cultivated rather than a defeated enemy to be punished. This led to a harsher treatment of the left and of trade unions and to a more favourable attitude towards the business and conservative elements. Washington was also tiring of paying the bill to keep Japan afloat and it was anxious for its economic recovery to take place. In this new atmosphere the old conglomerates, the former *zaibatsu* resumed operations. By 1949 the many thousands who had been purged because of their past links with the war government were beginning to be readmitted to civil and political life. And in July 1950, a month after the outbreak of the Korean War, permission was granted for the creation of a National Police Reserve, a para-military force 75,000 strong, in readiness to take over domestic security from the Americans.

The change in the American attitude accelerated the process of moving towards a peace settlement and bringing the occupation to an end. The Japanese left was embittered by the American change of course and it was also divided. But their increasingly anti-American posture paradoxically centred on the quintessentially American document, the famous Peace Article No. 9. In his negotiations with John Foster Dulles, who had come in 1950 to try and draw Japan into America's Cold War coalition, Prime Minister Yoshida was able to draw upon the opposition of the left as one of his key arguments against Japan being called upon to take an activist role. After protracted negotiations Yoshida made minimal concessions (for example he agreed to increasing the number of the police reserves who were to be called the National Security Force from 75,000 to 110,000 instead of the 350,000 demanded by Dulles) and secured an approach that was to prevail for the next four decades and beyond:

1 The principal national goal was Japan's economic rehabilitation and to this end economic and political cooperation with the United States was essential.
2 Japan was to remain lightly armed and free of entanglement in international strategic issues so as *inter-alia* to minimize internal divisions – what Yoshida called 'a 38th parallel' in the hearts of the Japanese people.
3 Bases would be provided for the American armed forces in order to gain a long term guarantee for the security of Japan.[17]

The approach was predicated on the conviction that the imperatives of the Cold War determined that the Americans would deploy significant forces in Japan and that they would suffice to deter the Soviet Union. Japan would be insulated from the hard choices of international politics and security while pursuing economic goals amid conditions of political stability. Indeed, by 1955 the domestic situation settled into an almost fixed pattern as the sets of political parties essentially polarized into a socialist party that became a permanent opposition and the Liberal Democrats who became the party of government. Meanwhile the myth took root of a Japan that, as a country that had been uniquely scarred by the atomic bomb and especially endowed by its peace constitution, was particulary committed to peace.

The negotiations with Dulles, however, also exacted a price for Japan's opting out of collective security responsibilities. The security treaty that was signed on the same day as the San Francisco Peace Treaty (8 September 1951) was unequal also in terms of security obligations and it preserved many of the prerogatives enjoyed by the United States during the occupation. Although together with the British the Japanese had been successful in barring both Chinas from attending the Peace Treaty (if the PRC were not to be allowed to attend by the United States, then the ROC should not attend either), Yoshida had no alternative but to recognize Chiang Kai-shek's ROC as the legitimate China.

There was, however, a substantive body of opinion in business circles that demanded economic access to the PRC as being necessary for Japan's recovery. Being alert to the needs of the Japanese economy the Americans facilitated the utilization of Japanese reparations as a way of gaining access to the resources and markets of the Southeast Asian countries.[18] This set a pattern of unbalanced trading relations as Japan exchanged raw materials for value added manufactures. However, not withstanding these arrangements an unofficial trade agreement was signed in Beijing on 1 June 1952 by Japanese businessmen. In September Japan joined the newly established CHINCOM the allied committee formed to limit trade with the PRC. The Japanese drew a balance between the conflicting pressures between the US and the ROC on the one side and the PRC on the other. In July 1953 the House of Representatives of the Japanese Diet unanimously passed a resolution calling for the development of trade with the PRC as the first step towards improving relations between the two countries. Indeed between 1952 and 1958 four unofficial trade agreements were signed. Although notionally trade and politics were separate, even in Japanese eyes the two were closely related.

Despite a hitch in relations in 1958 after the more right-wing former member of the war time cabinet, Kishi Nobusake, had visited Taiwan, trade relations gradually resumed and in 1962 they were formalized into two types of transactions, 'Memorandum Trade' and 'Friendly Trade'. Since Japan was precluded from normalising relations with the PRC because of its American sponsored recognition of the ROC, all sides understood that the Memorandum Trade offices in the respective capitals served the purposes of unofficial missions. MITI bureaucrats served in Beijing and foreign ministry officials served in Tokyo. Although relations were fraught with problems relating to PRC suspicions of Japanese ties with Washington, and especially Taipei, and to the consequences of political turmoil in the PRC itself, Japan remained China's most important capitalist trading partner and as Sino–Soviet circumstances changed in 1968 there were signs of a movement in Japan towards recognition of the PRC.[19]

Japan's relations with the Soviet Union during this period also followed a line independent of the United States. Yoshida was replaced as Prime Minister in 1954 by the more nationalistic Hayatoma Ichero. He tried to take advantage of the more relaxed international environment to pursue a peace treaty with the Soviet Union. In the event that fell through because of the territorial dispute over the four groups of islands immediately to the north of Japan. In Japan there was an underlying sense of betrayal at the Soviet occupation of the islands, which in the Japanese view were falsely claimed as part of the Kuriles group and that in any case had been acquired at the end of the war by a Soviet violation of their non-aggression pact which Japan had done nothing to provoke. But the two states were able to agree to normalize relations in 1956 and this paved the way for Japan's admission into the United Nations. A possibility for a compromise over the islands was floated for a while, but it came to nothing, in part because of pressure by an alarmed Dulles and the confusions of domestic Japanese politics.[20] After this brief opening, Japanese relations with the Soviet Union reverted to their previous levels of animosity as the Soviet Union was unable to loosen Japan's ties with the United States and the Japanese were unable to make progress on their claims to the northern islands or in gaining access to their traditional fishing grounds in the Sea of Okhotsk. There was little, therefore, to change their legacy of historical rivalry and suspicion. This reinforced the hostility that was embedded in their opposing alignments in the Cold War.

Japan's relations with the United States were not greatly affected by these divergences from core American policies. Throughout the 1950s and 1960s Japan enjoyed privileged access to American domestic markets without being required to reciprocate. In the 1950s and 1960s Japan was seen by the United States as the linchpin of the 'free world' in Asia. It was strategically located and it was a resounding success as a democracy and as a capitalist economy. The only 'hiccup' in the relationship during this period occurred when Prime Minister Kishi sought to renew the security treaty on a more equitable basis with the United States in 1960. It aroused the fury of the left and led to riots that caused American President Eisenhower to cancel his planned visit for the signing ceremony. But the rioting was aimed principally at Kishi himself and his handling of the episode, for it died down almost as quickly as it erupted and was not followed by further anti-American demonstrations. If anything the episode served to consolidate the Yoshida approach by impressing on the Americans the dangers of exerting pressure on Japan to adopt a more active strategic role.[21]

The United States instead encouraged Japan to join the several international economic organizations that shaped the international economic order. These included the OECD, the General Agreement on Tariff and Trade (GATT), and the International Monetary Fund (IMF). Japan was also a founder member of the Asia Development Bank (ADB). Moreover, Japan had benefited economically from the Korean War during its early stage of recovery and in the late 1960s as it had become an economy of the first rank it also benefited from the Vietnam War.

Typically, there was no question of Japan participating in the war, but American use of bases in Okinawa aroused both nationalist and pacifist sentiments within Japan. In 1947 Prime Minister Sato had raised the question of the reversion of Okinawa to Japanese sovereignty, during a summit meeting with President Johnson, but without success. But in a meeting with President Nixon in 1969 it was finally agreed that sovereignty would revert in 1972.[22] By this stage, however, the configurations of power had begun to change significantly especially in Asia and that was to bring a significant adjustment of Japanese policies towards the region.

AN INDEPENDENT FOREIGN POLICY, 1971–89

During this period Japan fashioned a number of foreign relations initiatives that collectively suggested a more active and independent foreign policy despite still sheltering under the American security umbrella and despite the central role that was still accorded to relations with the United States. These initiatives may be seen as a response to a relative decline in American hegemonic power as expressed in the Nixon Doctrine and in the removal of the American dollar from the gold standard. But they also reflected responses to the two oil crises of the 1970s and to the emergence of tripolarity in the Asia-Pacific. But more than just response was involved in Southeast Asia where Japan began to take a more active role with a view to contributing to regional order. This was also the period when the imbalance in Japanese–American trade relations began to inject a note of discord in their relations. Meanwhile Sino–Japanese relations began to move out from under the American shadow to acquire a character and dynamism of their own.

Although the Nixon Doctrine as it emerged from his press conference in Guam in 1969 had alerted the Japanese to the American intention to scale down their military commitments in Asia, his decisions in 1971 to open relations with China and to take the US dollar off the gold standard came as shocks. What was particularly galling was the failure to consult or inform them significantly in advance. The cavalier way in which fundamental Japanese interests were apparently overlooked was more than a blow to self esteem. To be sure, Japan hastened to normalize its own relations with Beijing, but Beijing's bargaining position was stronger and recognition was delayed until Prime Minister Sato, to whom Beijing objected as being sympathetic to Taiwan, was replaced by Tanaka Kakuei. The threat of damage to the international economic order that was implicit in the withdrawal of the US dollar from the gold standard was soon confirmed for Japan by the 1973 oil crisis. Japan quickly responded to the threat of the Arab oil embargo by abandoning the American pro-Israeli stance in favour of a pro-Arab position.

Forced in effect to adopt a more independently conceived foreign policy, Japan under the rubric of 'omni-directional' foreign relations fashioned a series of policies designed to protect its interests. These called for the insurance of having access to as many markets and sources of supply as possible so as to minimize vulnerability in the event of closure of any one source. But in the Asia-Pacific it was also necessary to develop means of treating with China and of contributing to order in Southeast Asia in the wake of the American withdrawal.

The relationship with China was highly complex in view of their emotionally charged history and the mixed feelings over superiority and inferiority stemming from Japan's cultural indebtedness and its greater economic modernity. The difficulties were further compounded by the suggested complementarities of their economies amid major differences in their political systems and by concerns about their potential rivalry as the major regional powers. The first step to be taken in the new international environment was to complete the process of normalizing relations. The key issue was that of Taiwan. Japan's basic policy since 1952 was to try to maintain relations with both Chinas. This accorded with history and with Japan's economic interests. Moreover, there was important support for Taiwan in sections of Japanese business and within the LDP. A clever formula was found by which Japan established formal diplomatic relations with Beijing and maintained an ostensibly unofficial mission in Taipei. Normalization was followed up by agreements on fisheries, air carriers, etc. An important territorial dispute emerged over sovereign claims to some rocky islands (Senkaku in Japanese and Diaoyudao in Chinese) which would determine the division of the continental shelf and rights to possible oil and other reserves. Typically, the issue was left to be resolved by future generations. From a Japanese perspective the relations with China were troubled by a Chinese tendency to seek to exploit differences between Japanese domestic factions and interests. The Japanese were also irritated by what was regarded as politically inspired, rather than genuinely felt, Chinese sensitivity to periodic attempts by Japanese nationalist members of the Cabinet to play down the significance of Japanese aggression during the Pacific War. Nevertheless trade rapidly grew between the two sides, enhancing Japan's position as China's most important trading partner. But this too gave rise to friction, in part because the Chinese side felt entitled to favourable treatment on account of past wrongs from the war for which they had not claimed reparations and in part because of the favourable balance enjoyed by Japan. But the greatest concern of Japan was to avoid being drawn into Beijing's anti-Soviet coalition.[23]

Japan's first and perhaps most ambitious foreign policy initiative emerged with regard to Southeast Asia. Known as the Fukuda Doctrine after the prime minister who enunciated it in Manila on 18 August 1977 the policy was designed to signify a *political* commitment by Japan to contribute to stabilizing Southeast Asia. The initiative was stimulated by the confluence of a number of developments, notably the American disengagement from the sub-region following its debacle in Vietnam in 1975; the emergence of three communist states in Indo-China; and the resurgence of ASEAN as a more self conscious political entity, as signified by its first summit in Bali in 1976 and the concomitant treaties designed to set the principles for the conduct of relations in Southeast Asia. Fukuda in fact attended the second ASEAN summit held in Kuala Lumpur in August 1977. Specific Japanese concerns arose from the growing significance of the sub-region for the Japanese economy; and from the perceived need to improve the poor image of Japan as shown in the 1974 demonstrations in Thailand and Indonesia which, despite their local causes, took an anti-Japanese dimension. More broadly, Japan has a direct interest in the stability of the sub-region and, in the absence of American leadership, the Japanese prime minister, supported by more domestic parochial interests and encouraged by approaches from within ASEAN, felt emboldened to take the initiative.

The Doctrine was phrased in typically Japanese diplomatic language. Its first principle emphasized Japan's commitment to peace and to the rejection of military power as a basis on which it would contribute to peace and prosperity elsewhere. The second, committed Japan to develop trust and mutual confidence to include social and cultural areas as well as the political and economic. Finally, and to the point, Japan was declared to be an equal partner with ASEAN pledged with others to strengthen its solidarity and resilience and aimed at 'fostering a relationship with the nations of Indochina' so as to contribute to peace and prosperity 'throughout Southeast Asia'.[24] In other words, Japan sought to bring about an accommodation between Vietnam and the ASEAN countries.

Considerable diplomatic effort was directed towards implementing the new policy: exchange visits were arranged with Vietnamese and ASEAN leaders; Washington was cajoled to recognize Vietnam; and Japan tried to use its economic instruments to promote its goal of bridging the gap between Vietnam and ASEAN and of weaning Vietnam away from the Soviet Union. But the larger strategic and political momentum was moving in the opposite direction. A polarization was beginning to form between the Soviet Union and Vietnam on the one side and the United States and China on the other with ASEAN increasingly being drawn towards the latter. Although the die was cast by the Vietnamese invasion of Cambodia in December 1978 it was not until the Soviet invasion of Afghanistan a year later that the Japanese government finally gave up on its attempts to draw Vietnam away from dependence on the Soviet Union.[25] But Japanese prime ministers continued to cultivate ASEAN. Indeed one of the effects of the Fukuda Doctrine was to begin the process of what became the annual Post Ministerial meetings Conferences (PMCs) which began in 1977 and also included Australia and New Zealand. Japan had become a regular political and security dialogue partner of ASEAN as well as a dominant economic influence in the region.

In view of the thrust of its diplomacy in Southeast Asia, it was perhaps ironic that the conclusion of the peace and friendship treaty with China in August 1978 contributed to the polarization of international politics in East Asia and to the tightening of ties between the Soviet Union and Vietnam. Perhaps it illustrated Japan's inexperience (in contrast to the PRC) in conducting a coordinated international political and strategic set of policies. But the treaty with China may also be seen as indicative of Japanese difficulties in dealing with both the Soviet Union and China.

Following the changes in the international environment in the early 1970s the Soviet Union attempted to engage Japan with a mixture of enticement and implied threats. Seeking to play on a section of Japanese business that was interested in contributing to the development of Siberia and gaining access to resources there, Moscow held out the promise of participation in oil projects. Moscow also hinted that it might re-open discussions about the disputed islands with the objective of signing a peace treaty. Meanwhile Moscow had not abandoned its long standing aim of loosening Japanese ties with the United States. But it also had a more immediate aim of heading off Chinese attempts to secure their own peace treaty with Japan that would include a clause committing the two to oppose 'hegemony' which Moscow, with good reason, thought was directed against the Soviet Union. In the event the Soviet Union overplayed its hand. The project for oil development was shifted further west in Siberia and the terms offered to the Japanese became confused. It also became clear that no concessions were to be offered on the disputed islands. The Soviet Union then proposed that in lieu of a peace treaty the two sides could sign a treaty of good neighbourliness. When the Japanese balked, the Soviet side published their draft in order to bring pressure to bear on Japan. Not surprisingly, the attempt back-fired and Japan signed a treaty with the PRC. Although this involved a face-saving compromise that placed the 'anti-hegemony' clause in the preamble and, for good measure, added that the treaty was not directed at any third party, the die was effectively cast. Whether or not this was immediately appreciated in Japan, it was effectively thrust into an anti-Soviet coalition including the PRC and the United States.

But strains soon developed in relations with China. Japanese firms had eagerly responded to the overblown plans announced by the temporary leader Hua Guofeng in early 1978 and by the following year had got their fingers badly burnt as the Chinese defaulted on various projects. The Japanese business community was appalled by the lack of an appropriate investment infrastructure in China, with the absence of appropriate laws and dispute settlement procedures, and by the complexities of bureaucratic procedures. The Chinese side, however, suspected darker motives at work on the Japanese side. The result was that despite the enormous increase in trade and the regular payments of large amounts of Official Development Aid (ODA) Japanese firms throughout the 1980s did not directly invest in China in a big way. Although trade continued to expand rapidly between the two sides, by the late 1980s Hong Kong replaced Japan as the PRC's leading trader. China's leaders professed to see evidence of the re-emergence of militarism in Japan in revisions of school textbooks to gloss over Japanese aggression and atrocities in the Pacific War and in the statements and actions of leading politicians to the same effect. Moreover, China's leaders seemed to find that fierce public denunciations could bring about retractions in Japan. In 1985 Chinese students demonstrated against the 'second (economic) invasion' by Japan. They complained about allegedly unfair Japanese trade practices and compared Japan unfavourably with other developed countries for holding back on the transfer of technology. The Japanese for their part resented what they regarded as Chinese interference in their domestic affairs. Such complaints were resonant of the deeper problems at issue between the two sides.[26]

Meanwhile, in 1979–80 Prime Minister Ohira Masayoshi commissioned a number of high-powered studies to debate and to formulate a new national agenda for Japan as it approached the twenty-first century. By common agreement Japan was seen to have gone beyond the process of 'catching-up' and that as one of the world's most powerful economies and a leader in many aspects of advanced technology it should no longer follow the established practices of its foreign relations. The result was the emergence of a new slogan of 'comprehensive security' which ostensibly stressed the multi-dimensional quality of security. As noted by a Japanese scholar, 'concealed in this idea is the hope that Japan's contributions to international betterment such as foreign aid, debt rescheduling, and contributions to international agencies will be considered supportive of American policy'.[27] By the time of the accession of Prime Minister Nakasone (1982–87) the emphasis had become one of both responding to a more assertive nationalist mood and to demonstrating Japan's value as a partner of the United States through economic liberalization and upgrading the defence capabilities of the Self Defence Forces. The latter was aimed at 'overcoming the previously strong image of Japan as an economic spoiler and military free rider and at creating an image of Japan as an economic and military supporter'.[28] But it did not involve the assumption of a conventional security role. This attempt to gain American approval while simultaneously responding to the more assertive nationalist mood could and did backfire. American complaints at allegedly unfair Japanese trading practices did not abate. Indeed in 1989 they led to the so-called Structural Impediments Initiative that involved each side suggesting to the other that it change fundamental aspects of its domestic system, which in turn only served to accentuate the nationalistic distaste for the other that exists in both countries.

Interestingly, one of the more successful attempts to tackle the enormous and deep-seated trade imbalance between the US and Japan that was to transform Japan's relations with the ASEAN countries in particular was the so-called Plaza Agreement of 1985 that resulted in a significant re-valuation of the Japanese Yen. In order to remain competitive Japan exported considerable manufacturing capacity to the so-called 'four Asian tigers' and to the increasingly stable and investment friendly ASEAN countries. This has resulted in a complex economic triangle involving Japan, the East Asian countries and the United States, with the latter serving as the principal market.[29] The result has been to modify America's trade deficit with Japan at the cost of increasing it with the other economies of Pacific Asia.

Japan's independent foreign policy during this twenty-year period was still predicated on the American security guarantee which was in turn anchored in the Cold War order. Japan had become an independent contributor to stability in ASEAN, but it had no means of pursuing the agenda of the Fukuda Doctrine in the teeth of the determination of China and the United States to isolate Vietnam. Within certain strategic limits set by its security dependency on the United States, Japan had fashioned an independent relationship with China (and Taiwan) and its poor relations with the Soviet Union were the product of bilateral factors as well as the antagonism caused by its alliance with the United States. More generally, Japan's neo-mercantilist policies had been modified rather than transformed and that was evident in the Asia-Pacific as well as in the wider world.

TOWARDS A NEW ROLE AFTER THE END OF THE COLD WAR, 1989–95

Japan's security relationship with the United States has ostensibly remained intact despite the end of the Cold War. American forces have continued to be stationed on bases in Japan while Japan has persisted in its previous low key defence posture. But circumstances have changed and Japan has begun to pursue a more activist foreign policy that has included the token despatching of naval vessels to the Gulf and the limited deployment of armed service personnel in UN Peace Keeping Operations (PKO). Japan has also played a high profile economic role in contributing to the UN brokered peace settlement in Cambodia. The relationship with the United States has remained central to Japan's international position, but it has been subject to new strains. Ostensibly relations with China have improved, while relations with Russia remain stalled on the territorial dispute. Japan's importance in Southeast Asia has increased in correspondence with the growing significance of economics in stabilizing the region. In 1993 Japan formally applied to become a permanent member of the UN Security Council and set in motion a far-reaching debate about the country's new international role. This in turn must be understood against the context of a major change in the domestic alignments of Japanese politics. It remains to be seen whether that will lead to a change of the domestic political system. Japan is clearly poised on the edge of a major transition.

Within the post Cold War context Japan has developed a more active role as a facilitator of enhanced regionalism. The Japanese were quietly but effectively instrumental in the establishment of both the Asia-Pacific Economic Cooperation forum (APEC) and the ASEAN Regional Forum (ARF) – the two first inter-governmental institutions of the region. Ostensibly, it was an Australian initiative to establish APEC in 1989, but it was Japan in the shape of the Ministry of International Trade and Industry, together with the USA, that was the prime mover behind the scenes. Fearful of the possible emergence of more protective trade blocks, the so-called 'fortress Europe' in particular, MITI was keen to establish a trans-Pacific association to safeguard its position. Being aware of ASEAN suspicion of such an enterprise especially if sponsored by Japan, MITI was content to let Australia play the role of its promoter in public, especially as its prime minister, Bob Hawke, was keen to do so.

By 1991 Japan had become mindful of the greater strategic latitude afforded to China by the disappearance of the Russian threat and the end of the Cold War. The then Japanese Foreign Minister, Taro Nakayama, proposed in July in Kuala Lumpur at the ASEAN Post Ministerial Meeting that a regional security dialogue be held in conjunction with the annual post ministerial external dialogue meetings. Washington was initially opposed to multilateral security projects, but relented by the following year when the decision was made by the ASEAN heads of government meeting in Singapore. The ARF was formally initiated in July 1993 with the active encouragement of Japan and the United States, with the declared purpose 'for ASEAN and its dialogue partners to work with other regional states to evolve a predictable and constructive pattern of relationships in Asia-Pacific'.[30] It was evident that the key object was to draw China into a pattern of constructive engagement.

If Japan had emerged as an active facilitator of regional consultative institutions, its relations with the major powers showed considerable continuity as well as a degree of change. This was a necessary corollary of the refusal by the Japanese to assume a more conventional security role. The first impact on Japan of the end of the Cold War affected its relations with Russia and China. Although the level of hostility in relations with the Soviet Union/Russia was reduced at an early stage, it has not proved possible to settle the northern islands dispute and neither the Japanese government nor Japanese business has been keen to invest much in the country despite pleas from the Western allies. Since the end of the Cold War the differences with Russia have become primarily a Japanese affair and no longer directly involve the American security guarantee. If the previous Soviet intransigence on the disputed islands may have been a function of its relative strength, the subsequent position of Russia must be seen as a function of its relative weakness. Russian fears about the possible disintegrative implications and/or domestic nationalist opposition has made the prospects of a settlement remote. The impasse has nevertheless not prevented both sides from including the other in collective institutional arrangements in the Asia-Pacific.

Japan's relations with China differ also from those with the United States although they are more alike than those with Russia. Because of its less pronounced interest in human rights and because of the greater priority given to regional stability as expressed in orderly economic relations, Japan did not share the same enthusiasm for imposing sanctions on China after 4 June 1989 as did its American ally. Indeed Japan was the first of the G-7 countries to resume ODA. In fact Sino–Japanese relations rapidly improved after 1990 and have reached what both sides regard as the best period of their relations yet. After a certain delay Japanese FDI in China reached new heights and in 1993 Japan once again became China's most important trading partner. The emperor has visited China and many-sided dialogues and exchanges take place between the two sides. These also include high level meetings between military representatives. There is also little that ostensibly divides the two sides about the issues in the Asia-Pacific such as Korea or the desirability of seeking peaceable solutions to territorial disputes in the region.

But at deeper levels problems remain. The two are incipient rivals within the region should the American commitment to remain militarily engaged be found to be less enduring than is currently asserted. With this in mind the Chinese worry whether Japan might seek military power once again if the Japanese were to be suddenly bereft of the American military presence. The Japanese are concerned as to what China's military modernization might portend and call in vain for greater transparency on the Chinese side. In 1995 following a Chinese nuclear test carried out only three days after the international agreement to renew the NPT indefinitely (and within a context in which the other declared nuclear powers had stopped conducting tests since 1992) the Japanese government took the unprecedented step of cancelling the aid of $92 million that had been promised for the year. Japan was also prominent in its sharp criticism of China's creeping assertiveness in the South China Sea in the dispute with the Philippines over Mischief Reef in March 1995. The Japanese government has also publicly expressed its concern about the possibility that China might use force to resolve the Taiwan question. Like China's other neighbours, Japan is also troubled by the possible destabilization of China and of the influence that may have upon the region and what the ramifications may be for Japan. More narrowly, will China welcome Japan's attempts to increase its international role and to become a permanent member of the UN Security Council?

Although the partnership with the United States has continued to remain central to the economies and security arrangements of both states, it has nevertheless been subject to new strains and old problems have acquired greater salience. The Gulf War created new strains as it exposed the continuing fundamental differences in outlook between the two sides. Regarding the war as essentially an American affair the Japanese assistance was late, grudging and largely confined to money – although the Japanese did send some mine-sweepers to the Gulf after hostilities had come to an end. The Japanese response puzzled and angered American opinion and revived the old suspicions about the Japanese as free loaders. The episode also served to fuel American disquiet about the terms of trade with Japan, especially as that was no longer tempered by Cold War considerations about Japan's strategic importance. The stage was reached when opinion polls on both sides of the Pacific showed that each regarded the other as their country's principal adversary. The advent of the Clinton Administration and its tendency to put even greater emphasis upon trade matters has not damaged the relationship even though at times it has subjected it to new stress. That is in part due to the fact that the Clinton approach has also been tempered by the importance it has attached to the Asia-Pacific in America's foreign relations and by its concern to increase US exports to Japan. Despite its inconsistencies the Clinton Administration has always stopped short of pushing the trade disputes to the point of threatening the coherence of the relationship itself. Perhaps too the recession in Japan since 1992 coupled with the resurgence of the American economy in the same period has contributed to an easing of tensions. The Japanese have become less triumphalist and the Americans less anxious. But the uncertainties about this crucial partnership in the Asia-Pacific have not aided either side in developing coherent policies in the post Cold War era.[31]

Japanese quiescence and what to Americans appears as excessive parochialism has also been evident in the diplomacy over the North Korean problem in 1993 and 1994. The Japanese government was aware that the PRC with its veto power was resisting the American-led attempt to get the UN Security Council to authorize the application of sanctions against the North should it continue to defy the International Atomic Energy Agency and the other international obligations to which it was committed. Nevertheless Japan insisted that it would apply sanctions only if authorized to do so by the United Nations. The government argued that otherwise they could not risk confronting the Korean organization operating within Japan that was responsible for transferring an estimated US$1–1.5 billion a year to the North – its main source of hard currency. Yet the Japanese government did not dispute that if the North were to acquire a nuclear capability the consequences for Japan would be too terrible to contemplate. The parochial Japanese approach seemed totally disproportionate to the issue at hand.

Japan, meanwhile, has contributed significantly to the UN peace process in Cambodia and through its main strengths in economics, manufacturing and advanced technology it has played a major role in accelerating the growth and upgrading the economies of Southeast Asian countries. This in turn has enhanced their political stability and national self confidence.

Perhaps the most significant development, however, is the domestic political change taking place within Japan and the broad debates about the international role the country should adopt in the new era. The two are clearly related since the character of political, administrative and economic structural change within Japan will inevitably lead to changes in dealing with the outside world. But perhaps the following points from the debate about Japan's future international role are significant:

1 The quest for enhanced UN status has raised afresh the question as to what the role and mission of the Self Defence Forces (SDF) should be. Various alternatives have been suggested, from those appropriate to a 'normal nation' at one extreme to those appropriate for a 'global civilian power' at the other.
2 Should Japan be more broadly engaged in global affairs or should it continue to limit its interests to Japan and its immediate region? Should it identify itself more with its Asian neighbours?
3 How should Japan's obligations to the United States be balanced with those to the United Nations?

4 Should Japan's role be primarily confined to financial and civil support for UN operations or should its SDF be placed at the disposal of the UN? And if so would that not require reform of the UN?

5 More generally, how can Japan's acknowledged economic, human and intellectual resources be translated into international political power?[32]

Some of these points and questions may seem removed from the contemporary realities of international politics in the Asia-Pacific and they still seem to be premised on the continuation of the American military presence in the Western Pacific and of its continued security commitment to Japan. There is little here that touches on what many in the region would regard as their immediate security problems and even less on how these can be addressed collectively. But it is possible that the basis of the post war consensus that has sustained Japan's quietist and neo-mercantilist role is changing. As we have seen, Japan has adopted the role of the facilitator of regional institutions of a consultative kind that are in accordance with the immense diversities within the Asia-Pacific. Whether Japan will adopt a more conventional security role may well depend on the long process of domestic political change that has begun in the new post Cold War context. It will also depend on future developments of the Chinese and American roles in the region.

NOTES AND REFERENCES

1 F. C. Jones, *Japan's New Order in East Asia* (London: Oxford University Press, 1954).
2 Kenneth B. Pyle, *The Japanese Question: Power and Purpose in a New Era* (Washington DC: The AEI Press, 1992) p. 26.
3 Cited in *ibid*. pp. 27–28.
4 There are two contrasting arguments about Japan's diplomacy in this regard: the first is impressed with its shortcomings and failures and the latter with its successes in achieving its relatively limited goals. For good examples of the two arguments, with the critical one first see Michael Blaker, 'Evaluating Japan's Diplomatic Performance' and John Creighton Campbell, 'Japan and the United States: Games That Work'. Both are in Gerald L. Curtis (ed.) *Japan's Foreign Policy After the Cold War: Coping With Change* (Armonk: M. E. Sharpe 1993) pp. 1–42 and 43–61 respectively.
5 Reinhard Drifte, *Japan's Foreign Policy* (London: Routledge for the Royal Institute of International Affairs, 1990) p. 35.
6 See scenarios two and three in Richard P. Cronin, *Japan, the United States, and Prospects for the Asia-Pacific Century, Three Scenarios for*

the Future (Singapore: Institute of Southeast Asian Studies, 1992) pp. 111–18.

7 Takashi Inoguchi, *Japan's International Relations* (London: Pinter Publishers, 1991) pp. 166–67, 172–73.

8 Takashi Inoguchi, *Japan's Foreign Policy in an Era of Global Change* (London: Pinter Publishers, 1993) p. 153 and p. 146 respectively.

9 For a clear account see Sueo Sudo, *The Fukuda Doctrine and ASEAN* (Singapore: Institute of Southeast Asian Studies, 1992) pp. 13–17. For an example of this in practice see pp. 136–46.

10 Respectively, Takashi Inoguchi and Nakatani Iwao, cited in *ibid.* p. 108.

11 For extensive analysis of Japan's 'immobilism' in key areas of domestic politics and foreign policy, see J. A. A. Stockwin *et al. Dynamic and Immobilist Politics in Japan* (London: Macmillan Press, 1988).

12 See for example, Sueo Sudo, *The Fukuda Doctrine and ASEAN: New Dimensions in Japanese Foreign Policy* (Singapore: Institute of Southeast Asian Studies, 1992) p. 14.

13 See Pyle, *The Japanese Question* (*op. cit.*) pp. 107–11; and Reinhard Drifte, *Japan's Foreign Policy* (*op. cit.*) pp. 17–19. See also the discussion of Donald C. Hellmann, 'The Imperatives for Reciprocity and Symmetry in U.S.–Japanese Economic and Defense Relations' in John H. Makin and Donald C. Hellmann (eds) *Sharing World Leadership? A New Era for America and Japan* (Washington DC: AEI, 1989) pp. 237–66.

14 Pyle, *The Japanese Question* (*op. cit.*) p. 110.

15 By Akio Morita and Shintaro Ishihara (New York: Simon and Schuster, 1991).

16 For elaboration see J. A. A. Stockwin, *Japan: Divided Politics in a Growth Economy* (London: Weidenfeld and Nicolson, 2nd edn, 1982) pp. 203–5, and more broadly, Chapter 10, pp. 196–218.

17 Pyle, *The Japanese Question* (*op. cit.*) p. 25.

18 For details see Lawrence Olson, *Japan in Postwar Asia* (New York: Praeger, 1970).

19 Wolf Mendl, *Issues in Japan's China Policy* (London: Macmillan Press, 1978) Chapter 1, pp. 1–31.

20 On the latter see Donald C. Hellman, *Japanese Foreign Policy: The Peace Agreement with the Soviet Union* (Berkeley and Los Angeles: University of California Press, 1969).

21 For accounts of their relations in this period see William J. Barnds (ed.), *Japan and the United States: Challenges and Opportunities* (New York: New York University Press, 1979); and Franklin B. Weinstein (ed.) *US–Japan Relations and the Security of East Asia: The Next Decade* (Boulder: Westview Press, 1978).

22 For details see Akio Watanabe, *The Okinawa Problem. A Chapter in Japan–US Relations* (Melbourne: Melbourne University Press, 1970).

23 For an account from a Japanese perspective of this period in the relationship see, Wolf Mendl, *Issues in Japan's China Policy* (*op. cit.*).

24 This and the preceding paragraph drew on Sueo Sudo, *The Fukuda Doctrine and ASEAN* (*op. cit.*).

25 *ibid.* p. 204.

26 For accounts of the problematic relationship (as viewed primarily through Chinese perspectives) see Allen S. Whiting, *China Eyes Japan*

(Berkeley and Los Angeles: University of California Press, 1989); and Laura Newby, *Sino–Japanese Relations: China's Perspective* (London: Routledge for the Royal Institute of International Affairs, 1988). For an account of the problems of the economic relations in the early 1980s see Chae-Jin Lee, *China and Japan: New Economic Diplomacy* (Stanford: Hoover Institution Press, Stanford University, 1984).
27 Takeshi Inoguchi, *Japan's International Relations* (*op. cit.*) p. 26.
28 Takashi Inoguchi, *Japan's Foreign Policy in an Era of Global Change* (*op. cit.*) pp. 37–38.
29 Mitchell Bernard and John Ravenhill, 'Beyond Product Cycles and Flying Geese: Regionalization, Hierarchy, and the Industrialization of East Asia', *World Politics* Vol. 47, No. 2, January 1995, pp. 171–209.
30 Michael Leifer, *Dictionary of the Modern Politics of South-East Asia* (London: Routledge, 1995) p. 52.
31 For varied analyses of these complex issues see Gerald L. Curtis (ed.) *Japan's Foreign Policy After the Cold War: Coping with Change* (*op. cit.*); Takashi Inoguchi, *Japan's Foreign Policy in an Era of Global Change* (*op. cit.*) relevant chapters; and Kenichiro Sasae, *Rethinking Japan–US Relations* (London: IISS/Brassey's, Adelphi Paper 292, December 1994).
32 These points have been extracted from Kenichiro Sasae, *Rethinking Japan–US Relations* (*op. cit.*) pp. 55–61.

8 Conclusion
The post Cold War period, 1990–95

The end of the Cold War in the late 1980s followed in 1991 by the disintegration of the Soviet Union itself signified the end of the bipolar era. That era was distinguished by a central strategic balance that spanned the world. Although the United States seemingly emerged as the clear victor from the Cold War, especially as this was rapidly followed by the military triumph in the Gulf War, it apparently had neither the strength nor the will and indeed not the vision either to establish what its President briefly invoked as a 'new world order'. But it must be conceded that the basis for such a vision was not readily to hand. No clear pattern of alignments had emerged to characterise the new era. Nor had a new main axis of conflict appeared to replace the old East–West divide. Moreover, none of the leading states seemed likely to confront another with the threat of war.[1] No set of issues had emerged that might serve as a focal point for focusing domestic and international attention in such a holistic way as the defunct Cold War. There was no doubt that the United States had emerged as the sole superpower, but this did not mean that it was either able or willing to exercise universal hegemony in the sense of being able to lay down the law to the rest of the world.[2]

As a result considerable uncertainty exists among scholars as well as among practitioners as to how to understand the structure of international politics in the new era. In fact the new era is commonly referred to as the 'new world disorder'. The current period has been variously described as a transitional one prior to the emergence of a stable multipolar system; as a new system altogether in which a new international fault line has emerged between the forces of integration and disintegration; and as yet a different kind of world in which the main lines of conflict are between the heirs to the Western, Islamic and Confucian civilizations.[3]

Despite these uncertainties and wide differences of view, it is possible to identify particular changes and trends since the end of bipolarity that have been of special significance for the Asia-Pacific. It is also possible to outline their impact on the region and the changes that have taken place in the region as a result.

First, a repositioning of the major powers in the region is under way. Post Soviet Russia has declined absolutely. The United States is perceived to have declined relatively even though it is still the dominant power. China, which has been freed from the threat of conventional military attack for the first time in more than 150 years and which is modernizing at an extraordinary rate is regarded as the new rising power with a degree of strategic latitude unprecedented since 1949; and Japan is still regarded enigmatically as a major economic power that has yet to determine its international political role. Much depends upon the willingness of the United States to remain as the major military power deploying overwhelming force in the Western Pacific.

Second, the end of the bipolar structure itself has dissipated the central strategic balance to which regional and sub-regional conflicts had been attached before. This has tended to localize conflicts. However, the prospect of the acquisition of nuclear weapons by North Korea has given a new international dimension to the Korean conflict, which by virtue of the involvement of the United States, Japan, China and Russia cannot be considered as a conflict of only local significance. Nevertheless the ending of the Cold War has profoundly changed the context of that conflict too.

Third, the countries of Pacific-Asia have for the first time sought to establish multilateral mechanisms – albeit of a consultative kind – with which to address the new security challenges of the region. It was only in 1989 that it was agreed to establish an inter-governmental regional economic association. Known as the Asia-Pacific Economic Cooperation forum (APEC), it is primarily consultative in character. It may be seen as an appropriate response to the possible emergence of trade blocs in Europe and North America by a region whose members at this point neither wish nor can aspire to establishing a free trade area, let alone an integrated economic community. In 1993 the consultative approach was extended to security matters with the establishment of the ASEAN Regional Forum (ARF) with eighteen members, which owed much to Japanese initiative and American encouragement, with the constraint of China in mind.

Fourth, in contrast to the situation in Europe the end of bipolarity was not, strictly speaking, simultaneously marked by the end of the ideological Cold War in the Asia-Pacific. China, Vietnam and North Korea continue to be ruled by communist parties. Notwithstanding China's adoption of a more market oriented economy and its growing integration into the capitalist international economy, conflicts of a Cold War kind continue to affect Sino–American relations in particular. This has also changed the context of the Taiwan problem as the democratization taking place on the island has added a new dimension to its appeal for recognition by the international community and to the character of the support it enjoys within the United States.

Fifth, in the aftermath of bipolarity China is re-emerging as the great power of the region. Freed of the Soviet military threat, and with a vast and fast growing economy that according to an IMF study based on purchase power parity calculations already ranks as second only to the United States,[4] China's leaders have pursued a policy of good neighbourliness with a view to enhancing their country's economic integration into the region. Yet disputes over sovereignty, especially in adjoining seas have acquired a new salience and the question of Taiwan continues to loom large notwithstanding its changing character. Uncertainty exists as to how China will behave in its new enhanced role and attention has focused on the acrimonious process of its regaining sovereignty of Hong Kong due in 1997. For their part the other Asian–Pacific countries have tried to engage China and its various bureaucracies and regions in more interactive relationships, most visibly in the consultative processes of APEC and ARF. But concern prevails as to how to accommodate a new, nationally assertive and militarily modernizing China whose political stability cannot be taken for granted.

THE REALIGNMENT OF POWER

The disintegration of the Soviet Union in 1991 and its replacement in the Asia-Pacific by Russia only confirmed the precipitant decline from power that had already become apparent in the previous two years. The once awesome Pacific Fleet now lay rusting in their Pacific waters bereft of fuel, maintenance and the capacity even to carry out exercises. The capacity to project power in the Indian Ocean and the Western Pacific that had shaped the regional power balance in the 1970s and 1980s had suddenly ended. With it had ended much of Russia's significance in the Asia-Pacific as a whole. To be sure Russia was important to its immediate neighbours China and Japan and of course to the United States as Russia still deployed continental range ballistic nuclear missiles in its Pacific waters. But lacking sufficient economic weight and now having lost its edge as a military power in the region, Russia had declined absolutely as a power capable of shaping events throughout the Asia-Pacific region.[5]

If Russia had ceased to be a power of major regional significance it still exercised residual importance by reason of geography in Northeast Asia. Moreover, it could affect immediate arms balances through sales of advanced weapons systems and affect diplomacy in the region. Beyond that its *potential* as a great power was generally recognized in the region as it was thought that it was just a question of time before Russia would recover from its domestic turmoil. Meanwhile its very weakness was turned to diplomatic advantage in its dealings with Japan as President Yeltsin has been able to argue in effect that domestic nationalist opposition coupled with regional sentiment in the Russian far east has prevented him from ceding to Japan the disputed 'northern territories' at the southern tip of the Kurile Islands. The Japanese in turn have withheld contributing major investment funds to Russia which in view of the uncertainties in that land they were loath to provide in any case. But it has left the issue unsettled and troublesome to a Japan that is unable to translate its perceived greater weight in international affairs to tangible gain against a crippled Russia.[6]

By contrast Russia has been more yielding in its relations with China. Confidence building measures have been agreed between the armed forces across their borders and the two sides have reached agreements about their hitherto disputed borders largely upon terms agreeable to the Chinese. Trade has grown between the two so that in 1993 Russia ranked as China's fifth largest partner and China as Russia's second. Furthermore Russia agreed to sell China two squadrons of the advanced SU-27 aircraft which should increase China's strike power significantly. Similarly, China's capacity to project force at sea has been augmented by the purchase of 10–12 *kilo* class submarines from Russia. According to American sources, China has also recruited hundreds and perhaps thousands of redundant Russian specialists from the former Soviet military–industrial complex to assist in the technological upgrading of China's own weapons establishment. It is assumed that the Russian motivation is commercial rather than strategic. But it is obvious that the Russian government has every interest in cultivating good relations with China rather than risk potential disruption along their 4000-mile long border. Within the relatively under-populated Russian far east region anxieties have been expressed about illegal Chinese migration and unfair Chinese trade practices. The disparities in trading conditions and the problems of smuggling led Moscow in 1994 to tighten its controls and to negotiate a new trading regime. This had the temporary effect of reducing the volume of trade, but there can be little doubt that for the first time in at least 150 years the advantage lies with China and the momentum of the growth of trade will be continued with a strong regional dimension especially on the Chinese side. In broader terms, the Russian interest in cultivating good relations with the West, especially in the European sector, limits the Chinese capacity to use such leverage as it may possess with Russia in their dealings with the United States. But the possibility that both may wish to utilize each other in order to improve their respective manoeuvrability with the United States in particular should not be excluded in the future.[7]

Russia's role in Southeast Asia can only be considered to be marginal at best since it is confined primarily to the diplomatic. But here too Russia has found a new role as a salesman of advanced aircraft. It has agreed to sell to Malaysia a consignment of Mig-29s – Russia's most advanced fighter aircraft. Again the motive would appear to be commercial, but the deal and the prospect for more such deals offers Russia a point of re-entry into the strategic calculations of the regional states – albeit on a different basis. Nevertheless there can be no doubt that Russia has declined to being at best a 'bit' player in the affairs of the region.[8]

The United States remains by far the most dominant power in the region. With bases in Japan and South Korea its naval and air power are unrivalled in Northeast Asia; and, despite the loss of the bases in the Philippines, the United States still exercises predominant military power in the seas of Southeast Asia where it enjoys partial access to basing facilities in some of the ASEAN countries. The United States is still the principal economic power in the region both in the sense of being the ultimate guarantor of the international economic system that has served the region so well, and being the most important economic partner for many of the countries in the Asia-Pacific. The United States may have suffered a relative decline in the sense that it is no longer as dominant as it was in the 1950s and 1960s, but it is still the main provider of leadership and of public goods in the region. In short, despite the legacy of Vietnam, the United States continues to play a vital role in sustaining the economic and security structures of the Asia-Pacific that have provided the platform on which the economic dynamism of the region has been built.[9]

The demise of the Soviet Union has meant that the United States can no longer base its strategy upon the concept of the Soviet threat. The American role in the Asia-Pacific has evolved into a more complex and variegated one of providing strategic stability and political balance while simultaneously being an economic competitor and collaborator. However, within the United States there has been a distinct shift to defining national security interests in economic terms. Given the adverse balances of trade that the United States experiences with most of its East Asian partners, notably Japan, a stronger element of rancour is evident in American relations with its Asian allies than obtained in the Cold War period when different strategic priorities prevailed. Consequently uncertainties exist within the region as to the precise value of the American current strategic commitment to the region and as to its durability. No matter how often the Bush and Clinton Administrations have assured their Asian allies of America's long term commitment to being militarily engaged in the region they have been unable to expunge the doubts that at some point domestic American support for sustaining recalcitrant allies and economic rivals in Asia could suddenly be withheld.

The ASEAN countries tend to regard the American presence as critical to their overall sense of security, particularly as its withdrawal would leave them vulnerable to the possible rivalries between China and Japan. Hence even Malaysia and Indonesia – the ostensibly non-aligned states – have publicly called for American troops to continue to be deployed in the region. But it was an indication of the new mood of anxiety about the possible American withdrawal in the long term and the prospect of the rise of Chinese power that Thailand refused to welcome a US plan to pre-position military supply ships off-shore to cope with a crisis in the region or in the Gulf. Malaysia and Indonesia supported the Thais, but interestingly, Singapore had already offered limited logistics facilities. At the same time few believe that the United States would come to their assistance in the event that the Chinese sought to pursue their sovereign claims in the South China Sea by force. The United States, however, could be expected to help to sustain a balance of a kind through judicious arms sales and an interest in the freedom of sea lanes. Indeed that was precisely the American response to the Sino–Filipino incident of March 1995 arising from China's assertiveness over Mischief Reef in the Spratlys. Meanwhile something of an arms build-up has begun in the region.[10]

Taiwan also faces uncertainties about the American readiness to come to its aid in the event of a Chinese attempt to use force. Much would depend on the precise circumstances. Meanwhile as China has lost something of its strategic significance to the United States since the end of the Cold War the United States became emboldened to sell Taiwan arms that went beyond the limited terms agreed with Beijing in the August 1982 Communique. The agreement by President Bush to sell 150 F-16 aircraft has been followed up by ancillary agreements by the Clinton Administration. Taiwan's increasing democratization, especially as contrasted with China's continued adherence to communist party rule and its attendant human rights violations, has found increased support within the American Congress. In May 1995 President Clinton bowed to Congressional pressure and, against the advice of the State Department, he agreed to allow President Lee Teng-hui to visit the US in a private capacity. This evoked an angry reaction from Beijing which saw the decision as part of a wider concerted strategy by Washington to obstruct China's modernization, divide the country and generally limit its rising power. In America, however, this was seen as yet another example of the *ad hoc* way in which important foreign policy moves were made in response to domestic politics. Little thought appears to have been given to the possible consequences. For example, Taiwan is widely regarded as able to defend itself against invasion and the United States is clearly committed to ensuring that it will continue to possess the military capacity to continue to do so. But uncertainty remains as to how America would respond to more limited use of force such as naval harassment or attempts at blockade.

The relationship with Japan may still be regarded as the linchpin of the American strategic commitment in Asia. But the persistent economic and trade disputes risk undermining domestic American support for sustaining the commitment. Although the relationship is highly interdependent and multifaceted, the American security guarantee has served to limit Japan's political and strategic engagement in the region. Fears still exist in the Asia-Pacific that further American retrenchment could lead once again to a resurgent Japan. These fears could be possibly allayed were Japan to develop closer political links with neighbouring states to match, say, its economic ties. The Japanese initiative to promote ARF may be taken as a step in that direction. Deeper political ties with Japan would doubtless ease anxieties about further American military withdrawals from the region. Interestingly, it was the Thais who suggested to a visiting

Japanese military delegation that joint naval exercises might be possible, only to have the offer turned down in the end. But paradoxically the continued American security guarantee militates against the prospects for a Japanese re-evaluation of its national security and of its role in Asia, which the Americans would very much like to see.[11]

In 1992 concern about the possible development of a nuclear capability by North Korea provided a new basis for linking American international commitments with its interests within the region. It once again accentuated the significance of American leadership in both arenas and reduced the immediate fears about further withdrawals. At the same time the uncertainties of the approach by the Clinton Administration which alternated tough with conciliatory approaches to the North not only exemplified the difficulties of pursuing a consistent strategy in this more indeterminate period, but it also raised further doubts about the foreign policy qualities of the administration.[12] Nevertheless the significance of the American role was highlighted by the inability of Japan to take an initiative and the unwillingness of the Chinese to support sanctions against the North even though it was abundantly clear that these two together with South Korea would be the first to suffer the consequences of an acquisition of nuclear weapons by the North.

The significance of China's status as a rising power in the region and perhaps in the world as a whole will be treated at greater length below. The focus here will be on Japan which may be considered to be the only country capable of balancing Chinese power in the event of a major American military withdrawal. Despite the attention that is regularly given to the relatively high defence budget in Japan, which in 1993 was calculated at US$39.71 billion – second only to the United States – its Self Defence Force 'could not fight a war without the USAF's direct support'.[13] Apart from operating as an auxiliary to the US military forces, the SDF also has a role in territorial defence. However, there is neither support at home nor within the region for Japan to assume a more assertive military role. Although Japan has taken a more active role in international diplomacy, especially within the framework of the United Nations, where it has demanded a permanent seat on the Security Council, and in international economic fora, there is no sign yet of the emergence of an independently active Japan in the strategic arena.[14]

However, Japan is widely regarded within the region as possessing the technological capabilities to transform itself very rapidly indeed into a major strategic power. Should it be subject to the shock of

American withdrawal, such is the Japanese sense of vulnerability (or so it is thought), that it would become a major power in no time. Consequently, despite the Japanese public distaste for the military since the defeat in the Pacific War, and continual Japanese assurances to the contrary, the regional perception of Japan's capacity to become a military power very rapidly has induced a mood of continual wariness. This wariness is fuelled by the perception that the Japanese have not fully come to terms with their history of brutal aggression in the Pacific War. Thus both Japanese domestic caution and the unease of neighbours (even though imperfectly understood within Japan) have combined to constrain the country from developing what might be called 'normal' relations within the region except in the economic sense. Notwithstanding the ending of the Cold War, the continuation of the American presence under the terms of the US–Japan Security Treaty has had the effect of perpetuating the long standing position of Japan while heightening regional uncertainties about its future. The prospect remains that there may yet be a political and perhaps strategic rivalry between China and Japan.

In sum the United States is still the major guarantor of strategic security in the Asia-Pacific. But uncertainties exist about the extent to which the American public will continue to support that role. Moreover, East Asian security may be regarded as in a period of transition as China's power is seen to rise and new forms of multilateralism are being explored.

THE LOCALIZATION OF REGIONAL CONFLICTS

The end of the bipolar period meant that regional conflicts ceased to be part of a larger structure of conflict involving the global powers. In that sense they could be seen as having been regionalized or localized. It did not mean, however, that the United States, as the surviving global power with an array of interests and commitments throughout the world, had suddenly disengaged itself altogether from such conflicts. Nor did it mean that other great powers were not also engaged. But what it did mean was that the pattern by which local disputants or regional rivals were tied into a structure of conflict of global dimensions was no more. It also meant that the United States and the remaining great powers no longer possessed the mechanism of the central balance by which to calculate the relative significance of lesser conflicts or the geopolitical weight of different regions. Thus even where the United States, for instance, may have an interest, uncertainty would probably arise about the intensity of commitment that may exist to sustain that interest and the character of the domestic support or opposition at home for upholding it. Moreover, American regional and global interests were no longer as congruent as before. Thus the urgency of upholding the nuclear non-proliferation regime and the patience required for addressing the problem of the two Koreas raised new dilemmas for the US. Similarly, the concern to uphold international norms of human rights in dealings with China raised new difficulties in developing cooperative relations with that country on many other issues. In short, the international significance of regional issues and local conflicts varied in new and less predictable ways.

The Korean conflict may be seen as the last hang over from the Cold War era in which a totalitarian communist regime with a failing command economy confronts a democratizing regime with a highly successful market economy. Moreover, the commitment of the United States to the South has remained intact. But the 'defection' of the North's great allies, China and the Soviet Union/Russia has shown that the ending of the Cold War has had an impact even here. With the end of bipolarity there was no longer any compelling strategic or political logic for the Soviet Union to continue to lend costly support to an ally whose leader and regime it disliked, especially as North Korea had the capacity to drag the Soviet Union into conflicts that were highly damaging to the new Soviet interests. Moreover, the Soviet Union had every reason to develop cooperative relations with the South in the hope of attracting much-needed investment and managerial know-how and as part of demonstrating to the United States and the West in general that the Soviet Union had genuinely put the Cold War behind it. As the successor state, Russia had even less reason to accommodate the interests of the North. China's leaders had already shown the high priorities they attached to economics in the conduct of foreign relations by developing economic ties with the South as from 1985. But once the Soviet Union had declared its hand in Korea it ended the competitive edge that had long existed between the two giant neighbours regarding the North and allowed the Chinese to follow suit. Since the North continued to be of geopolitical significance to China's national security and since it was one of the few surviving fellow communist regimes the Chinese leaders were more committed to its survival than the Russians. But like the Russians, the Chinese felt that at long last they no longer had to underwrite a regime they disliked and which could involve them once again in a war that would be highly detrimental to Chinese interests.

In 1990 the Soviet Union normalized relations with the South after the meeting of the two presidents on the west coast of the United States. The following year China made it clear that it would not veto the application of the South to membership of the United Nations and thereby gave the North little option but to agree to enter the UN simultaneously. This contributed to the erosion of the North's claim to exclusive legitimacy as the authentic Korean state. In 1992 the Chinese angered the North still further by recognizing the South as a state and its government as its legitimate representative. This produced an asymmetry by which the South was recognized by China and Russia, but the North was not recognized by either the United States or Japan.[15]

These developments not only undermined the credibility of the commitment of the North's great power backers, but they also eroded the credibility of the North's case against the South. That had turned on the claim that the South lacked authenticity as a legitimate representative of Korea or any of its parts since it was in effect a creature of the United States. The problems of the North were not confined to the diminishing credibility of its claims, but perhaps more importantly they embraced those of the economy.

The Soviet Union/Russia insisted that as from January 1991 economic relations would be handled only on the basis of hard currency. The effect on trade was catastrophic: the North's imports almost ceased altogether as they declined to only 2 per cent of the previous year while its exports were cut to a third.[16] The Chinese too reduced their subsidized exports to the North and raised their 'friendship prices' for oil closer to prevailing world prices. Kim Il-Sung visited China in October 1991, but his pleas for continued economic support elicited only friendly lectures about the desirability of carrying out careful economic reforms and opening up to the outside world as the answer to his country's economic problems. These had become acute partly because the domestic Stalinist type economy had become stultified and partly because the lifelines from the giant neighbours had been cut. The North then attempted in vain to interest the Europeans and the Japanese in investment and trade. The claims of the North to have been economically self-reliant in accordance with its much vaunted *juche* ideology were shown to be false. Indeed in December 1993 the North officially and unprecedentedly acknowledged huge economic failings.[17]

The problems of the North were further compounded by the

imminence of the political succession to Kim Il-Sung. His death on 8 July 1994 came at a point when diplomacy was being tried yet again as a means of breaking the deadlock. Although his son and successor Kim Jong-Il had long been groomed as heir apparent much uncertainty was involved. The problems that have been generally attendant upon such events in communist countries have been further compounded in this case by doubts about the survivability of the regime itself in what is for the most part the post communist world. The South, having been enthused initially about the prospects for unification at the time of the fall of the Berlin Wall, has become very wary about the costs that might arise from a rapid process of unification arising from the collapse of the North. The subsequent German experience of the economic and social difficulties of precipitate unification has proved to be most sobering.

In fact it was within this context that the first and sudden breakthrough originally took place in the slow moving North–South dialogue when the North agreed in the autumn of 1991 (i.e. after the collapse of the diehard coup against Gorbachev and the subsequent disintegration of the Soviet Union) to restart prime ministerial meetings. This led to an Agreement on Reconciliation and Non-Aggression that was signed on 13 December and to the issuing on 31 December of a joint Declaration on a Non-Nuclear Korean Peninsula.

By this stage both North and South may be said to have gained from this limited accommodation. The South had accepted the North's concept of non-aggression and hoped to have found a way for gradual evolution of the North through establishing a broad range of contacts and linkages that in time would soften its totalitarian features, introduce market features into the economy and gradually diminish the gap between the two sides of the Korean divide. The North, aware of some of these dangers, refused to countenance unrestricted exchanges of newspapers and television programmes, but hoped to have escaped from its international isolation and to have gained access to economic infusions from the South. A greater stabilization of the regime in the North was in the interests of both sides. But the North evidently hoped that its accommodation with the South would open the door to relations with Japan and above all the United States. That would at least restore a degree of symmetry with the South which enjoyed good relations with Russia and China. But the negotiations with Japan proved fruitless in part because of the North's demands for economic largesse by way of compensation for Japanese wrong doing during the period of annexation of 1910–45 and more controversially for alleged wrong doing in the post war years. The talks with the United States were also held up by differences between the two sides about the status of the South as well as about the American military presence on the peninsula. But above all negotiations with both Japan and the United States came to founder on the question of the North's alleged acquisition of military nuclear power and of its obligation to allow unfettered investigation by the International Atomic Energy Agency (IAEA).

Whatever expectations about new forms of cooperation between North and South had been engendered by the 1991 agreements had been dashed by the end of 1992. The proposed North–South nuclear inspection regime had foundered. By 1993 it had become clear that inspections by the IAEA that had begun in 1992 had also run into trouble. The IAEA had found evidence to show that the North had used nuclear materials in ways that they had tried to conceal. The North also denied access to certain sealed sites in Yongbyon that the IAEA demanded to inspect. Meanwhile the United States and the South had announced their intention of resuming the large scale military exercise known as Team Spirit. The North had long objected to this, arguing that it constituted a military threat, but now it also claimed that it was a form of nuclear blackmail. When the IAEA issued a demand for compliance by the end of March 1993 to its request to inspect Yongbyon the North simply suspended its membership and refused to acquiesce. Opinion in the US government was divided on how best to approach the North, and whether it had a nuclear weapon. At issue now was not only the problem of the two Koreas but the credibility and effectiveness of the international non-proliferation regime itself.

The United States, however, was in effect responsible for managing both the regional and international dimensions. Japan and the South urged a cautious approach. China, which also had no interest in either seeing the Korean peninsula become nuclearized or in seeing the non-proliferation regime founder, urged caution and the pursuit of a settlement through dialogue. Although it lacked effective power over the North, China nevertheless exercised a good deal of influence. But Chinese interests required the gradual evolution of the North towards economic reform and integration into the wider international community rather than its humiliation and possible sudden disintegration. The Chinese leaders made it clear that they would not support the issuing of sanctions against the North by the UN Security Council. By early 1994 the preference for a conciliatory rather than a confrontationist approach had prevailed. The North agreed to allow the renewal of inspections by the IAEA, but once again in effect denied access to the Yongbyon sites.

Notwithstanding the death of Kim Il-Sung the previous month, North Korea and the United States eventually reached a framework agreement on 13 August 1994 by which the North would forego its current nuclear programme in return for the supply of two modern nuclear reactors that could not be used for military purposes and for the provision of oil supplies to meet the energy shortfall in the interim. The agreement was scheduled to be implemented over five years, by which time the United States undertook to recognize the North and to remove remaining barriers to trade and investment. The agreement did not fully resolve differences about the inspections of all nuclear facilities in the North by the IAEA and the agreement was also criticized for leaving open other issues that could lead it to unravel. For example, as a bilateral agreement it still left unresolved how an accommodation could be made between the two Koreas. The American side anticipated that the South would build and provide much of the $4 billion cost of the new reactors, but it was unclear whether that would be accepted by the North. At the initiative of the United States and Japan a North Korea Energy Development Organization (NEDO) was established in order to provide an institutional basis for a wider international participation (including that of European states) in the process of implementing the framework agreement that would also facilitate the process of implementation. Stability on the peninsular does not only depend on resolving the nuclear issue (in which the international community is most interested), but also on resolving the North–South conflict.[18]

Meanwhile the survival of the regime in the North is shrouded in uncertainty. Despite concern about the prospect of the outbreak of new hostilities between North and South, especially in view of occasional bellicose threats from the North, such a prospect is unlikely in view of the opposition of the major powers including China. Yet tensions remain high as the North has deployed up to a million men at a high state of readiness with armour, artillery, missiles and chemical weapons along the de-militarized zone within easy reach of Seoul. These are opposed by a corresponding force of the South Korean and American armed forces. Were a war to break out the United States would become engaged automatically because of its deployment of 30,000 troops as a concomitant of its commitment to the South. Unlike in the early 1950s any such war under current conditions would not necessarily engage other regional and international states in active and immediate belligerence.

The localization of regional conflicts is perhaps even more evident in the case of Cambodia. As was noted in the previous chapter, the basis for a settlement emerged after the disengagement of the Soviet Union in 1988–89. That effectively detached the conflict from Soviet–American and Soviet–Chinese relations. Deprived of Soviet support the Vietnamese had little alternative but to remove their forces and make their peace with China. The reconciliation was achieved in stages. Meetings were held in July 1989 between deputy foreign ministers. These were followed in September 1990 by a secret meeting of senior leaders in the Chinese city of Chengdu, which issued a memorandum based on a United Nations plan for power sharing in Cambodia. In the event the Cambodian factions could not agree until the following year. By this time both the Chinese and Vietnamese sides actively sought a settlement. In July 1991 a meeting of the Cambodian Supreme National council was held in Beijing with a Chinese representative attending uniquely as an observer. It signified Chinese acceptance of Hun Sen as an authentic Cambodian representative and not as a Vietnamese puppet. This was followed by meetings of increasingly senior Chinese and Vietnamese leaders culminating in a summit meeting in November 1992.[19]

The actual settlement was brokered through an international conference co-chaired by France and, significantly, by Indonesia – now that Thailand was no longer the ASEAN frontline state under threat. The conference was held effectively under the auspices of the United Nations. Undaunted by the failure of its first meeting in Paris in July 1989 negotiations continued until they bore fruit at a second meeting in October 1991. The basis for a settlement had been established, as we have seen, as a result of an accommodation between China and Vietnam and a corresponding adjustment in the positions of the Cambodian factions they had previously patronized. This effectively provided a basis for a settlement that would uphold the independence and neutrality of Cambodia now that it had been freed from the 'special relationship' that Vietnam had previously imposed. But the actual settlement required an arrangement agreeable to all sides on how power could be shared between the competing factions and, crucially, how such power sharing could be brought into existence. An unprecedented solution was devised through the establishment of a Supreme National council comprising all factions, including the Khmer Rouge, which would delegate responsibility to a United Nations Temporary Authority in Cambodia (UNTAC) as an impartial body that could disarm the disputants, oversee elections and help establish a new government for the country.

In the event UNTAC could not quite carry out the initial mandate particularly with regard to disarming the different armies. But to the surprise of many it succeeded in organizing and carrying out the elections despite their repudiation by the Khmer Rouge. Although the incumbent government of Cambodia put in by Vietnam was unhappy with the result, in which it came second in the polls to Prince Sihanouk's party, it nevertheless accepted it in the end in large part at the instigation of UNTAC. But not before Vietnam had demonstrated its final unwillingness to become re-engaged. A break-away group from the government of Cambodia was openly refused Vietnamese support in seeking to challenge the election results. This led to the establishment of a government headed by two prime ministers under the constitutional monarchy of Norodom Sihanouk. The Khmer Rouge after not allowing UNTAC access to its administered territory in areas near the Thai border have continued to resist the new government. A low intensity civil war is being waged and order is precarious. But an authority exists which is recognized as sovereign by the international community. The international and regional powers that were previously the patrons of the warring factions in Cambodia have largely disengaged. Doubtless they continue to maintain a wary eye on developments, but it is clear that the ending of the bipolar configuration of international politics has facilitated if not a fully operational settlement of the Cambodian conflict at least one that has localized any residual conflict. Cambodia has ceased to be at the fulcrum of regional and international concerns in Southeast Asia. It has become possible for the governments of Indo-China and especially ASEAN to think afresh about the questions of security and order in the region as a whole.

Conflicting claims to maritime territories, extensions of the continental shelf and associated rights also took on more local and regional dimensions in the aftermath of the Cold War.[20] As noted earlier, the Russo-Japanese dispute over the islands immediately to the north of Japan has been denuded of its previous global strategic aspects and has become a largely bilateral affair. Other maritime disputes in Northeast Asia about fishing rights, smuggling and piracy involving China, Russia, Japan, the two Koreas, and Taiwan have tended mainly to be confined to bilateral matters to be handled by the resident states on a case by case basis without affecting overall relations unduly.

A partial exception is the disputed claim to sovereignty over the Senkaku or Diaoyudao rocky islands between the PRC (and Taiwan) on the one side and Japan on the other. Its resolution would determine the allocation of much of the continental shelf of the Yellow Sea. At stake is not only the potentially oil rich sea bed, but a matter of national pride and relative status. Although at the time of mutual recognition in 1972 Beijing and Tokyo agreed to set aside the dispute over sovereignty, to be settled by future generations, incidents have occurred from time to time. The ending of the Cold War has diminished the larger international strategic scope of the dispute and there is concern in Japan in particular that this may provide a context in which the Chinese may be emboldened to utilize its increasing capacity to project force at sea at a time of growing national assertiveness at home. But generally, it is believed that the significance of the economic relationship between the two great East Asian powers – especially for China – militates against precipitant action.

Anxieties about Chinese maritime claims have become even greater among the littoral states of the South China Sea. Sovereignty over all or part of the Spratly Islands which consist of a numerous series of loosely connected islets, reefs and shoals sprawled along the southern section of the South China Sea are disputed between the PRC, Vietnam, Malaysia, Brunei, the Philippines and Taiwan (in its guise as the Republic of China). All except Brunei have troops stationed on various islands, some of which are located within the 200–mile Exclusive Economic Zones (EEZs) of littoral states. Even though China's claims are based on long historical ties and were advanced earlier than the others, the bulk of the islands are up to a 1,000 miles from the Chinese mainland's island of Hainan, and China has been relatively late in establishing a presence. Were these claims to be realized China would reach right into the heart of Southeast Asia and would exercise command of the South China Sea through which pass vital shipping lanes linking the Pacific and Indian Oceans. The PRC is the only country to have used force to uphold its claims in the South China Sea in 1974 and 1988. Although these two occasions involved only Vietnam, with whom the Chinese were in conflict over other matters, China's creeping assertiveness, with increasingly more vigorous patrolling, intensive surveying (technically, on behalf of the United Nations) and the construction of facilities on various islets is disturbing to its neighbours, especially in view of the rise of China's power generally. As seen from China's point of view, these are islands to which the Chinese have long laid claim and others have taken advantage of particular international contexts and of China's technological backwardness in earlier years to establish illegitimate claims and occupations of their own. At stake are significant off-shore energy resources and potential control of the strategically important shipping lanes of the South China Sea.[21]

Attempts to establish a multilateral regime for the management of the South China Sea have so far been resisted by China. Moreover the United States – the only country capable of providing effective countervailing power – indicated long ago to the Philippines that its security commitment did not extend to the Spratlys. The PRC, however, professes to be committed to the principle of the peaceful settlement of disputes and to what it calls the setting aside of conflicting sovereign claims in favour of the joint development of the islands and their resources. Within China there has been evidence of a difference between the more accommodating Chinese Ministry of Foreign Affairs and the more assertive Chinese high military command. The latter has developed a consistent policy of naval expansion.[22] By 1995 a more concerted Chinese practice had emerged of quietly expanding its presence in the Spratly group by fixing markers on tiny islets and erecting facilities (ostensibly for fishermen, but replete with satellite dishes) on others. This may be seen as a policy designed to establish new *fait-accompli* and to probe local reactions. Upon the discovery of Chinese constructions on Mischief Reef within its claimed 200-mile EEZ the Philippines made a point of making highly publicized protests. Significantly, none of its ASEAN partners nor the United States chose to lend the Philippines public support. ASEAN confined itself to reiterating support to the Manila Declaration of 1992 on the peaceful settlement of maritime disputes and the United States did no more than affirm its interest in ensuring that access to the vital sea lanes would remain unaffected. The general approach within the region has been two pronged: an attempt has been made to bind the Chinese side into a variety of networks of association, notably through the establishment of the ASEAN Regional Forum (ARF) in 1993, with the aim of enmeshing the Chinese state and its relevant agencies in mutual interactions with neighbouring countries so as to minimize hostile unilateral ventures; and at the same time the littoral states have strengthened and modernized their defence forces. Perhaps the key factor constraining the Chinese is the need to maintain good working relations with neighbours in order to uphold the peaceful international environment deemed essential for the continued promotion of a high rate of economic growth that is regarded by the leaders as crucial for the survival of the communist regime.

TOWARDS MULTILATERAL SECURITY ARRANGEMENTS

The history of security arrangements in the Asia-Pacific have tended to be of a bilateral kind. The United States had its series of essentially bilateral treaty obligations running north to south along the western littoral of the Pacific. The Soviet Union in its heyday had separate treaties with its Asian allies. Such multilateral security treaties as did exist tended to be less than tightly binding on members to come to the assistance of each other in the event of aggression. This was true of the long defunct SEATO and it continues to apply to the essentially consultative Five Power Defence Arrangements that notionally tie Britain, Australia and New Zealand to the security needs of Singapore and Malaysia. Until the end of bipolarity neither the United States nor ASEAN expressed much interest in moving towards multilateral security institutions. As the dominant power in East Asia the United States had often expressed an interest in 'burden sharing' especially with regard to Japan, but it had adamantly opposed all proposals for new multilateral arrangements lest these diminish its freedom of operation without compensatory benefits to multilateral security.

The American objections to multilateral arrangements weakened as it became clearer that the effective power of the Pacific Fleet of the former Soviet Union had waned and that American international interests in the post Cold War era would in fact be best served in the Asia-Pacific by new kinds of multilateral arrangements that under the new conditions could be seen as supplementing rather than undermining its existing bilateral security treaties. In particular the United States was concerned about the problems of the proliferation of weapons of mass destruction, about the rapidly escalating arms race in East Asia and about the desirability of re-emphasizing the American commitment to the region at a time when its relative decline in the Asia-Pacific was widely anticipated.[23]

The new departure by ASEAN in openly addressing security issues of a larger Asian geographical span was itself a product of the perceived changes in the international and regional strategic environment that had made the agreements on a Cambodian settlement possible. Although the October 1991 Paris Peace Accord on

Cambodia brought to an end ASEAN's diplomatic role which for a long time had been regarded as the political glue that held the association together, the new situation opened the way for the Association to address openly security issues that it had previously chosen to put aside. With the disappearance of Russia as an effective military force in the region, with the perception of a reducing American military presence and of a friendlier Vietnam that was committed to economic development, ASEAN felt less inhibited from publicly taking the initiative in focusing upon more general regional security issues. In doing so it had benefited from the long experience of regular discussions between ministers and senior civil servants and more recently, by the institutionalized cooperation between the major quasi autonomous security and foreign affairs think tanks of the various capitals including some of the dialogue partners.[24]

The first indication of the new approach came at the ASEAN summit in January 1992 that was followed up at the annual ministerial meeting in July. The association issued a separate statement urging that the competing sovereign claims to the Spratlys be settled without the use of force and calling for cooperation between all interested parties to ensure safety of navigation, communication and protection of the environment. This was drafted principally with China in mind. ASEAN also took the unprecedented step of publicly calling upon the United States to retain a military presence in the region. Hitherto Malaysia and Indonesia had been reluctant to compromise their non-aligned status, but the new international realities brought their true concerns out into the open, especially in the light of the American withdrawal from its Filipino bases.[25]

In essence the end of the Cold War and the retreat of the Western powers has left ASEAN increasingly concerned about a possible power vacuum in the region. Cognizant of the growing power of China – the only country to have used force in the prosecution of its claims in the South China Sea in recent years (in 1974 and again in 1988) – the ASEAN countries have sought to encourage their giant neighbour to integrate with the institutions of the Asia-Pacific so as to become more tightly enmeshed with the countries of the region in the hope that this will give rise to cooperative rather than confrontational behaviour. Accordingly, the establishment of ARF in July 1993 should not be understood as a new security system designed to deal with the problem of China or indeed as a security system at all. It is principally a forum for what might at best be described as preventive diplomacy.

The aim of ARF is 'to engage the wider region in a dialogue on political and security issues. Other elements include a plan to develop ASEAN's Treaty of Amity and Cooperation into a regional code of conduct'.[26] Consequently, its membership is broad as it consists of all six ASEAN members; the observers Vietnam, Laos and Papua New Guinea; the dialogue partners, the US, Japan, Canada, the EU, South Korea, Australia and New Zealand; and Russia and China. Although ARF is an important new departure for ASEAN and indeed for the Asia-Pacific as a whole, it is neither comprehensive in membership, nor even a forum where its members can be expected to bring all their regional security concerns for general discussion. Unlike APEC, it does not include Hong Kong or Taiwan, and North Korea also is not a member. The problems of Northeast Asia are unlikely to be addressed in any meaningful way in the forum and the great powers are likely to continue to prefer to handle their main regional security concerns on a bilateral basis. Indeed it remains to be seen whether even the ASEAN members themselves will bring their particular security problems before the forum. After all no ASEAN government has yet invoked the machinery for settling disputes provided by the Treaty of Amity and Cooperation of 1976. But ARF is an important first step in establishing a pan-regional security institution. Perhaps like ASEAN itself it will evolve into an institution whose informal procedures for discourse among members have led to conflict avoidance if not conflict resolution. The difficulty here is that its wide membership includes even greater diversity than that of ASEAN and it remains to be seen whether ARF can establish even the informal *modus operandi* of ASEAN that was based on the shared perception that national and regional resilience were threatened by similar destabilizing forces. Such a perception is unlikely to be shared by all the ARF members.

It should be appreciated however that many of the principal security problems of the Asia-Pacific are still handled bilaterally or by *ad hoc* procedures. For example, the Korean issue may involve the four great powers and the two disputants, but, despite the Russian call in March 1994 for a multilateral approach, there is no immediate prospect for any such formula to be accepted. North Korea has so far preferred to deal with each of its interlocutors separately and China has evinced no interest in multilateralism on the Korean issue. Russia and China continue to explore confidence building measures along their borders on a bilateral basis, but where appropriate they include Kazakhstan and Kyrghistan in discussions about common borders. Similarly, despite its security alliance with the US, Japan is on its own in negotiating with Russia over the 'northern territories'. The Taiwan question nominally involves the island and the Chinese mainland, but the United States plays an important role as the ultimate protector of Taiwan. In other words, most of the conflicts in the Asia-Pacific are disaggregated. It is within that context that the ASEAN Regional Forum constitutes a new, if tentative, and above all consultative approach to multilateral security problems in the post Cold War era.

The ARF may be seen as an attempt to extend the precepts of ASEAN to a wider geographic setting. But it remains to be seen whether the pattern of conflict avoidance, preventive diplomacy and perhaps conflict management that has been the practice of ASEAN will be applicable to the conduct of relations with China especially following the incorporation of Vietnam within ASEAN from July 1995. Moreover it remains to be seen whether incentives can be offered to China to exercise unilateral restraint in the prosecution of its maritime claims as seems to be envisaged by the founders of ARF.

APEC: INSTITUTIONALIZING ECONOMIC COOPERATION

The Asia-Pacific Economic Cooperation forum was inaugurated in 1989. It was the first time that a trans Pacific inter-governmental organization had been established. It was a condition of its establishment that it should be only consultative in character. One of the distinctive features of the astonishing economic dynamism of the Asia-Pacific has been the absence of multilateral organizational structures of the kind that typified the development of the Western European economies and trans-Atlantic relations after 1945. The critical if often unacknowledged reason for this has been the role of the United States. Paralleling its strategic role in providing regional security through bilateral alliances, the United States also provided a favourable regional economic environment through the provision of unfettered access to American capital, technology and above all to its domestic market. As we have seen, the policy of containment also aimed at developing the economies of America's allies so as to enhance social stability and reduce their vulnerability to communist subversion and insurgency. The result has been that through enjoying favoured access to the American market on a non-reciprocal basis they have been able to follow export-led economic growth behind various tariff and non-tariff barriers. In effect they have been the unique beneficiaries of the international economic institutions and arrangements established primarily by the United States at the end of the Second World War as they have not been bound by the principles of reciprocity built into them. A considerable part of the American agenda in the Asia-Pacific since the 1980s has been to address the consequences of the success of those policies which have resulted in huge trade surpluses for several of these countries, notably Japan.[27]

The ending of the Cold War provided an opportunity for the United States to modify its reluctance to engage in multilateral arrangements in the Asia-Pacific. To be sure it continued to deal with its economic problems with Japan and others primarily on a bilateral basis where its bargaining power could be employed to best advantage. Where appropriate it also continued to invoke inter-national global institutions for such purposes. But the American interest was in moving forward to establish a regional economic institution that would seek to underscore its general approach to the need for common rules on investment, trade, financial services and the protection of intellectual property rights.

Meanwhile the pattern of economic regionalism that had emerged in the Asia-Pacific had been business-led. That accounted for the growing proportion of trade, investment and technology transfers that was taking place between Asian countries as opposed to that carried out with Western countries. Unlike the development in Europe where the legal and political structures were put in place before economic integration began to take effect, in the Asia-Pacific the economic underpinning was established first. Interlocking busi-ness networks have emerged linking different divisions of multi-national corporations, many of them based in the region, and smaller firms, as well as a variety of more informal networks based on ethnicity, family and geographical ties, particularly of the disparate Chinese communities.

In fact there had long been an interest within the region in multilateral institutions. More than twenty years of effort had been exerted by senior politicians, officials, academics and business people notably in Japan, Australia, Canada and the United States to organ-ize such an institution with little to show for their endeavours. Businessmen of the five OECD countries in the region established the Pacific Basin Economic Council (PBEC) in 1967. The following year under the sponsorship of Japan's Foreign Minister Takeo Miki the organization of Pacific Trade and Development (PAFTAD) was established primarily for academics. In 1980 the more promising

Pacific Economic Cooperation Council (PECC) was inaugurated for officials, academics and businessmen. None of these involved the formal participation of governments and, however useful they were in providing points of contact and in generating ideas and blue-prints through study groups, none of the resolutions or recommenda-tions they adopted were binding on governments.[28] The primary reason for the failure to develop an inter-governmental organization was the resistance of the ASEAN countries who feared that such an institution would be dominated by the US or Japan to the detri-ment and possible marginalization of ASEAN itself.

The Australian initiative in founding APEC in 1989, at the insti-gation behind the scenes of the United States and Japan through its Ministry of Trade and Industry (MITI) in particular, was successful primarily because its timing coincided both with the ending of the Cold War and with the fear of the emergence of international trad-ing blocs. It also built on the unofficial governmental patterns of cooperation established in the PECC where a variety of consul-tations and study groups helped to provide for better understanding of the different perspectives and interests of the various states.[29] Indeed its membership, like that of the PECC, included the rep-resentatives of Hong Kong and Taiwan as well as those of the PRC so that although membership was limited to governing authorities it was not a membership of sovereign states.

It was a condition of the membership of the ASEAN countries that APEC should remain a loosely consultative forum only and that it should not compete with their Association. As if to signify its separate quality, ASEAN in January 1992 committed its members to establishing an exclusive free trade area (AFTA) over a fifteen-year period. Indeed even after the establishment of APEC the Malaysian Prime Minister Dr Mahathir Mohamad proposed to establish an East Asian Economic Grouping that would have excluded the Western countries. In response to the unease of fellow ASEAN states and the refusal of Japan, especially in the light of outright opposition to the concept by the United States, the proposal was modified to become the East Asian Economic Caucus (EAEC) and eventually through the good offices of President Suharto of Indonesia the EAEC became attached to APEC through ASEAN. But this was a matter of form only.

By this stage the American president had developed a new approach that was to transform APEC. Determined to demonstrate the depth of his recognition of the significance of Asia to the United States, the value of whose trade now exceeded that of trans-Atlantic trade by some $100 billion, President Clinton proposed at the G-7 meeting in Tokyo in July 1993 that the Asian leaders should meet him at a summit following the APEC ministerial meeting scheduled to be held in Seattle in November that year. Because of Beijing's sensitivities about Hong Kong and Taiwan the meeting was designated as an informal one. Yet there was much discussion in Washington about the desirability of establishing an Asian–Pacific Community. This was treated warily by the ASEAN states who had no wish to see the significance of their Association downgraded or diluted. Dr Mahathir, in particular, took offence and refused to attend the summit. In the event little came of the summit, but it was agreed that the leaders should convene at the next ministerial meeting of APEC in Jakarta scheduled for November 1994. Suitably mollified Dr Mahathir agreed to attend, but not before he took offence at a remark by the Australian Prime Minister, Paul Keating. Matters were duly settled, but the episode reflected some of the rifts between the Western and Asian members of APEC. The vision of an Asian–Pacific Community became tarnished as the Clinton Administration soon found itself in dispute on different grounds with significant APEC members. Nevertheless the next ministerial meeting at Bogor, Indonesia, built further on the earlier Clinton initiative to issue the Bogor Declaration pledging the members to free trade among the eighteen APEC members. The industrialized economies would do so by 2010 and the developing ones by 2020. Malaysia and China modified their commitment to the dates by labelling them as 'indicative' rather than 'binding'. More to the point, as APEC lacks an effective secretariat it does not have the necessary bureaucratic resources to transform the general declaration of principles into specific guidelines for member countries.[30]

There can be no question that as a forum where economic ministers and even heads of government can meet APEC is an important advance on previous arrangements. The forum can be seen as something more than an extension of the principle first established in the Post Ministerial Conferences that followed annual ASEAN meetings. It provides opportunities for developing better personal relations between leaders which in the Asian context is a necessary but not a sufficient basis for developing a sense of community. It remains to be seen whether APEC will evolve into a forum in which procedural rules for economic exchanges can be established and where incipient conflicts of interest can be addressed.

THE NEW COLD WAR

From the perspective of the Asia-Pacific the ending of the Cold War is better depicted as the ending of bipolarity. The changes that occurred under Gorbachev's leadership, culminating in the disintegration of the Soviet Union itself in 1991, effectively removed the Soviet Union and its successor state Russia from the position of a major power in the international politics of the Asia-Pacific. This left the United States not only as the sole remaining superpower in the world as a whole, but also as the unchallenged dominant military power in the Asia-Pacific too. However, with the exception of Mongolia (the only true satellite of the Soviet Union in Asia) the collapse of the communist regimes in Europe and the Soviet Union has not been matched by a similar collapse in Asia. Communist party rule has survived in China, North Korea and Vietnam. In their own separate ways the communist parties of these states claim that the ideological and political conflict with the Western world is far from over. North Korea with its egregious personality cult and autarkic Stalinist command economy is almost a throwback to the communist style regimes of the 1950s. Although both China and Vietnam have opened their doors to the international capitalist economy and have carried out economic reforms that have begun to transform their societies, their leaders argue that there are forces in the United States and elsewhere in the Western world who seek to undermine and overthrow communist rule. These forces, they claim, may have given up the confrontationist policies of military threats and trade embargoes, but their strategy of 'peaceful evolution' (which the Chinese have traced back to John Foster Dulles) poses a serious danger to the survival of communist regimes particularly at a time of economic reform.

In this sense the Cold War is not over in the Asia-Pacific. Moreover it is mirrored on the American side by an insistence that these countries improve their human rights practices, in particular by tolerating peaceful dissent and by following the rule of law. It is difficult to determine which of these would contribute more to the unravelling of communist party rule. China, which, unlike the Soviet Union, was spared these pressures in the 1970s because of its value as an ally against the Soviet Union and in the 1980s because it was believed to be embarked on a more liberal road, has been the main target of American human rights concerns since the Tiananmen killings of 4 June 1989.

This new Cold War should not be confused with the one associated with the bipolar era. It does not involve a comprehensive conflict between two camps. In fact the Chinese in 1989, in the aftermath of the Tiananmen crisis, decisively rejected the opportunity to establish a new Asian communist united front. There are differences of interest and security perspectives between the communist states, but more importantly, the Chinese and the Vietnamese wish to be integrated into the international economy of the Asia-Pacific and they wish to have access to the American market and to American advanced technology. Similarly the major companies and entrepreneurs of the Western powers vie with each other in investing and trading with China and Vietnam. The United States wishes to encourage them to participate in arrangements to limit the spread of weapons of mass destruction and it seeks their agreement to participate in the various rules and norms of international economic relations. The pro Western countries of the Asia-Pacific are anxious to enmesh both China and Vietnam in a web of mutually beneficial relations so as to encourage their peaceful integration into the region. Clearly the new Cold War in the Asia-Pacific is highly complex and is mediated by a web of interdependencies. Other Asian governments, notably those of Singapore and Malaysia, resent what they regard as unwarranted interference in their affairs by the West and the United States, in particular through the use of the banners of human rights and democracy. They have countered with a campaign to promote the superior virtues of what are presented as Asian values.[31] But the issue is nevertheless an important dimension in the relations between the United States and China, which by virtue of their significance as great powers in the region has ramifications for the Asia-Pacific as a whole.

Sino–American relations have been shaped by deep historical and cultural forces that are the product of totally different historical experiences.[32] Although the oscillations in their relations since 1949 may be seen as the product of changes in the international strategic environment, the ways in which each side conducted the relationship reflected these deep differences in political culture between them. The latest clash between them since the Tiananmen killings which has been depicted here as a new kind of Cold War must be understood against this complex historical background.

In his authoritative account of the two decades since Kissinger and Nixon opened relations in 1971–72 Harry Harding has charted a cyclical pattern by which periods of warm and even euphoric embrace have been followed by periods of disenchanted confrontation that in turn have led to reconciliation and then to a renewal of the cycle.³³ Although each side has recognized that deep differences exist between their two societies in terms of values, political systems and levels of economic development they have not found ways to limit the extent to which these can threaten to undermine interests which they share in common. On the contrary, the Chinese side has tended to accentuate the problem by continually depicting the United States as an imperialist power that is opposed to China and its communist system, while simultaneously demanding the transfer of advanced military technology, the provision of vast economic assistance and unhindered access to the American market as proof of American sincerity in treating China as a friendly and equal power. The Americans in turn have contributed to these problems through a continual redemptionist trend in the way they have tended to treat China's economic reforms as a movement towards capitalism and liberal democracy and in a tendency to caricature contemporary China in either excessively bright or dark colours.

The Tiananmen crisis and the collapse of communism in Eastern Europe coincided with the removal of the strategic structures of the bi-polar period and as a result the underlying cultural and political divisions between the two sides came to the fore. Domestic factors in each country became more important in shaping foreign policy and these two contributed to the new Cold War atmosphere. In Washington the increased importance of Congress, lobbyists, single issue groups and inter-agency rivalries made it difficult to coordinate policy. In Beijing the fears about the possible collapse of the regime and a relapse into chaos were augmented by the uncertainties of the imminence of political succession. The American response to Tiananmen was to introduce three kinds of sanctions that were all in the control of the government: end high level exchanges, stop concessionary loans and grants and call a halt to military exchanges and sales of military or military related technology. Since President Bush also feared the consequences of isolating the Chinese side he secretly sent his National Security Adviser to Bejing the following month. This emerged as he sent another high level delegation in December. In anger Congress then passed resolutions that sought to deny China the tariff concessions granted to most other countries (Most Favoured Nation or MFN) until it should improve its human rights performance. The president vetoed the bill. At issue was not a disagreement about whether the United States should seek to change the Chinese system along more law abiding and democratic lines, but rather what was the best way to achieve this. Congress favoured the exercise of open pressure through the use of economic sanctions, whereas the president favoured a process of constructive engagement. The latter envisaged that profound democratic change would take place as a result of economic and other exchanges with China which in time would see a new entrepreneurial middle class pressing for a greater say in public affairs. In other words both Congress and the president were possessed of the 'missionary spirit' and both were confident of their capacity to bring about change in China. The difference between them was on how best to do so.

The conflict between President Bush and Congress became an annual exercise until the election of President Clinton. By agreement with Congress he renewed MFN in 1993, but made its renewal in 1994 conditional on the Chinese government making satisfactory progress on a number of designated human rights matters. In the event in May 1994 he decided to renew MFN despite acknowledging that the Chinese had failed to make the necessary progress. The reversal of policy was due in part to pressure from American business lobbies, but it was also due to Clinton's recognition that the United States could not subordinate all dealings with a country of China's significance to the human rights factor alone. Clinton nevertheless promised to prosecute human rights concerns by other means.

The new Cold War is in essence a conflict between the norms that underlie the China of Deng Xiaoping and those of the international community and the West in particular. It is manifest in the disputes concerning the reversion of the sovereignty of Hong Kong to China in 1997 and in those that centre on the Taiwan question. China's leaders have long distrusted the British authorities as long time imperialists of immense cunning, but they had come to view Britain as a declining power and were nevertheless able to agree terms with them about the return of Hong Kong. Since Tiananmen in 1989 the Chinese leaders have tended to fear that the emergence of democracy in Hong Kong could be politically subversive on the Chinese mainland. Several liberal politicians in the territory have been accused by name of the offence and the Chinese side is pledged to abolish the elected institutions in 1997 because of disagreement with Governor Chris Patten about his constitutional reforms deemed to have been advanced in contravention of previous agreements. While the Chinese leaders wish to reap the benefits of the territory's economic significance, they do not wish to do so at the cost of what they see as political upheaval.

The Taiwan problem has also been affected by the new Cold

War. As the island has become more democratic the prospects of reunification with the mainland have receded. A vigorous opposition party demands outright independence, while the government demands acceptance by Beijing of its separate existence, but still nevertheless a part of China. Designating itself as the Republic of China on Taiwan it claims to represent only the people on its electoral roll, rather than the whole of China as before, and it seeks greater international recognition for its separate status, including a voice in the United Nations. Beijing still demands re-unification under the sovereignty of the PRC while promising the island considerable autonomy under the policy of 'one country two systems'. Taiwan's claims for international recognition of its special status have acquired greater appeal because of its more democratic character, but Western governments have withheld open recognition because of the greater international weight of the PRC. They have responded, however, with gestures such as raising the quality of their unofficial representation on the island. Beijing has been much troubled by the relative success of Taiwan's flexible diplomacy that has considerably raised its economic and political profile especially in Southeast Asia. As a democracy Taiwan is better placed to resist the blandishments of Beijing and to attract support from the United States which is still the significant external power with obligations towards the island arising from the 1979 Taiwan Relations Act. As long as the PRC remains ruled by a communist dictatorship an element of Cold War politics will continue to be played out in the unresolved Taiwan question.

REGIONAL SECURITY IN THE NEW ERA

The region is in a state of flux, or perhaps it is better depicted as being in a process of transition between the bipolar era and a new pattern of the distribution of power that has yet to take shape.[34] The process is complicated for several reasons. First, power is increasingly understood to embrace a wider range of factors than the military. Economic and technological factors as well as other 'soft power' considerations such as scientific capabilities and the capacity of societies to participate in the information revolution, are all germane to identifying the relative powers of states in the new era.[35] Second, the capacity of the great powers to manage international order has been questioned as the world's only superpower, the United States, finds it increasingly difficult for domestic and external reasons to define its international priorities and to impose

its will on lesser recalcitrant powers. Third, the significance of the
rising power of China is doubly unclear, in part because of uncertainty as to how its enormous domestic problems including the
decline of central authority are to be addressed, and in part because
of the uncertainties as to the extent to which the Chinese will
cooperate with their neighbours in approaches to regional problems.
Finally, it remains to be seen whether Japan will develop a more
assertive foreign and strategic policy.

Earlier it was argued that the emergence of the Asia-Pacific as a
region of relative security and dynamic economic development owed
much to the favourable containment policies which the United
States pursued during the Cold War. It follows that neither security
nor economic dynamism can be taken for granted in the post Cold
War period. Much of the stability that has been provided so far
stems from the continued military engagement of the United States.
It is a measure of the appreciation of this by the states in the region
that they all express concern about the willingness of the American
public to continue to sustain that role. For its part the United
States in the new era has recognized the need for more cooperative
institutional arrangements in the region and lent its support to the
establishment of ARF and APEC. But these are slender reeds on
which to build new security arrangements. ARF was found to be
less than cohesive and relevant when the Chinese challenged the
Philippines over Mischief Reef in 1995. Nor has it responded to
the Chinese declared intention of seeking separate bilateral settlements of disputes as opposed to the ARF's preference for multilateral cooperative approaches. Moreover, the United States confined
itself to seeking assurances from the Chinese about keeping open
the trade routes of the high seas. Not surprisingly, the East Asian
states, unlike their Western counterparts, have increased their military spending since the end of the Cold War.[36]

The development of regional patterns of consultation on security
matters through ARF and CSCAP meetings are important in the
sense that they help to deepen awareness within the region of
the perspectives and problems of other states. They may even lead
to the establishment of confidence building measures. But in themselves they are no guarantee of security. However, the deeper purposes of these multilateral consultative institutions are first, to
engage the major powers (principally China) who could pose threats
to regional security, in a process of dialogue that will enmesh them
in cooperative patterns of behaviour; and second, it is seen as a way
of retaining American involvement in regional security. Chinese

interest in cooperation is underpinned by the importance of the Asia-Pacific to the continued development and modernization of the economy which the communist leaders regard as crucial for their own survival in power.

Regional security will ultimately depend upon the evolution of the great powers and the relations between them. As has been argued in previous chapters, China as the rising power faces immense problems as it grapples with the succession to Deng Xiaoping that will shape its coherence as an international actor in ways that cannot be predicted with any confidence. But what is of concern is the irredenta claims to Taiwan and maritime territories especially in the South China Sea that are being advanced amid an increasingly assertive nationalist outlook. Japan too is undergoing a systemic change that may have profound foreign policy implications. Much will depend upon Chinese sensitivity to Japanese concerns. But the critical factor will turn on Sino–American relations.

The United States is a major factor in most aspects of China's foreign relations especially on issues to do with strategy, modernization and integration into the international community. As we have seen, Sino–American relations have tended to be problematic as they reflect the contrast between the deeper historical and cultural forces that have shaped the two states. With the ending of bipolarity these differences have emerged into sharper focus and as China's leaders seek to consolidate their new and growing position in the world they find the United States to be their principal obstacle. China's relations with the United States in the first half of the 1990s has combined both elements of cooperation and incipient conflict, but as China grows stronger the latter may become more prominent and it may provide a new basis for linking local, regional and international issues in the Asia-Pacific.

NOTES AND REFERENCES

1 For a more extended argument along these lines see Robert Jervis, 'A Usable Past for the Future' in Michael J. Hogan (ed.) *The End of the Cold War: Its Meanings and Implications* (Cambridge: Cambridge University Press, reprinted 1993) pp. 257–68.
2 For an account of this concept see Martin Wight, *Power Politics*; and the discussion of the role of great powers in Hedley Bull, *The Anarchical Society* (*op. cit.*) Chapter 9, pp. 200–29 and especially on 'hegemony' pp. 215–19.
3 For the first view see Kenneth W. Waltz, 'The New World Order' *Millennium, Journal of International Affairs* Vol. 22, No. 2, Summer 1993,

pp. 187–95; for the second, John Lewis Gaddis, 'The Cold War, the Long Peace, and the Future' in Hogan (*op. cit.*) pp. 21–38; and for the third, Samuel P. Huntingdon, 'The Clash of Civilizations?' in *Foreign Affairs* Vol. 72, No. 3, Summer 1993, pp. 22–49; and 'If Not Civilizations, What? Samuel P. Huntingdon Responds to His Critics' in *ibid.* Vol. 72, No. 5, November/December 1993, pp. 186–94.

4 See 'A Survey of China', *The Economist* 28 November 1992.

5 For a general account of Russia in relation to the three major powers in East Asia that also considers the terms under which Russia may eventually reassert a more active role in the region see Robert Legvold, 'Russia and the Strategic Quadrangle' in Michael Mandelbaum (ed.) *The Strategic Quadrangle: Russia, China, Japan, and the United States in East Asia* (New York, Council on Foreign Relations Press, 1955) pp. 16–62. For regular accounts of Russia's relations in Asia see the January issue of *Asian Survey* every year.

6 For Russo–Japanese relations in the 1990s see Legvold, *ibid.* pp. 51–54; and Leszek Buszynski, 'Russia and Japan: the Unmaking of a Territorial dispute' *World Today* March 1993.

7 For accounts of Sino–Russian relations in the early 1990s see Legvold (*loc. cit.*) pp. 22–27; and Gary Klintworth, *The Practice of Common Security: China's Border With Russia and India* (Taipei: Council of Advanced Policy Studies, CAPS Papers No. 4, 1993).

8 For an account of Russia and Southeast Asia in the 1990s see Bilveer Singh, *Moscow and Southeast Asia Since 1985: From USSR to the CIS* (Singapore: Singapore International Affairs, 1992).

9 For a general account of the United States relationship with the major powers in East Asia see Michael Mandelbaum, 'The United States and the Strategic Quadrangle' in Mandelbaum (ed.) *The Strategic Quadrangle* (*op. cit.*) pp. 154–95. For regular accounts of American relations in Asia see the January issue of *Asian Survey* and the first issue of *Foreign Affairs* every year.

10 For details and discussion see Andrew Mack and Desmond Ball, 'The Military Build-up in the Asia-Pacific', *Pacific Review* Vol. 5, No. 3, 1992; and 'The Power Game' *Asia 1994 Yearbook* (Hong Kong: The Far Eastern Economic Review, 1994) pp. 18–23.

11 For a brief discussion of the prospects for US–Japan security relations after the Cold War see Jonathan Pollack, 'The United States in East Asia' in *Asia's International Role in the Post-Cold War Era*, Part 1, (London: IISS/Brassey's, Adelphi Paper 275, March 1993) especially pp. 75–76. See also Mandelbaum (*loc. cit.*) especially pp. 176–84.

12 See, for example, the criticisms by Henry Kissinger, 'Tell It Straight to North Korea – But Talking May Not Be Enough' *International Herald Tribune* (4 July 1994).

13 Takashi Inoguchi, 'Japan in Search of a Normal Role' in *Asia's International Role . . .* Adelphi Paper 275 (*op. cit.*) p. 59.

14 See Mike M. Mochizuki, 'Japan and the Strategic Quadrangle' in Mandelbaum (ed.) *The Strategic Quadrangle* (*op. cit.*) pp. 107–53.

15 The following account of the Korean question draws on successive issues of *Strategic Survey* (*op. cit.*) for the relevant years.

16 *Strategic Survey 1991–1992* (London: Brassey's for the International Institute of Strategic Studies, 1992) p. 136.
17 Communique of the Central Committee Plenum in BBC *SWB* FE/1866, 9 December 1993. See also reports in *The Times* and *International Herald Tribune* 10 December 1993.
18 Nigel Holloway and Shim Jae Hoon, 'North Korea: The Price of Peace' *Far Eastern Economic Review* 25 August 1994, pp. 14–15.
19 The above discussion draws heavily on Michael Leifer, 'Powersharing and Peacemaking in Cambodia?' *SAIS REVIEW*, Winter/Spring 1992, Vol. 12, No. 1, pp. 139–54.
20 For a full account of the disputed claims see Douglas M. Johnson and Mark J. Valencia, *Pacific Ocean Boundary Problems* (Dortrecht: Martinus Nijhoff, 1991).
21 For an account of the legal dimensions of the Chinese position see Jeanette Greenfield, *China's Practice in the Law of the Sea* (Oxford: Clarendon Press, 1992).
22 John W. Garver, 'China's Push Through the South China Sea: The Interaction of Bureaucratic and National Interests', *The China Quarterly* No. 132, December 1992, pp. 999–1028.
23 See the comments to this effect by Secretary of State Warren Christopher at the ASEAN Post Ministerial Conference in July 1993, cited in Michael Vatikiotis 'ASEAN Uncharted Waters', *FEER*, 5 August 1993, p. 11.
24 The Council for Security Cooperation in the Asia Pacific (CSCAP) was formally established in June 1993 at a meeting in Kuala Lumpur. See papers by Desmond Ball and Paul M. Evans of August and July 1993 respectively, available from the Strategic and Defence Studies Centre, Australian National University, Canberra.
25 Rodney Tasker, 'ASEAN Facing up to Security,' *FEER*, 6 August 1992, pp. 8–9.
26 Vatikiotis, 'Uncharted Waters' (*op. cit.*) pp. 11–12.
27 For further discussion see Michael Yahuda, 'The "Pacific Community": Not Yet', *The Pacific Review* Vol. 1, No. 2, 1988.
28 For contemporary accounts that reflect both optimistic and more cautious views of the prospects see Hadi Soesastro and Han Sung-joo (eds) *Pacific Economic Cooperation: The Next Phase* (Jakarta, Centre for Strategic and International Studies, October 1983).
29 For an account see Stuart Harris, 'Varieties of Pacific Economic Cooperation', *The Pacific Review* Vol. 4, No. 4, 1991.
30 John McBeth and V.G. Kulkarni, 'APEC: Charting the Future' *FEER* 24 November 1994, pp. 14–15.
31 For two contrasting views by two Asian leading figures see the interview with Lee Kuan Yew in *Foreign Affairs* (March/April 1994) and the riposte by Kim Dae Jung in *Foreign Affairs* November/December 1994.
32 See Warren I. Cohen, *America's Response to China: A History of Sino–American Relations* (New York: Columbia University Press, third edition, 1990); Michael Hunt, *The Making of a Special Relationship: the United States and China to 1914* (New York: Columbia University Press, 1983); and Harold Isaacs, *Scratches on Our Minds: American Images of China and India* (New York: John Day, 1958).

33 Harry Harding, *A Fragile Relationship: The United States and China since 1972* (Washington DC: The Brookings Institution, 1992).
34 For a forceful discussion of the continuing importance of military power in the circumstances see Paul Dibb, *Towards A New Balance of Power in Asia* (London: IISS/OUP, Adelphi Paper 295, 1995).
35 Chinese strategists have tried to capture these broader dimensions of power in their term 'comprehensive strength'. There are other schools of thought which see more fundamental changes inherent in the challenges to the state system itself from the globalization of a wide range of issues such as finance and the environment.
36 For further discussion see Dibb, *Towards a New Balance...* (*op. cit.*) pp. 56ff.

Select bibliography

GENERAL, ASIA-PACIFIC

Bellows, Michael D. (ed.), *Asia in the 21st Century: Evolving Strategic Priorities* (Washington DC: National Defense University Press, 1994).

Borthwick, Martin, *Pacific Century* (Boulder, CO: Westview Press, 1992).

Chan, Steve, *East Asian Dynamism, Growth, Order and Security in the Pacific Region* (Boulder, CO: Westview Press, 1993).

Dibb, Paul, *Towards a New Balance of Power in Asia* (London: Adelphi Paper 295, IISS/Oxford University Press, May 1995).

Gibney, Frank, *The Pacific Century: America and Asia in a Changing World* (New York: Charles Scribner's Sons, 1992).

Godement, François, *The New Asian Renaissance: From Colonialism to the Post-Cold War*, trans. Elisabeth Parcell (London and New York: Routledge, 1996).

Gourevitch, Peter A. (ed.), *The Pacific Region: Challenges to Policy and Theory*, The ANNALS of the American Academy of Political Science (Newbury Park, CA: Sage Publications, September 1989).

Leifer, Michael (ed.), *The Balance of Power in East Asia* (London: Macmillan, 1986).

Mack, Andrew and Ravenhill, John (eds), *Building Economic and Security Regimes in the Asia-Pacific* (Boulder, CO: Lynne Rienner, 1994).

Mandelbaum, Michael (ed.), *The Strategic Quadrangle: Russia, China, Japan and the United States in East Asia* (New York: Council on Foreign Relations Press, 1995).

Millar, T. B. and Walter, James (eds), *Asian-Pacific Security After the Cold War* (NSW, Australia: Allen & Unwin, 1993).

Segal, Gerald, *Rethinking the Pacific* (Oxford: Oxford University Press, 1990).

GENERAL, THE COLD WAR IN THE REGION

Barnett, A. Doak, *China and the Major Powers in East Asia* (Washington DC: The Brookings Institution, 1977).

Cohen, Warren I. and Iriye, Akira (eds), *The Great Powers in Asia 1953–1960* (New York: Columbia University Press, 1990).

Gaddis, John Lewis, *The Long Peace: Inquiries into the History of the Cold War* (Oxford: Oxford University Press, 1987).

Goncharov, Sergei N., Lewis, John W. and Xue Litai, *Uncertain Partners: Stalin, Mao and the Korean War* (Stanford, CA: Stanford University Press, 1993).

Jansen, G. H., *Nonalignment and the Afro-Asian States* (New York: Praeger, 1966).

Kim, Ilpyong, *The Strategic Triangle: China, the United States and the Soviet Union* (New York: Paragon House, 1987).

Nagai, Yonosuke and Iriye, Akira (eds), *The Origins of the Cold War in Asia* (Tokyo: University of Tokyo Press, 1977).

Ross, Robert S., *China, the United States and the Soviet Union: Tripolarity and Policy Making in the Cold War* (New York: M. E. Sharpe, 1993).

GENERAL, NORTHEAST ASIA

Barnds, William J. (ed.), *The Two Koreas in East Asian Affairs* (New York: New York University Press, 1976).

Clough, Ralph A., *Embattled Korea: The Rivalry for International Support* (Boulder, CO: Westview Press, 1987).

Harris, Stuart and Cotton, James (eds), *The End of the Cold War in Northeast Asia* (Boulder, CO: Lynne Rienner, 1991).

Mack, Andrew (ed.), *Asian Flashpoint: Security and the Korean Peninsula* (Canberra: Allen & Unwin in association with the Department of International Relations, RSPacS, ANU, 1993).

Scalapino, Robert A., *Major Powers in Northeast Asia* (Lanham: University Press of America, 1987).

Weinstein, Martin E., *Northeast Asian Security after Vietnam* (Urbana: University of Illinois Press, 1982).

GENERAL, SOUTHEAST ASIA

Acharya, Amitav, *A New Regional Order in South-East Asia: ASEAN in the Post-Cold War Era*, Adelphi Paper 279 (London: IISS/Brasseys, 1993).

Buszynski, Leszek, *SEATO: The Failure of an Alliance Strategy* (Singapore: Singapore University Press, 1983).

Colbert, Evelyn, *Southeast Asia in International Politics 1941–1956* (Ithaca, NY: Cornell University Press, 1977).

Jeffrey, Robin, *Asia, The Winning of Independence* (London: Macmillan Press, 1981).

Leifer, Michael, *Foreign Relations of the New States* (Australia: Longman, 1974).

Leifer, Michael, *ASEAN and the Security of Southeast Asia* (London and New York: Routledge, 1989).

Leifer, Michael, *Dictionary of the Modern Politics of South-East Asia* (London and New York: Routledge, 1995).

Lyon, Peter, *War and Peace in South-East Asia* (Oxford: Oxford University Press, 1969).

Neher, Clark D., *Southeast Asia in the New International Era* (Boulder, CO: Westview Press, 1991).

Vatikiotis, Michael, *Political Change in South East Asia: Trimming the Banyan Tree* (London and New York: Routledge, 1996).

Wang Gungwu, *Community and Nation: Essays on Southeast Asia and the Chinese* (Singapore: Heinemann Educational, 1981).

THE UNITED STATES

Buckley, Roger, *US–Japan Alliance Diplomacy, 1945–1990* (Cambridge: Cambridge University Press, 1992).

Chang, Gordon H., *Friends and Enemies: the United States, China and the Soviet Union, 1948–1972* (Stanford, CA: Stanford University Press, 1990).

Cohen, Warren I., *America's Response to China* (New York: Columbia University Press, 3rd edn 1990).

Gaddis, John Lewis, *Strategies of Containment* (Oxford: Oxford University Press, 1982).

Gordon, Bernard H., *New Directions for American Policy in Asia* (London and New York: Routledge, 1990).

Harding, Harry, *A Fragile Relationship: The United States and China Since 1972* (Washington DC: The Brookings Institution, 1992).

Iriye, Akira, *Mutual Images: Essays in American–Japanese Relations* (Cambridge, MA: Harvard University Press, 1975).

Kissinger, Henry, *Diplomacy* (New York and London: Simon & Schuster, 1994).

Litwak, Robert S., *Detente and the Nixon Doctrine: American Foreign Policy and the Pursuit of Stability, 1969–1976* (Cambridge: Cambridge University Press, 1984).

Oye, Kenneth A. *et al.* (eds), *Eagle in New World: American Grand Strategy in the Post-Cold War Era* (New York: Harper & Collins, 1992).

Tow, William T., *Encountering the Dominant Player: US Extended Deterrence Strategy in the Asia-Pacific* (New York: Columbia University Press, 1991).

Tucker, Nancy Berkop, *Patterns in the Dust: Chinese American Relations and the Recognition Controversy* (New York: Columbia University Press, 1983).

THE SOVIET UNION/RUSSIA

Buszynski, Lezek, *Gorbachev and Southeast Asia* (London and New York: Routledge, 1992).

Ellison, H. (ed.), *The Sino-Soviet Conflict: A Global Perspective* (Seattle: University of Washington Press, 1982).

Goncharov, Sergei, Lewis, John W. and Xue Litai, *Uncertain Partners: Stalin, Mao and the Korean War* (Stanford, CA: Stanford University Press, 1993).

Hasegawa, Tsuyoshi, Haslam, Jonathan and Kuchins, Andrew (eds), *Russia and Japan: An Unresolved Dilemma Between Distant Neighbours* (Berkeley: University of California Press, 1993).

Segal, Gerald, *Sino-Soviet Relations After Mao*, Adelphi Paper 202, (London: IISS/Brasseys, 1985).

Segal, Gerald, *The Soviet Union and the Pacific* (London: Unwin Hyman, 1990).
Ulam, Adam, *Expansion and Coexistence: Soviet Foreign Policy, 1917–73* (New York: Praeger, 2nd edn 1976).
Ulam, Adam, *Dangerous Relations: The Soviet Union in World Politics 1970–1982* (Oxford: Oxford University Press, 1983).
Zagoria, Donald S., *The Sino-Soviet Conflict 1956–1961* (Princeton, NJ: Princeton University Press, 1962).
Zagoria, Donald S. (ed.), *Soviet Policy in East Asia* (New Haven, CT: Yale University Press, 1982).
Ziegler, Charles E., *Learning and Adaptation in the Gorbachev Era* (Cambridge: Cambridge University Press, 1993).

CHINA

China Quarterly, 'China And Japan', Special Issue, No. 124 (Dec. 1990).
China Quarterly, 'Greater China', Special Issue, No. 136 (Dec. 1993).
Hao Yufan and Huan Guocang (eds), *The Chinese View of the World* (New York: Pantheon Books, 1989).
Harding, Harry (ed.), *China's Foreign Relations in the 1980s* (New Haven, CT: Yale University Press, 1984).
Garver, John W., *Foreign Relations of the People's Republic of China* (Englewood Cliffs, NJ: Prentice-Hall, 1993).
Gittings, John, *Survey of the Sino-Soviet Dispute 1963–1967* (Oxford: Oxford University Press, 1968).
Grant, Richard (ed.), *China and Southeast Asia* (Washington DC: Center for Strategic and International Studies, 1993).
Gurtov, Melvin, *China and Southeast Asia – The Politics of Survival: A Study of Foreign Policy Interaction* (Lexington, MA: D.C. Heath & Co., 1971).
Kim, Samuel S., *China and the World: Chinese Foreign Relations in the Post-Cold War Era* (Boulder, CO: Westview Press, 3rd edn 1994).
Robinson, Thomas W. and Shambaugh, David, *Chinese Foreign Policy* (Oxford: Clarendon Press, 1994).
Shambaugh, David, *Beautiful Imperialist: China Perceives America, 1972–1990* (Princeton, NJ: Princeton University Press, 1991).
Taylor, Jay, *China and Southeast Asia: Peking's Relations with Revolutionary Movements* (New York: Praeger, expanded and updated edn, 1976).
Whiting, Allen S., *China Crosses the Yalu: The Decision to Enter the Korean War* (Stanford, CA: Stanford University Press, 1960).
Whiting, Allen S., *China's Calculus of Deterrence* (Ann Arbor: University of Michigan Press, 1975).
Whiting, Allen S., *China Eyes Japan* (Berkeley: University of California Press, 1989).
Yahuda, Michael, *Towards the End of Isolationism: China's Foreign Policy after Mao* (London: Macmillan Press, 1983).

JAPAN

Cronin, Richard P., *Japan, the United States, and Prospects for the Asia-Pacific, Three Scenarios for the Future* (Singapore: Institute of Southeast Asian Studies, 1992).

Curtis, Gerald L. (ed.), *Japan's Foreign Policy After the Cold War: Coping With Change* (Armonk, NY: M. E. Sharpe, 1993).

Drifte, Reinhard, *Japan's Foreign Policy* (London: Routledge, 1990).

Hellman, Donald C., *Japanese Foreign Policy: The Peace Agreement with the Soviet Union* (Berkeley: University of California Press, 1969).

Inoguchi, Takashi, *Japan's International Relations* (London: Pinter Publishers, 1991).

Inoguchi, Takashi, *Japan's Foreign Policy in an Era of Global Change* (London: Pinter Publishers, 1993).

Kenichiro, Sasae, *Rethinking Japan–US Relations*, Adelphi Paper 292 (London: IISS/Brasseys, 1994).

Makin, John H. and Hellman, Donald C. (eds), *Sharing World Leadership? A New Era for America and Japan* (Washington DC: The AEI Press, 1989).

Mendl, Wolf, *Issues in Japan's China Policy* (London: Macmillan Press, 1978).

Orr, Robert M., Jr, *The Emergence of Japan's Foreign Aid Power* (New York: Columbia University Press, 1990).

Pyle, Kenneth B., *The Japanese Question: Power and Purpose in a New Era* (Washington DC: The AEI Press, 1992).

Sueo, Suedo, *The Fukuda Doctrine and ASEAN: New Dimensions in Japanese Foreign Policy* (Singapore: Institute of Southeast Asian Studies, 1992).

Index